The Development of the Unconscious Mind

The Norton Series on Interpersonal Neurobiology

Louis Cozolino, PhD, Series Editor
Allan N. Schore, PhD, Series Editor, 2007–2014
Daniel J. Siegel, MD, Founding Editor

The field of mental health is in a tremendously exciting period of growth and conceptual reorganization. Independent findings from a variety of scientific endeavors are converging in an interdisciplinary view of the mind and mental well-being. An interpersonal neurobiology of human development enables us to understand that the structure and function of the mind and brain are shaped by experiences, especially those involving emotional relationships.

The Norton Series on Interpersonal Neurobiology provides cutting-edge, multidisciplinary views that further our understanding of the complex neurobiology of the human mind. By drawing on a wide range of traditionally independent fields of research—such as neurobiology, genetics, memory, attachment, complex systems, anthropology, and evolutionary psychology—these texts offer mental health professionals a review and synthesis of scientific findings often inaccessible to clinicians. The books advance our understanding of human experience by finding the unity of knowledge, or consilience, that emerges with the translation of findings from numerous domains of study into a common language and conceptual framework. The series integrates the best of modern science with the healing art of psychotherapy.

A NORTON PROFESSIONAL BOOK

The Development of the Unconscious Mind

ALLAN N. SCHORE

W. W. Norton & Company
Independent Publishers Since 1923
New York • London

Note to Readers: Standards of clinical practice and protocol change over time, and no technique or recommendation is guaranteed to be safe or effective in all circumstances. This volume is intended as a general information resource for professionals practicing in the field of psychotherapy and mental health; it is not a substitute for appropriate training, peer review, and/or clinical supervision. Neither the publisher nor the author(s) can guarantee the complete accuracy, efficacy, or appropriateness of any particular recommendation in every respect.

Printed in the United States of America
First Edition

For information about special discounts for bulk purchases, please contact W. W. Norton Special Sales at specialsales@wwnorton.com or 800-233-4830

Manufacturing by Lake Book Manufacturing, Inc.
Production manager: Katelyn MacKenzie

ISBN: 978-0-393-71291-9

W. W. Norton & Company, Inc., 500 Fifth Avenue, New York, N.Y. 10110
www.wwnorton.com

W. W. Norton & Company Ltd., 15 Carlisle Street, London W1D 3BS

1 2 3 4 5 6 7 8 9 0

The conscious mind may be compared to a fountain playing in the sun and falling back into the great subterranean pool of the subconscious from which it rises.

—Sigmund Freud

Man's task is . . . to become conscious of the contents that process upward from the unconscious . . . his destiny is to create more and more consciousness.

—Carl Jung

To all our children

Contents

Acknowledgments

In 1994, I overviewed twentieth century developmental science to offer my first book *Affect Regulation and the Origin of the Self.* In the opening sentence of that volume, now published as a Classic Edition, I boldly asserted that "the understanding of early development is one of the fundamental objectives of science. The beginnings of living systems set the stage for every aspect of an organism's internal and external functioning throughout the life span." In that inaugural volume of regulation theory, as well as three that followed, I articulated and elaborated the interpersonal neurobiological thesis that runs throughout my work: that events occurring during human infancy, especially emotional transactions with the social environment, are indelibly imprinted into the brain structures that are maturing in the first years of life. This book and its companion, *Right Brain Psychotherapy,* further expand regulation theory and continue to delve, deeply and widely, into a number of essential brain/mind/body functions, all operating at levels beneath conscious awareness, that are central to the human condition.

Since my 2012 volume, *The Science of the Art of Psychotherapy,* I continue to write, research, lecture, and share my work with audiences around the world. I take great pride in the fact that my publications over a variety of disciplines have increased to now well over 20,000 citations in Google Scholar. In my global travels over the past decade, I have also been very interested in finding new authors for the rapidly expanding field of interpersonal neurobiology. More times than not these individuals have sought me out, and many have actively participated in my Study Groups, which have spanned from Los Angeles and Vancouver to Boulder and Melbourne.

Even more so than before I spend time mentoring individuals in a number of disciplines, especially mental health professionals who are adept at integrating science and clinical work, describing the coupling between biological and psychological processes, and combining an objective perspective with one steeped in bodily-based emotional subjectivity. Indeed, these mentoring efforts are in part reflected in the forewords I've written for a number of Norton authors.

I would like to express my gratefulness to a group of remarkable conference organizers who have sponsored a number of important national and international personal appearances, including Marion Solomon, Jane Ryan, Joe Tucci, Ravi Kumar, Alessandro Carmelita, and Dan Hill. I also greatly value the contributions of my research partners, Ruth Lanius in Canada, and Jennifer Mcintosh and Craig Olsson in Australia. I'd like to thank the Norton staff, especially Mariah Eppes and Sara McBride for the work they've done on this book. Most notably, I express deep appreciation to my publisher and valued colleague Deborah Malmud for not only two decades of a productive and gratifying business and personal relationship, but for her continual advocacy of not only my work but the Norton Series.

Once again, I offer my love and gratitude to family: to David, for his professional computer skills; to Beth, for her talents in computer graphics and the design for the cover and a number of illustrations within this book; and to Judy, for providing so many forms of essential support for my life's work. The words I wrote to her in my first book twenty-five years ago still ring true: Through her intellectual keenness and emotional honesty, she continues to reflect and reveal to me those essential reciprocal emotional processes that are, willingly and unwillingly, most clearly exposed in an intimate human relationship.

The Development of the Unconscious Mind

CHAPTER 1

Early Emotional Attachment, the Development of the Right Brain, and the Relational Origins of the Unconscious Mind

IN RECENT YEARS THE UNCONSCIOUS, the central theoretical construct of psychodynamic theory, has reappeared in a new form in the scientific and clinical literatures. Psychoanalysis has been called the scientific study of the unconscious mind (Brenner, 1980), clearly implying both that the unconscious is its definitional realm of study and that this realm is accessible to scientific analysis. Although originally closely tied to the psychoanalytic theory of repression, the construct of the unconscious is now being used across a number of psychological and neurobiological disciplines to describe essential implicit, spontaneous, rapid, and involuntary processes that act beneath levels of conscious awareness. Yet, despite current significant advances in brain laterality research, many clinicians and social scientists continue to hold older and now unsupported ideas that the "primitive" nonverbal unconscious mind is a miniature of the "more complex" verbal conscious mind, and that the "nondominant" right hemisphere is a lesser mirror of the "dominant" left hemisphere.

In my last book, I asserted that a deeper understanding of human development can never be attained by narrowly focusing infant studies on the precursors of language, voluntary behavior, and conscious thought (Schore, 2012). This book, *The Development of the Unconscious Mind,* offers chapters on the early maturing yet long enduring essential impact of the unconscious mind on all later aspects of human development. In the following, I will offer a large body of evidence indicating that the development of the unconscious mind begins in the prenatal, perinatal, and postnatal stages of human infancy and continues across all later stages of the life span. This model supports Freud's description of the human mind: "Every earlier stage of development persists alongside the later stage which has arisen from it . . . the primitive stages can always be re-established; the primitive mind is, in the fullest meaning of the word, imperishable" (1915a/1957, p. 285). Indeed, in 1920 Freud proclaimed that "*the unconscious is the infantile mental life.*"

In expanding Freud's thesis, I will suggest that an integration of current findings in the neurobiological and developmental sciences can offer a deeper understanding of the origins and dynamic mechanisms of the system that represents the core of psychoanalysis, the system unconscious. The construct of the unconscious has thus shifted from an intangible, immaterial, metapsychological abstraction of the mind to a psychoneurobiological heuristic function of a tangible brain that has material form. The direct relevance of this reformulation to a deeper understanding of clinical phenomena is a central theme of *Right Brain Psychotherapy*, the companion to this volume.

In my inceptive 1994 volume, *Affect Regulation and the Origin of the Self*, I first integrated developmental psychology, developmental neuroscience, and developmental psychoanalysis in order to tie together the conceptual, clinical, and research links between early attachment, psychoanalytic object relational development, the experience-dependent maturation of the right brain, and the origins of the human unconscious. This first relationship, the one with the mother, acts as a template, as it permanently shapes the individual's capacities to enter into all later emotional relationships. These early experiences shape the development of a unique personality, its adaptive capacities as well as its vulnerabilities to and resistances against particular forms of future psychopathologies, much of which are expressed at unconscious levels. Indeed, they profoundly influence the emergent organization of an integrated system that is both stable and adaptable, and thereby the formation of the subjective self.

This conceptualization was the first expression of interpersonal neurobiology, a perspective of human development that enables us to understand that the structure and function of the mind and brain are shaped by experiences, especially those involving emotional relationships. To put this concisely, "the self organization of the developing brain occurs in the context of a relationship with another brain, another self" (Schore, 1996, p. 60). Over the past three decades, a huge body of interdisciplinary evidence across all mammalian species, including humans, documents the indelible, enduring impact of specifically the mother on the infant's prenatal and postnatal subcortical and cortical brain development (Schore, 1994, 2003a,b, 2012). Thus I have continued to offer data supporting the organizing principle that the "first relationship" (Stern, 1977), "the earliest relationship" (Brazelton & Kramer, 1990) with another human is mediated by unconscious right brain-to-right brain attachment communications between the mother and infant, and that this primordial bond is mediated by rapid emotional communications between the mother's right brain unconscious and the infant's emerging right brain unconscious (Schore, 1994, 2003a, 2003b, 2012). In other words, early affective experiences during critical periods of right brain development permanently influence the development of the right-lateralized psychic structures that process unconscious information.

Thus, a central thesis of my work dictates that the right brain represents the psychobiological substrate of Freud's unconscious. Recent information suggests maternal-fetal placental transactions occurring in the last trimester *in utero* may shape the primordial emergence of the deep unconscious (Schore, 2017). The continuity of this right brain unconscious mechanism across the life span underscores Fischer and Pipp's observation, "A young infant functions in a fundamentally unconscious way, and unconscious processes in an older child or adult are to be traced back to the primitive functioning of the infant or young child" (1984, p. 88). These authors also conclude that *unconscious thought does not remain static during childhood but undergoes subsequent systematic developments.*

Although a number of important developmental psychoanalysts studied the critical role of the unconscious in human infancy (see the companion volume *Right Brain Psychotherapy*), John Bowlby integrated psychoanalysis and contemporary ethology and neuroscience to propose that in intimate emotional attachment contexts, human feelings are detected through "facial expressions, posture, tone of voice, physiological changes, tempo of movement, and incipient action" (1969, p. 120). In a number of contributions,

I have offered neurobiological evidence that attachment communications are expressed in right-lateralized visual-facial, tactile-gestural, and auditory-prosodic emotional nonverbal communications (Schore, 1994, 2003a, 2003b, 2012). As opposed to later forming left-hemispheric secondary process verbal communication, right-hemispheric nonverbal attachment communication has been described by Dorpat as "primary process communication" expressed in "both body movements (kinesics), posture, gesture, facial expression, voice inflection, and the sequence, rhythm, and pitch of the spoken words" (2001, p. 451). The right hemisphere is dominant for the perception of nonverbal emotional expressions embedded in facial and prosodic stimuli, even at unconscious levels (Blonder, Bowers, & Heilman, 1991; George et al., 1996; Wexler et al., 1992), for primary process cognition (Galin, 1974; Joseph, 1996), and for nonverbal communication (Benowitz et al., 1983). At all later stages of human development, "The neural substrates of the perception of voices, faces, gestures, smells, and pheromones, as evidenced by modern neuroimaging techniques, are characterized by a general right-hemispheric functional asymmetry" (Brancucci et al., 2009, p. 895). At levels beneath awareness, humans tend to display right hemispheric "Left Gaze Bias," whereby they direct their initial gaze to the left side of the other's face, and look longer exploring the left side (Salva et al., 2012).

In classic studies of the two-person psychology of the early mother-infant face-to-face protoconversation, Trevarthen (1993) observed that visual eye-to-eye messages are coordinated with auditory vocalizations (tone of voice, "motherese") and tactile and body gestures as a channel of communication, and that the resultant dyadic resonance ultimately permits the intercoordination of positive affective brain states (Figure 1.1). This interactive mechanism requires older brains to engage with mental states of awareness, emotion, and interest in younger brains and involves a *synchronized* coordination between the motivations of the infant and the subjective feelings of adults. In this manner, "The emotions constitute a time-space field of intrinsic brain states of mental and behavioral vitality that are signaled for communication to other subjects and that are open to immediate influence from the signals of these others" (p. 155). In other studies, Trevarthen asserted that "the intrinsic regulators of human

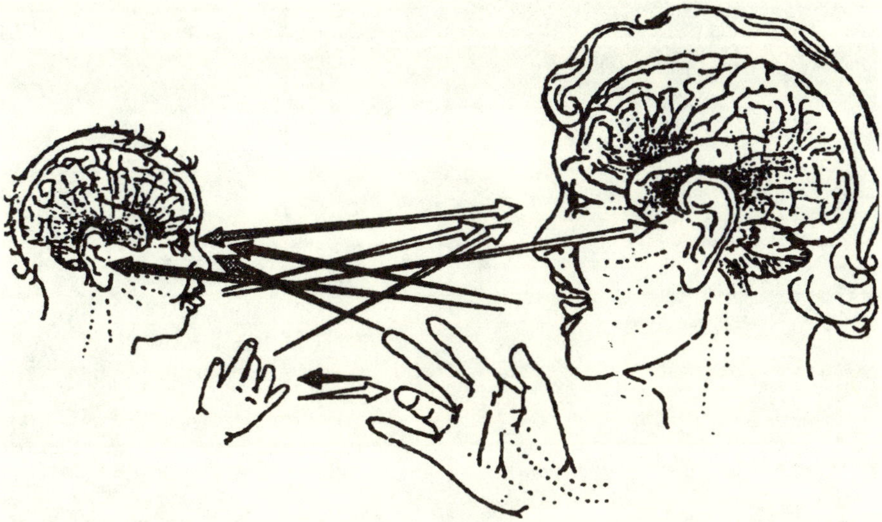

FIGURE 1.1 Channels of face-to-face communication in protoconversation mediated by eye-to-eye orientations, vocalizations, hand gestures, and movements of the arms and head, all acting in coordination to express interpersonal awareness and emotions. From Aiken, K.J. and Trevarthen, C. (1997), Self/other organization in human psychological development, Development and Psychopathology 9: 653-677. Reprinted with permission of Cambridge University Press.

brain growth in a child are specifically adapted to be coupled, by emotional communication, to the regulators of adult brains" (1990, p. 357), and that "The right hemisphere is more advanced than the left in surface features from about the 25th (gestational) week and this advance persists until the left hemisphere shows a post-natal growth spurt starting in the second year (1996, p. 582). In contemporary writings, Meares offered interdisciplinary evidence to show that the protoconversation mechanism continues in later development and is an essential element in not only communication but also the human capacity for symbolization. He describes protoconversation as "a conversation between two right brains" (2016, p. 52).

Twenty-five years after Trevarthen's pioneering work, advances in technology now present another image of the attachment communication system embedded in this primordial relationship. In an article in *Annals of*

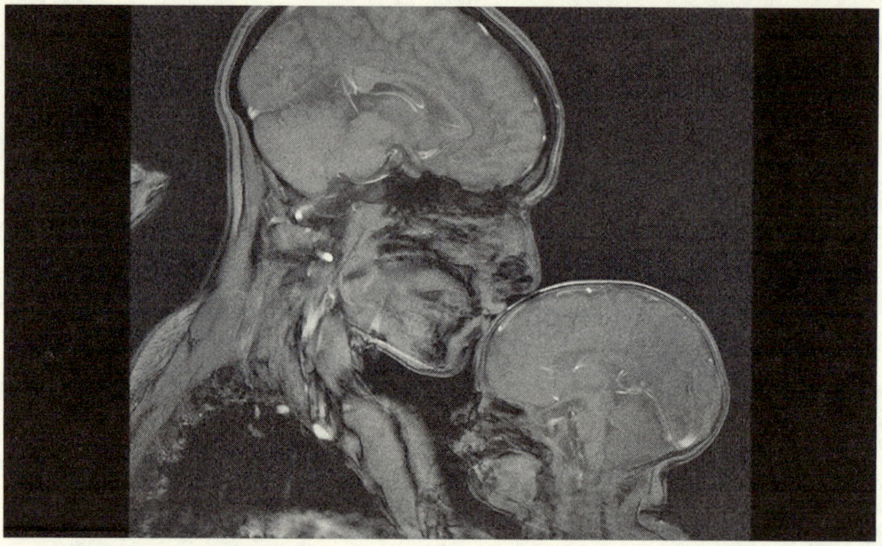

Figure 1.2 Mother and child in an MRI scanner. From Rebecca Saxe and Atsushi Takahashi | Department of Brain and Cognitive Sciences, MIT | Athinoula A. Martinos Imaging Center at the McGovern Institute for Brain Research, MIT.

Family Medicine, Ungar offered a two-person psychological image of the neuroscientist Rebecca Saxe and her infant in an MRI scanner (Figure 1.2). Commenting on this emotionally evocative image, Ungar (2017) concluded,

> The image depicts the mother-infant bond at the level of its most basic neuroanatomy. Through a grainy spectrum of black and grey, the infant brain—seemingly exposed and vulnerable—is held by a larger and more robust adult brain. The two are in close communication through a kiss to the infant's forehead, giving merit to the statement of Allan Schore, certainly to apply to our little patients in the office, that the developing brain forms in the setting of a relationship—a bonding relationship, with "another self—another brain." (p. 82)

Describing the prototypical dynamics of this mother-infant communication system, Walker-Andrews and Bahrick asserted, "From birth, an infant is plunged into a world of other human beings in which conversation, gestures, and faces are omnipresent during the infant's waking hours. Moreover, these harbingers of social information are dynamic, multimodal, and reciprocal" (2001, p. 469). In these rapid attachment communications, the infant's early maturing right hemisphere, which is dominant for the child's processing of visual emotional information, the infant's recognition of the mother's face, and the perception of arousal-inducing maternal facial expressions, is psychobiologically attuned to the output of the mother's right hemisphere, which is involved in the expression and processing of emotional information and in nonverbal communication. The right cortex is known to be specifically affected by early social experiences, to be activated in intense states of emotion, and to contribute to the development of reciprocal interactions within the mother-infant regulatory system. The child uses the output of the mother's emotion-regulating right cortex as a template for imprinting—the hard wiring of circuits in his own right cortex that will come to mediate his expanding affective capacities.

Via this interpersonal neurobiological mechanism, the parenting environment influences the developing patterns of neuronal connectivity that underlie implicit nonverbal communication and spontaneous emotional behavior (Schore, 2003a). Thus, the early maturing, visuospatial, emotional, right cerebral cortex (as opposed to the later developing lexical-semantic left cortex), which stores and processes self-and-object images, has been suggested to be responsible for the manifestations of unconscious processes (Galin, 1974; Hoppe, 1977; Miller, 1991; Schore, 1991; Watt, 1990). This data fits nicely with Bowlby's (1969) description of unconscious internal working models of the attachment relationship. These models, which operate outside of conscious awareness (Bretherton, 1985; Main, Kaplan, & Cassidy, 1985) are guides for future interactions, and the term "working" refers to the individual's unconscious use of the model to interpret and act on new experiences. They contain affective as well as cognitive components and are unconsciously accessed and utilized in the generation of internal strategies of implicit affect regulation, especially during times of stress. Unconscious attachment working models are thus encoded not in the left-hemispheric strategies of conscious emotion regulation, but in right-hemispheric unconscious, implicit (Schore, 1994), "subliminal affect regulation" (Jostmann et al., 2005), which does not rely on the limited capacity of the conscious mind and resists conscious intervention.

Alluding to the differences between the hemispheres, Freud described the unconscious as "a special realm, with its own desires and modes of expression and peculiar mental mechanisms not elsewhere operative" (1920). In *The Ego and the Id*, Freud proposed that "thinking in pictures . . . approximates more closely to unconscious processes than does thinking in words, and it is unquestionably older than the latter both ontogenetically and phylogenetically" (1923/1961, p. 21). This speculation is now confirmed by a body of data suggesting that the right hemisphere, the biological substrate of the unconscious, matures before the left (Gupta et al., 2005; Mento et al., 2010; Sun et al., 2005), and that the right brain is dominant in human infancy (Chiron et al., 1997; Schore, 1994). These neurobiological data also support Freud's suggestion that highly visual, nonverbal, primary process cognition, dominant in infancy, ontogenetically precedes later forming, verbal, secondary process cognition. Indeed, because of its central role in unconscious functions and primary process activities, psychoanalysis has been intrigued with the unique operations of the right brain since the last quarter of the 20th century (Hoppe, 1977; McLaughlin, 1978; Miller, 1986; Watt, 1986).

In my own developmental neuropsychoanalytic work, I have suggested that during rapid, dyadic attachment transactions, the sensitive primary caregiver's right brain implicitly (unconsciously) attends to, perceives, recognizes, monitors, appraises, and regulates nonverbal expressions of the infant's more-and-more intense states of positive and negative affective arousal. Neuroscientists are now asserting that at all stages of the life span, the right hemisphere specializes in implicit learning (Hugdahl, 1995). The temporal dynamics of these implicit, rapid, spontaneous, intersubjective, bodily-based, emotional, right brain nonverbal face-to-face communications have been described by Lyons-Ruth (1999), who observed that implicit, nonconscious processing of nonverbal affective cues in infancy "is repetitive, automatic, provides quick categorization and decision-making, and *operates outside the realm of focal attention and verbalized experience*" (1999, p. 576, italics added).

In this mutually reciprocal face-to-face intersubjective context of right brain-to-right brain nonverbal visual-facial, tactile-gestural, and auditory-prosodic communications, the caregiver and infant learn the rhythmic structure of the other and modify their behavior to fit that structure, thereby co-creating a moment-to-moment specifically fitted interaction. All of this is occurring rapidly and spontaneously, as the intuitive mother is co-creating this emotional relationship unconsciously, beneath levels of conscious awareness. Freud proposed that "everyone possesses in his own unconscious an instrument with which he can interpret the utterances of the unconscious of other people" (1913/1958, p. 320). Thus, the attachment relationship reflects a coordination and alignment between the mother's right brain unconscious and the infant's developing right brain unconscious. In face-to-face (as well as body-to-body) transactions, the mother is implicitly shaping her infant's unconscious mind, which as Freud observed develops before the conscious mind.

Indeed, the mother's emotionally expressive face is, by far, the most potent visual stimulus in the infant's environment, and the child's intense interest in her face, especially in her eyes, leads him to track it in space and to engage in periods of intense mutual gaze. The infant's gaze, in turn, reliably evokes the mother's gaze, and this dyadic system forms an efficient interpersonal channel for the transmission of reciprocal mutual influences. These mutual gaze interactions represent the most intense form of interpersonal communication, and in order to enter into this affective communication, the mother must be psychobiologically attuned not so much to the child's overt behavior as to the reflections of his internal state. The more the mother tunes her activity level to the infant during periods of social engagement, and the more she allows him to recover quietly in periods of disengagement, the more *synchronized* their interaction. This psychobiological synchronization mechanism allows the attuned dyad to be "on the same wavelength."

According to Manini and her colleagues,

> Synchronization of the mother's responses to infant signals in typical dyadic interaction can be considered a key aspect of sensitive parenting, as it implies the promptness of the mother's response and the adaptation moment by moment to the child's emotional state …

> which contributes to a unique bond between them. The autonomic nervous system seems to represent an elementary mechanism supporting emotional synchrony between mother and infant (p. 2).

Secure attachment thus depends on the mother's psychobiological attunement not with the infant's cognition or behavior, but rather with the infant's dynamic alterations of autonomic arousal, the energetic dimension of the child's affective state. To enter into this rapid communication, the mother must resonate with the dynamic crescendos and decrescendos of the infant's bodily-based internal states of peripheral autonomic nervous system (ANS) arousal and central nervous system (CNS) arousal. This autonomic activity occurs at an unconscious level. In these mutually synchronized social interactions, the psychobiologically attuned mother of the securely attached child not only minimizes the infant's negative states in comforting transactions but also maximizes his or her positive affective states in interactive play. Regulated and synchronized affective interactions with a familiar, predictable primary caregiver create not only a sense of safety but also a *positively charged curiosity, wonder, and surprise* that fuels the burgeoning self's exploration of novel socioemotional and physical environments. This ability is a marker of adaptive infant mental health.

TWO-PERSON NEUROIMAGING OF RIGHT-LATERALIZED INTERBRAIN SYNCHRONIZATION AND THE INTERPERSONAL NEUROBIOLOGY OF UNCONSCIOUS COMMUNICATION

Advances in neuroimaging technology now allow for hyperscanning methodologies that can directly study two brains in real-time social interactions with each other, including during rapid emotional attachment communications (see Chapter 1 in the companion volume *Right Brain Psychotherapy* on simultaneous electroencephalography, functional magnetic resonance imaging, near-infrared spectroscopy, and magnetoencephalography measurements). For example, Dumas and his colleagues reported simultaneous measurement of brain activities of each member of a dyad during interpersonal communications, wherein "both participants are continuously active, each *modifying* their own actions in response to the continuously changing

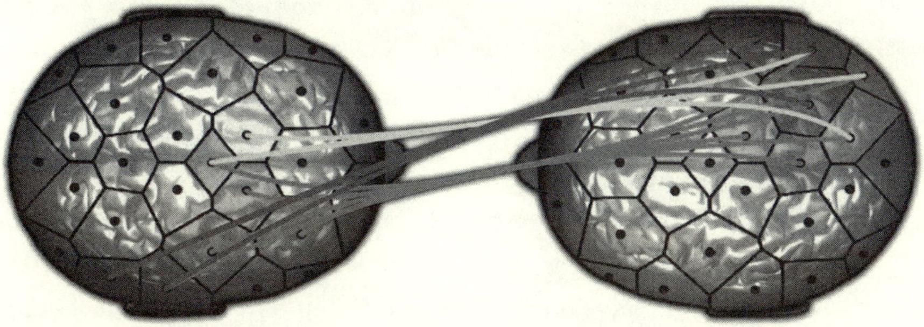

FIGURE 1.3 Right-lateralized interbrain synchronization of a spontaneous nonverbal communication. Adapted from "Toward a Two-Body Neuroscience" by Dumas (2011). Copyright 2011 by Landes Bioscience. Adapted with permission. See insert for color.

actions of their partner" (2010, p.1). Inspired by studies of nonverbal communication and coordination between a mother and her infant (see Figure 1.1, Trevarthen's protoconversation as "a conversation between two right brains) and by research on spontaneous imitation in preverbal infants, these authors offered a dual electroencephalography (EEG) study of *interbrain synchronization during a spontaneous social interaction*, characterized by reciprocal communication and turn taking. In this relational context, both implicitly share attention and compare cues of self and other's actions.

These researchers documented specific changes in both brains during nonverbal imitation, a central foundation of socialization and communication, specifically an interbrain synchronization of the right centroparietal regions on a milliseconds timescale in both interacting partners. Furthermore, they documented that the right temporoparietal cortex in one partner is synchronized with the right temporoparietal cortex of the other (Dumas et al., 2010). They pointed out that the right temporoparietal (TPO) junction is known to be activated in social interactions and is centrally involved in states of attention processing, perceptual awareness, face and voice processing, and empathic understanding. The right TPO integrates input from visual, auditory, somesthetic, and limbic areas and is thus a pivotal neural locus for self-functions. This right-lateralized system also allows for "making sense of another mind" (Saxe & Wexler, 2005). Figure 1.3 illustrates this interbrain synchronization, which is lateralized to the right hemispheres of each member of a communicating dyad (Dumas, 2011). Note this lateralized communication system also represents what I have called "right brain-to-right brain" interaction within the mother-infant attachment system between one subjective self and another subjective self (intersubjectivity).

In a very recent overview of current hyperscanning research Minagawa, Xu, and Morimoto (2018) described current studies of synchronized brain activity between mothers and infants, expressed in bidirectional exchanges of sensory signals, continuous interactive behavior, contingent live social signals, and rapid implicit processing of perceptual cues within the dyad. In one study of mother-infant bonding, Minagawa (2016) performed functional near-infrared spectroscopy hyperscanning neuroimaging during which mothers at rest held their sleeping 3–4 month old infants. This author reported, "The largest synchronization of the holding condition was observed . . . to be near the anterior orbitofrontal cortex (OFC) for both mother and infant . . . As the OFC is known to be a significant cerebral area engaged in maternal attachment (Minagawa-Kawai et.al, 2009; Schore, 2010), the results may further support its role" (p. 19). Note the attachment dyad is communicating when the mother is at rest and the infant is asleep.

Furthermore, Minagawa and colleagues offered the statement (applicable to the attachment system in both mother-infant and therapist-patient familiar dyads),

> As evidenced by several studies, regardless of their measurement modality, inter-brain coupling is more easily observed between a familiar dyad than an unfamiliar dyad. Accordingly more effective synchronization could be assumed between family members . . . Although such a synchronization network among familiar members could be regarded as an automatic process modulated partly in a top-down fashion, it could have been organized as a result of a bottom-up type of associative learning (Minagawa et al., 2018, p. 23).

In another hyperscanning study, Koike et al. (2016) established the central role of the right inferior frontal gyrus in joint attention, a function associated with eye blink synchronization that onsets at 7–12 months in the developing infant.

In summarizing hyperscanning research in infants, children, adolescents, and adults, Minagawa et al. (2018) concluded,

> enhanced interpersonal synchronization was often found in the right hemisphere, primarily the right prefrontal cortex, during cooperative behaviors with coordinated goals, whereas verbal-based communication typically induced inter-brain coherence in the left hemisphere, primarily the left prefrontal cortex and temporoparietal function" (p. 16)

The demonstrations by Dumas', Minagawa's, and Koike's laboratories of right-lateralized interbrain *synchronization* of a spontaneous nonverbal communication, inspired by nonverbal communication and coordination between a mother and her infant, directly applies to my characterization, in 1996, of the role of the mother-infant attachment bond in the early self-organization of the nonlinear right brain (Schore, 1996). During attachment affective communications, the psychobiologically attuned mother unconsciously *synchronizes* the spatiotemporal patterning of her exogenous sensory stimulation with the infant's spontaneous expressions of endogenous organismic rhythms. In 1997, I expanded this conception and proposed a model of attachment dynamics as *synchronized energy exchanges* that co-create nonlinear changes of state. Thus, emotional transactions involving synchronized ordered patterns of energy transmissions (directed flows of energy) represent the fundamental core of the attachment dynamic: "In this mutually *synchronized* attunement of emotionally driven facial expression, prosodic vocalization, and kinesic behaviors, the dyad co-constructs a mutual regulatory system of arousal which contains a positively amplifying circuit mutually affirming both partners" (Schore, 1997, p. 600).

In 2001, I directly alluded to spontaneous right-lateralized interbrain synchronization in my description of an attachment "right brain-to-right brain" nonverbal system of "spontaneous emotional communication," described by Buck as "a conversation between limbic systems" that is the interactive output of each member's right hemisphere (Schore, 2001). Acting at levels beneath conscious awareness, the mother-infant attachment system is transacted in rapid right brain-to-right brain communications of *implicit visual* facial expressions, *tactile* gestures, and *auditory* prosodic expressions, which *when synchronized can act as an integrated, optimally functioning self-system*. It is now well established that synchronization occurs at different levels, from neural activity (Anders et al., 2011), to physiological states such as heartbeat rhythm (Levenson & Gottman, 1983), to pupil size (Hess, 1975), to facial expressions and body postures (Chartrand & Bargh, 1999; Dimberg, 1982). Indeed, mother-infant physiological synchrony has been documented in infants at 3 months (Feldman et al., 2011; Moore & Calkins, 2004), 6 months (Moore et al., 2009), and 12 months (Ham & Tronick, 2006) of age. Studying mother-infant affect synchrony at 3 and 9 months, Feldman, Greenbaum, and Yirmiya assert,

> Synchrony in dynamic systems . . . reflects the degree to which interactants integrate into the flow of behavior the ongoing responses of their partner and the changing inputs of the environment (p. 224).

This right-lateralized interbrain synchronization, initiated in infancy, continues in later stages of development. Research by Feldman and her colleagues showed that mother and infant coordinate heart rhythms in moments of interaction synchrony (Feldman et al., 2011), and that mother-child behavioral synchrony is individually stable from infancy through adolescence (Feldman, 2010). In a magnetoencephalography (MEG) study of social synchrony in mother-child dyads (as opposed to mother-infant dyads), this laboratory called for a "move from focus on one-brain functioning to understanding how two brains dynamically coordinate during real-life social interactions" (Levy, Goldstein, & Feldman, 2017, p. 1036). In this recent work, the researchers observed,

> The mother-child context provides a prototypical, developmentally salient context where synchrony is first experienced and encoded in the brain during early sensitive periods (Feldman, 2015a, b). As mammals, our brain develops in the context of the mother-infant "nursing dyad" through processes of biobehavioral synchrony, the

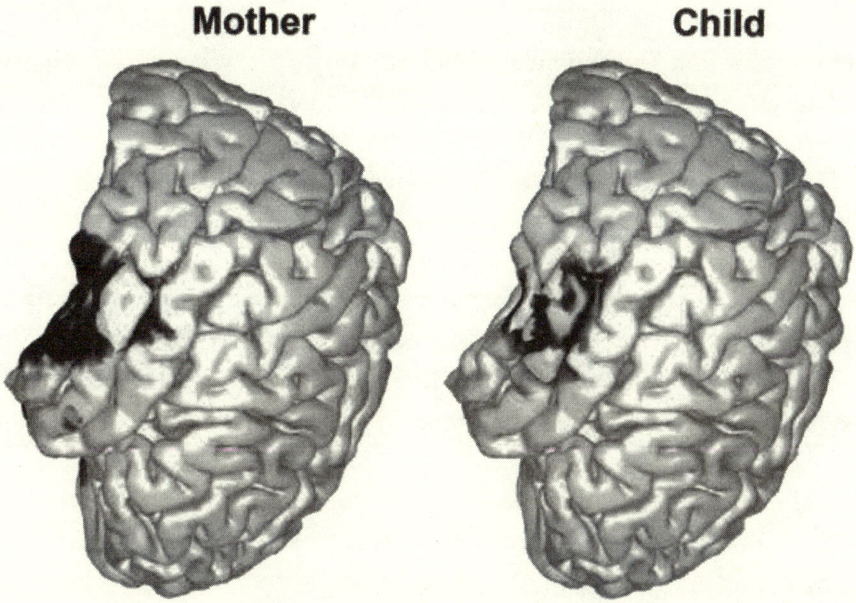

FIGURE 1.4 Brain responses of mother and child to vignettes of their interactions probing social synchrony. The brain responses of the child (right panel) and the mother (left panel) to episodes of own social synchrony were expressed in the right superior temporal sulcus. From Jonathan Levy et al. Perception of Social Synchrony Induces Mother-Child Gamma Coupling in the Social Brain. SCAN (2017) 12 (7): 1036-1046. See insert for color.

> coupling of mother's and child's physiological and behavioral signals during moments of social contact (Feldman, 2012, 2016). (p. 1037)

In research on mothers' synchronized interactions with their 9-year-old children, these researchers demonstrated brain-to-brain coordination during episodes of mother-child affective synchrony, as measured during an emotional "positive dialogue" and a "conflict dialogue" in the home, which then were viewed by each member of the dyad during the MEG scan (Levy et al., 2017). They reported that affective synchrony in such nonverbal social communications is associated with rhythmic processes in the social brain, specifically documenting that the brain responses of the child and the mother in episodes of social synchrony were expressed in heightened activity in the right superior temporal sulcus in both partners, thus implying "a form of communication" between them. Importantly, the extent of activity in the right superior temporal sulcus was significantly coupled only in mothers and their own children (Figure 1.4).

In an adult study titled "Brain Mechanisms Underlying Human Communication," Noordzij and colleagues (2009) offered research demonstrating that planning new communicative actions (by a sender) and recognizing the communicative intention of the same actions (by a receiver) relied on spatially overlapping portions of their brains, specifically the right posterior superior temporal sulcus (pSTS). The response of this region was lateralized to the right hemisphere, modulated by the ambiguity in meaning of the communicative acts. Via this right-lateralized system, the sender of a communicative signal uses his own intention recognition system to make a prediction of the intention recognition performed by the receiver. The authors concluded that these data confirm the crucial role of the right pSTS for processing novel metaphors and pragmatic aspects of linguistic information (Jung-Beeman et al., 2004; Mashal et al., 2007), an instance of the right-hemispheric dominance for inferring the communicative intentions of a conversational partner (Sabbagh, 1999).

Synchrony also operates within verbal interactions, as in a conversation where both members alter their posture and fixate their gaze simultaneously (Shockley et al., 2003; Richardson et al., 2007). This interactive mechanism co-creates an alignment that supports mutual understanding, what Clark and Brenman (1991) call "common ground," a shared function that correlates with synchrony at the neural level. Commenting on these studies, Jasmin et al. (2016) observed "when listening to a speaker tell a story, the listener's brain activity is synchronized with that of the storyteller's, both simultaneously and at a delay, and the degree of coordination predicts understanding and alignment of mental states" (Stephens, et al., 2010; Huhlen et al. 2012). (Note the direct relevance of this synchronization to conversations within the therapeutic interaction, in which among other things the therapist processes the patient's emotional narrative, and the patient processes the therapist's interpretation).

Utilizing functional magnetic resonance Jasmin et al. (2016) offered an fMRI study of "Cohesion and Joint Speech: Right Hemisphere Contributions to Synchronized Vocal Production." In this neurobiological research on "interactive," "joint," "synchronous" speech they concluded "our data suggest that the lateralization of speaking may vary with the interactive context in which the speech is spoken. Synchronous speech, especially with a live talker, recruits additional right hemisphere regions in frontal cortex (right inferior frontal gyrus), temporal cortex (superior temporal gyrus) and parietal cortex (somatosensory cortex)" (p. 4678). In addition, these authors suggested that turn-taking in an interactive context may depend on a right-lateralized network involved in the "unconscious detection of a live speaker," an assertion that fits with my interpersonal neurobiological construct of a therapeutic "conversation between two right brains" and a right brain "relational unconscious" (Gerson, 2004) that synchronizes and communicates with another relational unconscious, especially in an emotional context.

In further support of this model of right-lateralized interbrain synchronization, functional neuroimaging research is now exploring the critical role of the right hemisphere in adult social interactions (Semrud-Clikeman, Fine, & Zhu, 2011). Indeed, live face-to-face interaction during functional magnetic resonance imaging (fMRI) shows "greater activation in brain regions involved in social cognition and reward, including the right temporoparietal junction, anterior cingulate cortex, right superior temporal sulcus, ventral striatum, and amygdala" (Redcay et al., 2010, p. 1639). This clearly describes events within the attachment face-to-face context (as well as in the psychotherapeutic relationship). Another imaging study now demonstrates that emotions promote social interactions by synchronizing brain activity across individuals (Nummenmaa et al., 2012). In this manner, the right brain attachment dynamic continues throughout the life span as an unconscious mechanism that mediates the interpersonal and intrapsychic events of all relationships, especially intimate relationships.

CURRENT REFORMULATIONS OF FREUD'S UNCONSCIOUS

In classic writings, Orlinsky and Howard contended that the "non-verbal, prerational stream of expression that binds the infant to its parent continues throughout life to be a primary medium of intuitively felt affective-relational communication between persons" (1986, p. 343). The developmental scholar Ellen Dissanayake (2001) has reflected on this continuity of the early developing unconscious mind over all later developmental stages:

> [W]e tend to assume that analytic, abstract, verbalized cognition is dominant. Certainly for scientific and academic investigation and communication it is essential. But *we forget, at our peril, how much of our thinking and communication is imbued with analogical, unverbalizable, unconscious content* . . . our original analogical, nonverbal, intersubjective mind persists after infancy, but it is usually consciously overridden by 'cognition' and language (which are necessarily coupled to the real world) so that we are generally unaware of it (pp. 95–96, italics added).

Other infant researchers are asserting,

> Preverbal communication . . . is the realm of non-consciously regulated intuitive behavior and implicit relational knowledge. Whether information is transferred or shared, which information gets across, and on which level it is "understood," does not necessarily depend on the sender's intention or conscious awareness. (Papousek, 2007, p. 258)

In a study, "Unconscious Discrimination of Social Cues from Eye Whites in Infants," Jessen and Grossmann (2014) describe the essential role of eyes during communications within human social encounters of 7-month-old infants (a developmental period of "stranger anxiety"). These authors observe that this "emotion perception," "a vital part of any social interaction, heavily relies on information from the eye region. This is especially important for the detection of fear in others, as one of the most basic forms of identifying threatening situations . . . This mechanism operates exceptionally fast, and occurs irrespective of conscious awareness" (p. 16208). On the other side of the mother-infant dyad, a large body of adult research indicates that the right occipital-temporal cortex generates a holistic face representation at 170 milliseconds after stimulus onset, beneath conscious awareness (e.g., Jacques & Rossion, 2009; Yovel, 2016). In an adult study of voice processing, another central mechanism of preverbal communication, Schepman, Rodway, and Pritchard (2016) offered a study titled "Right-Lateralized Unconscious, but Not Conscious, Processing of Affective Environmental Sounds." According to the neuropsychologists Tucker and Moller, "The right hemisphere's specialization for emotional communication through nonverbal channels seems to suggest a domain of the mind that is close to the motivationally charged psychoanalytic unconscious" (2007, p. 91).

The unconscious early right brain-to-right brain communication system continues to operate at later stages of the life span, and these right-lateralized interbrain synchronizations continue to affect the development of the right brain, the psychobiological substrate of the human unconscious. This interpersonal neurobiological mechanism allows for the attachment system and indeed the unconscious to develop to more neuroplastic complexity. Indeed, research now indicates that "the right hemisphere is significantly more efficient and interconnected than the left hemisphere" (Iturria-Medina et al., 2011, p. 56). Although the predominant current developmental neurobiological methodology for studying infants is having the infant sit on the mother's lap and responding to video social cues, hyperscanning is now available for a relational two-person perspective. Research should now turn to investigations of the interpersonal neurobiology of spontaneous right brain-to-right brain face-to-face attachment mechanisms, from infancy, childhood, adolescence, and adulthood through old age. This calls for more applications of nonlinear statistical analyses that can measure and document both the reciprocal dynamic changes between as well as within each of two brains interacting in real time.

This conceptualization links the central role of the attachment relationship in the structural connectivity of the right hemisphere, in the infant's emerging abilities to experience, communicate, and regulate emotional self-states, and ultimately in the development of the implicit, subjective self, which throughout the life span operates unconsciously, beneath levels of awareness. It also underscores the fact that the human unconscious, a central construct of developmental psychoanalysis for the past hundred years, needs to be reinserted into academic developmental psychology from which it has almost been banished. Although the field's response to neuroscience has been tepid, its interest in early evolving "implicit" functions are in fact directly associated with operations of the early developing right hemisphere. Recall the right hemisphere specializes in implicit learning (Hugdahl, 1995), including "implicit relational knowing" (Boston Change Process Study Group, 2007; see also Schore, 2003a, 2003b).

In recent neuroscience, authors have reported studies on "Right Hemisphere Dominance in Nonconscious Processing" (Chen & Hsiao, 2014), concluding that the right hemisphere has an advantage in shaping behavior with implicit information, whereas the left hemisphere plays a greater role in expressing explicit knowledge. Another study on "the unconscious guidance of attention" documents that the right hemisphere temporo-parietal junction plays an essential role in implicit attentional functions that operate outside conscious awareness (Chelazzi, Bisley, & Bartolomeo, 2018). Hassin (2013) cited a large body of research documenting the adaptive functions performed by the human unconscious:

> The function of extracting patterns from our environment, also known as implicit learning, has been repeatedly demonstrated; maintaining evidence from past experience, also known as memory, can happen outside of conscious awareness; people can extract information about emotion and gender from subliminally presented facial expressions; comparing oneself with others, a central social function, occurs nonconsciously and even with subliminally presented others; and physical sensations affect perception and social perception. . . . A review of the literature through functional glasses quickly reveals that many functions that were historically associated with conscious awareness can occur nonconsciously. (p. 200)

In an earlier study, Hassin and his colleagues showed that in contrast to (left hemispheric) explicit working memory, implicit working memory operates unintentionally and outside of conscious awareness (Hassin et al., 2009). Note that each hemisphere has its own working memory system, one verbal, the other nonverbal.

A central theme of both my ongoing clinical and developmental studies dictates that the human brain and mind are in actuality a dual system. Toward that end, across all my writings I have been offering a continuous stream of clinical data and experimental research to show that the conscious mind resides in the left hemisphere, while the unconscious mind operating at levels beneath awareness resides in the right hemisphere (Schore, 1994, 2003a, 2003b, 2012). This hierarchical model traces back to the foundations of brain laterality research in the 19th century and to the origins of psychoanalysis in the early 20th century. It not only emphasizes the functional differences between the hemispheres, but also models the relationships between the cerebral hemispheres, as well as the relationships between the conscious and unconscious minds.

The current expanding body of knowledge of neuroscience and neuropsychoanalysis now suggests a major alteration in Freud's conceptualization of a "dynamic unconscious," a central construct of psychoanalysis, "the science of unconscious processes." For most of the past century, the contents of the dynamic unconscious were thought to be the products of repression. And yet, in classic writings Freud emphasized, "Everything that is repressed must remain unconscious; but let us state that at the very outset that the repressed does not cover everything that is unconscious. The unconscious has the wider compass: the repressed is a part of the unconscious" (1915b/1957, p. 166). In my earlier neuropsychoanalytic studies, I offered the following update of this "wider compass:" Freud's seminal model of a dynamic, continually active unconscious mind describes the moment-to-moment operations of a hierarchical, self-organizing implicit-procedural regulatory system that is located in the "emotional" right brain (Schore, 2003b). The dynamic unconscious processing, organization, communication, and regulation of emotional and relational stimuli is specifically associated with activation of the right and not left hemisphere. The right hemisphere generates implicit, unconscious, nonverbal emotion regulation (Schore, 1994, 2003a, 2003b, 2012) as opposed to the left hemisphere's explicit, conscious, verbal emotional regulation (Gross, 2008). This contemporary reformulation of Freud's theories also indicates that not only thoughts but also affects can be unconscious (Schore, 2012).

Indeed, with the establishment of modern trauma theory, it is now established that affects can not only be repressed but also dissociated (Schore,

2003a, 2003b). Current additions to clinical theory clearly suggest that the unconscious contains not only defensively repressed dysregulated emotional memories but also defensively dissociated traumatic emotional memories (Schore, 2012). Thus, not only early experiences of attachment trauma but also the defense against early overwhelming trauma—dissociation—is stored in unconscious implicit-procedural memory.

Furthermore, because of the incorporation of neuroscience and neurophysiology, psychoanalytic theory is now being transformed from a theory of the unconscious mind into a theory of brain/mind/body: unconscious systems operating beneath levels of conscious awareness are inextricably linked into the body. Spontaneously released "bottom-up" bodily-based autonomic and hormonal systems including stress steroids such as cortisol, sex steroids such as androgens and estrogens, and neuroendocrines such as oxytocin and vasopressin are now understood to operate at levels beneath conscious awareness. These neurochemical products of what were previously known as id processes are thus also part of the domain of the right brain unconscious system.

Indeed over the past three decades, the conceptualization of the unconscious system has been significantly revised within both psychoanalysis and academic psychology. In an article in the *American Psychologist*, Bargh and Chartrand contended that "most of moment-to-moment psychological life must occur through nonconscious means if it is to occur at all . . . various nonconscious mental systems perform the lion's share of the self-regulatory burden, beneficently keeping the individual grounded in his or her current environment" (1999, p. 462). In a further update of the unconscious, Winson concluded, "Rather than being a cauldron of untamed passions and destructive wishes, I propose that the unconscious is a cohesive, continually active mental structure that takes note of life's experiences and reacts according to its scheme of interpretation" (1990, p. 96). At about the same time, Dimberg and Ohman (1996) described that

> long sequences of interactions between people may be partly determined by nonconscious perceptions and automatic responses on the part of both the sender and receiver. Their conscious understanding of what is going on in the interaction that they can formulate ver-

> bally, on the other hand, may be quite independent of this basic level of interaction. (p. 177)

The authors specifically implicated right-hemispheric processes in these events.

In an even more complex characterization from within psychoanalysis, Davies (1996) described a "relational unconscious," one that

> evolves out of an ever present, yet constantly changing, system of affective, cognitive, and physiologically based self-experiences in ongoing interactive and dialogic discourse with a host of significant internally and externally derived objects. . . . Not one unconscious, not *the* unconscious, but multiple levels of consciousness and unconsciousness, in an ongoing state of interactive articulation as past experience infuses the present and present experience evokes state-dependent memories of formative interactive representations. (p. 197)

In my own writings on the "two-person psychology" of a relational unconscious, I have suggested that just as the left brain communicates its states to other left brains via conscious linguistic behaviors, so the right nonverbally communicates its unconscious states to other right brains that are tuned to receive these communications. This right-lateralized communication system evolves in the mother-infant attachment relationship, which shapes emotional circuits in early critical periods of right brain development that generate unconscious working models used to navigate the subjective self through the social world.

Thus, for better or for worse, the maternal-infant attachment relationship structuralizes the developing right brain unconscious via an implicit intergenerational transmission of resilience against or vulnerability to later psychiatric, personality, and developmental disorders. In those with the most difficult attachment histories, enduring unconscious representations of dysregulating relational emotional stressors and of early relational traumas are stored in unconscious implicit-procedural working models. The primordial, subjective autobiographical representational system of the earliest nonverbal emotional interactions is imprinted into the early developing right brain implicit self-system (in contrast to a later forming left-hemispheric verbal representational explicit self-system). Although by age 4, the left brain becomes the dominant hemisphere, under stress the right brain unconscious system shifts into the foreground of consciousness.

Bowlby (1973) described these dual representational systems:

> When *multiple models* of a single figure are operative they are likely to differ in regard to their origin, *their dominance* and the extent to which the subject is aware of them. In a person suffering from an emotional disturbance, it is common to find that *the model that has had greatest influence on his feelings and behavior, is one developed during his early years* and is constructed along fairly primitive lines, but that the person may be relatively unaware of while simultaneously there is operating within him a second, and perhaps radically incompatible, model, that developed later, that is much more sophisticated, and that the person is more clearly aware of and he may mistakenly assume to be dominant. (p. 205, italics added)

In classic neuropsychological writings on the right brain and the unconscious, Joseph (1992) characterized these lateralized, implicit and explicit self-representational systems, located in the "nondominant" right and "dominant" left hemispheres:

> Just as we have a conscious and an unconscious mind, as well as a right and left brain, we also have two self-images. One is consciously maintained and the other is almost wholly unconscious. The *conscious self-image* is associated with the left half of the brain in most people. However, this self-image is also subject to unconscious influences. By contrast, the *unconscious self-image* is maintained within the right brain mental system and is tremendously influenced by current and past experiences . . . the two self-images . . . interact. Indeed, sometimes the conscious self-image is fashioned in reaction to unconscious feelings, traumas, and feared inadequacies that the

> person does not want to possess, but that nevertheless, are unconsciously maintained. (p. 181, italics added)

In an earlier work, Joseph described "early emotional learning occurring in the right hemisphere unbeknownst to the left; learning and associated emotional responding may later be completely unaccessible to the language centers of the brain" (1982, p. 243).

The relationship of the conscious to the unconscious mind was initially discussed by Freud (1900/1953) in his topographical model of a stratified conscious, preconscious, and unconscious systems, and later in his structural model (1923/1961) of "higher" superego and ego functions that sit astride the id. My own neuropsychoanalytic conceptualization of an integration of Freud's topographical and structural models dictates a hierarchical organization of the conscious, preconscious, and unconscious minds. Freud's tripartite taxonomy of a conscious, preconscious, and subliminal unconscious is now reappearing in the scientific literature (Dehaene et al., 2006).

In terms of the sequence of neurobiological maturation, note in Figure 1.5 that the brain evolves in a caudal to rostral direction, subcortical to cortical, with the brain-stem autonomic and arousal structures maturing earliest, then the emotion-processing limbic system, then the earlier maturing right hemisphere, and lastly the verbal functions of the left hemisphere. This translates into an early evolution of the deep unconscious, then to the unconscious, then preconscious, and finally the higher levels of the conscious mind. In earlier work, I suggested that the deep unconscious represents activity of the subcortical amygdala, unconscious, and the anterior cingulate medial frontal system, and the preconscious represents activity of the right orbitofrontal corticolimbic system (Schore, 2003b).

The dual-brain, dual-mind systems shift from conscious to unconscious functions via the mechanism of regression. A modern neuropsychoanalytic translation of Freud's metapsychological model describes two different mechanisms of regression from the later forming conscious mind to the earlier evolving unconscious right mind. In this hierarchical model, an evolving higher level of functioning supplants and inhibits lower levels, which are more automatic and more organized. Reversing the sequence in the Figure 1.5 regression from "higher" to "lower" functional levels rep-

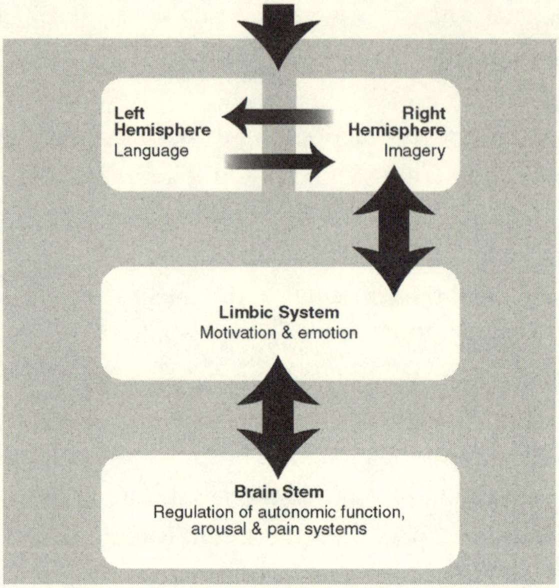

FIGURE 1.5 Unconscious implicit processing of the "lower," early developing right brain and subsequent connections into the "higher," later developing left brain conscious explicit system. Note the vertical axis of the right brain on the right side of the figure. From *The Science of the Art of Psychotherapy*, pg. 82, by Allan N. Schore (2012).

resents a "*taking off of the higher*" and "*at the very same time a letting go, or expression of the lower.*"

In a further reformulation of Freud's concept of regression, I propose two types of neurobiological regressions: an interhemispheric *topographical* form (a horizontal state switch from conscious left prefrontal cortical to preconscious right prefrontal cortical system) and an intrahemispheric *structural* regression (a vertical hierarchical state switch from higher to lower right brain, downward cortical to subcortical, from preconscious to deeper unconscious levels of the right brain (see the horizontal and vertical arrows on Figure 1.5). A topographical regression thus represents an intrapsychic shift from the later developing conscious "left mind" to the earlier developing unconscious "right mind." In contrast, a structural regression represents a shift from "higher right" to "lower right" levels of emotion-processing unconscious mind.

Thus, in my neuropsychoanalytic models, I describe a left-lateralized conscious mind and a right cortical preconscious mind behind the left cortical surface mind that is accessed via a shift in hemispheric dominance in a topographical regression. And another mind beneath conscious awareness, the bodily-based unconscious–deep unconscious mind, which is accessed via a structural regression. With respect to "horizontal" topographical regressions, Kane (2004) stated that the shift in hemispheric dominance in a creative moment of a regression in the service of the ego involves a callosal disinhibition, "a sudden and transient loss or decrease of normal interhemispheric communication, removing inhibitions placed upon the right hemisphere and allowing it to function at a greater-than-normal . . . activity level" (p. 52). In the clinical literature, Sandler and Sandler (1986) defined regression as "a process of release and disinhibition of past modes of functioning."

This updated integration of Freud's topographical and structural models also can be represented in a neurobiological update of Freud's iceberg visual metaphor of the unconscious (Figure 1.6). This model incorporates the previous discussions of repression, dissociation, internal working models, and implicit functions of the right-lateralized unconscious system.

In very recent writings on the clinical application of current psychoanalytic theory to psychotherapy, McWilliams (2018) overviews the field's conception of the dynamic unconscious system:

> Most fundamentally, psychoanalytic practitioners take seriously the evidence that the sources of most of our behaviors, feelings, and thoughts are not conscious … Yet, to psychodynamic therapists, it is not merely that these phenomena are nonconscious; there is a dynamic organization of how we unconsciously register experience, an organization that prompts analysts to refer to the unconscious, both generically and in each of us. In any individual, this schema is seen as the result of unfolding interactions between the growing child and significant people in that child's world. Features of, and relationships with, those early figures come to be internalized in stable ways (McWilliams, 2018, p. 88).

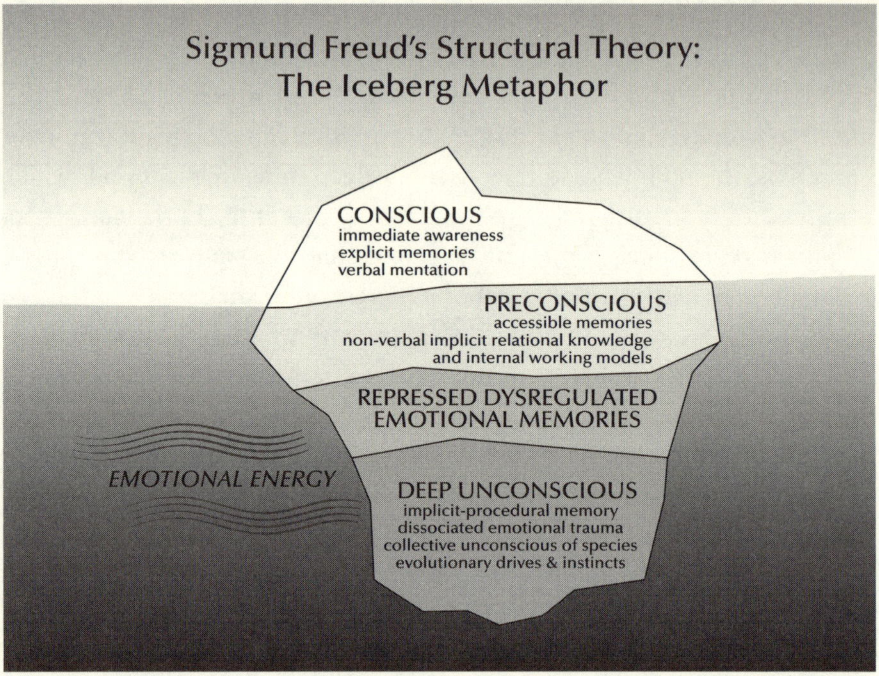

FIGURE 1.6 Revised update of Freud's iceberg metaphor.

These early internalizations of the right brain unconscious system play an essential role in psychotherapy (Schore, 2014).

In *Right Brain Psychotherapy*, the companion to this volume, I discuss the importance of patient-therapist mutual regressions from "higher," later evolving conscious to "lower," earlier evolving unconscious levels. These synchronized mutual regressions allow the dyad to access, communicate, and regulate the early unconscious self-image of the patient, which is dominant in determining the individual's emotional well-being and mental health. I continue to assert that much of the mental health field's research overemphasizes measures of the left brain conscious self and underappreciates the power of unconscious implicit motivational and emotional systems in the human experience (Schore, 2012). There is now agreement that affect dysregulation is a fundamental mechanism of all psychiatric disorders, that right brain deficits in implicit and relational processes are the key to all personality disorders, and that all psychotherapies show a similarity in promoting affect regulation.

With this introduction in mind, the following chapters are a continuation of a series of contributions directed toward elucidating the mechanisms that link early interpersonal processes with the organization of intrapsychic unconscious structural systems. Specifically, I am proposing that knowledge of the experience-dependent maturation of the right brain ("right mind") offers us a chance to more deeply understand not just the contents of the unconscious, but its origin, structure, and dynamics. Indeed, the mental health and the developmental fields are now both extremely interested in the clinical applications of neurobiological sciences to the problems of optimizing relational origins of the self in early prevention and intervention. Toward that end, in the second chapter I offer an elaboration of modern attachment theory, applying regulation theory to the developmental interpersonal neurobiology of relational trauma and dissociation, and the third chapter is a contribution on the early assessment of disorganized attachment disorders and autistic spectrum disorders.

In the fourth chapter, "All Our Sons: The Developmental Neurobiology and Neuroendocrinology of Boys at Risk," I propose that significant gender differences are seen between male and female social and emotional functions in the earliest stages of development, and that these result not only from differences in sex hormones and social experiences but also in rates of male and female brain maturation, specifically in the early developing right brain. I present interdisciplinary research that indicates the stress-regulating circuits of the male brain mature more slowly than those of the female in the prenatal, perinatal, and postnatal critical periods, and that this differential structural maturation is reflected in normal gender differences in right brain attachment functions and in increased vulnerability of males to autism, early onset schizophrenia, attention deficit hyperactivity disorder, and conduct disorders. Many of these affective gender differences are expressed at the implicit level.

Other chapters focus on not only minimizing risk but also maximizing resilience. The fifth chapter, "Early Right Brain Regulation and the Relational Origins of Emotional Well-Being," asks how the relational experiences at the beginning of life, especially in intimate contexts, fundamentally influence the growth of the self's subjective, unconscious mind? In that work, I suggest that an essential function of the right brain subjective self is to unconsciously generate a background sense of emotional well-being, an implicit sense of security that operates beneath levels of conscious awareness. In the sixth chapter—"The Development of the Right Brain across the Life Span: What's Love Got to Do with It?"—I present evidence indicating that during the critical period of development of the deep unconscious levels of the psyche, the resonant and amplified and thereby intense emotional energy shared within the loving mother-infant dyad structuralizes the infant's evolving right brain. This allows the developing unconscious to attain more structural coherence and thereby more functional complexity. At all points of the life span, in any heightened affective moment of mutual love, two deep unconscious systems are communicating, synchronizing, resonating, and co-regulating each other. Lastly, in an interview in the final chapter, I offer more personal reflections about my own unconscious creative processes over the course of my career.

A large body of studies now demonstrates that the "emotional," "social" right brain is centrally involved in not only affects and stress regulation but also empathy, intuition, creativity, imagery, symbolic thought, insight, play, humor, music, compassion, morality, and love (Schore, 2012). In light of the essential role of the right brain in unconscious functions, these studies alter previous conceptions of the unconscious as exclusively involved in "lower," less socially evolved functions. The common thread throughout the following chapters is that right brain fast-acting implicit functions mediate the deeper mechanisms of the invisible, omnipresent unconscious in everyday life, and thereby validate and expand upon Freud's enduring and fundamental contribution to science. This statement clearly implies my intention to reach the reader's unconscious as well as conscious mind.

CHAPTER 2

Modern Attachment Theory

OVER THE PAST THREE DECADES, I have elaborated modern attachment theory, a neurobiologically informed update of John Bowlby's pioneering attempts to integrate Freud's psychology and Darwin's biology in order to model the evolutionary origins of early human development. Grounded in developmental, affective, and social neuroscience, this interdisciplinary theory posits that the hard wiring of the infant's early developing right brain, which is dominant for the processing of emotional and social information, is imprinted in implicit, intersubjective, psychobiological transactions embedded in the attachment relationship with the mother. A primary focus is on the nonverbal communication of emotional states and the relational regulation of the infant's developing brain/mind/body. At the most fundamental level, modern attachment theory is a self-regulation theory (Schore, 1994, 2003a, 2003b, 2012; Schore & Schore, 2008, 2014a).

Modern attachment theory also explicates the mechanisms by which attachment shapes, for better or worse, the survival functions of the right brain. It is now clear that the developing brain is not "resilient" but "malleable" (Schore, 2013b). The theory offers a conceptualization of individual differences in attachment, of the interpersonal neurobiological origins of both secure and insecure attachments, as and of the etiology of a vulnerability to later disorders of emotion dysregulation and social information processing. Thus, the evolutionary mechanism of attachment is critical to more than just the development of overt behaviors and cognitive mental functions but also to self-regulating emotional and social capacities that are essential for adaptive organismic functioning.

The theory utilizes an interpersonal neurobiological perspective of development, one that describes how brains align their neural activities with other brains in not only early but all social interactions, and how the structure and function of the brain and mind are shaped by social experiences, especially those involving emotional relationships. Bodily-based attachment communications are transacted between the right brains of the mother and infant, thus facilitating the relational experience-dependent maturation of the infant's early developing right brain. In this manner, "The self-organization of the developing brain occurs in the context of a relationship with another self, another brain" (Schore, 1996, p. 60).

In the following, I will offer an overview of my studies on the developmental interpersonal neurobiology of a secure attachment and its growth-facilitating effect on the early development of the right brain. I will then discuss the developmental interpersonal neurobiology of attachment relational trauma and the growth-inhibiting effects of disorganized, disoriented, insecure attachment on developing right brain structure and function.

DEVELOPMENTAL INTERPERSONAL NEUROBIOLOGY OF SECURE ATTACHMENT

The essential task of the first year of human life is the creation of a secure attachment bond of emotional communication and interactive regulation between the infant and primary caregiver (Schore, 1994; Schore & Schore, 2008). Secure attachment depends on the mother's psychobiological attunement with not the infant's cognition or behavior, but rather in her regulation of the infant's dynamic alterations of autonomic arousal, the energetic dimension of the child's affective state. In order to enter into this communication, the mother must be psychobiologically attuned to the dynamic crescendos and decrescendos of the infant's bodily-based internal states of peripheral autonomic nervous system (ANS) arousal and central nervous system (CNS) arousal. Through right brain-to-right brain nonverbal visual-facial, tactile-gestural, and auditory-prosodic communications, the caregiver and infant learn the rhythmic structure of the other and modify their behavior to fit that structure, thereby co-creating a moment-to-moment specifically fitted interaction. All of this is occurring rapidly and spontaneously, as the mother is co-creating this emotional relationship unconsciously, beneath levels of conscious awareness. Thus, the attachment relationship reflects a coordination between the mother's right brain unconscious and the infant's developing right brain unconscious. Indeed, the mother is implicitly shaping her infant's unconscious mind, which as Freud observed develops before the conscious mind.

During these affective communications, the psychobiologically attuned mother synchronizes the spatiotemporal patterning of her exogenous sensory stimulation with the infant's spontaneous expressions of endogenous organismic rhythms. Via this contingent responsivity, the mother appraises the nonverbal expressions of her infant's internal arousal and affective states, regulates them, and communicates them back to the infant. To accomplish this, the sensitive mother must successfully modulate nonoptimal high *or* excessively low levels of stimulation that would induce supra-heightened or extremely low levels of arousal in the infant.

Research now clearly demonstrates that the primary caregiver is not always attuned and optimally mirroring, that there are frequent moments of misattunement in the dyad—ruptures of the attachment bond. The disruption of attachment transactions leads to a transient regulatory failure and an impaired autonomic homeostasis. In this pattern of "interactive repair" (Tronick, 1989; Tronick & Gianino, 1986) following dyadic misattunement, or "disruption and repair," (Beebe & Lachmann, 1994) the "good-enough" caregiver who induces a stress response through misattunement will in a timely fashion reinvoke a re-attunement—a regulation of the infant's negatively charged arousal. This repair process allows the infant to cope with stressful negatively charged affects and to gain self-regulatory skills in the form of maintaining persistent efforts to overcome interactive stress. Modern attachment theory utilizes a two-person interpersonal neurobiological perspective to model right brain-to-right brain communications of affect synchrony and positively valenced states and interactive repair of negatively valenced states.

In his seminal first volume, Bowlby proposed that mother-infant attachment communications are "accompanied by the strongest of feelings and emotions, and occur within a context of facial expression, posture, tone of voice" (1969, p. 120). Following his lead, in my first book I suggested that during attachment episodes of right brain *visual-facial, auditory-prosodic, and tactile-gestural* affective communications, the primary caregiver regulates the infant's internal states of ANS peripheral and CNS central arousal:

> The infant's early maturing right hemisphere, which is dominant for the child's processing of visual emotional information, the infant's recognition of the mother's face, and the perception of arousal-inducing maternal facial expressions, is psychobiologically attuned to the output of the mother's right hemisphere, which is involved in the expression and processing of emotional information and in nonverbal communication. (Schore, 1994, p. 63)

In order to process these nonverbal communications, the infant seeks proximity to the mother, who in an optimal context must be subjectively perceived as predictable, consistent, and emotionally available. During dyadic attachment transactions, the prereflective sensitivity of the primary caregiver's right brain implicitly (unconsciously) attends to, perceives (recognizes), appraises, and regulates nonverbal expressions of the infant's more-and-more intense states of positive and negative affective arousal. The temporal dynamics of these implicit, rapid, spontaneous, intersubjective, bodily-based emotional right brain nonverbal communications are described by Lyons-Ruth, who observed that implicit, nonconscious processing of nonverbal affective cues in infancy "is repetitive, automatic, provides quick categorization and decision-making, and *operates outside the realm of focal attention and verbalized experience*" (1999, p. 576, italics added). In the following, I describe current developmental neuroscience findings on these unconscious communications. Because of space limitations, I refer the reader to Schore (2012, 2013a) for specific references to the following.

With respect to *visual-facial attachment communications*, it is now established that mutual gaze is critical to early social development. The emergence of the capacity to efficiently process information from faces requires visual input to the right (and not left) hemisphere during infancy. At 2 months of age, the onset of a critical period during which synaptic connections in the developing occipital cortex are modified by visual experience, infants show right-hemispheric activation when exposed to a woman's face. Using electroencephalography (EEG) methodology, Grossmann and colleagues (2007) reported that 4-month-old infants presented with images of a female face gazing directly ahead show enhanced gamma electrical activity over right prefrontal areas. Near-infrared spectroscopy (NIRS) research (perhaps the most suitable of all neuroscience techniques applicable to human infants) revealed that specifically the 5-month-old's right hemisphere responds to images of adult female faces. By 6 months, infants show a right-lateralized, left gaze bias when viewing faces, right temporal activation when looking at angry faces, and significantly greater right frontotemporal activation when viewing their own mother's (as opposed to a stranger's) face (Carlsson et al., 2008).

Note the developmental progression over the first year to more complex visual-affective functions. These research data indicate that the future capacity to process the essential social information expressed in face-to-face communications, a central aspect of all later intimate relationships, is dependent on caregiver-infant eye contact and visual gazing during early critical periods. Thus, how often and in what contexts the mother and infant *spontaneously* look (and not look) directly at each other is of key importance to an infant's development and the emotional health of the dyadic relationship.

Ongoing studies of prenatal, perinatal, and postnatal *auditory-prosodic attachment communications* also highlight the role of the right brain. In an EEG study of auditory pitch processing in preterm infants born at 30 gestational weeks, Mento and colleagues concluded, "the earlier right structural maturation in foetal epochs seems to be paralleled by a right functional development" (2010, p. 1). A functional magnetic resonance imaging (fMRI) study of 1- to 3-day-old newborns documented that music evokes right-hemispheric activation in the auditory cortex (as do lullabies). Using NIRS with 2- to 6-day-old neonates, Telkemeyer and colleagues observed, "responses to slow acoustic modulations are lateralized to the right hemisphere" (2009, p. 14726). This same optical brain-imaging technology revealed that prosodic processing of emotional voices in 3-month-old and 4-month-old infants activates the right temporoparietal region. Grossmann and colleagues (2010) reported that 7-month-old infants respond to emotional voices in a voice-sensitive region of the right superior temporal sulcus, and happy prosody specifically activates the right inferior frontal cortex. These authors concluded, "The pattern of findings suggests that temporal regions specialize in processing voices very early in development and that, already in infancy, emotions differentially modulate voice processing in the right hemisphere" (2010, p. 852).

Furthermore, neuroscience now supports the principle that the caregiver's use of infant-directed speech ("motherese") is critical for the development of the posterior areas of the right hemisphere that process prosodic-emotional functions. Independent of culture, infant-directed speech, which Darwin (1877) referred to as "the sweet music of the species," is preferred over adult-directed speech as early as a few weeks after birth. Compared to adult-directed speech, motherese, the vocal expression of emotion to infants, is higher in pitch, has a wider pitch range, and exhibits exaggerated pitch contours. In addition, it is shorter, slower, and separated by longer pauses than adult speech. Developmental neurobiological research demonstrates that maternal infant-directed speech activates the right temporal area of 4- to 6-month-old infants, and that this activation is even greater in 7- to 9-month-old infants (Naoi et al., 2011). In 11-month-old infants, the voice of a woman's infant-directed speech (i.e., with somewhat exaggerated prosody) elicits a right-lateralized event-related potential.

Note the developmental progression of auditory affective functions that allow for more complex communication. The emotional quality of what infants hear in the early stages of infancy affects the development of the voice-processing areas of the right hemisphere, especially the temporal voice areas in the upper banks of the right superior temporal sulcus. These studies indicate the importance of not the verbal content but the melody of the mother's voice, and whether or not she's using infant-directed versus adult-directed speech in her interactions with her child, especially in both arousal-reducing calming-soothing and arousal-amplifying playful contexts. This use of infant-directed speech is essential to the development of the infant's right temporal areas, and the burgeoning ability of reading the emotional tone of the voice of others is an essential element of all later social relationships.

In terms of *tactile-gestural attachment communications*, Sieratzki and Woll (1996) describe the effects of touch on the developing right hemisphere and assert that the emotional impact of touch is more direct and immediate if an infant is held to the left side of the body (see studies of "left-sided cradling" found in 70–80 percent of mothers, regardless of handedness, e.g., Bourne & Todd, 2004; Vauclair & Donnot, 2005; Hendriks, van Rijswijk, & Omtzigt, 2011). Infants spend large amounts of their waking (and sleeping) activity in the arms of their mothers, and this makes cradling one of the main social contexts where mother-infant body-to-body interaction takes place (Suter, Huggenberger, & Schächinger, 2007). Clinical research demonstrates the essential role of maternal "affective touch" on human infant development in the first year of life (Ferber, Feldman, & Makhoul, 2008; Jean Stack, & Fogal, 2009). This allows the infant and mother to create a system of "touch synchrony" in order to alter vagal tone and cortisol reactivity (Feldman, Singer, & Zagoory, 2010). The dyad thus uses "interpersonal touch" as a communication system (Gallacet & Spence, 2010), especially for the communication and regulation of emotional information (Hernstein, 2002; Hernstein & Campos, 2001). Other studies report that high levels of tactile stimulation and mutual touch occur in breast-feeding, and an increase in EEG amplitude in right posterior cortical areas occurs in 6-month-old infants during the intense somatosensory tactile contact of breast-feeding. This research supports the infant's need for affectionate touch for healthy right hemisphere development.

With respect to gestures, to Nagy demonstrated a "lateralized system for neonatal imitation" and concluded, "The early advantage of the right hemisphere in the first few months of life may affect the lateralized appearance of the first imitative gestures" (2006, p. 227). Moreover, Montirosso, Borgatti, and Tronick documented left-sided regulatory gestures when infants are stressed. In summarizing their work on gestures, they stated, "these findings suggest that the right hemisphere is more involved in the social and biological functions regarding infant caregiver emotional bonding (Schore, 2005; Siegel, 1999)" (2010, p. 108).

Confirming this model of the critical importance of right brain-to-right brain attachment communications in the progressive social experience–dependent lateralization of the right brain, neuroscientists now document that the right hemisphere matures before the left in prenatal and postnatal stages of human development (Gupta et al., 2005), that the strong and consistent predominance for the right hemisphere emerges postnatally (Allman et al., 2005), and that the mother's right hemisphere is more involved than the left in emotional processing and mothering (Lenzi et al., 2009). This body of research clearly indicates that attachment transactions influence the "early life programming of hemispheric lateralization" (Stevenson et al., 2008) that underlies the dominance of the right hemisphere in the first year of life (Chiron et al., 1997).

Studying structural connectivity asymmetry in the perinatal brain with newborn infants *at the beginning of the first year,* Meaney and his colleagues concluded,

> In early life the right cerebral hemisphere could be better able to process . . . emotion (Schore, 2000; Wada & Davis, 1977). This idea appears consistent with our findings of rightward asymmetry in . . . limbic structures. . . . These neural substrates function as hubs in the right hemisphere for emotion processes and mother and child interaction. (Ratnarajah et al., 2013, p. 193)

Tronick and colleagues' research on infants *in the middle of the first year* reported that 6-month-old infants use left-sided gestures generated by the right hemisphere in order to cope with the stressful face-to-face still-face paradigm, one that severely reduces the mother's communication and regulation of the infant's distressed state. They interpreted these data as being "consistent with Schore's (2005) hypotheses of hemispheric right-sided activation of emotions and their regulation during infant–mother interactions" (Montirosso et al., 2012, p. 826). Using near-infrared spectroscopy, Minagawa-Kawai and colleagues' study of infant mother attachment *at the end of the first year* observed, "Our results are in agreement with that of Schore (2000) who addressed the importance of the right hemisphere in the attachment system" (2009, p. 289).

ENDURING EFFECT OF SECURE ATTACHMENT: OPTIMIZED DEVELOPMENT OF THE RIGHT BRAIN

As the securely attached infant enters toddlerhood in the second year, his or her interactively regulated right brain-to-right brain visual-facial, auditory-prosodic, and tactile-gestural communications become more and more holistically integrated, allowing for the emergence of a coherent right brain emotional and corporeal subjective sense of self (Devinsky, 2000). Like myself, Meares posits that "The right side of the brain seems to be more involved than the left in the creation of an 'inner,' emotionally laden experience," and that the right brain self-system generates "a background state of well-being" (2012, p. 296), an implicit sense of a secure attachment.

This right-lateralized system stores a vocabulary of nonverbal affective facial expressions, prosody, and gestures—right brain signals used in implicit bodily-based attachment communications. Secure, interactively regulated attachment histories are imprinted into developing right cortical-subcortical circuits in implicit-procedural memory, thus generating an internal working model of attachment that encodes strategies of affect regulation that nonconsciously guide the individual through interpersonal contexts. These adaptive capacities are central to the dual processes of self-regulation: interactive regulation, the ability to flexibly regulate psychobiological states of emotions with other humans in interconnected contexts; and autoregulation, which occurs apart from other humans in autonomous contexts. For the rest of the life span, attachment dynamics are expressed in right brain-to-right brain communications of affect and the interactive regulation of affective arousal, and thereby the regulation of biological synchronicity between and within organisms (Bradshaw & Schore, 2007; Schore, 1994).

An essential tenet of the interpersonal neurobiological perspective of modern attachment theory is that during early critical periods, affective attachment transactions shape the cortical-subcortical emotion- and stress-regulating circuits of the developing right brain. Indeed, there is now extensive evidence confirming the developmental principle that the regulatory functions of mother-infant social-emotional right brain-to-right brain attachment interactions imprint right brain circuits in critical periods of infancy (see Ammaniti & Trentini, 2009; Cozolino, 2002; Schore, 1994, 2003a, 2003b, 2012; Siegel, 1999). Basic research now confirms that optimal stress regulation is dependent on "right hemispheric specialization in regulating stress- and emotion-related processes" (Sullivan & Dufresne, 2006, p. 55).

Modern attachment theory also specifies that the postnatal organization of the right brain and the progressive assembly of limbic-autonomic circuits that process essential brain-body psychobiological functions occur in a very specific pattern. During a critical period of regional brain growth, genetic factors are expressed in an initial overproduction of synapses. This is followed by an epigenetic process that is driven by the social environment: the pruning and maintenance of synaptic connections and the organization of functional circuits involved in the processing, communication, and regulation of essential social and emotional information. Over the first 2 years, a hierarchy of regulatory centers emerges in the developing right brain (Schore, 2003b, 2012, 2013a, 2014b).

Specifically, the subcortical amygdala, especially the right central amygdala with its connections into the insula, periaqueductal gray, and hypothalamus and thereby into the autonomic nervous system and the hypothalamic-pituitary-adrenal (HPA) axis, is functional at birth. At 3 to 9 months of age, the basolateral amygdala and the ventral anterior cingulate (Brodman areas 24, 25, 32 of the medial frontal cortex)—a corticolimbic regulatory structure that is associated with responsivity to social cues, autonomic control of sympathetic states, emotional and motivational arousal, and the generation of integrated bodily responses (Bush et al., 2000; Ongur & Price, 2000)—comes into a critical period of maturation, giving the infant even greater self-regulatory capacities. From 10 to 12 months of age, the regulatory center in the orbitofrontal cortex begins its developmental growth period. This ventromedial prefrontal cortex, especially in the right hemisphere, is the locus of Bowlby's attachment control system, and it contains the brain's most complex affect- and stress-regulating mechanisms (Schore, 1994, 2003a, 2003b). Supporting this model, developmental neurobiological research now confirms that the dendritic and synaptic maturation of the anterior cingulate and orbitofrontal cortices is specifically influenced by the social environment (Bock et al., 2008). A review of the functional neuroanatomy of the parent-infant relationship by Parsons and colleagues concluded, "the same adult brain networks involved in emotional and social interactions are already present in immature and incomplete forms in the infant" (2010, p. 235), specifically mentioning amygdala, hypothalamus, insula, cingulate cortex, and orbitofrontal cortex.

With optimal attachment experiences, the vertical axis that connects the orbitofrontal and medial prefrontal cortices with multiple cortical and subcortical areas is well developed, allowing the "higher" centers of attachment control in the right orbitofrontal cortex to efficiently regulate the "lower" centers in the subcortical amygdala that are centrally involved in the generation of attachment security (Lemche et al., 2006). Developmental neurobiological research reveals that the process of coping with early life stress increases the myelination of the ventromedial cortex, a prefrontal region that controls arousal regulation and resilience (Katz et al., 2009). For the rest of the life span, the right, and not left, lateralized prefrontal regions are responsible for the regulation of affect and stress (Cerqueira, Almeida, & Sousa, 2008; Czeh et al., 2008; Quirin et al., 2013; Schore, 1994; Sullivan & Dufresne, 2006; Wang et al., 2005).

Thus, the enduring legacy of an early secure attachment with a psychobiologically attuned mother is an efficient right brain that can resiliently cope with the novelty and stress that is inherent in all human interactions. Ongoing neuroscience research continues to describe the adaptive socioemotional functions of the right brain. According to Decety and Chaminade, "self-awareness, empathy, identification with others, and more generally intersubjective processes are largely dependent upon . . . right hemisphere resources, which are the first to develop" (2003, p. 591). At all later stages of human development, "The neural substrates of the perception of voices, faces, gestures, smells, and pheromones, as evidenced by modern neuroimaging techniques, are characterized by a general right-hemispheric functional asymmetry" (Brancucci et al., 2009, p. 895). This perception of emotional stimuli takes place within the first attachment and all subsequent social contexts.

Indeed, a large body of studies now demonstrates the dominance of the right hemisphere in adults for the nonverbal, implicit, holistic processing of emotional information and social interactions (e.g., Decety & Lamm, 2007; Schore, 2012; Semrud-Clikeman, Fine, & Zhu, 2011). In a comprehensive overview of laterality research, Hecht (2014) stated, "Mounting evidence suggests that the right hemisphere has a relative advantage over the left hemisphere in mediating social intelligence, identifying social stimuli, understanding the intentions of other people, awareness of the dynamics in social relationships, and successful handling of social interactions." Another current EEG study of resting brain asymmetry demonstrates that the right hemisphere is centrally involved in implicit affiliation motivation that has "its evolutionary roots in parental care and social relationships" and is defined as "the tendency to establish, maintain, or recover affectively positive relationships with other individuals" (Quirin et al., 2013, p. 1). And a third neuroimaging study in the *Journal of Cognitive Neuroscience* now confirms that specifically right brain circuits are responsible for "interpersonal competence," which encompasses "the capacity to interact and communicate with others, to share personal views, to understand the emotions and opinions of others, and to cooperate with others or resolve conflict should it occur" (De Pisapia et al., 2015, p. 1257). This growing body of studies clearly suggests that the right hemisphere is dominant for socioemotional competence, another functional expression of a secure attachment.

DEVELOPMENTAL INTERPERSONAL NEUROBIOLOGY OF RELATIONAL ATTACHMENT TRAUMA AND DISSOCIATION

Optimal attachment communications directly affect the maturation of the CNS limbic system, which processes and regulates socioemotional stimuli, and the ANS, which generates the somatic aspects of emotion. It is important to stress that a growth-facilitating emotional environment is required for a child to develop an internal system that can adaptively regulate arousal and an array of psychobiological self-states (and thereby affect, cognition, and behavior). The empathic good-enough mother implicitly offers her securely attached infant access to her after a stressful separation; she tends to respond appropriately and promptly to his or her emotional expressions of a need for attachment repair. She also allows high levels of positive affect to be generated during co-shared play states that create a positively charged curiosity and sense of wonder, which fuels the burgeoning self's exploration of novel socioemotional and physical environments. Such events scaffold and invisibly support (Bolger, Kessler, & Zuckerman, 2000) an expansion of the child's right brain regulatory coping capacities and underlie the developmental principle that secure attachment is the primary defense against trauma-induced psychopathology.

In contrast to caregivers who foster secure attachment, in histories of attachment trauma an abusive or neglectful caregiver not only plays less, but also induces enduring negative affect in the child. In contexts of relational trauma, the caregiver is either hyperintrusive or emotionally inaccessible and disengaged, given to inappropriate or rejecting responses to her infant's expressions of emotions and stress, and provides minimal or unpredictable regulation of the infant's states of overarousal or underarousal. Instead, she induces extreme levels of stimulation and arousal (i.e., the very high stimulation of abuse or the very low stimulation of neglect). Because she provides no interactive repair of frequent significant affective ruptures of the attachment relationship, she leaves the infant to endure extremely stressful, intense negative states for long periods of time. Indeed, caregiver-induced relational trauma is qualitatively and quantitatively more potentially psychopathogenic than any other social or physical stressor (aside from those that directly target the developing brain). In an immature organism with undeveloped and restricted coping capacities, the primary caregiver is the source of the infant's stress regulation, and therefore sense of safety. When not safety but danger emanates from the attachment relationship, the homeostatic assaults have significant short- and long-term consequences on the maturing psyche and soma (for an extensive discussion of relational trauma, see Schore, 2001, 2003a, 2012, 2013a, 2013b).

In terms of the short-term effects, interdisciplinary evidence indicates that the infant's psychobiological reaction to severe interpersonal stressors is composed of two separate response patterns: hyperarousal and dissociation. In the earliest stage of threat, the child's sudden alarm or startle reaction indicates activation of the infant's right hemisphere. This, in turn, evokes a sudden increase of the energy-expending sympathetic branch of the ANS, resulting in significantly elevated heart rate (cardiac acceleration), blood pressure, and respiration. Distress is expressed in crying and then screaming. The infant's state of "frantic distress," or fear-terror, is mediated by sympathetic hyperarousal that is expressed in increased secretion of corticotropin releasing factor (CRF), the brain's major stress hormone. CRF regulates sympathetic catecholamine activity, and thus noradrenaline; dopamine and adrenaline levels are significantly elevated, creating a hypermetabolic state within the developing brain and body. Increased concentrations of cortisol and of glutamate, the major excitatory neurotransmitter in the brain, also accompany the state of hyperarousal.

But a second, later forming reaction to relational trauma is dissociation, in which the child disengages from stimuli in the external world—traumatized infants are observed to be "staring off into space with a glazed look." The child's dissociation in the midst of terror involves numbing, avoidance, compliance, and restricted affect. This energy-conserving parasympathetic-dominant state of conservation-withdrawal occurs in helpless and hopeless stressful situations in which the individual becomes inhibited and strives to avoid attention in order to become "unseen" (Schore, 1994, 2003a, 2003b). This defensive state of metabolic shutdown and cardiac deceleration is a primary regulatory process that is used throughout the life span. In conservation-withdrawal, the stressed individual passively disengages in order "to conserve energies . . . to foster survival by the risky posture of feigning death, to allow healing of wounds and restitution of depleted resources by immobility" (Powles, 1992). This parasympathetic mechanism mediates the "profound detachment" of dissociation. If early trauma is experienced as "psychic catastrophe," then dissociation is a "detachment from an unbearable situation," "the escape when there is no escape," a "last resort defensive strategy" (Schore, 2003a).

The neurobiology of dissociative hypoarousal is different from that of hyperarousal. In this passive state of pain-numbing and pain-blunting, endogenous opioids are elevated. In addition to alterations in dopamine and noradrenaline, serotonin levels are increased (see Tops et al., 2009, on serotonin as a modulator of a drive to withdraw). The dorsal vagal complex in the brain-stem medulla is activated, which decreases blood pressure, metabolic activity, and heart rate—despite increases in circulating noradrenaline. This elevated parasympathetic arousal is a survival strategy that allows the infant to maintain homeostasis in the face of the internal state of sympathetic hyperarousal. The traumatized infant's sudden switch from high-energy sympathetic hyperarousal to low-energy parasympathetic dissociation is reflected in Porges's characterization of "the sudden and rapid transition from an unsuccessful strategy of struggling requiring massive sympathetic activation to the metabolically conservative immobilized state mimicking death associated with the dorsal vagal complex" (1997, p. 75). This prolonged dorsal vagal parasympathetic activation explains the lengthy "void" states that are associated with pathological dissociative detachment.

How are the trauma-induced alterations of the developing right brain expressed in the socioemotional behavior of a traumatized toddler? Main and Solomon's (1986) classic study of attachment in traumatized infants revealed a new attachment category, type D, an insecure-disorganized/disoriented pattern that occurs in 80% of maltreated infants. These authors concluded that type D infants have low stress tolerance and that their disorganization and disorientation indicate that the infant is alarmed by the parent, the child's haven of safety. Because infants inevitably seek the parent when alarmed, these authors assert that parents that are frightening place infants in an irresolvable bind wherein they can neither approach the mother, shift their attention, nor flee. These infants are utterly unable to generate a coherent strategy to actively cope with their frightening parents.

Main and Solomon (1986) detailed the uniquely bizarre behaviors of 12-month-old type D infants in the "strange situation" procedure. These infants displayed brief (frequently only 10–30 seconds) but significant interruptions of organized behavior. Maltreated infants exhibit apprehension, confusion, and very rapid shifts of state during the strange situation. They describe the child's entrance into a dissociated state:

> One infant hunched her upper body and shoulders at hearing her mother's call, then broke into extravagant *laugh-like* screeches with an excited forward movement. Her braying laughter became a cry and *distress-face* without a new intake of breath as the infant hunched forward. Then suddenly she became silent, blank and dazed. (p. 119)

Hesse and Main (1999) note that type D disorganization and disorientation is phenotypically similar to dissociative states. Subsequent developmental research underscores a strong link between frightening maternal behavior, dissociation, and disorganized infant attachment (MacDonald et al., 2008).

In my original research on relational trauma, I described the intergenerational transmission not only of the intense emotional distress of relational trauma but also of the defensive response of pathological dissociation (Schore 2001, 2003a, 2009, 2012). Beebe and colleagues (2010) described studies of mothers of 4-month-old infants who later show disorganized attachment. They reported these caregivers show intrusive (as opposed to affectionate) touch, as well as engage in dyadic dysregulating "mother-chase-infant dodge" and "mother positive/surprised while infant distressed" (p. 355). They concluded that the mothers of these infants are overwhelmed with their own unresolved abuse or trauma and therefore cannot bear to intersubjectively engage with their infants' distress. Because these mothers are unable to regulate their own distress, they cannot regulate the distress of their infants. This type of mother is unable to allow herself to be emotionally affected by the dysregulated state of her infant, thus she shuts down emotionally, looking away from the infant's face and failing to coordinate with the infant's emotional state. Beebe interprets this fearful maternal behavior as a defensive dissociation, a strategy that protects the mother from the facial and visual intimacy that would come from joining the infant's distressed moments. This type of mother thus shows disrupted and contradictory forms of affective communication (abuse-intrusiveness-hyperarousal *and* neglect-disengagement-hypoarousal), especially around the infant's need for comfort when distressed.

More recent groundbreaking research by Beebe et al. (2012) on the dyadic origins of disorganized attachment highlights not only the infant's unresolved fear linked to the mother's fear-arousing behaviors, but also the mother's defensive emotional withdrawal in response to the infant's distress. These authors described maternal emotional withdrawal in response to infant distress:

> Clinically we observed that this maternal "closing up" of her face often occurred at moments of infant distress, as if mother is "going blank." If she remained empathic to infant distress, she might fear finding herself in the original traumatized state of her own history. . . . For example, as one future disorganized infant sharply vocalized distress and turned his head abruptly away with a *pre-cry* face, the mother's head jerked back, as if "hit" by the infant's

> distress; she then looked down with a "*closed-up*" face . . . these mothers . . . may shut down their own emotional processing and be unable to use the infant's behaviors as communications in a momentary dissociative process. (p. 364)

These observations fit well with my interpersonal neurobiological model of the intergenerational transmission of both trauma and the dissociative defense against trauma.

In an early history of traumatic attachment, the developing infant/toddler is thus too frequently exposed to a massively misattuning primary caregiver who triggers and does not repair long-lasting, intensely dysregulated states. The growth-inhibiting environment of relational trauma generates dense and prolonged levels of negative affect associated with extremely stressful states of hyperarousal and hypoarousal. And so for self-protective purposes, this relational context severely restricts the infant's overt expressions of an attachment need for dyadic regulation. The child thus significantly reduces the output of its right-lateralized, emotion-processing, limbic-autonomic attachment system. When stressed, defensive functions are rapidly initiated that quickly shift the brain from interactive regulatory modes into long-enduring, less complex autoregulatory modes.

During these episodes, the child is matching the rhythmic structures of the mother's dysregulated states, and this synchronization is registered in the firing patterns of the stress-sensitive cortical and limbic regions of the infant's brain, especially in the right brain, which is in a critical period of growth. An EEG study of 5-month-old infants observed increased theta activity over the right posterior temporal area while the infants were looking at a blank face (Bazhenova et al., 2007). At 6 months, the still face elicits right lateralization (Montirosso et al., 2012), and withdrawal behavior is associated with elevated cortisol and extreme right frontal electroencephalographic activity (Buss et al., 2003). Infants designated as "very fearful" at 7 months show larger evoked response potentials (ERPs) over the right hemisphere when viewing fearful facial expressions (de Haan et al., 2004). Thus, the chaotic and dysregulated alterations of state induced by relational trauma become imprinted into the developing right brain self-system of the child.

From a developmental psychopathological perspective, the immediate detrimental psychobiological impact is the generation of the altered metabolic processes that poorly sustain critical-period growth of the developing right brain, and the lasting impairment is an immature and functionally limited right brain capacity to regulate later life stressors that generate intense affect states (Schore, 2003b). Offering research data, Montirosso, Borgatti, and Tronick (2010) concluded, "Infants cope with the emotional distress caused by unresponsive mothers through self-regulation behaviors associated with a greater activation of the right hemisphere. In sum, this finding supports the view that during a stressful condition there is a state-dependent activation of the right hemisphere" (p. 108). According to Dutra et al. (2009), "parental affective unresponsiveness can be conceptualized from a psychobiological viewpoint as a form of "hidden trauma" specific to infancy—trauma that has the potential to hyperactivate the infant's response to stress over time (p. 388).

Relational traumatic experiences are stored in imagistic procedural memory of the visuospatial right hemisphere (Schiffer, Teicher, & Papanicolaou, 1995), the locus of nonconscious implicit (Hugdahl, 1995) and autobiographical (Markowitsch et al., 2000) memory. Recent models of early life trauma are altering their focus from deficits in later maturing conscious, verbal, explicit and voluntary behavior to impairments of early maturing nonconscious, nonverbal, implicit and automatic adaptive socioemotional functions (Schore, 2010). These psychological and biological perspectives converge on a basic developmental principle of modern attachment theory: early traumatic sundering of right brain-to-right brain attachment bonds is critical to the genesis of an enduring predisposition to a variety of early forming severe psychopathologies that characterologically access the autoregulating, affect-deadening defense of pathological dissociation.

ENDURING EFFECT OF RELATIONAL ATTACHMENT TRAUMA: IMPAIRED RIGHT BRAIN EMOTION PROCESSING, STRESS REGULATION, AND PATHOLOGICAL DISSOCIATION

Neurobiological data are also used by modern attachment theory to create models of the psychopathogenetic mechanism by which attachment trauma negatively affects right brain development. Current workers in the field of developmental traumatology now agree that the overwhelming socioemotional stress of maltreatment in childhood is associated with adverse influences on not only behavior but also brain development. Adamec, Blundell, and Burton reported experimental data that "implicate neuroplasticity in right hemispheric limbic circuitry in mediating long-lasting changes in negative affect following brief but severe stress" (2003, p. 1264). According to Gadea and colleagues, mild to moderate negative affective experiences activate the right hemisphere, but an intense experience "might interfere with right hemisphere processing, with eventual damage if some critical point is reached" (2005, p. 136). I suggest this right brain "damage" is most operative during intensely dysregulating experiences of hypermetabolic hyperarousal and hypometabolic hypoarousal.

In attachment contexts that generate too frequent, intense, unrepaired, and enduring relational trauma, dissociative defensive functions are rapidly initiated that quickly shift the brain from interactive regulatory modes into long-enduring, less complex autoregulatory modes. These patterns are primitive strategies for survival that remain online for long intervals of time, periods in which the developing brain is in a hypometabolic state, detrimental to the substantial amounts of energy required for critical-period biosynthetic processes of myelination and synaptogenesis. The dysregulating events of abuse and neglect thus create chaotic, severe biochemical alterations in the infant brain, and this homeostatic stressor intensifies the normal process of apoptotic programmed oxidative cell death and thereby alters the developmental trajectory of the right brain. This disruption of energy resources for the biosynthesis of right-lateralized limbic connections would be expressed in a critical-period developmental overpruning of the corticolimbic system, especially one that contains a genetically encoded underproduction of synapses (see Schore, 1994, 2002, 2003a, 2009, 2012 for the neurochemistry of apoptosis, oxidative stress, and excessive parcellation of limbic-autonomic circuits).

It is now accepted that "psychological factors" "prune" or "sculpt" neural networks in specifically not only the postnatally developing occipital and parietal cortices but also the frontal, limbic, and temporal cortices. Excessive pruning of cortical-subcortical limbic-autonomic circuits occurs in early histories of trauma and neglect. This severe growth impairment represents the mechanism of the genesis of a developmental structural defect. Because this defect is in limbic organization, the resulting functional deficit will specifically be in the individual's ability to cope with intense affects. In this manner, the stressful interpersonal context of a disorganized-disoriented attachment context acts as a growth-inhibiting environment for the experience-dependent maturation of right-lateralized CNS-ANS circuits and a predisposition to a number of early forming developmental psychopathologies. An extensive apoptotic parcellation of vertical circuits in the developing right brain would lead to an inefficient regulation of the ANS by higher centers in the CNS, functionally expressed as a dissociation of central regulation of sympathetic and parasympathetic systems.

Recall that "higher" right cortical areas and their connections with "lower" right subcortical structures are in a critical period of growth during early human development. If the primary caregiver chronically dysregulates and fails to repair the child's arousal and affective states during early critical periods of these cortical-subcortical circuits, this inhibits the experience-dependent maturation of the right brain, leading to enduring inefficient capacities for coping with interpersonal stressors and a predisposition to later psychiatric disorders. There is now agreement that early stress is associated with alterations in the control system of attachment, the orbital (ventromedial) frontolimbic cortex, and that individuals who experience early adversity such as childhood maltreatment are at a heightened risk for a wide range of psychopathologies (Hanson et al., 2010). Research now describes the detrimental effects of deficits of maternal care in the alteration of specifically the right and not left ventromedial cortex (Lyons et al., 2002) and the creation of a vulnerability to future psychopathologies (e.g., Schore, 2003a). All psychopathologies of the right brain emotion-processing limbic system involve disturbances of affect regulation, and they reflect an inefficient regulation of the right orbitofrontal cortex of the right amygdala, the major fear center of the brain.

In my 1994 volume, I proposed that orbitofrontal deficits lie at the core of a number of psychiatric disorders (Schore, 1994), and in 1996 I cited a small but expanding number of studies that reported orbitofrontal involvement and regulation disturbances in a number of developmental psychopathologies (Schore, 1996). During the past decade, altered structural and functional development of the orbitofrontal cortex has been documented in a wide variety of psychiatric disorders: schizophrenia, autism, affective psychosis, bipolar disorder, borderline personality disorder, psychopathic personality disorder, aggression and violence, alcohol and drug addiction, posttraumatic stress disorder, dissociative identity disorder, panic disorder, and depression (see references in Schore, 2012).

The massive psychobiological stress associated with attachment trauma not only impairs the development of this attachment control system but also sets the stage for the characterological use of the right brain defense of pathological dissociation when encountering later socioemotional stressors. In the developmental psychological literature, Dutra and colleagues observed that maternal disrupted affective communications and lack of involvement in the regulation of stressful arousal are associated with the child's use of dissociation, "one of the few available means for achieving a modicum of relief from fearful arousal." This in turn leads the child "not to acknowledge pain and distress within a set of caregiving relationships that are vital for survival" (2009, p. 388). In the clinical literature, Kalsched (2005) described operations of defensive dissociative processes used by the child during traumatic experience by which "Affect in the body is severed from its corresponding images in the mind and thereby an unbearably painful meaning is obliterated." A dissociatively detached individual is thus not only detached from the environment but also from the self—his body, his actions, and his sense of identity.

A large body of psychiatric, psychological, and neurological studies supports the link between childhood trauma and pathological dissociation (see Schore, 2012). Indeed, converging evidence indicates that early relational trauma negatively affects limbic and autonomic nervous system maturation, producing enduring neurobiological alterations that underlie right brain affective instability, inefficient stress tolerance, memory impairment, and dissociative disturbances. In this manner, traumatic stress in early childhood leads to self-modulation of painful affect by directing attention away from internal emotional states (Lane et al., 1997). The right hemisphere is dominant not only for the processing of social interactions but also for maintaining a coherent sense of one's body (Tsakiris, Costantini, & Haggard, 2008), for the subjective experience of body ownership, which makes bodily sensations unique to oneself (Tsakiris, 2010), for bodily self-consciousness (Ionta, Martuzzi, Salomon, & Blanke, 2014), for attention (Raz, 2004), and for pain processing (Symonds et al., 2006), and so the right brain strategy of dissociation represents the ultimate defense for blocking emotional bodily-based pain from consciousness. The characterological use of dissociation thus represents a deficit in the right-hemispheric "corporeal self" (Devinsky, 2000) and thereby in maintaining a coherent, continuous, and unified sense of self (McGilchrist, 2008).

At the most fundamental level, the early forming dissociative defense against attachment trauma reflects the inability of the right brain cortical-subcortical implicit self-system to adaptively recognize and process external stimuli (exteroceptive information coming from the relational environment) and on a moment-to-moment basis integrate them with internal stimuli (interoceptive information from the body, somatic markers, the "felt experience"). This failure of integration of the higher right hemisphere with the lower right brain induces an instant collapse of both subjectivity and intersubjectivity. Stressful affects, especially those associated with emotional pain, are thus not experienced in consciousness.

Confirming this principle of modern attachment theory, an fMRI study of traumatized post-traumatic stress disorder (PTSD) patients by Lanius and her colleagues (2005) showed right-hemispheric activation during dissociation. These authors concluded that patients dissociate in order to escape from the overwhelming emotions associated with the traumatic memory. Using transcranial magnetic stimulation, Spitzer et al. (2004) similarly reported that dissociation is associated with right hemisphere dysfunction in the form of lack of integration in the presence of emotionally distressing or threatening stimuli. Enriquez and Bernabeu also offered research showing "dissociation is associated with dysfunctional changes in the right hemisphere which impair its characteristic dominance over emotional processing" (2008, pp. 272–273). Helton, Dorahy, and Russell reported that high dissociators have difficulty in specifically coordinating activity within the right hemisphere, and that such deficits become evident when this hemisphere is "loaded with the combined effects of a sustained attention task and negative emotional stimuli. . . . Thus, the integration of experiences, which rely heavily on right hemispheric activation (e.g., negative emotion, sense of self with reference to the experience) may be compromised in high dissociators" (2011, p. 700). These findings are echoed in current neurological research. Brand et al. (2009) and Stanilou, Markowitsch, and Brand (2010) documented right temporofrontal hypometabolism in cases of dissociative amnesia, which is clinically expressed as an inability to recall important personal information of a traumatic nature: a failure of integration of consciousness, emotion, and cognition and a "constricted self."

At all points of the life span, although dissociation represents an effective short-term strategy, it is detrimental to long-term functioning, specifically by preventing exposure to potential right brain socioemotional learning experiences embedded in intimate intersubjective contexts that are necessary for emotional growth. In clinical writings, Bromberg (2006) linked right brain trauma to autonomic hyperarousal, "a chaotic and terrifying flooding of affect that can threaten to overwhelm sanity and imperil psychological survival." He observed dissociation is then automatically and immediately triggered as the fundamental right brain defense to the arousal dysregulation of overwhelming affective states. It is often overlooked that to some individuals intimacy represents an overwhelming state of arousal.

The end point of chronically experiencing catastrophic states of relational trauma in early life is a progressive impairment of the ability to adjust, take defensive action, or act on one's own behalf, and a blocking of the capacity to register affect and pain, all critical to survival. Clinical research shows pathological dissociation, a primitive defense against overwhelming affects, is a key feature of not only reactive attachment disorder of infants and pediatric maltreatment disorder but also autism spectrum disorders, psychotic disorders, dissociative identity disorder, post-traumatic stress disorder, eating disorders, substance abuse and alcoholism, somatoform disorders, and borderline personality disorders.

Psychotherapy with such patients needs to attend to the severe dysregulation of affect that characterizes the developmental self-pathologies associated with histories of relational trauma. In light of the commonality of nonverbal, intersubjective, implicit right brain-to-right brain emotion-transacting and -regulating mechanisms in the caregiver-infant and the therapist-patient relationship, developmental attachment studies have direct relevance to the treatment process. In recent writings, I have suggested that the right hemisphere is dominant in psychotherapy (Schore, 2014a; Schore & Schore, 2014). Experiences of relational trauma and attachment dysregulation appear in the therapeutic alliance as clinical enactments (Schore, 2012). Beneath the words, implicit right brain-to-right brain nonverbal bodily-based affective communications (facial expressions, prosody–tone of voice, gesture) convey unconscious transference-countertransference transactions, which revive earlier attachment memories, especially of intensely dysregulated affective states. Working with borderline personality disorders, Meares (2012) now describes "a form of therapeutic conversation that can be conceived . . . as a dynamic interplay between two right hemispheres" (p. 315).

Right brain-to-right brain transferential-countertransferential unconscious communications between the patient's and the therapist's "internal worlds" also represents an essential relational matrix for the therapeutic expression of dissociated affects that accompany early attachment trauma. Psychotherapy with such patients must also address the early forming dissociative defense that blocks these overwhelming affects from reaching consciousness, thereby denying the possibility of interactive regulation and the organization of more complex right brain stress regulation. The clinical research of Spitzer et al. (2007) demonstrated that insecurely attached dissociative patients dissociate as a response to negative emotions arising in psychodynamic psychotherapy, leading to a less favorable treatment outcome. It thus represents a major obstacle to the intersubjective change process in all affectively focused psychotherapies, but especially in patients with a history of early relational trauma (Bromberg, 2011; Schore, 2012, 2014a).

CHAPTER 3

Early Interpersonal Neurobiological Assessment of Attachment and Autistic Spectrum Disorders

INTRODUCTION

In a study on the developmental neurobiological basis of attachment that was published in the journal *Neuropsychopharmacology,* the researchers boldly asserted, "Understanding the motivational basis of healthy and at-risk parenting may open new theoretical vistas and clinical opportunities and may lead to the construction of more specific interventions that can target disruptions to maternal–infant bonding at an earlier stage and in a more accurate manner" (Atzil, Hendler, & Feldman, 2011, p. 11). And in a concurrent editorial in the *Journal of Child and Psychiatry,* "Developmental Neuroscience Comes of Age," Leckman and March articulated the well-established developmental principle that underlies the current intense interest in early assessment: "A scientific consensus is emerging that the origins of adult disease are often found among developmental and biological disruptions occurring during the early years of life" (2011, p. 333). Researchers as well as clinicians are now eagerly looking for clinical applications of current knowledge about the critical biological and psychological aspects of early attachment experiences, both in optimal and nonoptimal relational contexts.

Toward that end, I have offered my own contributions. Over the past two decades I have articulated and expanded regulation theory in order to model how early, emotionally laden attachment experiences indelibly impact and alter the early developing right brain, which for the rest of the life span is dominant for the nonverbal, holistic, spontaneous (unconscious) processing of emotional information and social interactions, for enabling the organism to regulate affect and cope with stresses and challenges, and thereby for emotional resilience and emotional well-being in later stages of life (Schore, 1994, 2003a, 2003b, 2012a). Modern attachment theory (Schore & Schore, 2008, 2010) represents a neurobiological update of John Bowlby's seminal work. The more comprehensive model, regulation theory offers an overarching interpersonal neurobiological model of the development, psychopathogenesis, and treatment of the early forming subjective self-system. In a number of current publications in the clinical literature, I use my work on regulation theory as a guide for formulating early assessments of mother-infant attachment relationships (Schore, 2012a, 2013; Schore & Newton, 2012. In this chapter, I describe my ongoing attempts to apply the theory to clinical practice in order to generate more effective evidence-based models of early assessment, intervention, and prevention.

The assessment model of regulation theory emerges from a foundation of three organizing principles. *First* is the construct of interpersonal neurobiology: that the structure and function of the mind and brain are shaped by social experiences, especially those involving emotional relationships. The fundamental core principle of the body of my work dictates that "the self-organization of the developing brain occurs in the context of a relationship with another self, another brain" (Schore, 1996, p. 60). A number of research and clinical disciplines now emphasize the "relational" or "intersubjective" principle in models of human development over the life span (Schore, 2014). Regulation theory describes the interpersonal neurobiology of attachment and the development of intersubjectivity. This clearly implies that a central focus of an early assessment is on the dynamics of the attachment *relationship* and on the developing infant's evolving capacity for *intersubjectivity* (Ammaniti & Gallese, 2014; Schore, 2012a).

Second, advances in our understanding of the ontogeny of brain lateralization now indicate that a critical period of growth in the right hemisphere precedes that in the left in human infancy. Two decades ago, I proposed that attachment experiences specifically impact the early developing right brain (Schore, 1994). I also presented extant studies reporting that the infant's right hemisphere begins a growth spurt in the last trimester of pregnancy and ends in the middle/end of the second year, when the left hemisphere begins its own, a period that also marks the end of the human brain growth spurt. A number of anatomical and imaging studies now document earlier maturation of the right hemisphere in prenatal and postnatal stages of human development (Gupta et al., 2005; Mento et al., 2010; Sun et al., 2005). This body of research clearly indicates that attachment transactions influence the "early life programming of hemispheric lateralization" (Stevenson et al., 2008) that underlies the dominance of the right hemisphere in the first year of life (Chiron et al., 1997).

In addition to laterality research on the developing brain, studies on the adult brain are now shifting the classical "single brain" paradigm to a "dual-brain" paradigm and exploring precisely how the two cerebral hemispheres mediate different modes of experiencing and coping with the external world. In his monumental overview of current brain asymmetry research, neuropsychiatrist Iain McGilchrist put forth the argument that the difference between the two brain hemispheres is profound. The right and left hemispheres create coherent, utterly different, and often incompatible versions of the world with competing priorities and values, and indeed two modes of being. He concluded that when the right-hemispheric mode is dominant, "we experience—the live, complex, embodied world of individual, always unique beings, forever in flux, a net of interdependencies, forming and reforming wholes, a world with which we are deeply connected" (2009, p. 31). Hecht (2014) cited even more recent lateralization research indicating that the right hemisphere is the primary driver of the innate psychobiological need for affiliation and social connection, and thereby for emotion regulation and personal growth. The essential adaptive right brain functions of interdependence, social connection, and emotion regulation emerge out of early attachment experiences, and they need to be assessed during the critical period.

Third, on the basis of the principle of hierarchical brain organization, I have offered a model of the ontogeny of the emotion-processing limbic system, which is shaped by the mother-infant attachment relationship (Schore, 2000, 2005). It is well established that the right cortical hemisphere, more so than the left, is particularly well reciprocally connected with limbic and subcortical regions, and that the functional maturation of corticolimbic circuits is significantly influenced by early socioemotional experience. In his classic volume, Bowlby (1969) speculated about an attachment "biological control system" that regulates the limbic system and is structured as a "hierarchical mode of organization." Following this idea in a pair of articles in the 2001 issue of the *Infant Mental Health Journal*, I articulated a model of the prenatal and postnatal ontogeny of the hierarchically organized limbic system, which suggests that a number of discrete limbic components come online and develop connectivity in a defined sequence in the first year (Schore, 2001a, 2001b). The model proposes that the neuroanatomy of the emotion-processing limbic system is characterized as a series of hierarchically organized "control systems" or "hubs" in the right amygdala, right anterior cingulate, and right orbitofrontal cortex (Schore, 2003a, 2012a, 2012b, 2013).

In line with the morphogenetic principle of caudal to rostral brain development, regulation theory proscribes a maturational sequence over prenatal to postnatal stages of more complex right-lateralized control (regulatory) systems in the amygdala, then anterior cingulate, then orbitofrontal cortex. This hierarchical circuit of emotion regulation is imprinted in affective attachment transactions over the course of the first year, bottom-up; that is, subcortical to cortical, amygdala at the beginning of the first year to orbital prefrontal cortical at the end of infancy. Research now demonstrates that subcortical components of the limbic system (e.g., amygdala) mature earlier than the cortical components, and that their maturation is influenced by attachment experiences. It is often overlooked that the first year is a time of tremendous expansion of subcortical brain areas. Knickmeyer et al. (2008) reported that the volume of the human subcortical area (including brain stem) increases by 130% in the first year of human life. Early assessments need to shift from later maturing cortical executive functions to earlier developing subcortical functions.

Integrating the preceding three developmental organizing principles of interpersonal neurobiology, right brain lateralization, and ontogenetic progression of hierarchical regulatory systems, I offer a psychoneurobiological model that can be used to evaluate the burgeoning attachment system as it is evolving in real developmental time. This interpersonal neurobiological assessment of socioemotional development attempts to observe and document, in any specific case, the dynamic impact of the right brain emotion-transacting attachment relationship on the infant's developing right-lateralized limbic system. Modern attachment theory also offers a heuristic model of both optimal and less than optimal early right brain development. The model suggests that optimal development in infancy reflects a growth-facilitating relational context that promotes the progression of more complex limbic social-emotional control systems in the right brain that support a *foundation* of later emotional well-being, one that can adaptively alter its internal function in response to changes in the external environment, especially while under stress. This secure attachment function is described by Bob Dylan's "Forever Young," where he lyrically states, "May you have a strong *foundation* when the winds of changes shift" (italics added).*

On the other hand, less than optimal right brain development is associated with various growth-inhibiting relational contexts that generate altered subcortical-cortical patterns of limbic-autonomic connectivity, or even structural and neuropathological alterations within the regulatory hubs themselves, and thereby inefficient control functions. Interpersonal neurobiological assessments of both the infant-mother relationship and the infant's socioemotional development should be done over the course of the first year, during the critical periods of maturation of right-lateralized amygdala, anterior cingulate, and orbitofrontal limbic-regulating control systems.

But how can an individual infant's right brain socioemotional development be compared to a psychobiological standard of optimal normative versus nonoptimal "high-risk" socioemotional development? In my pair of *Infant Mental Health Journal* articles, I contrasted optimal right brain development in secure attachments with nonoptimal right brain development in contexts of relational trauma (abuse or neglect) associated with disorganized-disoriented insecure attachments. In subsequent work, I utilized the perspective of regulation theory and the construct of "relational trauma" to model the role of right brain attachment trauma in the psychopathogenesis of a DSM axis I disorder (post-traumatic stress disorder; Schore, 2003a,b) as well as axis II disorders

---

(borderline personality disorder and antisocial personality disorder; Meares, Schore, & Melkonian, 2011; Schore, 2002, 2003a).

In this chapter, I apply the regulation model of early assessment to another axis I "developmental disturbance," autistic spectrum disorders, which manifest both early appearing neurobiological disturbances and severe developmental psychopathology. In light of the long-standing gap, indeed disconnect between the attachment and autism worlds, it may seem surprising that attachment theory can make important contributions to a deeper understanding of autism. This work bears directly upon the clinical need for the early identification of what has previously been called "infantile autism."

Indeed, echoing the call for early interventions by attachment scientists cited earlier, autism researchers studying "the very early autism phenotype" now assert, "One purpose of the earlier identification is that treatments delivered at very young ages, when the brain is most plastic, may ultimately lessen or prevent the lifelong challenges associated with autism" (Yirmiya & Ozonoff, 2007, p. 9). The fact that both fields are intensely focused on socioemotional development in the prenatal, perinatal, and postnatal stages of human infancy highlights the problem of the early differential diagnosis of these developmental disorders. In classic writings on childhood autism, Rutter observed "there is a lack of attachment behavior and a relative failure of bonding," but also noted that "a failure of bonding is also seen in conditions other than autism," which show a different "style of social interaction" (1978, pp. 146–147). At present, there is agreement that most children who experience attachment disorders do not develop autistic spectrum disorders, and that attachment disorders are much more common than autism. That said, both fields have now embraced an epigenetic perspective, which suggests that they may share at least some common psychoneurobiological etiological factors.

In the upcoming first section of this chapter, I describe how the first 2 years of life represents a sequence of critical periods for the relationally driven maturation of the right brain, the "emotional brain." More and more complex rapid, spontaneous, and thereby implicit right-lateralized visual-facial, auditory-prosodic, and tactile-gestural communications lie at the psychobiological core of the emotional attachment bond between the infant and primary caregiver. These affective communications can in turn be interactively regulated by the primary caregiver, thereby expanding the infant's developing right brain regulatory systems. Regulated and dysregulated bodily-based communications can be assessed in order to determine the ongoing status of both the infant's emotional and social development and the quality and efficiency of the infant-mother attachment relationship. In the second section, I offer an overview of current research from developmental neuroscience on the early stages of autism. I also report recent studies on alterations of right brain limbic structures in developing autistic brains, as well as a growing body of research demonstrating early appearing deficits in intersubjective behavior in autistic mother-infant dyads. This work suggests that the emotion-processing limbic system and the "emotional" right brain may bridge not only attachment and autism neurobiology but also attachment and autism models of early intervention.

CLINICAL IMPLICATIONS OF REGULATION THEORY FOR EARLY ATTACHMENT ASSESSMENTS

Neurobiologically informed models of modern attachment theory advance Bowlby's (1969) basic tenet that attachment is biological in nature and underscore the morphogenetic role of the attachment relationship in the structural connectivity of the right brain, the emergence of emotional regulation, and the development of the implicit subjective self. J. Schore and I have suggested that the current expansion of Bowlby's seminal ideas allows for "new understandings in *clinical assessments, shaping therapeutic interventions* from relevant theory" (2008, p. 17, italics in original). Toward that end, regulation theory can be used to guide the assessment of attachment episodes of rapid, spontaneous, implicit *visual-facial, auditory-prosodic, and tactile-gestural* affective communications, in which the primary caregiver interactively regulates the infant's internal states of peripheral and central arousal. In this section, I describe current developmental neuroscience findings on the infant and maternal processing of these sensoriaffective communications. These studies are organized as a temporal sequence over the course of the first year. I also offer clinical implications of the research studies for assessments of socioemotional development. Because of space limitations, I refer the reader to Schore (2012a, 2013) for specific references to what follows.

As previously discussed with respect to *visual-facial attachment communications,* it is now established that mutual gaze is critical to early social development. The emergence of the capacity to efficiently process information from faces requires visual input to the right (and not left) hemisphere during infancy. At 2 months of age, the onset of a critical period during which synaptic connections in the developing occipital cortex are modified by visual experience, infants show right-hemispheric activation when exposed to a woman's face. Using electroencephalography (EEG) methodology, Grossmann et al. (2007) reported that 4-month-old infants presented with images of a female face gazing directly ahead show enhanced gamma electrical activity over right prefrontal areas. Near-infrared spectroscopy (NIRS) research (perhaps the most suitable of all neuroscience techniques applicable to human infants) reveals that specifically the 5-month-old's right hemisphere responds to images of adult female faces. By 6 months, infants show a right-lateralized, left gaze bias when viewing faces, right temporal activation when looking at angry faces, and significantly greater right frontotemporal activation when viewing their own mother's (as opposed to a stranger's) face.

Note the developmental progression over the first year to more complex visual-affective functions. These research data indicate that the future capacity to process the essential social information expressed in face-to-face communications, a central aspect of all later intimate relationships, is dependent on caregiver-infant eye contact and visual gazing during early critical periods. Thus, how often and in what contexts the mother and infant *spontaneously* look (and not look) directly at each other is of key importance to a clinician when evaluating both an infant's development and the health of the dyadic relationship. When there is mutual infant-caregiver visual gazing that looks and feels natural, the clinician implicitly knows that the infant's brain is likely developing well in this area.

A body of studies of prenatal, perinatal, and postnatal *auditory-prosodic attachment communications* also highlight the role of the right brain. In an EEG study of auditory pitch processing in preterm infants born at 30 gestational weeks, Mento et al. concluded, "the earlier right structural maturation in foetal epochs seems to be paralleled by a right functional development" (2010, p. 1). A functional magnetic resonance imaging (fMRI) study of 1- to 3-day-old newborns reported that music evokes right-hemispheric activation in the auditory cortex. Using NIRS with 2- to 6-day-old neonates, Telkemeyer et al. observed, "responses to slow acoustic modulations are lateralized to the right hemisphere" (2009, p. 14726). This same optical brain imaging technology reveals that prosodic processing of emotional voices in 3-month-old and 4-month-old infants activates the right temporoparietal region. Grossmann and colleagues reported that 7-month-old infants respond to emotional voices in a voice-sensitive region of the right superior temporal sulcus, and happy prosody specifically activates the right inferior frontal cortex. These authors concluded, "The pattern of findings suggests that temporal regions specialize in processing voices very early in development and that, already in infancy, emotions differentially modulate voice processing in the right hemisphere" (2010, p. 852).

Neuroscience now supports the principle that the caregiver's use of infant-directed speech ("motherese") is critical for the development of the posterior areas of the right hemisphere that process prosodic-emotional functions. Independent of culture, infant-directed speech is preferred over adult-directed speech as early as a few weeks after birth (Cooper & Aslin, 1990). Compared to adult-directed speech, motherese—the vocal expression of emotion to infants (Trainor, Austin, & Desjardins, 2000)—is higher in pitch, has a wider pitch range, and exhibits exaggerated pitch contours. In addition, it is shorter, slower, and separated by longer pauses than adult speech (Fernald, 1989). Developmental neurobiological research demonstrates that maternal infant-directed speech activates the right temporal area of 4- to 6-month-old infants, and that this activation is even greater in 7- to 9-month-old infants (Naoi et al., 2011). In 11-month-old infants, the voice of a woman's infant-directed speech (i.e., with somewhat exaggerated prosody) elicits a right-lateralized event-related potential (Thierry, Vihman, & Roberts, 2003).

Again, note the developmental progression of auditory affective functions that allow for more complex communication. The emotional quality of what infants hear in the early stages of infancy affects the development of the voice-processing areas of the right hemisphere, especially the temporal voice areas in the upper banks of the right superior temporal sulcus (Bestelmeyer, Belin, & Grosbas, 2011). Clinically, these studies indicate the importance of assessing not the verbal content but the melody of the mother's voice, and whether or not she's using infant-directed versus adult-directed speech in her interactions with her child, especially in both arousal-reducing calming-soothing and arousal-amplifying playful contexts. This use of infant-directed speech is essential to the development of the infant's right temporal areas, and the burgeoning ability of reading the emotional tone of the voice of others is an essential element of all later social relationships.

With respect to *tactile-gestural attachment communications*, Sieratzki and Woll (1996) described the effects of touch on the developing right hemisphere, and asserted that the emotional impact of touch is more direct and immediate if an infant is held to the left side of the body ("left-sided cradling" associated with the functional activation of the right cerebral hemisphere; Bourne & Todd, 2004; Huggenberger et al., 2009, Hendriks, van Rijswijk, & Omtzigt, 2011; Forrester et al, in press). Touch is the first medium of communication (Stack, 2001), and Moszkowki and colleagues (2009) demonstrated the importance of touch for infant communication and regulation during early social interactions. Indeed, Ludwig and Field 2014) reviewed the literature to argue that touch is essential to parent-infant mental health. Hertenstein (2002) articulated a model of tactile communications in infancy, offering evidence that it regulates not only arousal levels but is capable of communicating valenced and discrete emotions. He suggested the tactile communication that the infant receives transpires within the context of a larger infant-caregiver communications system composed of several sensory modalities, and that this bi-directional and relational dyadic system represents a dynamic of mutual regulation (Tronick, 1989). I suggest mutual touch is embedded in the larger bidirectional right brain-to-right brain communication system.

This research supports the infant's need for affectionate touch for healthy right hemisphere development, which can be observed in an infant-caregiver assessment. Clinicians need to appraise not only the quality and amount of *spontaneous* direct pupil-focused eye gazing and auditory communications between caregiver and infant but also the quality and amount of sensitive interpersonal touch the infant is receiving and expressing. Left-versus right-sided cradling, which is mostly subconscious (Vervloed, Hendriks, & van den Eijnde, 2011) should be assessed, as right cradling has been associated with maternal depression and maternal stress (Reissland, Hopkins, Helms, & Williams, 2009; Suter, Huggenberger, & Schachinger, 2007; Weatherill et al., 2004). The finding that adults who cradle on the right are more detached and less responsive to their infants than those who cradle on the left (Turnbull & Collins, 2000), and that poor levels of left cradling are typically associated with reduced emotional sensitivity and responsiveness (Morgan et al., 2018) can also be used diagnostically (see Schore, 2013). Indeed, these latter researchers are now asserting "cradling preference may possibly be an easily observable meaningful behavior trait signaling possible maternal emotional disengagement and its well-known heightened risks for adverse child development outcomes" (Morgan et al., 2018, p. 18).

As the securely attached infant enters toddlerhood, his or her interactively regulated right brain visual-facial, auditory-prosodic, and tactile-gestural communications become holistically integrated, allowing for the emergence of a coherent right brain emotional and corporeal subjective sense of self. Confirming this model of the critical importance of right brain-to-right brain attachment communications in the progressive social experience–dependent lateralization of the right brain, neuroscientists now document that the right brain hemisphere is dominant in human infants, that the strong and consistent predominance for the right hemisphere emerges postnatally, and that the mother's right hemisphere is more involved than the left in emotional processing and mothering. Studying structural connectivity asymmetry in the perinatal brain with newborn infants *at the beginning of the first year*, Michael Meaney and his colleagues concluded,

> In early life the right cerebral hemisphere could be better able to process . . . emotion (Schore, 2000; Wada & Davis, 1977). This idea appears consistent with our findings of rightward asymmetry in . . . limbic structures. . . . These neural substrates function as *hubs in the right hemisphere for emotion processes and mother and child interaction.* (Ratnarajah et al., 2013, p. 193, italics added)

Tronick and colleagues' research on infants *in the middle of the first year* reported that 6-month-old infants use left-sided gestures generated by the right hemisphere in order to cope with the stressful face-to-face still-face paradigm. They interpreted these data as being "consistent with Schore's (2005) hypotheses of hemispheric right-sided activation of emotions and their regulation during infant–mother interactions" (Montirosso et al., 2012, p. 826). Using near-infrared spectroscopy, Minagawa-Kawai and colleagues' study of infant mother attachment *at the end of the first year* observed, "Our results are in agreement with that of Schore (2000) who addressed the importance of the right hemisphere in the attachment system" (2009, p. 289).

Consonant with Bowlby's deduction that the hierarchically organized attachment control system is centrally involved in the organism's states of arousal, my work indicates that at the most fundamental level, the attachment mechanism is expressed as right brain-to-right brain interactive regulation of affective arousal, and thereby the regulation of biological synchronicity between and within organisms. Bowlby speculated that the "upgrading of control during individual development from simple to more sophisticated is no doubt in large part a result of the growth of the central nervous system" (1969, p. 156). Earlier, I described the emergence of a hierarchical sequence of interconnected limbic "control systems" or "hubs" in the right amygdala, right anterior cingulate, and right orbitofrontal cortex. These three systems interconnect with each other and with arousal-regulating bioaminergic neuromodulatory dopaminergic, noradrenergic, and serotonergic nuclei in the brain stem and midbrain, as well as with neuroendocrine nuclei in the hypothalamus, the "head ganglion" of the autonomic nervous system, and therefore each inputs the stress-regulating hypothalamic-pituitary-adrenal (HPA) axis.

Each hierarchical level of the three-tiered limbic system processes and imprints a positive or negative hedonic charge on current exteroceptive information about changes in the external social environment and then integrates it with interoceptive information about concurrent alterations in internal bodily states. Although all process exteroceptive and interoceptive information, the later maturing systems in the cortex process this information in a more complex fashion than do the earlier subcortical components.

The output of the lowest limbic levels is expressed as automatic innate reflexes, while higher processing produces more flexible intuitive responses that allow fine adjustment to environmental circumstances (intuitive affect regulation; Koole & Jostman, 2004). In three dimensions, the attachment control system is hierarchically structured as an outer, later developing orbitofrontal-limbic regulated core; an inner, earlier developing cingulate-limbic regulating core; and an earliest evolving amygdala-regulated core, like nested Russian dolls.

In my most recent articulation of this model of the ontogenetic progression of hierarchical limbic-autonomic regulatory centers, I offer evidence showing that the amygdala (especially the central nucleus), the paraventricular areas of the hypothalamus that produce the stress-reducing neuropeptide oxytocin and the stress-intensifying neuropeptide corticotropin releasing factor, and the insula (involved in stress-responsive visceroautonomic functions) begin their maturation prenatally and are functional at birth and over the ensuing perinatal stage (Schore, 2012a). In light of the fact that the emotional state of the mother influences the fetus, assessing the emotional well-being of the mother-to-be in pregnancy is critical.

At 2–3 months, the right basolateral amygdala, which densely connects with higher cortical areas, begins a critical period of growth, initiating the infant's burgeoning intersubjective functions. From 3 to 9 months, the anterior cingulate—a corticolimbic structure associated with responsivity to social cues—comes online, giving the infant even greater capacities for intersubjectivity and for receiving nonverbal communications of "good-enough" caregiver interactive regulation. From 10 to 12 months of age, the regulatory center in the orbitofrontal cortex, the attachment executive control system, begins its developmental growth period, which spans until the end of the second year (Schore, 2000). With optimal relational attachment experiences, the vertical axis that connects the right orbitofrontal cortex with subcortical areas is well developed, allowing the right orbitofrontal cortex to regulate (and be regulated by) the right amygdala.

Indeed, developmental neurobiological research reveals that the most rapid change in brain maturation occurs in the first 3–6 months of life, followed by slower change until 24 months, and relative stability after 24 months (Hermoye et al., 2006). Other studies demonstrate that amygdala function contributes to human attachment security (Lemche et al., 2006), and that the process of coping with early life stress increases the myelination of the orbitofrontal cortex, which controls arousal regulation and thereby promotes emotional resilience (Katz et al., 2009). For the rest of the life span, the right, and not left, lateralized prefrontal regions are responsible for the most complex regulation of affect and stress (Cerqueira, Almeida, & Sousa, 2008; Czeh et al., 2008; Quirin et al., 2013; Schore, 1994; Sullivan & Gratton, 2002). The right orbitofrontal cortex imprints internal representations of attachment experiences in implicit-procedural memory, thereby generating an internal working model that encodes nonconscious strategies of affect regulation. This regulatory system, the hierarchical apex of the limbic system, is responsible for the adaptive capacities of emotional communication and regulation that are found in secure children. On the other hand, functional limitations of the orbitofrontal system are seen in insecure attachment and a wide variety of psychiatric disorders (see Schore, 2003a, 2003b, 2012).

This ontogenetic hierarchical model suggests that right brain assessments need to be timed to crucial period transitions of the three regulatory systems (2–3 months, 10–12 months, and 18–24 months), periods of complex reorganizations of the emotion-processing limbic system. As the securely attached infant moves through infancy and toddlerhood, his or her interactively regulated intersubjective right brain visual-facial, auditory-prosodic, and tactile-gestural attachment communications become holistically integrated, allowing for the emergence of a right brain coherent emotional and corporeal subjective sense of self and a background state of well-being. The nonverbal implicit socioemotional capacities and deficits of both the infant's and the mother's right-lateralized self-system are a central focus of attachment assessments. Left-hemispheric verbal explicit measures cannot tap into these implicit psychoneurobiological mechanisms. In addition to ongoing clinical intersubjective evaluations, clinicians should investigate the use of current research methodologies as a potential source of developmental neuropsychological assessment tools.

CLINICAL IMPLICATIONS OF REGULATION THEORY FOR THE EARLY ASSESSMENT OF AUTISTIC SPECTRUM DISORDERS

As previously mentioned, there is now intense interest in the problem of early intervention for and assessment of not only burgeoning attachment disorders but also the earliest expression of autistic spectrum disorders: infantile autism. Autism is now viewed as a lifelong, complex neurodevelopmental disorder that severely impairs social interaction. Core symptoms include abnormal or unreciprocated interpersonal and emotional interactions, disordered social communication, and repetitive and stereotypic behaviors and restricted interests. At present, it is believed that the onset of autism most likely occurs in the latter part of the first year of life (Hazlett et al., 2005), although the field is now searching for neurobiological expressions of autism in even earlier periods of development. In a review, Yirmiya and Charman (2010) highlighted the importance of "brain development and the prodrome of autism spectrum disorders," noting that the finding of abnormal brain growth has "attracted enormous interest."

A large body of neurobiological studies reveals gross, widespread abnormalities in multiple areas of the autistic brain, including larger global brain volume in the first year (Courchesne, Carper, & Akshoomoff, 2008. Autism is now characterized as a disorder of aberrant neural circuitry, and research with infants at 6 months shows atypical patterns of connectivity of a number of white matter fiber tracts "not specific to any single brain region or behavioral domain" (Wolff et al., 2012, p. 596). These authors note that the earliest stages of infancy represent periods when "dramatic changes in behavior are paralleled by dramatic changes in the brain" (p. 590), and so "Extending neuroimaging downward to infants younger than 6 months would help clarify the temporal origin of diverging trajectories" (p. 597). The field is currently poised to begin more comprehensive studies of the prenatal, perinatal, and early postnatal periods. Yirmiya and Charman asserted, "Prenatal and perinatal environmental challenges during the course of pregnancy are likely causes of deleterious epigenetic modifications to the fetal brain with long-term developmental consequences, including risk and to autistic spectrum disorders" (2010, p. 446).

Recall Kanner originally suggested that autistic individuals "come into the world with an innate inability to form the usually biologically provided *affective contact* with other people" (1943, p. 250, italics added). Although the past two decades of autism research have been influenced almost exclusively by cognitive developmental psychology and cognitive neuroscience, there is currently a growing interest in altered development within autistic emotion-processing "limbic circuitry" (Haznedar et al., 1994). Yirmiya and Charman (2010) observed,

> The window of this abnormal brain growth coincides with the period of synaptogenesis and subsequent pruning when cortical connections are developed, refined and stabilized. *This process is interactive with the infant's experience of the environment* . . . and the consequences of a developing brain whose connections are not undergoing the usual refinement on information processing . . . may result in . . . the emergence of the ASD phenotype." (p. 443, italics added)

This clearly implies that updated models of autistic etiology are now shifting into the interactive relational model used in other developmental neuropsychiatric disorders; that is, the infant's interactions with the socioemotional environment (the attachment relationship) directly influence the development of the autistic infant brain.

In their overview of the field, Yirmiya and Charman referred to "an intriguing finding" that by the age of 2 years, children with autism had "enlarged amygdala, particularly in the right hemisphere" (2010, p. 443). Indeed, six studies now document a "pathological enlargement of the amygdala" in autistic infants, toddlers, and young children (Kim et al., 2010; Mosconi et al., 2009; Munson et al., 2006; Nordahl et al., 2012; Schumann et al., 2009; Sparks et al., 2002). Mosconi and colleagues suggested "failure to orient to faces and, more specifically, the eye region of the face is inherent in multiple aspects of social impairment unique to autism (e.g., joint attention, facial emotion processing) . . . may be linked to amygdala abnormalities" (2009, p. 510).

Studying children as young as 18 months, Munson and colleagues (2006) reported an association between enlarged right (and not left) amygdala volume with poorer socialization and communication development as measured on the Autism Diagnostic Interview and Vineland Scale. They speculated that right amygdala enlargement may reflect "right-sided amygdala activation in response to conditioned fear" (p. 690). Commenting on this amygdala enlargement in 18-month-old toddlers, Schumann and colleagues stated, "The amygdala has long been a site of intense interest in the search for neuropathologic markers for autism, given its well-established role in the production and recognition of emotions and modulatory role in social behavior. Initial signs of autism in toddlers include unusual affective behavior, reduced social interest, and poor eye contact, which are all suggestive of aberrant amygdalar function." (2009, p. 942). The problem of diminished attention to faces early on "may be the first in a cascade of problems that lead to later emotional and social impairments" (p. 947). Furthermore, they concluded that the autistic toddler's dysfunctional hyperaroused amygdala "suggests a heightened emotional, or even fearful, response when autistic individuals look at another person's eyes, regardless of whether they are familiar or a stranger" (p. 947).

This body of research clearly implies that autistic infants and toddlers experience a chronic intense fear state in the first 2 years of infancy, and that this needs to be assessed. The finding that early developing right basolateral amygdalar enlargement, associated with amygdalar hyperreactivity and abnormal fear conditioning, persists in 6- to 7-year-old children (Kim et al., 2010) strongly suggests that a chronic fear–based subjectivity continues in the autistic child's mind. My own studies on early relational trauma, disorganized attachment, and the origins of post-traumatic stress disorder implicate the right amygdala in states of fear conditioning (Baker & Kim, 2004) and "unseen fear" (Morris, Ohman, & Dolan, 1999) in both hyperaroused amygdala terror states and hypoaroused amygdala dissociative, detached states of emotional withdrawal (Schore, 2001b, 2002, 2009, 2012a). This work describes not only attachment experiences of traumatic affective arousal but also the unique defenses that the infant (and mother) use to counteract traumatic hyperarousal: dissociation, "the escape when there is no escape," "the last resort defensive strategy," "detachment from an unbearable situation" (Schore, 2001a).

In the infant mental health and infant psychiatry literatures, Guedeney and Fermanian (2001) described the "sustained withdrawal" of the disorganized infant, manifested in frozen, absent facial expression; total avoidance of eye contact; immobile level of activity; absence of vocalization; absence of relationship to others; and the impression that the child is beyond reach. In a subsequent study, Guedeney and colleagues observed withdrawn social behavior from as early as 2 months in "*autism*, chronic or severe pain, failure to thrive, or posttraumatic stress disorder" (2008, p. 151, italics added). Other research reports hyporesponsiveness to social stimuli (e.g., lack of orienting to novel sounds and attention disengagement) in 6-month-old autistic infants (Baranek et al., 2013). In a case study, Dawson and colleagues (2000) documented an infant with autism's "checking out" after overstimulation at 2.5 months and presenting a "transfixed stare" during eye contact at 9 months. The right amygdala findings in autistic toddlers indicate that pathological dissociation needs to be recognized and studied by autism researchers.

Developmental neuroscience also implicates another component of limbic circuitry, the right anterior cingulate (that is strongly connected with the right amygdala), in autism. Allman and colleagues (2005) described Von Economo neurons (VENs) in the anterior cingulate and fronto-insular cortex of humans that are part of the circuitry supporting social bonding. They observed that the VEN number is low at birth but increases in early development, that they are 30% more numerous in the right hemisphere than the left, and that this ratio develops in the early postnatal period. These authors stated the strong and consistent predominance for the right hemisphere emerges postnatally, that this right hemisphere VEN predominance may be related to the right-hemispheric specialization for the social emotions and therefore important for normal functioning, and therefore deviations from this ratio could be dysfunctional. Thus, "their emergence might be disrupted during postnatal development with dysfunctional consequences related to neuropsychiatric disorders" (p. 367). Functionally, this right anterior cingulate system is involved in the fast intuitive assessment of complex social situations. Allman and colleagues proposed that "in autism spectrum disorders the VENs fail to develop normally and that this failure could be partially responsible for the social disabilities in these disorders as a result of faulty intuition. Our theory predicts that autistic subjects will be abnormal in making intuitive decisions under conditions involving a high degree of uncertainty" (p. 372).

Von Economo neurons are also found in the human fronto-insular cortex. The right insula, a limbic structure that has extensive connections with the amygdala (Hoistad & Barbas, 2009, is involved in emotional and facial processing (Berthier, Starkstein, & Leiguarda, 1987), in integrating tonal structure with a speaker's emotions and attitudes (Riecker et al., 2000), and in visceral and autonomic functions that mediate the generation of an image of one's physical state (Craig et al., 2011). This limbic structure is activated by perceptual awareness of threat (Critchley, Mathias, & Dolan, 2002) and harm avoidance (Paulus et al., 2003). It is also implicated in pain processing and serves as an alarm center, "alerting the individual to potentially distressing interoceptive stimuli, investing them with negative emotional significance" (Banzett at al., 2000, p. 2120). These functions may be severely altered in the autistic brain. Research has documented that at 2 years, a group of autistic toddlers exhibited sensory abnormalities, hyperesthesia or hypoesthesia to pain and touch, and hyperactivity in the somatosensory (parietal) areas of the right (and not left) hemisphere (Miyazaki et al., 2007).

Along with the right anterior cingulate, the right insula is a "hub" of a "salience network" that integrates external sensory stimuli with internal states, and thereby is implicated in subjective awareness and interoception (Craig, 2011). Autistic children show alterations in connectivity between the insula and anterior cingulate (Uddin & Menon, 2009), reflecting disturbances in affective processes and difficulty with adapting to change, restrictive and repetitive behavior, and increased sensitivity to visual, auditory, and tactile stimuli (Uddin et al., 2013). These latter authors concluded that altered connectivity between the insula and anterior cingulate underlies a dysfunction in identifying relevant internal and extrapersonal stimuli to guide behavior, and therefore "dysfunction of the system may be part of the neurobiology of autism." Other studies of emotional face-processing deficits in autism show diminished activation in the right fusiform gyrus (Curby, Willenbockel, Tanaka, & Schultz, 2010), and increased activity in salience detection in the right amygdala and insula (Monk et al., 2010). The insular dysfunction of autism thus reflects an impairment in what Craig (2010) called "a sentient self."

With regard to the highest level of the hierarchical emotion-processing limbic circuit, Sabbagh (2004) asserted that the ability to decode others' mental states from facial expressions is mediated by the orbitofrontal/medial temporal circuit within the right hemisphere. Offering a neurobiological model of autism, he described a "core deficit" and concluded, "The developmental roots of autism might lie in abnormal functioning of the orbitofrontal/medial temporal circuit which may, in turn, underlie the abnormal development of social-cognitive skills among individuals with autism" (p. 209). Baron-Cohen, who first proposed the amygdala theory of autism, now postulates an atypical self-representation in autism, involving dysfunctional processing in the cingulate and ventromedial (orbitofrontal) cortex (Lombardo et al., 2010).

For more than two decades, I have offered interdisciplinary data indicating that the right-hemispheric orbitofrontal cortex and its cortical and subcortical connections support the adaptive functions of the implicit self-system (see Schore, 2012a, pp. 295–296, for a large body of research confirming right-hemispheric activity in generating self-awareness and self-recognition). The term "autism" is derived from the Greek word "autos," meaning self, and since Kanner's groundbreaking work autism has been associated with an atypical sense of self. In an extensive neurobiological overview of atypical development of self-related processes in autism spectrum disorders, Lyons and Fitzgerald (2013) cite my work and that of others and conclude,

> There is substantial evidence that the main components of self-awareness including self recognition, self-other differentiation, body awareness, theory of mind, intersubjectivity, emotion processing, language (pronoun reversal, inner speech, third person perspective), autobiographical memory and narrative self are impaired in ASD. Our review of neural substrates underlying these processes has highlighted the significance of the Right Hemisphere. (p. 753)

These authors contend that the developmental organization of the early developing self depends on relations with others, and that these early experiences are vital to right brain maturation. They concluded that "right hemisphere impairment leads to a dysfunctional self-development in autism spectrum disorders" (p, 754), and that "substantial behavioural evidence of infants who later developed autism is supporting the theory of *disrupted intersubjective behavior*" (p. 755, italics added).

In fact, a small but extremely important group of studies has explored very early deficits in "intersubjective communication" and "emotional attachment" in autistic infants. In groundbreaking clinical research using microanalytic analysis of home videos, Trevarthen and Daniel (2005) reported disorganized rhythm and synchrony in the dyadic play of an 11-month-old autistic infant and her father. Their interactional analysis also revealed reduced motor capacities, as well as "abnormal withdrawal or detachment," specifically documenting that the interaction was characterized by "long blank periods lacking in shared experience" (p. S29), clearly describing dissociative withdrawal. The authors asserted that these deficits in infant intersubjectivity and mutual reciprocity that underlie "asynchronous social behavior" reflect alterations in "both brain growth and early development of skills and sociability" (p. S25).

Expanding upon this work, Muratori's laboratory has offered the most productive studies of the very earliest manifestations of autism (Muratori et al., 2011). Analyzing home videos of *spontaneous* interactions of autistic infants and their caregivers over three trimesters of the first 18 months (0–6 months, 6–12 months, and more than 12 months), their video coding of interactions within a time window of 3 seconds included "maintain social engagement" (operationally defined as "The infant takes up an active role within a two-way interaction in order to keep the caregiver involved. The infant interacts, vocalizes and maintains turn taking") and "regulation" ("The caregiver modulates the infant's arousal and mood; the caregiver may act to either excite [up-regulation] or calm-down [down-regulation] the infant"). They documented that autistic infants show, in the first semester, a reduction in the duration of spontaneous social behavior "such as enjoying with people and maintaining social engagement" and "the capacity on the one hand to express and to repeat affective states, and on the other hand to be attentive and to read the affective states of the other" (p. 413). In the second semester, they observed further difficulties in the development of intersubjectivity, expressed in a decreased tendency of the infants to orient to their own name, typically seen at 9 months. They concluded,

> Different intersubjective abnormalities operate during the first year to impede its development. These abnormalities reduce the typical propensity of infants and toddlers to be active in seeking interactive experiences and in sympathizing intentions and feelings of others. Side-by-side, primary caregiver-infant interactions are shaped by the *lack of infant intersubjectivity*. (p. 409, italics added)

In a subsequent study, these researchers used more complex computational methods to analyze interaction synchrony from home movies in order to differentiate autism from intellectual disability and typical development over the first three trimesters (Saint-Georges et al., 2011). Summarizing caregiver-infant interactions in typically developing babies, Muratori and colleagues (2011) asserted,

> Vocalizations are predominant from birth. . . . While seeking people peaks significantly at second semester . . . intersubjective behavior continues to grow significantly over the semesters. Thus in the second semester, a typical child is rather seeking and attending to his caregiver and little by little turns to objects. . . . This pattern describes the typical development of shared or joint attention. (p. 10)

Describing typical caregiver behavior in these same two periods of the first year, they stated,

> [Caregiver] vocalizations are predominant from birth. We can assume that this type of stimulation which has its roots in animal communication is the more powerful way to strengthen child attention and affective communication. Probably it happens thanks to prosodic cues specific to infant directed speech . . . caregiver gestural solicitations increase during the first year. (p. 10)

Note this description echoes my studies of right brain prosody and gestures.

In contrast, "autistic children show less orienting toward people in the first semester, and thereafter they exhibit a much smaller increase of seeking people behaviors" (Muratori et al., 2011, p. 10). Importantly, orienting and being receptive toward people is not active, but passive. They concluded,

> Thus, it seems that the real marker for atypical social development is the weakness in initiating a social interaction: without the increase in social initiative the ability to be receptive and responding to others also become more severe. . . . All these results are consistent with the hypothesis of a *growing deviant development in autistic disorders.* (p. 10, italics added)

On the caregiver side, they observed that in response to a socially underactive autistic infant (lack of initiative, inability to provoke or to anticipate the other's aims, hypoactivity), the parent assumes that the infant needs to be more stimulated, and by the second trimester a parent adopts a hyperstimulating style. Trevarthen and Daniel (2005) and Doussard-Roosevelt et al. (2003) also reported that parents of autistic children overstimulate their infants as a result of their inactivity. (I'd suggest this could be a relational context that increases infant dissociative withdrawal.) On the basis of these data, Saint-Georges and her colleagues recommended assessment/screening in the first 6 months and parent-infant training in the second trimester.

In the most recent publication of Muratori's group, Apicella and colleagues (2013) again reported less infant motor activity in the first trimester and lower amounts of vocalizations in the second. They cited Grossmann and colleagues' (2010) study on right-lateralized voice processing in 4- and 7-month infants (described in the first section of this chapter) and proposed, "The reduced use of vocalizations to respond could suggest that, in infants with autistic spectrum disorders, the original vocalizations do not develop into a vocal communication able to respond, engage in dialogue" (Apicella et al., 2010, p. 8). As for caregivers' behaviors, they documented a reduction in affectionate touch (less caressing or kissing) in the second trimester, suggesting that it represents a response to the infant's atypically reduced motor and vocal development, and that this non-synchronic motor-vocal pattern may interfere with the development of reciprocity. On the other hand, they also reported an increase in caregivers' stimulating gestures (gesticulating, tickling, making faces, or presenting objects to the infant), which also may be "the way parents with infants with ASD adapt to their less responsive child" (p. 9).

It is interesting to note that the primary caregiver's reduction in affectionate, loving touch may be understood as a maternal coping mechanism of defensive withdrawal in response to the intense stressor of an increasingly emotionally unresponsive autistic infant, one who is becoming more and more unable to respond to the love of the mother. In other words, the intensely stressful interpersonal neurobiological context of the autistic infant-mother interaction may in some cases dyadically generate a detached "refrigerator mother." It is frequently forgotten that a dysregulated infant may be a source of relational stress for the mother.

These studies that directly assess real-life, real-time reciprocal social interactions represent a potential paradigm shift in autism research, assessment, and treatment. Saint-Georges and colleagues (2011) asserted that the use of engineering methods related to detecting *spontaneous* social signal processing allows "focusing on dynamic parent–infant interaction instead of single behaviors of the baby or of the parent" (p. 9). This methodology of studying interactions rather than discrete behaviors of each member of the dyad mirrors the theoretical perspective of my interpersonal neurobiological work on right brain-to-right brain intersubjective emotional communications. Trevarthen and Daniel (2005) stated that the "modern diagnosis of autism" reflects the prevailing view of psychological growth as "the development of cognition," and that to date it has ignored "the special significance of interpersonal factors" such as "infant subjectivity." They concluded that autism fundamentally represents "a failure in the integration of motives to move in purposeful ways with self awareness, and also to difficulties with intuitive awareness of other persons' motives and states of mind. The processes that make these functions possible are not explained by cognitive neuroscience" (p. S26). For some time now, both autism research and treatment have been dominated by cognitive science, cognitive neuroscience, and cognitive developmental psychology. But with a renewed interdisciplinary focus on the very early development of not left brain cognitive but right brain socioemotional survival functions and the emergence of the implicit self, there is now a possibility of reforging a bridge between autism and attachment-informed treatment models, including models of early assessment and intervention.

In light of the fact that the primordial etiology of autism, attachment disorders—and indeed of all early forming psychiatric disorders—takes place in universally shared prenatal, perinatal, and postnatal stages of human brain development, developmental neuroscience may play a key role in this rapprochement. According to regulation theory, all human infants, with whatever early genetic endowments and in both positive growth-facilitating or negative growth-inhibiting relational contexts, progress through the same critical periods of attachment-influenced right brain development and stages of self-organization. Both the significant degree of brain dysfunction and level of psychopathology of autistic disorders, which are essentially relational, intersubjective, socioemotional, and not merely cognitive disturbances, are clearly more widespread than attachment disorders or early forming personality disorders.

The neurobiological alterations of organized insecure attachments are mainly focal alterations of cortical limbic-autonomic circuitry, while disorganized attachments show more subcortical right amygdala dysfunction. Autistic disorders involve more global alterations of various brain circuits, both subcortical and cortical. Although the right amygdala is functionally deficient in both disorganized attachment disorders and autism, early pathological enlargement of the amygdala and brain hypertrophy are unique to autism. It is now thought that "the processes that lead to autistic spectrum disorders probably begin during fetal development" (Abel et al., 2013, p. 391). A study of RNA *in situ* hybridization of the brains of autistic children reported patches of pathological disorganization in regions mediating social and emotional functions. The authors concluded, "Our data are consistent with an early prenatal origin of autism or at least prenatal processes that may confer a predisposition to autism" (Stoner et al., 2014, p. 1216).

On the basis of these data, I would speculate that in autism, stressful alterations of the right central nucleus of the amygdala occur *prenatally* because of untoward intrauterine influences of the social and physical environment that substantially compromise the very early development of the midbrain reticular formation—bioaminergic (dopaminergic, noradrenergic, serotonergic) nuclei that innervate the fetal amygdala. These bioamines, central to emotional functioning, have energy regulating, arousal generating, and trophic functions. For example, *in utero* early pathological mechanisms within midbrain ventral tegmental dopaminergic subnuclei could alter dopamine's trophic functions and impair mesolimbic dopaminergic innervation of the central (and then basolateral) amygdala. These systems may also be sensitive to gestational neurotoxic pesticide exposure, which has also been implicated in autism (Shelton, Hertz-Picciotto, & Pessah, 2012).

On the other hand, right amygdala alterations in disorganized attachments may result from epigenetic mechanisms associated with stressful *perinatal and postnatal* social environments. Attachment disorders reflect delayed connectivity or "immaturity" of the limbic-autonomic circuits of the right brain, whereas the "complex neurodevelopmental" autistic disorders reflect altered connectivity and "developmental derangement" of the right brain. The biological mechanisms that underlie the neuropathology of the "growing deviant development in autistic disorders" are now thought to produce an individual deviation from normative developmental processes (Jones & Klin, 2013). In autism, developmental neuropathology is expressed not only in the right amygdala but also in all three regulatory control systems, again suggesting a progressive metabolic failure of bioaminergic innervation, even in postnatal critical periods. Research strongly suggests that during prenatal and postnatal critical periods, aberrant DNA methylation, excessive oxidative cell damage, apoptosis, and mitochondrial dysfunction may underlie the metabolic pathology of the developing autistic brain (e.g., Melnyk et al., 2012). In any event, the earlier described progression of right brain subcortical and cortical attachment functions and structures also apply to early assessments of the ontogeny of autism.

CONCLUSION

At the outset of this chapter, I described a major goal of autism researchers—to create "treatments delivered at very young ages, *when the brain is most plastic,* may ultimately lessen or prevent the lifelong challenge associated with autism" (Yirmiya & Ozonoff, 2007, p. 9, italics added). The importance of early intervention in not just autism but all developmental disorders is stressed in a number of disciplines: infant mental health, child psychology and psychiatry, pediatrics, clinical social work, and developmental neuroscience. Authors in this latter field assert, "Although the first year of life may be a period of developmental vulnerability, *it may also be a period in which therapeutic interventions would have the greatest positive affect*" (Knickmeyer et al., 2008, p. 12179–12180, italics added).

Regulation theory highlights the potentially optimizing effects of early interventions within prenatal, perinatal, and postnatal critical periods of brain development. The theory has recently been applied to using maternal-infant interactions as a mechanism for reducing the effects of allostatic load on premature infant neurodevelopment in neonatal intensive care units (Weber, Harrison, & Steward, 2012), for differentially diagnosing attachment disorders from infantile autism in the first year (Schore, 2013; Voran, 2013), and for generating an evidence-based interpersonal neurobiological model of attachment assessments and interventions (see Schore & Newton, 2012, for applications to a clinical case, the assessment and treatment of a 7-month-old infant and his mother).

Although left-hemispheric language disturbances appear later in the second and third year, the common underlying social impairment symptoms of autism spectrum disorders, abnormal or unreciprocated interpersonal and emotional interactions and disordered social communication, present in the first year. In human infancy, "communication" is not verbal but nonverbal communication, a specialization of the right hemisphere. Infants diagnosed with autistic spectrum disorder show an absence of the typical right hemispheric left visual field processing of faces (Dundas, Gasteb, & Strauss, 2012) and an atypical hemispheric specialization for faces (Keehn, Vogel-Farley, V., Tager-Flusberg, H., & Nelso, C.A. (2015). Importantly, *the left cradling bias is absent in children with autistic spectrum disorders* (Pileggi et al., 2013), and, indeed, the left cradling right hemisphere bias is now being suggested as an assessment for the early identification of children at risk for these disorders (Jones, 2014). Recent hyperscanning research demonstrates that adults with high-functioning autistic spectrum disorder also show a deficit in joint attention, associated with an impairment of early visual processing of gaze and a diminished intra-brain functional connectivity between the right inferior frontal gyrus and right superior temporal sulcus (Tanabe et al., 2012). Furthermore, a functional near-infrared spectroscopy study of children with autism spectrum disorders shows a hypoactivation of the right prefrontal cortex underlying motor-related inhibitory deficits (Ikeda et al., 2018).

The early evolving core symptomatology of infantile autism describes a developmental neuropathology and developmental psychopathology of the early developing right hemisphere, which for the rest of the life span is dominant for the *implicit* nonverbal, holistic processing of rapidly communicated emotional information and *spontaneous* social interactions (Decety & Lamm, 2007; Schore, 2012a; Semrud-Clikeman, Fine, & Zhu, 2011). Very recent research reveals decreased *spontaneous* attention to social stimuli in 6-month-old infants later diagnosed with autism spectrum disorders (Chawarska, Macari, & Shic, 2013). A developmental neuropsychological study of these implicit spontaneous functions demonstrates that "the social choices of children with autism were influenced less by emotional information presented subconsciously and suggest a subcortical contribution to the social/emotional processing deficits observed with autism" (Hall, West, & Szatmari, 2007, p. 100). Although both the analytic left hemisphere and holistic right hemisphere are affected by a common neuropathological process, at the core autism represents a severe impairment of the right-lateralized cortical-subcortical implicit self-system that acts unconsciously, beneath levels of conscious awareness (Schore, 1994, 2003b, 2012a).

Developmental assessments of human socioemotional (as opposed to cognitive) development need to focus attention on rapid dyadic right brain-to-right brain visual, auditory, tactile (and olfactory) attachment communications that can either facilitate or inhibit the experience-dependent maturation of the infant's developing right brain. Modern attachment theory can be used as a guide for assessing a misattuned infant-caregiver relationship by observing, experiencing and evaluating the intersubjective communication of affects and the interactive regulation of affective arousal between the infant's and mother's right brains (see Schore, 2012a, pp. 389–393, for schematics of regulated and dysregulated right brain attachment communications). Early chronic failures of interactive arousal regulation are expressed not only in intersubjective deficits but also in dysregulated fear-driven subjective states of consciousness in the infantile autistic brain.

Regulation theory dictates that assessments of infant mental health (Schore, 2001b) in the first and second year must be relational and need to utilize nonverbal, bodily-based measures of early forming right brain intersubjective relational affectivity (implicit affect regulation), and not later forming left brain verbal language-based measures (explicit mentalization).

Early assessments of "high-risk dyads" can easily transition into clinical interventions that potentially are able to expand the mother's implicit capacities for interactive affect regulation, the core of the attachment dynamic, thereby creating a growth-facilitating environment for infant right brain development. This work suggests that modern attachment theory can act as a catalyst for the potential cross-fertilization of the attachment and autism worlds, one that can lead to more effective clinical intervention models. In the case of infantile autism, timely neurochemical interventions may also be used to prevent oxidative damage of the developing brain (e.g., Main et al., 2012) and to enhance psychological interventions (Gordon et al., 2013).

The interpersonal neurobiological perspective of regulation theory supports the clinical principle that effective early intervention during critical periods of heightened brain plasticity can facilitate the expansion of the right brain not only in infancy but also over the course of the rest of the life span. A large body of developmental psychiatric research confirms the idea that "Most mental illnesses . . . begin far earlier in life than was previously believed" (Insel & Felton, 2005, p. 590). Neurobiologically informed programs of early intervention could thus bring us closer to a common goal of psychology and psychiatry, the optimization of emotional well-being and the prevention of emotional disorders.

CHAPTER 4

All Our Sons

The Developmental Neurobiology and Neuroendocrinology of Boys at Risk

THE IDEA THAT the growth and maturation of males is affected more adversely by early environmental stress than it is for females has a long history in the biological, medical, and anthropological literatures (e.g., Greulich, Crimson, & Turner, 1953; Tanner, 1978). The more modern concept of "*boys* at risk" clearly suggests the importance of gender in order to understand both the psychology and biology of human beings, especially early developing human beings. The term "at risk" implicitly implies a vulnerability not only in early development but also at some later stage of the life span, and it explicitly connotes that a certain group of "high-risk" male children will, as they enter adolescence, be highly susceptible to a number of psychiatric disorders in which the diagnostic symptomatology first appears in that period of human development. It also suggests a vulnerability of specifically developing boys and not girls to certain psychiatric disorders, and thus psychological difficulties that are more associated with the male versus the female gender.

The study of the differences (and similarities) between the sexes has long been a major focus of research in both psychology and biology. Indeed for most of the past century, there was a substantial divide between the psychological and biological sciences, and thus gender has a long history of controversy. The studies of psychology into the problem of gender have been substantially influenced by the theoretical models that were dominant at different points in the development of psychology as a discipline.

In recent writings, I have described three paradigm shifts: beginning in the 1960s with behavioral psychology; to the 1980s with cognitive psychology into the 2000s; and a shift to an emotional psychology (Schore, 2012). These disciplinary developmental transitions were manifest in changes in research and clinical focus from behavior to cognition to bodily-based emotion. They paralleled transformations in biology and neuroscience from the voluntary motor and language functions of the left brain to the emotional functions of the right brain. Each of these three psychological theoretical perspectives has dictated the research orientation and methodologies of gender studies: sexual differences in behavior, sexual differences in cognition, and gender differences between the sexes in terms of the emotional and social functions of a male or female bodily-based self. Over this time period, neurobiology, influenced by psychology, also has a history of studying similarities and differences between the male and female brains.

Earlier biological research focused on developing psychological gender differences in behavior and language and were paralleled by sex differences in the functional properties of the developing verbal left hemisphere. For the most part, this psychological research paid little attention to the very earliest stages of human development. Frequently, investigations were disconnected from studies that documented differences in emotional and social functions of developing male and female infants, from developmental neurobiological research on differences in early brain development between the genders, and from a substantial body of research documenting sex differences in psychiatric disorders. Indeed, gender studies in developmental psychology remained divorced from and frequently antithetical to biology. Because of the almost exclusive focus on late infancy and early childhood cognitive and behavioral differences, emotional differences were not measured or were ignored. Indeed, gender differences in early infancy were generally thought by developmental psychologists to be nonexistent and were not viewed as a relevant dimension of experimental research or clinical practice.

In contrast to earlier psychological studies that privileged social factors in generating sex differences in behavior and cognition (Money & Ehrhardt, 1972; Maccoby & Jacklin, 1974), my work has attempted to integrate the biological and social mechanisms that underlie the early origins of affective gender differences. In 1994, I cited extant 20th-century studies of the developing brain in order to offer a model of gender development centered in early sex differences in the emotional right brain, which is dominant in human infancy. In later chapters of that volume, I described the critical role of gonadal steroids in the organization of right brain circuits and proposed that the sexes differ in their experience-dependent patterns of the wiring of the limbic system and cerebral cortex and thereby in the regulation of emotional behavior (Schore, 1994). Importantly, I cited classical neurological research that indicated cerebral maturation as a whole is slower in males than in females, and therefore developing boys were more at risk. In 2003, I was an author of the Commission on Children at Risk (2003) report *Hardwired to Connect*, which concluded,

> In recent decades, many adults have tended to withdraw from the task of assigning prosocial meaning to gender, especially in the case of boys. . . . But neglecting the gendered needs . . . can be dangerous. As the medical world has discovered, the risk of not attending to real differences that exist between males and females can have dangerous consequences. (pp. 24–25)

Two years later in an influential article "Sex and the Suffering Brain" in the journal *Science*, Holden asserted, "For many years we were not even allowed to say there were sex differences in the brain" (2005, p. 1577). She observed, "It's easy to start a fight about whether there are gender differences when it comes to mental skills, but there's little debate that patterns of mental illness and disorders vary between the sexes" (p. 1574). On that point, she noted although culture helps shape how the two sexes express mental problems, some differences persist across cultures and across time; specifically, women are more likely to get depressed, while men are more severely afflicted by schizophrenia and exhibit more antisocial behavior, and most alcoholics and drug addicts are male. Holden cited Thomas Insel, the head of the National Institute of Mental Health, as saying "it's pretty difficult to find any single factor that's more predictive for some of these disorders than gender" (p. 1574).

If psychiatry had been ambivalent about gender studies, biology was less equivocal. In 2008, Sharpe offered a perspective on these gender differences in the extant biological literature:

> The difference between becoming a male rather than a female is about as fundamental as you can get, as it will alter that individual's place in society, transform the shape of his body, reshape his inherent abilities, his thought processes and his behaviors . . . when compared with the "set-up" program which would have led to a female, it is becomingly increasingly clear that "making a male" is a rather perilous process. (p. 1)

That same year, Zahn-Waxler, Shirtcliff, and Marceau offered a forward-looking "Disorders of Childhood and Adolescence: Gender and Psychopathology" in the psychological literature. Integrating psychiatry and developmental psychology, they concluded,

> Even toddlers and preschool children can have serious externalizing problems, and sex differences are already present at this time. This suggests an even earlier onset that may need to be incorporated into developmental models. *The delayed physical maturation and language development of boys, along with emotion regulation problems, may place young boys at greater risk than girls.* (p. 282, italics added)

A central theme of this chapter dictates that this increased maturational risk of males is expressed at the earliest stages of the life span, from the male fetus to the male infant to the boy in childhood and teen in adolescence, when classical psychiatric disorders first appear. Furthermore, this normative maturational delay is principally involved in a male-associated vulnerability to specific types of psychiatric disorders, especially to the externalizing psychopathologies and to deficits in the emotional and social functions of the early developing right brain. According to Holden (2005), "men are more prone to expressing unhappiness through an 'externalizing pathway' of physical behavior that includes drinking, drug abuse, and violence, whereas women are more likely to 'internalize,' leading to depression and disorders such as anorexia" (p. 1576). She also reported that more males than females are diagnosed with schizophrenia and have earlier, more severe symptoms, and intriguingly suggested "these deficits all begin prenatally during the period of sexual differentiation of the brain" (p. 1577).

In agreement with this development model, Zahn-Waxler and colleagues (2008) put forth the idea that the study of sex differences provides a means to identify the complex etiologies for different forms of emotional and behavioral problems, and that the origins of male and female dominant psychopathologies at later life are rooted in biological, physical, cognitive, and socioemotional differences in boys and girls that precede the expression of clinical problems. These psychiatric data have also become a focus of neuroendocrinology, where Kigar and Auger (2013) have documented differences in the diagnostic ratios between genders of male-dominant autism spectrum disorders (male to female = 80:20), early onset schizophrenia (80:20), and attention deficit hyperactivity disorder (ADHD; 58:42) versus female-dominant major depressive disorders (33:67) and anorexia nervosa (7:93). In the neuroscience literature, it is now agreed that "in humans, males are more prone to neuropsychiatric disorders that appear developmentally, whereas females are more vulnerable to those that appear later" (Llorente et al., 2009, p. 240).

These male gender–associated disorders have significantly increased recently. In the pediatrics literature, Boyle and colleagues (2011) reported that from 1997 to 2008, developmental disabilities rose dramatically, and that among this group boys had a higher prevalence overall for a number of select disabilities compared with girls. This 17% increase in all developmental disabilities is caused in large part by shifts in the prevalence of ADHD and autism. Echoing this in the *Annual Review of Public Health*, Lanphear (2015) cited psychiatric epidemiological data to show that the prevalence of developmental disabilities has recently dramatically increased in U.S. children. He cited data from the Centers for Disease Control and Prevention (CDC) indicating a 123% increase from 2002 to 2010 in the prevalence of autism spectrum disorder among 8-year-old children, the age of peak prevalence. With respect to another male-dominated disorder, he stated,

> ADHD, the most common brain disorder of childhood, affects about 1 in 10 children in the United States; boys are 2.5 times more likely

> to meet criteria for ADHD than are girls . . . these data indicate that we are in the midst of an epidemic of brain-based disorders. (p. 213)

Intriguingly, he links the sudden rise in developmental disabilities to the effects of environmental toxins on the developing brain.

Why are boys at risk? In order to address this question, I will use the perspective of regulation theory (Schore, 1994, 2003a, 2003b, 2012)—an evidence-based interpersonal neurobiological model of development and psychopathogenesis—to offer a model of the deeper psychoneurobiological mechanisms that underlie this vulnerability of the developing male. The central thesis of the following work dictates that significant neurohormonally driven gender differences are seen between male and female social and emotional functions in the earliest stages of development, and that these result not only from differences in sex hormones and social experiences but also in rates of male and female brain maturation, specifically in the early developing right brain. I will suggest that the stress-regulating circuits of the male brain mature more slowly than those of the female in the prenatal, perinatal, and postnatal critical periods, and that this is reflected in normal gender differences in right brain attachment functions.

I will also offer evidence to show that due to this maturational delay, developing males are more vulnerable over a longer period of time to stressors in the social environment (attachment trauma) and toxins in the physical environment (endocrine disruptors) that negatively impact right brain development. These right-lateralized structural alterations and deficits in social, emotional, and stress-regulating functions—more so than later maturing left brain language and motor functions—underlie the etiology of documented gender differences in neural response to psychological stress seen in developmental disabilities and psychopathologies (Wang et al., 2007). In earlier work, I have offered a large body of research and clinical data to show that the predisposition to various psychiatric and personality disorders is rooted in postnatal attachment trauma that alters the experience-dependent maturation of the early developing right brain (Schore, 1994, 2003a, 2003b, 2012), but I now expand that model to include the central role of gender. As I will soon describe, significant sex differences are operating early in the intrauterine period of development, and that *in utero* the male fetus and female fetus show differential rates of brain maturation and patterns of stress reactivity.

Thus, another major theme of this work is to move developmental etiological models even earlier in time, to the period of "life before birth" (Nathanielsz, 1998). There is now widespread acceptance of the fetal programming hypothesis (Barker, 1998; Barker et al., 2002; Gluckman & Hanson, 2004), and here I apply it to the problems of gender development and boys at risk. I will suggest that the developing male or female embryo/fetus undergoing rapid developmental changes is particularly vulnerable to organizing and disorganizing environmental influences during prenatal sensitive periods, and that these leave permanent imprints on later gender differences in both healthy emotional behavior and in susceptibility to certain psychiatric disorders.

Here, as in all my writings, I continue to use the device of citing verbatim the current voices of researchers across a number of disciplines in order to demonstrate an interdisciplinary convergence and agreement on the fundamental importance of gender, early brain maturation, neuroendocrinology, and socioemotional development in addressing the problem of why boys are at risk. In the following, I offer a number of hypotheses derived from regulation theory (Schore, 1994, 2003a, 2003b, 2012) for experimental validation. In line with my ongoing work on the clinical applications of the theory, this work also addresses a fundamental question: How can we use the recent rapid advances in knowledge in the developmental sciences not only to generate more efficient models of diagnostic and treatment interventions for *today's children and adults*, but also in prevention; that is, to improve the mental and physical health of *subsequent generations*?

SEX DIFFERENCES IN BRAIN MATURATION, EARLY APPEARANCE OF SOCIOEMOTIONAL FUNCTIONS, AND THE NEUROENDOCRINE ORIGINS OF GENDER

Almost 50 years ago, Taylor (1969) published "Differential Rates of Maturation between Sexes and between Hemispheres" in the journal *Lancet*, thus initiating the interest of neuroscience in the early emergence of gender differences in brain development. On the basis of clinical data regarding *cerebral maturation,* he concluded, "*This process proceeds more rapidly in girls than in boys,* a fact that is supported by general evidence of their physical, and behavioural development" (p. 141, italics added). This neurobiological mechanism of slower functional maturation in developing male brains compared to developing female brains is expressed immediately after birth.

Thirty years later in the developmental psychological literature, Tronick's lab offered the study "Gender Differences in Emotional Expressivity and Self-Regulation during Early Infancy" (Weinberg et al., 1999). Surveying the field, they cited research demonstrating that male newborns are less responsive to auditory and social stimuli and less able to maintain eye contact than female newborns, and that male newborns experience greater difficulties in maintaining affective regulation than female newborns (Hittelman & Dickes, 1979). Male infants smile less than female infants and display more irritability, crying, facial grimacing, and lability of emotional states (Call, 1978; Feldman, Brody, & Miller, 1980; Phillips, King, & DuBois, 1978). Male as opposed to female neonates show a more rapid buildup of arousal and a quicker peak of excitement (Osofsky & O'Connell, 1977) and engage in less self-comforting, a behavior that functions to regulate arousal, tension, excitement, or distress (Brazelton, Koslowski, & Main, 1974; Korner, 1974). On overviewing these studies, Weinberg et al. (1999) observed that *girls seemed "less vulnerable to interactive stresses,"* and therefore these gender differences in emotional expressivity and self-regulation differentially affected the regulatory demands of mothers and sons and mothers and daughters.

In more recent work, Tronick reported, "in 6-month-old infants . . . boys were more emotionally reactive than were girls during face-to-face social interactions with their mothers. Boys were more likely than were girls to show facial expressions and anger, to fuss and to cry, to want to be picked up, and to attempt to get away or distance themselves from their mothers by arching their backs and turning or twisting in their infant seats" (2007, p. 340). Interpreting these data, he suggested,

> These gender differences focused on differences in boys' and girls' self-regulation of affect. Boys' greater emotional reactivity suggested

> that *boys have greater difficulty self-regulating their affective states and that they need to rely more on maternal regulatory input than do girls.* (p. 340, italics added)

He concluded, “Boys . . . are more demanding social partners, have more difficult times regulating their affective states, and may need more of their mothers’ support to help them regulate affect. This increased demandingness would affect the infant boys’ interactive partner” (p. 345).

Other research confirms the continuity of these gender differences from the neonate to the toddler. A study of neonatal imitation in 1- to 3-day-old infants reveals that newborn girls are better at imitating fine motor extensions than are newborn boys (Nagy, Kompagne, Orvos, & Pat, 2007). These authors concluded that newborn girls, with their faster and more accurate abilities, may create a more responsive and interactive social environment that in turn leads to differences in socioemotional development at later stages of development. At 12 months, female toddlers show a greater preference for dyadic interactions (Benenson, 1993), make more eye contact (Lutchmaya, Baron-Cohen, & Raggart, 2002), spend more time watching a film of a face than of a car (Lutchmaya & Baron-Cohen, 2002), and show more affective empathy and prosocial behavior (Volbrecht et al., 2007) than do age-related males.

In terms of interpersonal neurobiology, from the beginning and throughout infancy boys show *functional* expressions of prolonged *structural* cerebral immaturity in affect and stress regulation, adaptive functions of the early developing right brain. Zahn-Waxler and colleagues noted, “The curve of *development of the frontal cortex, caudate, and temporal lobes in girls is considerably faster than in boys* (2008, p. 279, italics added). Integrating this with Taylor’s and Tronick’s work, the longer period of development of social responsiveness and regulating affect in male infants reflects the slower maturation rate of the male brain during the brain growth spurt, from the last trimester through the end of the second postnatal year (Dobbing & Sands, 1973).

Not only the regulation but the processing and expression of affect also shows this gender difference. McClure documented “significant female advantages for facial expressing processing in infants and in children and adolescents" (2000, p. 444). She asserted that this face-processing system may not be fully mature at birth, that it continues to develop throughout the first 6 months of life, and that the brain regions that respond to faces "*may develop more rapidly and earlier in females than in males* (p. 428, italics added). McClure proposed,

> Early developments in facial emotional processing depend heavily on maturational changes in a neurological subsystem specialized for recognition of complex patterns such as faces and selected facial features, including expressions. . . . Studies have implicated a variety of structures as participants in this subsystem. The bulk of research, however, has focused on the temporal cortex and the amygdala, as well as a variety of structures seated in *the right cerebral hemisphere.* (p. 426, italics added)

Over the past three decades, my work has documented the structure-function relationships of the early developing right hemisphere (Chi, Dooling, & Giles, 1977; Crowell et al., 1973; Geschwind & Galaburda, 1987; Gupta et al., 2005; Mento et al., 2010; Sun et al., 2005), which is dominant in human infancy (Chiron et al., 1997; Schore, 1994). The nonverbal right hemisphere is in a growth spurt in the first year, but the verbal left hemisphere not until the second year (Thatcher, 1994). Expanding my studies on early emotional development, I suggest that the right hemisphere, which is dominant for the processing, expression, communication, and regulation of emotion, develops more slowly in male than in female infants. The infant right brain becomes dominant for the processing of visual-facial (de Heering & Rossion, 2015), auditory-prosodic (Grossmann et al., 2010), and tactile-gestural (Montirosso, Borgatti, & Tronick, 2010) information, and although both sexes show the same sequence of posterior cortical to anterior cortical development, they do this at different maturational rates. In his classic study, Taylor concluded, "Cerebral maturation would be more rapid in girls, as are physical and psychological development, so that *boys would be at risk for a longer time*" (1969, p. 140, italics added). This means there is a more protracted period of vulnerability in the boy's slower maturing right hemisphere, and that the male compared to the female infant's prolonged immaturity is manifest in a less efficient processing and regulating of stressful negative affects, a dominant function of the right hemisphere (Schore, 1994, 2003a, 2012).

In my 1994 book on the neurobiology of emotional development, I cited Taylor's developmental neurobiological principle in a chapter, "The Origins of Infantile Sexuality and Psychological Gender" (Schore, 1994). Integrating psychology and biology, I reviewed extant 20th-century studies of the neuroendocrinology of the developing brain in order to describe the critical role of gonadal steroids in the organization of right brain circuits, and proposed that the sexes differ in their experience-dependent patterns of the wiring of the limbic system (Schore, 1994). I also reported a sexual dimorphism and feminized versus masculinized wiring patterns in the emotion-processing limbic system as well as gender differences in the regulation of the male infant's and female infant's emotional and social functions. Over the course of the following two decades, a massive body of research now unequivocally demonstrates that in prenatal and postnatal periods, the sex-specific gonadal steroids androgen (testosterone) and estrogen (estradiol) produced by the hypothalamic-pituitary-gonadal (HPG) axis play an essential organizing role in brain development and in the early evolution of gender-specific differences.

Both androgens and estrogens (which are derived from the aromatization of testosterone) are produced by the bodies of both sexes, although in different amounts. The action of sex steroids on the nervous system is classically described by two mechanisms. Organizational (programming) effects refer to the ability of gonadal steroids to permanently sculpt the nervous system during critical periods of development, thereby giving rise to both male and female physiology and behavior in adulthood, while activational effects of sex hormones are mediated through the acute and transitory actions on the fully developed nervous system, especially in social contexts. The focus of this work on boys at risk will be on the androgen testosterone, which causes male and female brains to develop differently in prenatal periods, infancy, childhood, adolescence, and adulthood (De Bellis et al., 2001; Hutchinson, 1997).

In current writings on early androgen exposure and human gender development, Hines, Constantinescu, & Spencer (2015) noted that literally thousands of studies document the organizational effects of early androgen influences on developing brain circuits, and thereby on enduring sex differences. In both the fetal and postnatal stages of early brain maturation, the gonadal steroid testosterone promotes neurite outgrowth, facilitates synaptogenesis and inhibits synapse elimination, regulates apoptotic developmental cell death and induces cell survival, and influences developing neurotransmitter systems. They noted that testosterone is significantly higher in males than in females during two specific periods of early human development: a prenatal surge from weeks 8–24 of gestation with maximal sex differences at 12 and 18 weeks, and a neonatal surge during the first months after birth, with the largest sex difference occurring in the first through the third postnatal month, a period also known as "mini puberty." They concluded, "These, therefore are the times when testosterone is likely to influence human gender development" (p. 3).

This enduring influence is not only on later sexual behavior but also on social, emotional, and stress-regulating differences between the genders. Fetal testosterone affects the developmental anatomy of the hypothalamus and thereby the stress-regulating hypothalamic-pituitary-adrenal (HPA) axis (Cunningham, Lumia, & McGinnis, 2012), as well as the limbic system (De Vries & Simerly, 2002). Notably, Sholl and Kim (1990) reported that androgens, which facilitate fetal synaptogenesis and inhibit synapse elimination, are highest in the right over left frontal primate fetal cortex, and higher in male than in female fetuses. Zahn-Waxler and colleagues asserted that *prenatal* exposure to testosterone accounts for the slower biological and physical maturation as well as greater disinhibition in boys than in girls, and that gender differences in social and emotional functions and in psychopathology "derive from sexual dimorphisms of the brain and body that begin *in utero*" (2008, p. 278). Indeed, authors studying sex differences in the developing human *fetal* brain also report "male brains develop more slowly than their female counterparts" (de Lacoste, Horvath, & Woodward, 1991, p. 844).

This clearly suggests that males are extremely susceptible to alterations or disruptions in testosterone levels during the prenatal and perinatal critical periods. Such alterations have not only detrimental short-term but also long-term effects on the development of specific emotion and stress-regulating functions, and thereby on the origins of a predisposition to male gender–related psychiatric disorders. In a recent article on the early etiology of sex differences in mental health, Kigar and Auger (2013) observed that the developing brain is exquisitely sensitive to the effects of circulating steroid hormones during sensitive periods of *perinatal* development, and that hormonal surges occurring during discrete windows of time can have long-term effects on an organism's behavior and physiology. They concluded, "Although neuronal sex differences are present at birth as a result of both genetic and hormonal organization, chemical and morphological changes continue to occur postnatally and into adulthood" (p. 1141). In upcoming sections, I will discuss the detrimental effects of antiandrogenic environmental toxins that specifically disrupt the testosterone surges and will link them with Lanphear's (2015) proposal that the current rise in developmental disabilities is associated with environmental toxins in the developing brain.

EARLY MALE BRAIN DEVELOPMENT AND SEX DIFFERENCES IN STRESS REACTIVITY AND REGULATION

At present, there is intense interest across disciplines in the problem of specifically how genetic, hormonal, environmental, and social factors influence brain development, and how these act in the causal pathways that link early development with a predisposition to later psychopathologies and disease. All fields are now converging on the centrality of epigenetic mechanisms—heritable changes in gene expression that occur without a change in DNA sequence. Epigenetic DNA methylation determines gene expression and silencing during both prenatal and postnatal periods. Sex steroids are known to influence the onset and off-set of gene expression and are essential candidates for exerting epigenetic effects on the sexually dimorphic developing brain (McCarthy et al., 2009). This mechanism has been implicated in the etiology of both sex differences in the brain and in mental health risk and resilience. Writing in the field of neuroendocrinology, Kigar and Auger asserted, "There is . . . growing support for the culpability of *hormones and the rearing environment* as organisers of an *epigenetic* framework that determines risk and resilience to disease between the sexes" (2013, p. 1147, italics added).

The epigenetic construct is now being used to understand not only the mechanism by which environmental neurotoxins in the physical environment that alter levels of gonadal steroids permanently influence brain development, but also how variations in the quality of maternal care in the social environment indelibly organize brain development. Indeed, there is now agreement that

> The enduring impact of early maternal care and the role of epigenetic modifications of the genome during critical periods in early brain development in health and disease is likely to be *one of the most important discoveries in all of science that have major implications for our field*. (Leckman & March, 2011, p. 334, italics added)

It is now established that postnatal changes in epigenetic programming of the infant's brain are directly linked to maternal behavior (Weaver et al., 2004), and that stress from the social environment embedded within the maternal-infant relationship activates epigenetic modifications (Gudsnik & Champagne, 2012). Over the course of my own writings, I have described how the unfolding of epigenetic programs that guide early brain development over the perinatal and postnatal stages of human infancy occur within mother-infant attachment transactions.

Epigenetic modifications also describe how regulated and dysregulated stressors in the social/maternal rearing environment and the attachment relationship differentially impact the developing male and female brains. Furthermore, an epigenetic perspective can be utilized to specify which particular neural circuits are hormonally activated and imprinted in specific critical periods. In my 1994 volume on the developmental neurobiology of emotional development, I suggested that in postnatal critical periods, *optimal levels of gonadal steroids* in the developing male and female brains epigenetically influence the maturational rates of limbic-autonomic neural circuits involved in regulating emotional stress (Schore, 1994). I also proposed the existence of early gender differences in the regulation of emotional behavior, and that this sexual dimorphism of emotional function reflects a sexual dimorphism of the limbic structures responsible for such function. Thus, the sexes differ in the experience-dependent temporal patterns of the wiring of the emotion-processing limbic system.

Even more specifically, I cited classic studies demonstrating sexual dimorphism in the medial and central amygdala, the core of the limbic system, and the orbitofrontal cortex, the hierarchical apex of the limbic system (Nishizuka & Arai, 1983; Van Eden, Uylings, & Van Pelt, 1984). Reflecting the maturational differences between the genders in brain development, I further suggested that the right orbitofrontal cortex, the attachment control system, functionally matures according to different timetable in females than in males and that differentiation and growth stabilizes earlier in females than in males. This interpersonal neurobiological system is responsive to early relational stress via the right orbitofrontal regulation of the right amygdala (Schore, 1994). In other words, the developmental rate of the emotion-processing and stress-regulating attachment system is faster in female and slower in male infants. Such epigenetic, hormonally influenced gender differences in limbic function are responsible for the earlier cited gender typical differences in socioemotional development and stress reactivity in the first year of life.

Confirming this model, Kunzler, Braun, and Bock (2015) reported basic developmental neurobiological research demonstrating the "male and female brain display differential sensitivity towards early life stress" and that relational stress specifically affects the maturation of prefrontal limbic regions. They observed, "Exposing newborn male . . . to separation stress causes an acute strong increase of cortisol and can therefore be regarded as a severe stressor" (p. 862). Repeated separation results in hyperactive behavior, and "changes . . . prefronto-limbic pathways, i.e. regions that are dysfunctional in a variety of mental disorders" (p. 862). Furthermore, the long-term outcome of these epigenetic stressors on the developing male brain are manifest in "impairments in behavioral flexibility, emotion processing and different aspects of executive control, which are mediated by the orbitofrontal and/or medial prefrontal cortex" (p. 866).

It is now well established that regulated levels of moderate stress facilitate normal brain development and account for the previously described normal gender differences in emotional and social development associated with delayed development of the male infant's right hemisphere (McClure, 2000). On the other hand, traumatic dysregulating levels of relational stress during the early stages of life exert an enduring detrimental epigenetic impact on the developing right brain, significantly altering the individual's emotional responsiveness and stress-coping strategies later in life. Writing in the neuroscience literature, McCarthy and colleagues proclaimed, "Epigenetic changes in the nervous system are emerging as a critical component of enduring effects induced by early life experience, hormonal exposure, trauma and injury, or learning and memory" (2008, p. 12815). They offered the important observation that stressful epigenetic changes are largely context dependent:

> The context may be variables in the internal or external environment, such as *steroid hormones or endocrine-disrupting chemicals,* respectively. *Alternatively the context may be experiences as profound as early child abuse, or events as mild as context-dependent learning* . . . the early *social/maternal environment* can modify sex differences in behavior, and recent evidence suggests that it may do so in an epigenetic manner. (p. 12816, italics added)

Epigenetic mechanisms are known to be activated in the perinatal programming of the stress-regulating HPA axis (Meaney, Szyf, & Seckl, 2007). This neuroendocrine system is centrally involved in regulating responses to stress by direct influences and feedback interactions between the hypothalamus, pituitary, and adrenal gland. Upon activation of the HPA axis, the paraventricular nucleus of the hypothalamus and the pituitary secrete corticotropin releasing hormone and adrenocorticotropic hormone, respectively, which then act upon the adrenal gland to produce glucocorticoid hormones, such as corticosterone and cortisol. Through a negative feedback cycle, glucocorticoids act on receptors in the hypothalamus and pituitary to suppress adrenocorticotropic hormone and corticotropin releasing hormone secretion.

Bingham and colleagues have demonstrated, "Manipulations that alter environmental variables, maternal-infant interactions, and the glucocorticoid and/or sex steroid hormone environment during the neonatal period permanently alter the magnitude of the hypothalamic-pituitary-adrenal axis response to stress" (2011, p. 250). They demonstrated that during the prenatal and postnatal periods, testosterone surges exert significant changes not only in male brain morphology but also in the maturation of developing HPA function. Furthermore, they proposed that "the masculinization of the HPA axis, at least with respect to acute stress, is affected by testosterone and androgen receptors *prior to parturition*" (p. 255, italics added). I would add that in addition to the earlier-mentioned maturational differences between the postnatal male and female brains, in the prenatal period the primordial male HPA matures more slowly than the female HPA, thus accounting for gender differences in stress regulation before birth.

A large body of studies now demonstrates that gender differences in stress reactivity and regulation are expressed *in utero* in the earliest stage of brain development, the prenatal period. Buss and colleagues (2009) reported that in response to a stressful, startling vibrotactile stimulus, the male fetus at 31–37 weeks gestation expresses a twofold larger heart rate and a slower neurodevelopmental trajectory compared to those in females. They concluded that fetuses present "different neurodevelopmental trajectories for males and females that result in sex-specific developmental intervals of maximum susceptibility to environmental exposures" (p. 634), and that "there may be both optimal and detrimental endocrine influences on fetal behavior" (p. 637). Buss and her colleagues stated that the gender differences in the magnitude and the timing of the male and female fetal brains' response to prenatal stress reflect "significant differences in the trajectory of maturation which may contribute to sex-specific time windows when the developing fetus is vulnerable to programming influences" (p. 637), echoing the previously mentioned proposal by Taylor that males' slower brain maturation in the later stages of infancy and childhood "puts them at risk for a longer time" (1969, p. 140).

Indeed, boys are at risk in the womb. In fact, clinical and experimental research indicates that male more than female fetuses are vulnerable if their nutrition is compromised (Pedersen, 1980), and that the incidence of preterm birth, which involves the maternal and fetal HPA, is higher in pregnancies carrying a male (Brettell, Yeh, & Impey, 2008; Challis et al., 2013). Weber, Harrison, and Steward (2012) have elegantly applied my work to premature infants in neonatal intensive care units. I would now add that these high-risk male preterms who are born in the early or mid third trimester may be even more vulnerable in the short- and long-term than females. Indeed, research shows that the risk for preterm birth is increased in male fetuses (Zeitlin et al., 2002), that preterm males have a less effective stress response than females (Greenough et al., 1987), and that prematurely born boys have significantly more neurological handicaps, subnormal development, and developmental disability than girls (Hoffman & Bennett, 1990). In female preterms, the surface of the right hemisphere is larger than the left, whereas no difference is found in male preterms (Dubois et al., 2008), suggesting less structural development. In light of the extreme immaturity of these preterm males at birth, their fragile socioemotional repertoire is much less developed, and therefore they are not as well equipped to spontaneously enter into interactive dialogue with their primary caregiver, the maternal attachment object. That being the case, sensitive interactive regulation is essential to their further development.

Other studies show that during human fetal brain development, male brains develop more slowly than female brains (de Lacoste et al., 1991), that sex-specific differences in the cortisol stress response are present before birth with the output of cortisol being much greater in male than female fetuses (Giussani, Fletcher, & Gardner, 2011), that full-term males are more at risk for pregnancy outcome (Di Renzo et al., 2007; Eriksson et al., 2010), and that fetal distress during labor and low Apgar scores are more common in males (Bekedam et al., 2002). In a study of sex differences in electrocortical activity in human neonates, Thordstein and colleagues (2006) documented an earlier maturation of cortical function in girls than in boys, indicating that at birth,

> The CNS of newborn full-term girls is more mature than that of boys. . . . This may be part of the reason for the larger vulnerability of the CNS in boys than that of girls in the perinatal period manifested both in an increased tendency for brain damage and in higher mortality. Moreover, many neurodevelopmental disorders are over-represented in boys. (p. 1167)

Indeed, a large body of literature indicates that newborn males are at risk, and that these increased risks continue during later development (see Elsmen, Steen, & Hellstrom-Westas, 2004).

In support of this model of the continuity of gender differences in reactivity to stressors in the social and physical environment from the prenatal, to perinatal, to postnatal periods, Davis and Emory (1995) showed that healthy, term male and female neonates respond differently to the mildly stressful behavioral assessment procedure, the Neonatal Behavior Assessment Scale (Brazelton, 1973). One-day-old males react with elevated cortisol levels, most marked at 10–15 minutes, while females do not show this elevation. Females exhibit a greater change in heart rate immediately after the assessment, returning to baseline within 10 minutes, while males show little change, a finding that reflects more immature regulation. Indeed, the authors proposed that the etiology of these gender differences reflects the effects of sex hormones, especially testosterone, which is known to be at higher levels at birth in males than in females (Hammond et al., 1979).

At 3–4 months, male infants with increased levels of postnatal testosterone display higher levels of negative affectivity, as reflected in their greater frustration tendency expressed in fussing or crying during caretaking activities, when failing to achieve a goal, or when placed in a confining position (Alexander & Saenz, 2011). At 6 months, male infants are less able than females to physiologically regulate frustration (Calkins et al., 2002). These physiological data are consonant with the previously mentioned gender studies of neonates that describe male newborns as showing greater difficulties in maintaining affect regulation (Weinberg et al., 1999). The fetal and perinatal gender differences in stress reactivity and regulation continue in the middle of the first year, as Tronick (2007) documented. At 12 months, boys are more likely than girls to become stressed when placed in a context in which they cannot control the onset of a potentially frightening stimulus, suggesting that they have a greater readiness for negative emotional responding under fearful arousal conditions (Gunnar-Vongnechten, 1978). This trend is seen in the second year, where Bergman and colleagues (2010) reported a significant association between prenatal amniotic fluid testosterone but not fetal cortisol and fear reactivity in 17-month-old boys and not girls. They proposed that fear reactivity in males may reflect a joint activity of cortisol and testosterone, and that this interaction may underlie the general predisposition to greater arousal and reactivity in boys. Indeed, a body of basic research now demonstrates that throughout development, the hypothalamic-pituitary-adrenal and hypothalamic-adrenal-gonadal axes interact and influence each other (Cunningham et al,, 2012).

Furthermore, in the postnatal period males are more sensitive than females to not only environmental stressors but also infectious agents and immune challenges. Exposure of male neonates to a low dose of a bacterial endotoxin during the perinatal period (after the testosterone spike) has long-term effects on the neuroimmune system in adulthood, while the same dose at the same time in females does not (Bilbo et al., 2005, 2011). This endotoxin exposure in male neonates results in long-term changes in HPA axis activity expressed in elevated corticosteroid levels and increased stress reactivity (Bilbo et al., 2005), inhibited socioemotional behavior in dyadic contexts (Granger et al., 1996), and altered neuroimmune response in adulthood (Boisse et al., 2004). Schwarz and Bilbo (2012) cited research on sex differences in the regulation of immune functions being linked to gonadal steroid hormones, which shows that in general, testosterone depresses immunity and increases susceptibility to bacterial and viral infections, while estrogen enhances immunity. They concluded, "males and females may have a fundamentally different response to neonatal activation of the immune system. Specifically, females may be resilient to the long-term alterations in the immune system" (p. 248), and that males are more sensitive than females to early-life immune challenges.

These early appearing sex differences in immune function set the tone for all later stages of development. A large body of studies demonstrates that sex differences in the rates and severity of many infections are greater in human adult males than in human adult females (Klein, 2004; McMillen, 1979; Washburn et al., 1965), and that female adults exhibit an enhanced immune response and increased resistance to disease and infection compared to those of male adults (McClelland & Smith, 20011; Schuurs & Verheul, 1990). Indeed, there is now agreement that immune maturation in the prenatal and perinatal periods set individual trajectories toward health and disease susceptibility across the life span (Gollwitzer & Marsland, 2015).

EARLY DEVELOPMENT OF THE HPA AXIS, ATTACHMENT TRAUMA, AND THE EMERGENCE OF PSYCHIATRIC EXTERNALIZING PSYCHOPATHOLOGIES IN ADOLESCENCE

In the prenatal and postnatal periods, the male's slowly maturing stress-regulating HPA axis is more susceptible than that of the female to both external environmental stressors and internal significant and chronic hormonal alterations that accompany these social stressors. These include not only gonadal sex steroids but also stressful alterations in adrenal corticosteroids that accompany dysregulated and regulated maternal-infant interactions, and thereby both are etiologically involved in sex differences in later disorders of HPA dysfunction. Maternal emotional stress in the *prenatal period* releases high levels of corticosteroids into the mother's bloodstream, and substantial proportions of stress hormones cross the placenta. Intriguingly, recent research demonstrates gender differences in the placenta, a temporary organ that is designed for exchange of oxygen, nutrients, antibodies, and hormones between the mother and fetus, and that plays a key role in fetal growth and development. According to Di Renzo and colleagues (2015a),

> Female and male placentas have different strategies to optimize health. . . . The male strategy for responding to an adverse maternal environment is a minimalist approach: few genes, proteins or functional changes are involved in the placenta. . . . This specific male response is associated with a greater risk of intrauterine growth restriction, preterm delivery or death *in utero* if another adverse event occurs during the pregnancy. The female placenta responds to an adverse maternal environment with multiple placental gene and protein changes. . . . Thus, female adjustments in placental function and growth ensure survival in the presence of another adverse event which may further compromise nutrient or oxygen supply. (pp. 5–6)

Indeed, a large body of research now indicates that "male and female fetuses and neonates institute different mechanisms to cope with an adverse environment or event" (Saif et al., 2015, p. 724). The female placenta adjusts its glucocorticoid activity and inflammatory cytokine gene expression to high maternal glucocorticoid concentrations, as opposed to the male placenta, which does not adaptively change (Clifton, 2010), suggesting a maturational advance in female over male regulatory systems. Elevated cortisol levels interfere and reduce the fetus's production of testosterone (Kime et al., 1980; Ward & Weisz, 1984), especially during the prenatal testosterone surge. In the fetus, high plasma concentrations of corticosteroids are known to have deleterious effects on the nervous system (Sapolsky, 1996) via increased apoptosis and cell death (Gruver-Yates & Cidlowski, 2013). Androgenic steroids regulate the "programming" of developmental cell death (Evans-Storms & Cidlowski, 1995), and so reduced testosterone levels could alter cell survival in a critical period of fetal brain growth. Notably, maternal alcohol consumption suppresses both testosterone surges in the male fetus/neonate (Ward et al., 2003; Weinberg et al., 2008).

In the *perinatal period*, a time of the second testosterone surge, maternal stress is known to influence both the onset and duration of testosterone exposure and thereby permanently alter the organization of the androgen-sensitive pathways to the HPA axis (Bingham et al., 2011; Williamson, Bingham, & Viau, 2005). Over the course of the first year in the *postnatal period*, the developing male infant's extreme sensitivity to both stressful perturbations in the external social environment and hormonal changes in the internal environment makes him more vulnerable to early child abuse and neglect, extreme maternal-infant developmental stressors that alter the early organization of prefronto-limbic pathways into the HPA axis.

There is now widespread agreement that both prenatal and postnatal maternal-infant factors program the HPA axis, and that severe early-life stress permanently impairs this stress-regulating system over later stages of the life span, thereby jeopardizing the future mental and physical health of the individual (Schore, 2003a, 2003b; Welberg & Seckl, 2001; Weinstock, 2005). It has been suggested by a number of authors that neurodevelopmental disorders result from alterations of the set points of neuroendocrine systems and the HPA axis (de Kloet, Joëls, & Holsboer, 2005; Gunnar & Quevedo, 2007; Phillips, 2007). In light of the fact that sex hormones have "organizational" or "programming" effects on the development of the HPA axis generating enduring gender differences in HPA stress activity

(McCormick et al., 1998), this conception of psychopathogenesis needs to be updated in terms of the expression of gender differences in the expression of a dysfunctional HPA axis in a male and in a female infant. It is important to point out that under stress, HPA dysregulation can take two forms: underregulation and overregulation, which in turn underlie the susceptibility of males to externalizing and females to internalizing disorders.

Recall that exposing a newborn male to a separation stress triggers an acute, strong increase of cortisol (Kunzler et al., 2015), but in the case of severe attachment stressors such as abuse and neglect, the stressors are extreme and chronic and the stress hormones are elevated for long periods of time during a critical period, physiologically altering the HPA set point. Indeed, infants with disorganized-disoriented insecure attachment associated with abuse and neglect (and maternal alcohol consumption; O'Connor, Sigman, & Brill, 1987) exhibit the highest cortisol levels of all other attachment classifications (Hertsgaard et al., 1995). Such long-enduring, high levels of postnatal cortisol may be a continuation of elevated prenatal cortisol, associated with previously described highly stressful *in utero* experiences. In recent writings in the *Infant Mental Health Journal* concerning a clinical case of a boy with a history of maltreatment and disorganized attachment, Ribaudo observed, "For some, even the womb is not a safe haven. In the United States alone, as many as 500,000 children each year are exposed to interpersonal violence in utero" (2016, p. 91).

Earlier research shows that high maternal cortisol in late pregnancy is associated with more difficult behavior at birth (De Weerth, van Hees, & Buitelaar, 2003). At weeks 1–7 (the very time of the postnatal testosterone surge), these infants display more crying, fussing, and negative facial expressions, a description of what has been termed "a difficult temperament." It is usually not appreciated that "the fact of birth has apparently no significance for the brain developmental sequence" (Dobbing, 1974, p. 3). This continuity of brain development between the prenatal and postnatal stages clearly suggests that the long-held idea that fixed "inborn" temperament represents *genetic* factors that are first expressed at birth is incorrect. Rather, temperament at birth is a result of *epigenetic* mechanisms that have evolved prenatally and continue to be epigenetically shaped or misshaped by the postnatal socioemotional environment. In studies on "prenatal predictors of infant temperament," Werner and her colleagues concluded that "what has been termed 'constitutional' about temperament is emerging as identifiable in the prenatal period and may be, in part, the consequence of environmental influences before birth" (2007, p. 475).

In previous writings on the origins of "difficult temperament" dominated by states of negative emotionality, I proposed that due to delayed rates of cerebral maturation in male infants, gender differences must be considered in developmental traumatology (Schore, 2003a). In early studies, Carlson and colleagues (1989) documented that disorganized attachment is more frequent among boys in low-income maltreated infants. Ten years later, Lyons-Ruth, Bronfman, & Parsons (1999) found that infant boys displayed significantly more disorganized attachment behaviors and concluded that gender plays a role in the manifestation of disorganized behavior pattern in high-risk samples. More recently in studies of the early origins of disorganized attachment in an ethnically diverse group of highly educated mothers and their 4-month-old infants, Beebe and colleagues reported, "Male infants were overrepresented in future disorganized infants. . . . Moreover, male infants are more emotionally reactive than female (M. Weinberg, Tronick, Cohn, & Olson, 1999), so that they may be *more vulnerable to a disorganized form of insecurity*" (2012, p. 359, italics added). In light of the consequent increased risk of the developing male brain, these intense postnatal social stressors represent a significant etiological scenario of a vulnerability to later male-dominant externalizing psychopathologies in adolescence.

In support of this model, it is now thought that adolescence represents a developmental stage in which, like the earlier periods of prenatal and postnatal testosterone surges, there is a steroid-dependent organizational remodeling of the developing male brain, and thus it is a "vital junction during which carefully timed exposure to gonadal hormones permanently alter developmental trajectory to influence adult behavior" (Sisk & Zehr, 2005, p. 169). During puberty, a period of considerable biological and social change and sexual maturation, secretion of androgens significantly increases because of the maturation of the male gonads, leading to dramatic gender differences in testosterone. Adolescent boys and adult men produce far more testosterone than do adolescent girls and adult women.

Boys' testosterone levels, which have anabolic effects, increase at a more accelerated rate and are more variable during adolescence than girls' levels (Shirtcliff, Granger, & Likos, 2002).

As a result, puberty, a time of intense neurostructural and endocrine changes, has been identified as a risk factor for both male- and female-related psychopathologies (Hayward & Sanborn, 2002). During adolescence, conduct disorder, a prime example of externalizing behavior problems, increases in males (Moffitt, 1993), as opposed to depression, one of the main internalizing disorders, which increases from mid-puberty onward in females but not males (Angold & Costello, 2006). The higher testosterone levels found in male but not female adolescents with externalizing aggressive behavior have been linked to a risk of psychopathology for later antisocial behaviors (Maras et al., 2003). Attachment experiences significantly influence the relationship between high circulating testosterone and antisocial behavior in adolescence (Fang et al., 2009; Updegraff, Booth, & Thayer, 2006). The transition into adolescence thus represents a period of risk for boys, especially those who have experienced fetal or postnatal testosterone dysregulation as a result of antiandrogenic environmental toxins, prenatal alcohol, or traumatic attachments, including early abuse or neglect.

As an example, histories of early abuse and neglect are common in severe conduct disorders, and therefore in creating a predisposition to violence (Schore, 2003a). In a review article on life-course-persistent antisocial behavior, Yildirim and Derksen (2012) cited research showing that activational effects of high levels of testosterone and low HPA-axis responsivity is associated with psychopathy. Not moderate but elevated levels of fetal testosterone are consistently found in this disorder, which is 10–14 times more likely in males than in females. Indeed, they cited research indicating that heightened developmental testosterone is an essential biological determinant in the etiology of psychopathy, and that "fetal testosterone may inhibit the maturation of the right orbitofrontal cortex and circulating testosterone may subsequently dampen its responsivity to social cues, resulting in lower empathy and higher aggressive behaviors, processes that increase the risk for chronic antisocial behavior" (p. 999). These authors specifically noted the work of Yang and Raine (2009), who cited a number of studies showing functional impairments in specifically the right orbitofrontal cortex, the control center of attachment (Schore, 2000). They also pointed out that high fetal testosterone predicts less eye contact in infancy at 12 months (Lutchmaya & Baron-Cohen, 2002), and this impaired attention to the eyes of attachment figures is later associated with reduced affective empathy and psychopathic development in adolescence (Dadds et al., 2010). In this later stage of development, "cold-blooded" instrumental aggression, strongly linked to psychopathy, is directly related to high testosterone levels in males (Van Bokhoven et al., 2006). A study of incarcerated, late adolescent males reported that the testosterone-violence relationship is strongest at low cortisol levels (Dadds, Jurkovic, & Frady, 1991).

In other writings, Yildirim and Derksen proposed, "Since the life-long functioning of the ventromedial prefrontal (orbitofrontal) cortex is programmed and fine-tuned during the early years of life, traumatic and abusive experiences can permanently alter ventromedial cortex maturation and basal HPA-axis throughout life (Schore, 2001b)" (2013, p. 1261). They concluded that the interpersonal/affective facet of psychopathy arises from insecure/disorganized attachment in childhood, congruent with my own studies on early attachment trauma, right orbitofrontal dysfunction, and the development of a predisposition to violence that leads to the clinical expression of severe conduct disorders in adolescence (Schore, 2003a). In that work, I differentiated early histories of abuse and disorganized attachment associated with an elevated HPA set point of high resting arousal and elevated cortisol with impulsive aggression, versus neglect, disorganized attachment trauma, and an HPA set point of low resting heart rate, reduced cortisol, and predatory, callous, fearless, instrumental aggression. I would now add that in these most severe conduct disorders, high testosterone when coupled with a hyperactive HPA, high fear-reactivity, and hot-blooded rage reflects the impulsive aggression, but when coupled with low fear-reactivity and cold-blooded rage generates instrumental aggression. Recall testosterone dampens the HPA axis reactivity to stressors and threats. Notably, increased testosterone in adolescent boys and not girls is associated with reduced amygdala-orbitofrontal connectivity, which in turn is associated with increased alcohol intake (Peters et al., 2015).

In a study on androgen signaling and cortical maturation in adolescence, Raznahan and colleagues (2010, p. 16991) showed "a focally accentuated *delay of frontal maturation in males compared to females*" [italics added] in the orbitofrontal and ventromedial cortices. Note the delayed maturation of this emotion processing and regulating cortical system in males, earlier expressed in fetal development, infancy, and childhood, is still operating in adolescence. Citing studies documenting the rapid and disproportionately male increases in violent offenses and substance abuse with the onset and progression of puberty, these authors observed, "*protracted cortical maturation in males could also lead to a regionally specific broadening of the temporal windows through which detrimental genetic and environmental influences are accrued*" (p. 16991, italics added). They further observed that maleness is an especially potent risk for antisocial disorder and psychopathy in the next stage of development, adulthood, where these conditions manifest strong associations with aberrant structure and function.

Integrating the information in this section, I propose the fetal and neonatal developing male brain, especially its early emotion-processing limbic circuits that regulate the HPA axis, functionally develop at a slower rate than the female limbic system. In addition to accounting for normal gender differences in social and emotional functions and stress regulation in male and female infants, this longer period of developmental neurobiological immaturity is expressed in an oversensitivity to and inefficiency in regulating more intense and chronic forms of interpersonal stress. The slower maturation exposes the developing male brain to stressful altered levels of testosterone and corticosteroids during critical periods of right brain development. Attachment trauma such as abuse or neglect interfere with or preclude optimal interactive stress regulation, and because they occur in critical periods of right brain development, they epigenetically generate enduring maturational failures in the limbic system and the HPA, structural deficits that are reactivated in adolescence, a time of substantial remodeling of cortical and limbic circuits. This model supports the assertion by Zahn-Waxler and colleagues that "Gender intensification could result from earlier vulnerabilities such as insecure attachments" (2008, p. 285).

BOYS AT RISK: ENDOCRINE DISRUPTORS IN FETAL AND POSTNATAL DEVELOPMENT AND MALE PSYCHOPATHOGENESIS

According to Kigar and Auger, "Perinatal exposure to a *chemical* (e.g., testosterone, folic acid) *or* an *environmental* cue (e.g., *nurturance, maternal depression*) can create a lasting change in mental health risk or resilience" (2013, p. 1147, italics added). It is now established that the androgenic hormone testosterone regulates and interacts with neurotransmitters and neuromodulators and thereby influences the structural and functional organization of the developing brain, that androgen receptor functions in prenatal and postnatal periods are essential to "brain masculinization" and to male-typical behaviors in later stages, and that environmental "antiandrogens" interfere with androgen action by binding to and inhibiting androgen receptors and thereby contribute to abnormal development. There is currently intense interest across a large number of disciplines in "endocrine disruptors," environmental toxins that directly interfere with the synthesis, function, storage, or metabolism of natural hormones, including androgens and estrogens. These substances undergo bio-accumulation and at this point in time are so widespread in humans and animals that they are described as "ubiquitous" in the air, water, and the earth.

A large body of research in endocrinology—the study of the mechanisms by which hormones coordinate and control the functions of multiple organ systems and processes throughout life—now indicate that endocrine disruptors alter their normal regulatory functions, especially during early critical periods of brain development. Both environmental androgenic disruptors that mimic natural male androgenic hormones such as testosterone and estrogenic disruptors that mimic the female hormone estradiol have sex-specific effects, and they alter the normal balance between androgens and estrogens in the brain and body. Although developing male brains are vulnerable to both classes of environmental chemicals, in this work on "boys at risk" I shall focus on the enduring detrimental effects of masculine androgen disruptors.

In an article in *Journal of Neurological Sciences* titled "Endocrine Disruptors as a Threat to Neurological Function," Weiss noted, "Sex differences, taking root before birth, are planted by the actions of hormones. These actions can be modified during fetal life by exposure of the mother to environmental chemicals that mimic, inhibit, or otherwise distort normal hormonal function" (2011, p. 13). In terms of neurodevelopmental implications, he concluded that morphological differences between male and female brains translate into behavioral differences, and environmental endocrine disruptors transform these differences in various ways. He also documented that androgen disruptors are found in specific herbicides, fungicides, insecticides, and plasticizers, and that "Human exposure is universal" (p. 15).

Because sex hormones such as androgens and estrogens have different effects at different times of the life cycle, the timing and duration of exposure to endocrine disruptors is essential (Zoeller et al., 2012). Critical periods of fetal, infant, and pubertal development are more sensitive to low doses of hormones than are adult tissues, and thereby during these "critical windows of exposure" are more vulnerable to endocrine disruption (Selevan, Kimmel, & Mendola, 2000, p. 451). This fundamental biological principle applies to significant alterations in prenatal and postnatal androgen surges of the rapidly developing male brain, and it implies that endocrine-disrupting chemicals during early critical periods represent a major etiological factor of "boys at risk" and an important contributor to the current significant increase in male gender–related psychiatric disorders.

The association of endocrine disruptors, early brain development, and the link to later male-dominant psychopathologies is now receiving a great deal of attention from a number of different scientific disciplines. Discussing the detrimental effects of these environmental toxins on developmental programming in the neuroendocrinology literature, Gore (2008) offered the important observation:

> The developing fetus or infant is much more sensitive to endocrine-disrupting compounds than the adult, moreover, *effects early in life may not be manifested until adulthood*. Extremely low-dose exposures may exert significant effects on a developing organism, particularly if the exposure occurs during critical developmental periods. (p. 363, italics added)

She also noted that exposure to these "ubiquitous" chemicals occurs in critical developmental times, including maternal-fetal transfer through the placenta in perinatal periods and breast-feeding via lactation in postnatal periods. Clinical studies show fivefold higher concentrations of endocrine disruptors in human amniotic fluid at 15–18 weeks gestation (Ikezuki et al. 2002) and elevated concentrations in breast milk and lower testosterone level in 3-month-old male infants (Main et al., 2006). These and other studies clearly suggest that developing males are more at risk from exposures to environmental androgen disruptors than are females, especially during the prenatal testosterone surge at 12–18 weeks *in utero* and the postnatal surge at 1–3 months. They also imply that when a prenatal alteration in testosterone is combined with a suppression of the neonatal testosterone surge, there will be even more severe consequence on the developing male brain.

Indeed, writing in the journal *Neurotoxicology*, Miodovnik and colleagues asserted,

> The *prenatal* period is uniquely vulnerable to the effects of endocrine disruptors on maternal and fetal sex hormones in brain development . . . ongoing exposure to these endocrine disruptors in the *postnatal* period may be independently associated or may act cumulatively with prenatal exposure to increase the risk of atypical behavior. (2011, pp. 266–267)

They noted that the effects of these endocrine disruptors are seen in later stages as "impaired reciprocal social behaviors" in male-dominant autistic spectrum disorders, ADHD, and oppositional defiant conduct disorder. These sobering warnings are echoed in an article on "Neurobehavioral Effects of Developmental Toxicity" in *Lancet Neurology* by Grandjean and Landrigan, who described a "pandemic of developmental neurotoxicity" (2014, p. 330). They concluded,

> Neurodevelopmental disabilities, including autism, attention-deficit hyperactivity disorder, dyslexia, and other cognitive impairments, affect millions of children worldwide, and some diagnoses

> seem to be increasing in frequency. Industrial chemicals that injure the developing brain are among the known causes for this rise in prevalence. (p. 330)

The Centers for Disease Control and Prevention estimates the prevalence of developmental disorders at 1 in every 6 children (Boyle et al., 2011). In light of the fact that the prevalence of autism has dramatically escalated from 3 in 10,000 children in 1970 to 1 in 68 children in 2014, it is now thought that genetic factors alone cannot account for an epidemic that developed in the relatively short period of the past several decades, and that environmental toxins are considered to be a strong contributor to the increased prevalence of autism (Berg, 2009; Deth et al., 2008, Rossignol, Genuis, & Frye, 2014). Researchers are now linking perinatal exposure to androgenic (and ovarian estrogenic) endocrine disruptors to not only autism spectrum disorders (de Cock, Maas, & van de Bor, 2012) but also to ADHD (Zhou et al., 2011). These data are congruent with the idea that exposure of the developing male brain to environmental toxins that interfere with the functions of the endocrine system are associated with the current significant increase in a number of male-dominant psychiatric disorders.

Because these endocrine disruptors are known to act on and interfere with the programming effects of gonadal steroids in the primordial stages of brain development, it follows that their association with extensive neurobiological and hormonal dysregulation will have a substantial detrimental effect on the emotional survival functions of the early developing right brain. In classic writings, Geschwind and Galaburda (1987) linked early appropriate levels of testosterone with right-hemispheric growth. Following up on this early study, Toga and Thompson (2003) suggested that early testosterone levels favored structural and functional lateralization to the right hemisphere. More recently, Bourne and Gray (2009) showed that early prenatal and not later-life testosterone exposure is specifically associated with later right brain–dominant functions of processing positive and negative facial expressions. Thus, significantly altered levels of testosterone in prenatal and postnatal periods by endocrine disruptors would contribute to psychopathogenesis by negatively affecting the maturational trajectory of the socioemotional right brain in males at later stages of life, especially during the later testosterone surge in puberty and adolescence.

BOYS AT RISK: VULNERABLE RIGHT BRAIN FUNCTIONS IN PERINATAL AND POSTNATAL CRITICAL PERIODS

An overarching model of the neurobiological mechanisms that underlie why and when boys are at risk for later gender-related psychopathologies must address the fundamental question of specifically which brain circuits are shaped or misshaped by fetal and postnatal stressors, and how these systems show later deficits in social and emotional functions in adolescence and adulthood. The initial wiring of these circuits is influenced by regulated and dysregulated levels of organizational gonadal steroids and corticosteroids in the developing brain's evolving stress-regulating systems, first in dyadic fetal-maternal placental and then dyadic infant-maternal attachment transactions. In terms of the development of socioemotional deficits, subcortical and cortical circuits of the limbic-HPA system enter critical periods of maturation during the brain growth spurt, from the last trimester through the end of the second postnatal year, a period of maximal neuroplasticity. Indeed, research has documented rapid initiation of neural growth in the third trimester of gestation (Doria et al., 2010; Yu et al., 2016). These systems continue to evolve, especially in postnatal periods and adolescence, the time of the appearance of axis I psychiatric and axis II personality disorders. The brain growth spurt represents a stage of vulnerability in all humans (Dobbing, 1974), and during this period the slow maturation of the male brain makes it even more at risk during the period of maximal vulnerability. Recall, the CNS of both the male fetus and the male neonate is less mature than that in the female fetus and neonate. In other words, during developmental "windows of vulnerability," males are more vulnerable than females.

In terms of early intervention of boys at risk, the structure-function relationships of developing socioemotional systems, which are online significantly before later evolving language functions, need to be assessed in their critical periods. This applies to perinatal and postnatal interventions, but in the case of early male development, clinical attachment evaluations need to be informed by the slower maturation and gender differences in the processing and regulation of social and emotional information in the developing male's interactions with the mother. With respect to the maturation of the male fetal and postnatal brain, the early developing right brain, which for the life span is dominant for socioemotional functions and stress regulation, is more vulnerable to the previously described stress-related alterations in corticosteroids than is the later developing left brain.

Indeed, Trevarthen in 1996 proposed, "The right hemisphere is more advanced than the left in surface features from about the 25th (gestational) week and this advance persists until the left hemisphere shows a postnatal growth spurt starting in the second year" (p. 582). Supporting this, later studies by Schleussner and colleagues reported "an earlier maturation of certain right than homologous left hemispheric brain areas during fetal brain development" (2004, p. 133). Even more recently, Kasprian and colleagues documented that at 26 gestational weeks, the human fetal right superior temporal sulcus appears earlier and is deeper than that on the left and concluded, "Our structural data further support the findings of functional neuroimaging studies indicating an earlier maturity of right hemispheric function" (2011, p. 1081).

This maturation of the early developing right brain continues after birth, in infancy, a time of right brain dominance (Chiron et al., 1997), when the mother-infant attachment mechanism is activated. Attachment transactions thus influence the "early life programming of hemispheric lateralization" and the initiation of adaptive stress-regulating right brain functions (Stevenson et al., 2008, p. 852). Over the past three decades, I have offered a large body of studies to show that in right brain-to-right brain attachment communications, the mother regulates (for better or worse) the infant's stressful states of emotional arousal, and thereby influences the maturation of the infant's developing right-lateralized HPA axis (Schore, 1994, 2003a, 2003b, 2012). Research now clearly shows that maternal care within the attachment relationship shapes the infant's stress-regulating HPA axis (Gunnar, 2000), that specifically the right and not left prefrontal areas regulate the HPA axis (Sullivan & Gratton, 2002), and that for the rest of the life span, the right hemisphere regulates the HPA and thereby controls vital functions supporting survival, enabling the organism to cope with stresses and challenges (Schore, 1994; Wittling, 1997; Porges, 2011).

In an optimal developmental scenario, the evolutionary attachment mechanism, maturing during a period of right brain growth, thus allows epigenetic factors in the social environment to impact genomic and hormonal mechanisms at both the subcortical and then cortical brain levels. By the end of the first year and into the second, higher centers in the right orbitofrontal and ventromedial cortices begin to forge mutual synaptic connections with the lower subcortical centers, including the arousal systems in the midbrain and brain stem and the hypothalamic-pituitary-adrenal axis, thereby allowing for more complex strategies of affect regulation, especially during moments of interpersonal stress. That said, as I pointed out in 1994, the right orbitofrontal cortex, the attachment control system, functionally matures according to a different timetable in females and males, and thus differentiation and growth stabilizes earlier in females than in males (Schore, 1994). In either case, optimal attachment scenarios allow for the development of a right-lateralized system of efficient activation and feedback inhibition of the HPA axis and autonomic arousal, essential components for optimal coping abilities.

In marked contrast to this growth-facilitating attachment scenario, in a relational growth-inhibiting postnatal environment, less than optimal maternal sensitivity, responsiveness, and regulation are associated with insecure attachments. In the most detrimental growth-inhibiting relational context of maltreatment and attachment trauma (abuse or neglect), the primary caregiver of an insecure disorganized-disoriented infant induces traumatic states of enduring negative affect in the child (Schore, 2001b, 2003b). As a result, dysregulated allostatic processes produce excessive wear and tear on the developing brain, severe apoptotic parcellation of subcortical-cortical stress circuits, and long-term detrimental health consequences (McEwen & Gianaros, 2011). Relational trauma in early critical periods of brain development thus imprints a permanent physiological reactivity of the right brain, alters the corticolimbic connectivity into the HPA, and generates a susceptibility to later disorders of affect regulation expressed in a deficit in coping with future socioemotional stressors. Earlier I described that slow-maturing male brains are particularly vulnerable to this most dysregulated attachment typology, which is expressed in severe deficits in social and emotional functions.

On the basis of behavioral observations (the "Strange Situation"), it is now commonly assumed that there are no gender differences between the male and female attachment in the first 2 years of life. As opposed to classical attachment theory, neurobiologically informed, emotionally focused modern attachment theory asserts that this is incorrect (Schore & Schore, 2008). In both secure and insecure attachment scenarios, the male infant's right brain takes longer to mature and is less able to regulate stress than the female. Such epigenetic, hormonally influenced gender differences in limbic function are responsible for the earlier cited gender-typical differences in socioemotional development and stress reactivity at birth and through the first year of life. Thus, it takes longer for males to functionally express the efficient stress-regulating coping strategies of a secure attachment. Mature self-regulatory systems in secure infants utilize two complementary modes of action: interactive regulation and autoregulation. Over the life span, when under stress females initially interactively regulate, males autoregulate, a normal gender difference in affect regulation. This regulatory bias is shown in early development.

As I have indicated, the male fetus and the male infant exhibit androgenic-influenced gender differences in brain structural and functional systems that are responsive to stress. Insecure attachments, which are defined by dysregulated stress-regulating systems, show enduring altered patterns of inefficient right brain connectivity that lead to a vulnerability to later psychopathologies (Schore, 1994). Over the course of the life span, the right-lateralized and not left-lateralized prefrontal regions and their subcortical connections are responsible for the most complex regulation of emotion and stress (Cerqueira, Almeida, & Sousa, 2008; Czeh et al., 2008; Schore, 1994, 2003a, 2003b, 2012; Wang et al., 2005), and it is these circuits that are developmentally impaired in their earliest critical period of growth.

In order to understand a particular individual's right brain emotional response to the relational stressors of later developmental stages such as adolescence, it is necessary to take into consideration the preexisting right brain prenatal and postnatal attachment history, as well as gender. This includes the male infant's attachment transactions with the father in the second year, when the father is critically involved not only in androgen-controlled toddler rough-and-tumble play (Meaney et al., 1983) but also in facilitating the male (and female) toddler's aggression regulation (as opposed to the mother's earlier role in fear regulation). This same period (18–24 months) involves the initiation of a critical period of growth in the left hemisphere (Thatcher, 1994, 1996), and so the "paternal attachment system" of father-son interactions would presumably forge an androgenic imprint in the toddler's evolving left brain circuits, including the left dorsolateral prefrontal cortex (see Schore, 1994), allowing for the father's regulation of the male toddler's testosterone-induced aggression ("terrible twos") and rough-and-tumble play. That being said, in light of the male infant's slower brain maturation, the secure mother's attachment-regulating function as a sensitively responsive interactive affect regulator of his immature right brain in the first year is essential to optimal male socioemotional development. The misattuned insecure mother, on the other hand, is a source of considerable relational stress, especially when the immature male toddler is expressing high levels of dysregulated aggression or fear. That said, research documents that boys more so than girls raised in single-mother families show twice the rate of behavioral problems than boys in two-parent families (Bertrand & Pan, 2013), and that in the first 3 years, single mothers spend less time with their sons than with their daughters of the same age (U.S. Department of Labor, Bureau of Labor Statistics, 2014).

How can we clinically and experimentally access these immature, dysregulated states that will become the painful emotional core of male gender–related psychopathologies? There is much interest in the psychological and biological literatures in the formation of early phenotypes for specific neurodevelopmental psychiatric disorders. These phenotypes depict the range of regulatory failures of early developing systems, later expressed in affective "regressions" to highly dysregulated immature states. How can we observe changes in brain activity associated with dysregulated states, especially right brain circuits that are hyperaroused in high levels of fear and of aggression? It is important to remember that these are hyperactivated limbic circuits, and that they are therefore experienced by the developing feeling organism as a subjectively painful state. How would a dysregulated allostatic overload, both neurobiologically as well as hormonally, of the earliest evolving components of the emotion-processing limbic system be observed in terms of an individual's emerging predisposition for psychopathology? How does a clinician or researcher observe and take part in an array of right brain stress-regulating attachment emotional communications? At the most fundamental level, how can we access and study the adaptive and maladaptive attachment functions of the right brain limbic system as they operate in real time?

DEVELOPMENTAL NEUROBIOLOGY OF THE AMYGDALA COMPLEX, THE CORE OF THE RIGHT-LATERALIZED LIMBIC SYSTEM

The mental health field is now urgently calling for programs of early prevention. The scientific-clinical discipline of infant mental health can make important and valuable contributions in this effort, because the stages of human development that it studies are occurring in critical periods of brain maturation. In earlier contributions, I linked infant mental health to adult mental health (Schore, 2001a, 2001b). Here I apply regulation theory's developmental model to the earliest prenatal stage of human development and suggest that infant mental health rests upon preceding fetal health. In terms of brain development, this primordial stage represents the most rapid genesis of neurons. Indeed, neural proliferation before birth is estimated at 250,000 per minute (Cowan, 1979). This primordial stage of human development, described as "life before birth" (Nathanielsz, 1998), has been largely overlooked, both in neuroscience and in developmental psychology. As recently as 2009, Buss and colleagues proclaimed that, "Despite acknowledgement of the critical role the prenatal period plays for an individual's health outcome, little effort has been invested in studying human fetal behavior and its consequences" (2009, p. 633), and that "the study of fetal behavior has not progressed because it has been judged as insignificant" (p. 637).

The greatly enhanced rate of neuronal development continues in the perinatal period. From birth to 3 months, the total number of cortical neurons increases by 23% to 30% (Shankle et al., 1999). The earliest of human beginnings, the prenatal and postnatal stages of human development, are ones in which the fetus and then infant is evolving through a succession of critical periods in both the *in utero* and then extrauterine environments, experience-dependent stages of brain growth that can both support or inhibit the development of more complex brain structure and function. Because the brain evolves caudally to rostrally, subcortically to cortically, the question becomes what early evolving regions of the brain are in critical periods in fetal and postnatal stages of development? There is now agreement that "the ontogenetic neural timetable might have consequences for the timing of early intervention" (de Graaf-Peters & Hadders-Algra, 2006, p. 262). These authors suggested that the best opportunities for intervention occur between 28 weeks postmenstrual age and 15 months, the period of the brain growth spurt and right brain dominance.

Indeed, this information is useful in terms of generating evidence-based assessments that can tap into subcortical systems of the developing brain that are in critical periods *in utero*. The earliest evolving subcortical systems—including noradrenergic, dopaminergic, and serotonergic neuromodulatory bioaminergic systems that are essential to neurotransmission and the development of neuronal circuits in the embryo and later in generating emotional arousal in the neonate—evolve very early *in utero*, at 8–10 weeks gestational age (de Graaf-Peters & Hadders-Algra, 2006), the time of the first testosterone surge. Brain-stem catecholamine neurons are known to be target sites for androgenic and estrogenic hormones (Heritage et al., 1980). These neuromodulators are susceptible to fetal stress that can result in long-term changes in the structure and function of the organism (Herlenius & Lagercrantz, 2001). At birth there is a surge of the catecholamines noradrenaline and dopamine, which is important to neonatal adaptation. These subcortical arousal-generating systems continue to evolve in postnatal periods when they send axon collaterals up the neuraxis, thereby exerting trophic and regulatory roles on the development of the limbic system and cerebral cortex (Lambe, Krimer, & Goldman-Rakic, 2000; Schore, 1994). The volume of the subcortical area, including the brain stem, increases by 130% in the first year (Knickmeyer et al., 2008), and it is influenced by the attachment relationship.

In addition to the energy-regulating bioamines, what other subcortical regulatory systems are known to evolve in the fetal brain? For some time, I have used regulation theory to model the developmental progression of postnatal limbic-autonomic regulatory centers (Schore, 1994, 2003a, 2003b), but I now extend this model to prenatal regulatory systems. The insula, which begins its maturation at 13–18 gestational weeks (the time of the first testosterone surge) and shows earlier development in the right fetal hemisphere, becomes involved in stress-responsive visceroautonomic functions (Afif et al., 2007). At 22 weeks gestation, the human fetal adrenal gland develops and now produces cortisol in appreciable quantities (Mesiano & Jaffe, 1997). In the last trimester, the paraventricular areas of the hypothalamus that produce the stress-intensifying neuropeptide corticotropin releasing factor, and the sexually dimorphic androgen-imprinted ventromedial hypothalamus, later associated with aggression in males (Choate, Slayden, & Resko, 1998; Yang et al., 2013), are functional. But perhaps most important the amygdala complex, especially the central and medial nuclei that develop before the basolateral nucleus, is structurally mature (Humphrey, 1968), suggesting that at this point the fetus's right limbic-autonomic HPA axis is capable of processing negative and positive proto-emotional states.

During the last gestational trimester, while the above systems are in a critical period of maturation and the brain growth spurt commences, plasticity and pruning of the developing brain is at its highest, with almost 50% of neurons in the fetal brain experiencing apoptotic programmed cell death (Volpe, 2000). Apoptosis is regulated by the organizational function of gonadal steroids (Evans-Storms & Cidlowski, 1995) that allows for the preservation of developing sexually dimorphic nuclei and imprinting of gender-related limbic circuits. Circulating levels of androgens and tissue levels of estrogens are higher in males than in females in the late prenatal/early postnatal periods (Weisz & Ward, 1980). This is the exact time of the beginning of the second testosterone surge (Hines, 2015), and therefore the amygdala, which is known to contain many androgen receptors and is larger in males than in females (Nishizuka & Arai, 1981), is vulnerable to stress or endocrine disruptors that could amplify cell death in this critical period.

At the end of the fetal period, the medial and central amygdala, with their connections into bioaminergic arousal centers in the midbrain and brain stem, the sympathetic and parasympathetic components of the autonomic nervous system, and the insula, represent the hierarchical apex of the fetal regulatory system. The maturity/immaturity of this amygdala stress-regulating system is expressed at birth. In the normal developmental scenario, this system is less mature in the more slowly developing male fetus and neonate. In assessments of the earliest appearing, gender-specific socioemotional functions that I described at the beginning of this work, attention needs to be paid to the amygdala, which in optimal contexts is known to reach a high degree of maturity in the 8th gestational month (Ulfig, Setzer, & Bohl, 2003) and is therefore operational at birth, the very onset of the perinatal period. The more slowly evolving male right amygdala thus regulates the previously described social and emotional behaviors of the male neonate.

As opposed to optimal fetal development, a chronically stressful and thereby growth-inhibiting intrauterine context produces an immature amygdala-HPA regulatory system that has not only poor capacities for autoregulation of dysregulated states but also difficulty in entering into states of dyadic interactive regulation with the mother. Immediately after emerging from the womb, the infant is exposed to the novel stimulation of the outside world, especially the face (eyes), smell, and touch of the mother. The amygdala and subcortical sensory areas are involved in all of these functions. In high-risk infants, an immature, inefficient right amygdala is poor at eye gaze, an essential point of contact with another human being. In light of the extreme immaturity of these preterm males, their socioemotional repertoire is much less developed, and therefore they are not well equipped to enter into normal interactive dialogues with their caregivers. That being the case, interactive regulation is essential to their further development.

The amygdala system that first emerges in the prenatal period continues to rapidly evolve in the perinatal and postnatal periods. I have suggested that the later developing basolateral nucleus, with its extensive cortical connections, begins a critical period at about 2–3 months, when the infant is able to enter into more complex socioemotional interactions with the mother (Schore, 2012, 2013, 2014; see also Schore, 1994). Recall McClure's (2000) finding that the function of the infant's amygdala in right-hemispheric face processing develops faster in females than in males. This clearly suggests that the slowly developing male basolateral amygdala would be more vulnerable to certain perinatal stressors, especially neglect, which deprives him from receiving sufficient amounts of maternal interactive regulation (maternal postpartum depression).

Because this is the period of the second testosterone surge, the male basolateral amygdala is also more at risk for androgenic endocrine disruptors at this time. Indeed, research now indicates that perinatal exposure of the male brain to an endocrine disruptor is specifically associated with abnormal synaptic plasticity in the developing basolateral amygdala, especially in alterations in dopamine and gamma-aminobutyric acid (GABA) circuits (Zhou et al., 2011). This structural defect is accompanied by functional deficits, hyperactivity and attention deficit, leading these authors to suggest that a developmental mechanism is involved in the neuropathogenesis of ADHD. Other research demonstrates that in adults with ADHD, more hyperactivity and less inattention are associated with smaller right amygdala volumes (Frodi et al., 2010). Endocrine disruptors have also been implicated in schizophrenia pathogenesis (Brown, 2009). In an overview of abnormal amygdala structure and function in autism and schizophrenia, Schumann, Bauman, and Amaral concluded, "The amygdala, perhaps more than any other brain region, has been implicated in numerous neuropsychiatric and neurodevelopmental disorders. It is part of a system initially evolved to detect dangers in the environment and modulate subsequent responses" (2011, p. 745). This adaptive function is altered by early chronic exposure to endocrine disruptors.

Diagnostic evaluations of early socioemotional development would thus need to assess the early socioemotional and regulatory functions of the right amygdala. It is now thought that in human infancy, the right amygdala is more greatly affected by early rearing experiences than is the left (Joseph, 1992; Schore, 1994). A prime example of the enduring impact of severe early adverse experiences on brain development is seen in studies of infants who experienced institutional deprivation in Romania. As children, these individuals show greater activity in the right than in the left amygdala and decreased eye contact during a live dyadic interaction (Tottenham et al., 2011). In adolescence, Romanian orphans with histories of severe early deprivation and neglect show "reduced probability of connection to the frontal pole in the right hemisphere . . . associated with increased externalizing behavioral problems" (Behen et al., 2009, p. 295). Another study of this population reveals "greater amygdala volumes, especially on the right" (Mehta et al., 2009, p. 943).

The early expression of a structurally impaired right amygdala is also seen in autism. Studying children as young as 18 months, Munson and colleagues (2006) reported an association between enlarged right (and not left) amygdala volume with poorer socialization and communication development as measured on the Autism Diagnostic Interview and Vineland Scale. They speculated that right amygdala enlargement may reflect "right-sided amygdala activation in response to conditioned fear" (p. 690). Commenting on this amygdala enlargement in 18-month-old toddlers, Schumann et al. (2009) stated,

> The amygdala has long been a site of intense interest in the search for neuropathologic markers for autism, given its well-established role in the production and recognition of emotions and modulatory role in social behavior. Initial signs of autism in toddlers include unusual affective behavior, reduced social interest, and poor eye contact, which are all suggestive of aberrant amygdalar function. (p. 942)

The problem of diminished attention to faces early on "may be the first in a cascade of problems that lead to later emotional and social impairments" (p. 947). Furthermore, they concluded that the autistic toddler's dysfunctional hyperaroused amygdala "suggests a heightened emotional, or even fearful, response when autistic individuals look at another person's eyes, regardless of whether they are familiar or a stranger" (p. 947). That this early developing right basolateral amygdalar enlargement, associated with amygdalar hyperreactivity and abnormal fear conditioning, persists in 6- to 7-year old children (J. Kim et al., 2010) strongly suggests that a chronic fear-based subjectivity continues in the autistic infant's and child's mind.

Microstructural alterations of the right amygdala have been identified even earlier, in 6- to 14-day-old neonates of prenatally depressed mothers (Rifkin-Graboi et al., 2013). I suggest that at this perinatal stage, the dysfunction is mainly in the early developing central and medial rather than the later maturing basolateral amygdala, which initiates a critical period at 2–3 months (Schore, 2012, 2013). In discussing the functional expressions of this structural alteration, Rifkin-Graboi and her colleagues (2013) offered the important observation that amygdala dysregulation is expressed in increased negative emotionality, a state that also affects the quality of the interactions adults direct toward the infant. They propose a prenatal transmission for a vulnerability to depression:

> These findings suggest a cascade whereby maternal signals influence the *in utero* development of brain regions that regulate the emotional well-being of the infant, which, in turn, affect parent-infant interactions that reinforce negative emotionality and thus risk for mood disorders. (p. 842)

They cite the work of Tronick and Reck (2009), who stated that these infants develop negative affective states that bias their interactions with others, which in turn exacerbates their affective problems, and that male infants are more vulnerable than female infants to maternal depression. These data clearly suggest that early attachment assessments of boys at risk need to involve not only the infant and the mother but also the intersubjective socioemotional interactions between them.

FURTHER IMPLICATIONS FOR EARLY ASSESSMENT OF "BOYS AT RISK"

There is now agreement that at all stages of the life span, attachment security is mediated by the subcortical amygdala (Lemche et al., 2006; Schore, 1994, 2003a, 2003b, 2012), which is known to show sex differences (Hamann, 2005), and so very early attachment assessments of males in the perinatal and then postnatal critical periods are essential to early intervention. As an example, Beebe et al. (2012) offered a study of the origins of disorganized attachment in the microanalysis of dysregulated emotional interactions within the 4-month mother-infant interaction. I suggest that these assessments must be more than behavioral; they must also include an interpersonal neurobiological perspective that can track the development or failure of development of the right brain emotion-processing limbic system.

In the psychiatric literature, Schwartz and colleagues (2012) demonstrated that a phenotype of early infancy identified at 4 months predicts individual differences in reactivity of the right amygdala to faces *almost two decades later in adults*. The rapidly growing body of developmental neurobiological research emphasizes the important need for clinical assessment and early intervention for chronically misattuned caregiver-infant communications that are found in contexts of relational attachment trauma, especially for boys at risk.

In a pair of articles in the 2001 issue of *Infant Mental Health Journal*, I articulated a model of the prenatal and postnatal ontogeny of the hierarchically organized limbic system, which suggests that a number of discrete limbic components come online and develop connectivity in a defined sequence in the first year (Schore, 2001a, 2001b). The model proposes that the neuroanatomy of the emotion-processing limbic system is characterized as a series of hierarchically organized "control systems" or "hubs" in the right amygdala, right anterior cingulate, and right orbitofrontal cortex. In my most recent articulation of this model (Schore, 2012, 2013, 2014), I offered evidence showing that at 2–3 months, a transition occurs from the right central amygdala to a critical period growth spurt in the right basolateral amygdala, which densely connects with higher cortical association areas, initiating the infant's burgeoning intersubjective and regulatory functions. From 3 to 9 months, the ventral anterior cingulate, a corticolimbic structure associated with responsivity to social cues, comes online, giving the infant even greater capacities for intersubjectivity and for receiving nonverbal communications of "good-enough" caregiver interactive regulation. From 10 to 12 months of age, the regulatory center in the orbitofrontal cortex, the attachment executive control system, begins its developmental growth period, which spans until the end of the second year (Schore, 2000).

This ontogenetic progression of limbic-autonomic regulatory centers can serve as the foundation of an evidence-based clinical model of longitudinal assessments of the same dyad across the stages of infancy and toddlerhood over the first 2 years, the time of the brain growth spurt. Assessments of right brain nonverbal social/emotional functions can be used to clinically formulate specifically tailored interventions during these critical periods of interpersonal neurobiological maturation, which are timed differently in male and in female infants. The right hemisphere enters subsequent growth spurts but exhibits maximal plasticity during the brain growth spurt, from the last trimester through the second year. Furthermore, in light of the precedence of later maturing left brain cognitive development by earlier right brain emotional development, the focus should move from higher verbal cortical executive functions to lower subcortical limbic-autonomic circuits that are imprinted in the attachment transactions of infancy and toddlerhood. Evidence-based regulation theory formulates an assessment of attachment episodes of rapid, spontaneous, right brain visual-facial, auditory-prosodic, and tactile-gestural communications, in which the primary caregiver interactively regulates the infant's states of emotional arousal. In my most recent formulations of neurobiologically informed modern attachment theory, I conclude that attachment transactions influence the "early life programming of hemispheric lateralization" that, in turn, generates the dominance of the right hemisphere in the first year of life.

In support of this model, Meaney and his colleagues offered neuroimaging research of neonates at the beginning of the first year and concluded, "In early life the right cerebral hemisphere could be better able to process . . . emotion (Schore, 2000; Wada & Davis, 1977). . . . These neural substrates function as hubs in the right hemisphere for emotion processes and mother and child interaction" (Ratnarajah et al., 2013, p. 193). Research from Tronick's lab on infants in the middle of the first year demonstrated that under relational stress, 6-month-old infants use left-sided gestures generated by the right hemisphere. They interpret these data as being "consistent with Schore's (2005) hypotheses of hemispheric right-sided activation of emotions and their regulation during infant–mother interactions" (Montirosso et al., 2012, p. 826). Using near-infrared spectroscopy, Minagawa-Kawai and her colleagues' study of infant mother attachment at the end of the first year observed, "Our results are in agreement with that of Schore (2000) who addressed the importance of the right hemisphere in the attachment system" (2009, p. 289).

The evolving attachment system that is fundamentally expressed in right-lateralized visual-facial, auditory-prosodic, and tactile-gestural nonverbal communication functions of "the human social brain" can be assessed over the prenatal and postnatal stages of infancy to appraise the ongoing status of emotional and social development. Allman and colleagues articulated an organizing principle of developmental neuroscience: "The strong and consistent predominance for the right hemisphere emerges postnatally" (2005, p. 367). In an overview of their research on the development of voice-sensitive areas of the right hemisphere, Grossmann and colleagues proposed that in postnatal periods, "responses to voices and emotional prosody . . . might thus serve as one of potentially multiple markers that can help with an early identification of infants at risk for neurodevelopmental disorders" (2010, p. 856). With an eye to diagnostic implications, Montirosso and colleagues called for future study of different gestures with simultaneous measurement of brain functions and suggested that "such studies would also be useful with samples of high risk infants whose behavior and brain organization may be compromised" (2010, p. 109).

The growing body of research on the early developing right brain can serve as the foundation of an evidence-based clinical model of early intervention and prevention. Toward that effort, in a number of recent publications I have used a large body of neurobiological studies in order to outline a model of clinical assessments of the mother's right brain, the infant's right brain, and their right brain-to-right brain expanding capacity for intersubjectivity. With respect to the mother, I have suggested that the sensitive mother accesses not her left but right brain in attachment communications (Schore, 1994, 2003a, 2012). Studies indicate that "The right prefrontal cortex is involved in human maternal behavior concerning infant facial emotion discrimination" (Nishitani et al., 2011, p. 183). Killeen and Teti reported "greater relative right frontal activation in response to seeing one's own infant is related to maternal negative affect matching during times of infant distress, and greater perceived intensity of infant joy during times of joy" (2012, p. 18). Note that these findings (as well as the body of my work) do not support the idea that the left hemisphere is dominant for positive emotions and the right only for negative emotions (see my critique of valence theory in Schore, 2015a). Maternal assessments should thus evaluate the mother's capacity to access her right brain for interpreting her infant's spontaneous nonverbal communications, facial expression, vocal tone, and body posture.

With regard to the assessment of the infant's developing right brain, I refer the reader to my work on the ontogeny of an infant's increasing ability to process an expanding array of visual-facial, auditory-prosodic, and tactile-gestural attachment communications from birth through 18 months (Schore, 2012, 2013, 2014), thereby tracking the developmental progression to more complex sensoriaffective functions. The future capacity to receive and express essential visual-facial social information is expressed in face-to-face communications, a central aspect of all later intimate relationships, and is dependent on caregiver-infant eye contact and visual gazing during early critical periods. How often and in what contexts the mother and infant spontaneously look (and not look) directly at each other is of key importance to evaluating both an infant's development and the health of the dyadic relationship.

In addition, an assessment needs to be made of the infant's developmental progression to more complex auditory-prosodic attachment communications. The emotional quality of what infants hear in the early stages of infancy affects the development of voice-processing areas of the right hemisphere, especially the temporal voice areas in the upper banks of the right superior temporal sulcus. This underscores the importance of evaluating the infant's emotional response to not the verbal content but the melody of the mother's voice, and whether or not she's using infant-directed versus adult-directed speech in her interactions with her child, especially in both arousal-reducing calming-soothing and arousal-amplifying playful contexts. In addition, an assessment needs to be made of the infant's developmental progression to more complex tactile-gestural attachment communications ("affective touch"). This focuses on not only the quantity but also the quality and amount of sensitive interpersonal touch the infant is receiving and expressing.

Furthermore, in addition to the dyadic right brain-to-right brain expression, reception, and communication of bodily-based emotional information, an organizing principle of modern attachment theory dictates that the mother's attachment functions are expressed in her ability to interactively regulate various states of infant emotional arousal. Again, I refer the reader to my book *The Science of the Art of Psychotherapy* (see Table 11.1 therein for a model of mother-infant right brain regulation and dysregulation) and to Schore and Newton (2012). This assessment focuses on the mother-infant dyad's relational capacity to implicitly interactively up-regulate positive affect in a mutual play context and down-regulate negative affect in a relationally stressful context. The latter allows for an evaluation of the male infant/toddler's emerging capacity for right-hemispheric specialization in regulating stress and emotion-related processes, a developmental achievement that occurs later in male toddlers than in female toddlers. As mentioned earlier, there are gender differences in self-regulation: boys toward autoregulation, girls toward interactive regulation. Yet for both, accessing each is adaptive during times of stress. In the case of poorly developed right brain stress-regulating systems, an assessment should also be made of the child's defenses under intense relational stress, including dissociative withdrawal.

In addition, an evaluation should be made of the dyad's capacity for intersubjectivity, the contact of the infant's emerging emotional mind with the mother's mind. In other work, I have translated Trevarthen's and Stern's work on emerging intersubjectivity over the first year in terms of the development of more complex right brain-to-right brain psychobiological communications within the dyad. I refer the reader to see Schore (2014) for Saint-Georges's video coding of home movies of spontaneous, reciprocal infant-caregiver emotional interactions over the first and second postnatal semesters. The focus is on the dynamic parent-infant interaction instead of on single behaviors of infant or parent.

This assessment can be used with full-term or high-risk infants with an immature nervous system at birth. Mento et al. (2010) concluded,

> *The right hemisphere would sustain the functions necessary for the survival of the species,* such as visuospatial or emotional processes. Consequently the earlier and faster development of the neural substrates underlying these functions is needed to prevent possible impairment during infancy and childhood. (p. 571, italics added)

They further noted that "early alteration of the normal hemispheric asymmetry in terms of functional development in extremely immature infants has recently been related to several neurocognitive developmental impairments during childhood and adulthood" (p. 572). In concordant theoretical writings, Saugstad (1998) emphasized the importance of cerebral lateralization and the rate of that maturation and proposed that neurodevelopmental psychiatric disorders are associated with late and slow cerebral lateralization.

Most important, gender-informed assessments of all male infants need to be done in a sequence of right brain critical periods. As the preceding sections document, developmental neuroscience clearly suggests that both sexes move through a similar pattern of caudal to rostral brain development and subcortical to cortical limbic maturation. That said, the slower maturation of the developing male versus female brain indicates male infants and toddlers are more at risk to experience prenatal and postnatal exposure and vulnerability to stressful physical and social environments during the formation of right brain circuits that implicitly regulate affects. The ontogenetic progression of attachment imprinting of the evolving right-lateralized limbic system is universal. However, the timing and length of stages varies in male and female infants. The fact that there are different maturational rates in the brain growth spurt from last trimester pregnancy to second year suggests separate norms for each gender. These norms need to reflect normal gender differences in the slow-maturing male versus fast-maturing female infant's socioemotional functions. Risk would be demarcated at the extremes of normal ranges. These evaluations of efficient versus deficient right brain socioemotional functions may also be used to assess the development of evolving masculine versus feminine psychological gender identity in the second year.

An organizing principle of this work dictates that the prenatal and postnatal stages of human infancy represent critical periods of development of both the stress-regulating hypothalamic-pituitary-adrenal axis and the gender-determining hypothalamic-pituitary-gonadal axis, two neuroendocrinological systems that interact and influence each other. In the early developing male, the hormonal end-product of the former is cortisol, essentially involved in fear regulation, and of the latter testosterone, involved in aggression regulation. As previously described, the differences in rates of brain maturation between the sexes and the interaction of these two neuroendocrine axes account for gender differences in emotion regulation functions. The programming of regulatory limbic-autonomic circuits is epigenetically shaped by both classes of steroid hormones and imprinted prenatally and subsequently postnatally in the maternal and then paternal attachment relationship. In classical attachment theory, Bowlby (1969) heavily and almost exclusively emphasized the negative affect of fear, which is reduced by secure base behavior. Modern attachment theory emphasizes regulation of a large number of affects, including aggression, and suggests that the early endocrinological detection of infant boys at risk must include both salivary cortisol and testosterone levels. Early assessment needs to pay more attention to the primordial psychoneurobiological markers of both fearful impulsive and fearless instrumental aggression dysregulation of later appearing externalizing psychopathologies that are now significantly increasing in this and other cultures.

CULTURAL EPIGENETIC MECHANISMS OF INCREASED MALE GENDER PSYCHOPATHOGENESIS: EARLY CHILDCARE

Let me return to two questions I raised at the beginning of this chapter on boys at risk. What early developmental mechanisms are involved in the vulnerability of males to certain psychiatric disorders? What epigenetic mechanisms can account for their recent widespread increase in U.S. culture, and beyond? More than 20 years ago, in the last chapter of *Affect Regulation and the Origin of the Self,* I utilized a neurobiological perspective to overview disturbing research data on the documented increase of insecure, especially avoidant attachments and levels of aggression associated with early day care (Schore, 1994). I suggested that from a neurobiological perspective that focuses on not short-term cognitive but long-term enduring emotional effects, these findings were alarming. This problem has continued if not worsened since then.

In 2007, Dmitrieva, Steinberg, and Belsky reported,

> Evidence indicates clearly that care initiated early in life and experienced for many hours, especially in child-care centers, is associated with somewhat elevated levels of externalizing behavior problems (e.g., aggression and disobedience), and that these effects are not simply a function of low-quality care. (p. 1032)

In a later study, this group found that the effects of early childcare extend into late childhood and adolescence (Vandell et al., 2010). In a more recent developmental psychobiological study of older children in childcare outside the United States, Sajaniemi and colleagues (2011) observed a group of children with a cortisol pattern clearly indicating atypical HPA activity. They concluded,

> The number of physical and psychological stressors in the lives of children has multiplied in recent years as the number of children with various kinds of behavioural and developmental difficulties has increased. Besides other stressful childhood events such as family turmoil, disruptions or adverse social circumstances, day care may also be challenging for some children. (p. 56)

Citing my work, they concluded, "These findings should be considered alarming since developmental difficulties may be, at least partly, the consequence of chronically-induced stress which is known to have detrimental effects on brain activity, emotional well-being and development" (p. 56).

Indeed, the American Academy of Childhood and Adolescent Psychiatry is now asserting a "crisis" in children's mental health needs: One in every five children has a diagnosable psychiatric disorder, and one in every 10 suffers from a mental illness severe enough to impair everyday living (AACAP, n.d.). In a recent volume that I co-edited, *Evolution, Early Experience and Human Development* (Narvaez et al., 2013), I suggested that this large increase in child psychopathology in the United States is directly related to entry of many of our culture's infants into substandard early day care, at 6 weeks or less, due to the lack of national parental leave policy. In the United States, approximately 50% of 1-year-olds and 60% of 2-year-olds regularly attend some form of childcare (Hyson & Tomlinson, 2014). For many if not most parents, this placement so soon after birth is a highly stressful event, filled with conflictual emotions. It is at this very time that infants and mothers are just entering into the developmental phase "attachment in the making" (Ainsworth et al., 1978, p. 24).

In a number of contributions, I offer data indicating that at this same time, 6 weeks, right brain subcortical-cortical circuits in the right basolateral amygdala and right anterior cingulate begin a critical period of maturation (Schore, 2013, 2014). This pair of early emotion-processing limbic structures optimally evolve in an experience-dependent fashion, and these socioemotional experiences are embedded in a growth-facilitating, one-to-one, dyadic attachment relationship. On the other hand, early day care acts as an epigenetic social stressor. Experts in the field of maternal and child health are now asserting "[a] short maternity leave may detract from time available for mothers to care for themselves and their infants" (Guendelman et al., 2014, p. 201). This cultural mechanism promotes a premature disconnection of the burgeoning mother-infant emotional bond in the very earliest stage of their right brain-to-right brain intimate attachment relationship. This deprives the infant of the primary affect regulator, thereby providing less than an optimal context for ongoing right brain development. In discussing the neural and hormonal bases of the shift from parental to alloparental care, Rilling asserted "We need to study daycare and foster care workers who, despite the best intentions, may have limited amounts of empathy and compassion to partition among the many children they are caring for" (2013, p. 14).

Expanding my earlier work, I now suggest that this perinatal separation stress is amplified in male infants and puts them at even greater risk than that for female infants. Basic developmental neurobiological research demonstrates that "males appear to be more vulnerable to a unique long period of early maternal separation" and that this mechanism is associated with the fact that "males are more prone to neuropsychiatric disorders that appear developmentally" (Llorente et al. 2009, p. 240). Suomi's work on the late health effects of early-life adversity shows "males are much more affected by early deprivation than females" (Conti et al., 2012, p. 8870). Six weeks represents the exact time of the initiation of the postnatal testosterone surge found only in males, which Hines (2015) ascribed to the first months after birth, with the largest sex difference occurring in the first through the third postnatal month. This is a critical period for the ongoing formation of the HPA axis, and because of their slower brain development, male neonates are more at risk for social stressors, including the stressors that are associated with separation from the mother and the stressors associated with day care. I suggest that the heightened circulating androgenic steroids and stress-regulating corticosteroids in the male limbic brain at this very period act as a cultural psychopathogenetic mechanism for later externalizing disorders in males, including disorganized attachment etiologies of aggression dysregulation in conduct disorders.

In an article on how childcare affects child development, Crockenberg stated, "in view of an extensive vulnerability to stress (Zaslow & Haynes, 1986), when gender differences in children's reactions to childcare are identified, it is boys who show more negative behaviors" (2003, p. 1035). She cited the earlier work of Howes and Olenick (1986), who reported that boys are more adversely affected by lower-quality care than are girls; the NICHD Early Childcare Research Network (1998) finding that boys more than girls who experienced more than 30 hours a week of nonparental care are insecurely attached at 15 months; and Weinberg and colleagues' (1999) studies showing that by the middle of the first year, girls are better able to regulate negative arousal than are boys.

Over the past three decades, no studies have been done on the long-term effects, especially the enduring neurobiological effects of entrance at 6 weeks. In recent and relevant research on infants entering center care at 3 months (within the postnatal testosterone surge), Albers and colleagues (2015) followed these infants for the ensuing 9 months. Most mothers had completed higher professional education and had university degrees. Observing the infant both at home and in childcare, Albers and her colleagues reported that attending center care involves separation from the parents and exposure to a novel environment and professional caregivers, and that such experiences may be *especially stressful for young infants with both normal and limited coping capacities.* With respect to entrance at 14 weeks, they documented that infant morning and afternoon cortisol concentrations were higher on center care days compared to those on home days, and that infants receiving *higher quality of maternal behavior* displayed higher morning cortisol in center care compared to that in infants receiving lower quality of maternal behavior. They cited similar recent findings of Bernard et al. (2015), who also found afternoon cortisol levels to remain elevated throughout a 10-week transition to a new childcare setting, "possibly indicating that childcare continues to serve as a cortisol-eliciting context, even months into the transition" (Albers et al., 2015, p. 6).

Albers and her colleagues noted,

> On one hand, high quality of maternal caregiving behavior helps infants to regulate stress in challenging situations and, in the long run, to develop self-regulatory capacities (Loman & Gunnar, 2010; Schore, 2001a). On the other hand, young infants accustomed to receiving high-quality care at home may be less prepared to deal with challenges without such maternal aid, especially if the quality of the care provided by the caregivers in the center is relatively low. (p. 2)

Furthermore, higher concentrations of morning cortisol in this group remain stable throughout the first year of life. They speculate that these young infants have a history in which a *sensitive mother can be turned to for the interactive regulation of arousal* in stressful situations, and that *her unavailability in childcare* may induce increased levels of cortisol. I suggest that interactive regulation is at the core of the emerging interpersonal neurobiological attachment dynamic, and that these data indicate that early childcare represents a continual source of ongoing acute separation stress and therefore potentially less than optimal right brain development during the amygdala, anterior cingulate, and orbitofrontal critical periods of the first year. I also suggest it is for this reason that every other industrialized nation but the United States provides extensive policies of parental leave.

In addition, Albers and her group noted that entrance into center care at 3 months may be even more challenging for children high in negative emotionality (i.e., with a difficult temperament), and that heightened cortisol concentrations in this group may be indicating biologically significant chronic stress. Recall, temperament at birth is a result of epigenetic mechanisms that have evolved prenatally and continue to be shaped or misshaped by the postnatal socioemotional environment. These infants may experience a double stressor, first *in utero*, and then in the extrauterine environment of early childcare with its additional challenges of large group sizes, excessive noise, and multiple caregivers. Notably, in discussing difficult temperament, Albers and colleagues (2015) cited the above work of Crockenberg (2003), who emphasized the vulnerability of boys in childcare.

Early childcare thus represents a particularly severe stressor to a high-risk male infant with a poorly developed right-lateralized HPA axis and consequent immature capacities for both interactive regulation and autoregulation (see earlier discussion). These males use a primitive coping mechanism, dissociative disengagement, in order to cope with chronic stress, and so they may not behaviorally present with intense protest, yet are intensely homeostatically dysregulated (Schore, 2003a, 2003b, 2012). Furthermore, this gender difference in elevated cortisol during early critical periods is expressed in childhood in developing right brain–externalizing psychopathologies. The long-term effects of early childcare in this group of insecure disorganized attachment is further expressed in adolescence in the form of a predisposition to conduct disorders (Yildirim & Derksen, 2012). The detrimental impact of all-to-common inadequate early childcare on these high-risk male infants may be a later consequence of what Lanius, Vermetten, and Pain (2010) termed *The Impact of Early Life Trauma on Health and Disease: The Hidden Epidemic.*

Recent attention is being focused on the effects of early childcare at later stages, including adolescence (Vandell et al., 2010), but it is not integrating relevant findings in neuroscience nor disturbing current information from child psychiatry, especially the widely accepted tenet that "most mental illnesses . . . begin far earlier in life than was previously believed" (Insel & Fenton, 2005, p. 590). Earlier, I offered evidence to show that fetal and postnatal levels of testosterone have permanent organizational programming effects on the developing male limbic system, and that elevated levels of testosterone in adolescence are associated with the initiation of a number of male-dominant psychiatric disorders. Indeed, a psychiatric epidemiological study of 10,000 adolescents by Merikangas and colleagues (2010) documented a "high prevalence" of mental disorders in youth. These authors noted, "Approximately one in every four to five youths in the U.S. meets the criteria for a mental disorder with severe impairment across their lifetime" (p. 980).

In 1994, I reported studies showing childcare was specifically associated with an increase in avoidant (dismissive) attachment (Schore, 1994). Where does the increase in this attachment typology show up 20 years later? Indeed, the continuity of attachment styles over the life span has been an essential area of study in child development, attachment theory, and interpersonal neurobiology. A study of 10,000 Adult Attachment Interviews documented dismissing attachment in 35% of *nonclinical* adolescents, compared with that in only 23% of adults of the prior generation (Bakermans-Kranenburg & van IJzendoorn, 2009a). Research with more than 25,000 American college students by Konrath and colleagues (2014) reported that between 1988 and 2011, secure attachment decreased from 49% to 42%, while insecure attachment increased from 51% to 58%, with the largest rise (56%) in dismissing attachments. These authors pointed out that mothers' participation in the labor force rose from 38% in the late 1960s to 69% in the early 1990s, "straining parent's collective ability to invest quality time in their children" (p. 338), and suggested that "*changes in attachment related early childhood indicators may provide some explanation for changes in attachment styles*" (p. 338, italics added).

In a study of more than 75,000 American high school and college students from 1938 to 2007, Twenge and colleagues (2010) documented that the current generation of young adolescents report significantly higher symptoms of psychopathology on the Minnesota Multiphasic Personality Inventory (MMPI). In order to understand the underlying mechanism for this significant cultural change, they proposed that "*large changes over relatively short periods of time cannot be attributed to genetics*" (p. 152, italics added), and that "*there are also strong cultural influences on psychiatric symptoms—that is, an environmental influence outside of the individual family*" (p. 153, italics added). In agreement with Konrath and with Twenge, I suggest that the ongoing significant changes in insecure attachment status and reduced socioemotional health of our children are in part due to epigenetic cultural social stressors associated with early day care, which is in general substandard in the United States. This culturally sanctioned premature separation of the early developing brain from the primary caregiver occurs even before the attachment system is fully formed, thereby generating enduring future deficits in right brain social, emotional, and stress-regulating functions.

The sobering study by Albers and colleagues began with infants at 14 weeks and was done in the Netherlands, which has a comprehensive national policy of parental leave and a higher quality of childcare than that in the United States, where infants are placed at 6 weeks. Although both sexes are negatively affected, boys, with more slowly developing brains, are even more at risk, in both the short term and long term. Gunnar and colleagues (2010) asserted that U.S. childcare elevations of cortisol are associated with angry-aggressive behavior in boys, with anxious-vigilant behavior in girls, and that boys may experience more stress at childcare than girls. These gender differences reflect early expressions of externalizing and internalizing psychopathologies. Recall Holden's (2005) assertion that culture helps shape how the two sexes express mental problems.

Citing my work on brain development, Calnen (2007) asserted,

> It is biologically necessary that mothers be with their infants, especially during the *first few months postpartum*. This is not likely to become a reality until working families are granted a sufficiently long, and paid, maternity leave as a matter of national policy. (p. 39)

Because of its lack of support of a national policy of parental leave, unique within the industrialized world, and the poor quality of its early childcare, U.S. culture is now acting as a source generator of significant increases in the amount of mental problems in its child, adolescent, and adult citizens. That said, the science now exists to formulate evidence-based models of early intervention and indeed prevention of mental disorders.

On the basis of the developmental neurobiological data, I suggest that the United States should legislate and implement the strategies now operating in other industrialized nations: maternal leave of 6 months and paternal leave of 2 months. In addition, we must seriously address the problem of the training and the quality of childcare workers. Toward that effort, I have recently served as an independent reviewer of a volume published by the Institute of Medicine (2015), *Transforming the Workforce for Children Birth through 8: A Unifying Foundation,* although to my mind that work is still too focused on later developing left brain language and not right brain socioemotional functions. Furthermore, developmental neurobiological and neuropsychological studies of infants before, during, and after early daycare are now essential, and it should focus not on later maturing language or motor areas, but on brain systems responsible for socioemotional and stress-regulating functions, essential elements of well-being (Schore, 2015b). In a recent article, Layard and colleagues at the London School of Economics concluded, "The most important childhood predictor of adult life-satisfaction is the child's emotional health, followed by the child's conduct. The least powerful predictor is the child's intellectual development" (2015, p. F720).

CULTURAL EPIGENETIC MECHANISMS OF INCREASED MALE GENDER PSYCHOPATHOGENESIS: TOXIC ENVIRONMENTAL ENDOCRINE DISRUPTORS

In earlier sections of this chapter, I reported linkages between endocrine disruptors that are omnipresent not only here in the United States but worldwide and increased levels of male-dominant neurodevelopmental disorders such as autism and schizophrenia and psychiatric disorders such as ADHD and oppositional defiant conduct disorders (Grandjean & Landrigan, 2014; Lanphear, 2015; Miodovnik et al., 2011). I now offer some further thoughts on this second transcultural developmental mechanism that is amplifying male psychopathology in U.S. culture and beyond: widespread exposure of developing males to environmental toxins that interfere with the developmental programming of the structural brain systems that functionally regulate relational stress. The slower maturation of their fetal and postnatal brain puts males at even greater risk because of an extended window of vulnerability to these toxic environmental chemicals.

Recall, a large body of research in both animals and humans clearly demonstrates that the developing fetus and infant are much more sensitive to endocrine disruptors than are adults; that extremely low-dose exposure during critical periods exerts significant effects on a developing organism by inducing epigenetic modifications in the genome; that early exposure alters the androgen/estrogen balance in specific developing brain regions thereby changing the normally sexually dimorphic structures and behaviors that characterize boys and girls; that these xenobiotic agents have distinct effects on male and female limbic circuits; that male brains are particularly susceptible during the prenatal, postnatal, and pubertal testosterone surges;

that some of the effects in early life may not be manifest until adulthood; and that human exposure is "widespread."

Utilizing an evolutionary perspective in an ethotoxicological study of environmental endocrine-disrupting chemicals, Parmigiani, Palanza, and vom Saal concluded, "Pathological changes in behavior lead to reduced *social* adaptation and impaired responsiveness to environmental demands, with consequences for *social structure and population dynamics*" (1998, p. 333, italics added). Citing the current increased prevalence of developmental disabilities and autism, ADHD, and conduct disorders in U.S. children, especially boys, Lanphear asserted, "The impact of toxins on the developing brain is usually subtle for an individual child, but the damage can be substantial at the *population level*" (2015, p. 211, italics added). He also pointed out that causal mechanisms of these disorders are more than genetic, they are epigenetic, due to an interplay of genes and environment, including the physical environment. Indeed, most exposures to endocrine disruptors do not produce genetic mutations but promote effects on subsequent generations via "epigenetic transgenerational inheritance" (Skinner, 2016). In other words, the long-term effects of the early exposure of developing brains to these ubiquitous environmental toxins can account for not only significant increases in male (and female) gender-related psychopathologies at the individual level, but also for the significant increase of male-related psychopathologies in large numbers across a multitude of cultures.

A massive amount of basic and clinical research exists on early exposure to bisphenol A (BPA), an endocrine disruptor that has antiandrogenic effects on the androgen receptor (Lee et al., 2003) in both animals and humans. BPA is one of the highest-volume chemicals produced worldwide and is used in the manufacture of plastics and epoxy resins, including food and beverage containers. More than 90% of the U.S. population has measurable levels of BPA in bodily fluids, with children typically exhibiting higher internal levels than adults (Vandenberg et al., 2010). Exposure to BPA *in utero* inhibits the testosterone surge in the neonatal period, thereby disrupting the endocrine environment in the neonatal male (Tanaka et al., 2006). Females exposed to low doses of BPA during the last stage of pregnancy show altered maternal behavior in adulthood through an epigenetic mechanism that modifies gene activity (Palanza et al., 2002).

Note the negative effects on both sides of the mother-infant dyad, a focus of modern attachment theory (Schore, 2017; Schore & Schore, 2008). Palanza and his colleagues asserted that "slight perturbations of any of the components of the *mother-infant interaction* may result in alterations of the behavior of the mother and/or the offspring" (2002, p. 415, italics added). In more recent research on the impact of BPA on the social behaviors between infants and their mothers, Nakagami and colleagues reported prenatal exposure to a "relatively low dose" of this endocrine disruptor alters the behavior of the male infant toward its mother, and that "male infants and male-nursing mothers were more vulnerable to BPA exposure than female infants and female-nursing mothers" (2009, p. 1194). In this assessment, both showed more "outward looking" behaviors, suggesting an altered mother-infant interaction. It is important to emphasize that due to the epigenetic programming effects of sex steroids in critical periods, toxic endocrine-disrupting chemicals in the shared mother-infant physical environment induce the structural organization of a dyadic system that is functionally less adapted to deal with stressors in the mother-infant social environment.

These data regarding the detrimental effects of developmental endocrine disruptors on male social and emotional functions in postnatal periods reflect dysfunctions of gender-related attachment behaviors that I described earlier. These environmental toxins thus interfere with the necessary co-creation of the maternal-infant attachment relationship, and they preclude the interactive regulation that is required for the ongoing maturation of the slowly developing male limbic system. *In utero* and perinatal exposure to BPA alters spontaneous novelty seeking and impulsive behaviors (Adriani et al., 2003), decreases reception of fear-provoking stimuli (Negishi et al., 2004), and increases aggressiveness in males (Kawai et al., 2003). The reduction of postnatal testosterone caused by BPA also decreases the availability of androgens for regulating cell death in sexually dimorphic nuclei, such as the hypothalamic preoptic area, and for the imprinting and preservation of emerging right-lateralized corticolimbic regulatory circuits. These enduring structural defects and functional relational deficits represent the earliest etiological expressions of the previously mentioned gender-related predisposition to psychiatric disorders associated with endocrine-disrupting chemicals (Grandjean & Landrigan, 2014). Evans and colleagues (2014) documented that prenatal exposure to BPA is associated with externalizing aggression and oppositional defiant conduct disorder in 6- to 10-year-old boys but not girls.

In the study "Perinatal Exposure to Low-Dose Bisphenol A Affects the Neuroendocrine Stress Response in Rats," Panagiotidou and colleagues (2014) showed that low but chronic exposure throughout pregnancy and lactation alters the HPA axis at *puberty* in a sexually dimorphic manner. Exposed males exhibited a more active HPA axis under stress, reflected in a higher and more extended rise in plasma corticosterone, thus appearing "less mature regarding their pituitary stress responsiveness" (p. 216). Under resting conditions, exposed females had higher basal corticosteroid levels, and under stress the females did not down-regulate HPA activation. The researchers concluded that exposure of a pregnant female to this endocrine-disrupting chemical induces "a sex-specific effect on their offspring's physiology and behavior . . . including *reduction or reversal of existing sex differences*" (p. 210, italics added).

Chen and colleagues (2014) have demonstrated that sex differences in the *adult* HPA axis are altered by perinatal exposure to low-dose bisphenol A. These authors concluded that the hormonal basis of normal gender differences lies in different effects of estrogen and androgen upon the HPA's response to stress: "Ovarian steroids (estrogen) have been found to increase HPA-axis activity, and enhance the HPA-axis response to psychological stress. . . . Conversely, testosterone attenuates HPA-axis activity" (p. 13). They demonstrated that exposing the developing male brain to an endocrine disruptor in a perinatal period *reduces testosterone* and *increases corticosteroid* response to mild stress in adulthood, a *reversal of the normal male* HPA *pattern of affective behavior.*

As I mentioned earlier, there is now an intense interest in the impact of endocrine disruptors on early development across a very large number of scientific research and clinical disciplines, yet little to none of this has been incorporated into psychology and psychiatry, especially their developmental branches. To give an example of the wide range of these disciplines, in this work I have cited studies from such journals as the *Journal of Endocrinology, Brain Research, Neurotoxicology, Journal of Neurolog-*

ical Sciences, Lancet Neurology, Acta Paediatrica, Neuropharmacology, Environmental Health Perspectives, Toxicology and Industrial Health, and *Human and Experimental Toxicology,* among others. For some time, the field has been controversial, but now that the harmful effects of these developmental toxins has been firmly established and the research is directed toward the underlying neurobiological mechanisms, the main controversy is about what level can be considered a "safe dose" (see Grandjean and Ozonoff, 2013, for conflicts with industry and legal matters). At present, acceptable dose is designated at adult levels, which is considerably higher than maternal and infant levels and does not take into consideration the unique susceptibility of mothers and infants to very low levels of these environmental toxins.

In fact, the interdisciplinary findings are so convincing that a large number of different scientific and clinical disciplines are now simultaneously expressing a worldwide call for action on endocrine disruptors. To give some examples, in the *Journal of Steroid Biochemistry & Molecular Biology,* Rubin (2011) asserted,

> There is currently sufficient evidence to raise concern and to warrant practice of the precautionary principle, particularly for protection of the developing fetus, neonate and young children as they may be the most vulnerable to adverse effects of this ubiquitous compound. (p. 32)

A 2014 editorial in *Hormones and Behavior* signed by 20 journal editors-in-chief and 28 journal associate editors declared,

> Thousands of published studies have revealed the health effects of endocrine disrupting chemicals on wildlife and laboratory animals and, moreover, have shown associations of endocrine disrupting chemicals with effects in humans. . . . Of particular concern is incontrovertible evidence . . . that there are critical life stages, especially during early development, when hormones dictate the differentiation and development of tissues. Any perturbation of the delicate hormonal balance, whether due to the absence of natural

> hormones or presence of exogenous hormones, can have irreversible effects on endocrine-sensitive organs. Endocrine disrupting chemicals are known to upset the balance. (Gore et al., 2014, p. 190)

In a position statement in *Endocrinology*, authors have offered recommendations for strengthening the Endocrine Disruptor Screening Program (Zoeller et al., 2012), and in *Lancet Neurology*, Grandjean and Landrigan (2014) have called for an urgent formation of an international clearinghouse. Writing in *Annual Review of Public Health*, Lanphear (2015) has argued, “The optimal strategy to prevent the development of brain-based disorders is to identify and restrict or ban the use of potential toxins before they are marketed or discharged into the environment” (p. 222).

In the clinical literature, an international group of authors declared in a special communication in a 2015 issue of the *International Journal of Gynecology and Obstetrics*,

> Exposure to toxic environmental chemicals during pregnancy and breastfeeding is ubiquitous and is a threat to healthy human reproduction. . . . Exposure to toxic environmental chemicals and related health outcomes are inequitably distributed within and between countries; universally, *the consequences of exposure are disproportionately borne by people with low incomes*. . . . On the basis of accumulating robust evidence of exposures and adverse health impacts related to toxic environmental chemicals the International Federation of Gynecology and Obstetrics (FIGO) joins other leading reproductive health professional societies in calling for timely action to prevent harm. (Di Renzo et al., 2015b, p. 219)

In a recent issue of *NeuroToxicology*, Mustieles and colleagues (2015) applied science to practice: “Physicians, especially gynecologists and pediatricians, should be aware of the hazards of endocrine disrupting chemicals exposure, allowing them to make lifestyle recommendations for preventing and/or reducing exposure, *especially in high-risk populations*” (p. 182, italics added).

Although all mothers and their male and female infants are susceptible to the enduring untoward effects of early exposures to environmental toxins, those in lower socioeconomic groups are especially at high risk. Expanding upon studies demonstrating that toddlers from low-income families are at risk for poorer neurodevelopment (Black et al., 2000), research in the environmental health literature documents the enduring effects of environmental contaminants in American Indian and Alaska Native 24-month-old children (Hoover et al., 2012) and describes how prenatal and postnatal exposure to agricultural pesticides impairs neurodevelopment in Mexican American toddlers (Eskenazi et al., 2007). In an inner-city cohort of 3- to 5-year-old African American and Dominican children, Perera et al. (2012) observed that maternal bisphenol concentrations during the third trimester of pregnancy are associated with more problems with emotional reactivity and increased aggressive behavior syndromes in boys but not girls. Thus, economically disadvantaged boys, who all too frequently are exposed to low-quality early childcare, are most at risk to the long-term detrimental effects of environmental endocrine disruptors on stress regulation and affective behavior.

In 1962, Rachel Carson published the groundbreaking and transformational volume *Silent Spring*, which triggered a national debate on the worldwide unrestricted proliferation of environmental toxins (chemical pesticides) and on the role of the responsibilities of science, the chemical industry, and the government. She also questioned the wisdom of the government in allowing toxic chemicals to be so massively discharged into the environment before knowing the long-term consequences. This work rapidly galvanized a public environmental consciousness, and in the following decade DDT was banned in the United States and the Environmental Protection Agency was established. In this exceedingly forward-looking work, Carson proposed that one detrimental consequence of these toxins was the alteration of the proper balance between male and female hormones that would lead to an excessive accumulation of either, a foreshadowing of the later-discovered developmental toxicity of endocrine-disrupting chemicals, another aspect of human-induced environmental change.

Mothers and infants are vulnerable to low levels of a wide variety of environmental toxins that have lifelong impact on the ability to function, especially with respect to social dysfunction (Lanphear, 2015). Both the developing male and female brains are routinely exposed and therefore at risk for detrimental long-term effects in affective, social, and stress-regulating functions, but in a sexually dimorphic manner. The interdisciplinary integration of developmental neuroscience and developmental endocrinology has increased our understandings of both early human development and of the specific windows of vulnerability of specific, rapidly maturing brain systems to endocrine disruptors. These advances in science are in turn generating more powerful clinical models of the disturbing increased prevalence of gender-related developmental and psychiatric disorders. In addition to a more comprehensive and extended national policy and an improvement of childcare, a major contribution to our children's development of mental and physical health would be governmental regulatory policy measures that protect our future citizens from early exposure to environmental toxins.

CODA: DO BOYS EVER CATCH UP?

Throughout this chapter, I have provided evidence to show that the brain development of the male fetus, infant, and boy is slower than that in the female counterparts, and thereby more at risk. According to Zahn-Waxler and colleagues (2008), "The curve of development of the frontal cortex, caudate, and temporal lobes in girls is considerably faster than in boys, by as much as 20 months" (p. 279). At ages 7–12, boys lag behind girls by as much as 2 years in the development of social sensitivity (Baron-Cohen et al., 1999). Especially in terms of social and emotional development, do they ever catch up after childhood? What about the next phase, adolescence?

Recall the male brain experiences three testosterone surges, in prenatal, postnatal, and adolescent stages of development. The male brain initiates puberty through increased androgenic hormone release, leading to the maturation of the gonads and the production and release of increasing levels of these sex steroids. Earlier I offered evidence to show that the right orbitofrontal cortex, which regulates the right amygdala, matures later in male than in female toddlers. I also cited the study of Raznahan and colleagues (2010) on androgen signaling and cortical maturation in adolescence showing a focally accentuated "protracted cortical maturation" in males compared to females in the orbitofrontal and ventromedial cortices. I noted that the delayed maturation of this emotion-processing and emotion-regulating cortical system in males, earlier expressed in infancy and childhood, is still operating in adolescence.

In an MRI study of face processing in both male and female adolescents, Schneider and colleagues (2011) reported that 14-year-old males show a sex-dependent amygdala lateralization during the processing of faces, especially angry faces. They observed that the right amygdala is more strongly activated than the left in males but not females. They contrast this male gender–lateralized amygdala with females who exhibit a progressive increase in prefrontal relative to amygdala activation in the left hemisphere with age (Killgore, Oki, & Yurgelun-Todd, 2001), suggesting that "males and females might have different developmental gradients" (2011, p. 1852). The authors interpreted these gender data to demonstrate that the functional connectivity of the amygdala with the medial prefrontal cortex is reduced in normal male adolescents compared with that in adults, suggesting a weaker link between emotion, memory, and higher cognitive processes. This in turn is expressed in increased emotional vulnerability, one that is associated with a potential etiological pathway associated with mental disorders that are most frequent in adolescence, such as conduct disorders. They also note that this sex-dependent amygdala lateralization during basic emotional processes in adolescence is the precursor of the lateralization in emotional memory observed in adulthood. Clearly, the development of the male brain is still behind that of the female in early adolescence.

That said, testosterone levels rise dramatically in males over the course of adolescence. Testosterone starts to increase with the initiation of puberty and reaches adult levels by about 17 years of age (Griffin & Wilson, 1998), and so it is considerably higher in the 20- to 24-year-old adult than in the 15- to 19-year-old adolescent. In adult males, androgens suppress the HPA axis, and activation of the stress response results in the inhibition of glucocorticoid pathways (Clifton, 2010; Handa et al. 1994), thereby allowing for an increased gender-specific stress-regulating capacity. According to Davis and Emory, "sex differences in maturity eventually equalize, yet stress responses remain sexually dimorphic through adulthood" (1995, p. 24). Supporting this view that boys catch up in adulthood, Bakermans-Kranenburg and van IJzendoorn (2009b) documented studies indicating that at 6–14 years, 49% of boys compared with 64% of girls are securely attached, while in adulthood an equivalent 48% of males and 50% of females are securely attached on the Adult Attachment Interview.

Evidence that male socioemotional functions do mature in early adulthood is provided by De Pisapia and colleagues, who reported a neuroimaging study of "interpersonal competence" in healthy male young adults, defined as "the capacity to interact and communicate with others, to share personal views, to understand the emotions and opinions of others, and to cooperate with others or resolve conflict should it occur" (2014, p. 1257). They documented that an increased level of interpersonal competence is associated with higher white matter integrity in several major tracts of the right hemisphere, a finding that underscores its fundamental role in social cognition. De Pisapia and colleagues concluded,

> According to this line of research, the development of emotional and social intelligence in the individual—from childhood to adulthood—depends on the quality of their relationship with a principal caregiver and those socioemotional competencies heavily rely on right brain function. The finding may have implications for theories claiming that the right hemisphere plays a major role in modulating emotion and nonverbal communication during the first interpersonal relationship that every human being experiences, namely the infant–mother relationship (Schore, 1997, 2000, 2009). (p. 1262)

Hecht marshals a great deal of neurobiological studies to show that in adults, "the right hemisphere has a relative advantage over the left hemisphere mediating social intelligence—identifying social stimuli, understanding the intentions of other people, awareness of the dynamics in social relationships, and successful handling of social interactions" (2014, p. 1). These expanded right brain social and emotional functions allow the adult male to enter into an intimate emotional relationship with a same-aged female. Research describes important hormonal changes in men associated with marriage and fatherhood (both involving activation of right brain attachment mechanisms). Testosterone levels are lower in married versus single men (Booth & Dabbs, 1993) and in fathers (Gray, Yang, & Pope, 2006). Notably, fathers' testosterone levels drop during their partners' late pregnancy and early postpartum period (Perini et al., 2012; Storey et al., 2000), and men who provide more parental care have lower baseline testosterone levels than those of fathers who provide less care or fathers without children (Gettler et al., 2011). Lower levels of paternal testosterone have been linked with developing paternal nurturance by increasing empathy for and suppressing aggression toward infants. It is tempting to speculate that this socially mediated reduction of testosterone is the result of increased aromatization of testosterone into estrogen in the adult male that has become a father.

Authors now suggest an inverted U-shaped function in which moderate (regulated) levels of testosterone are associated with better infant care than are either high or low levels, and that the testosterone reduction in fatherhood seems to be a consequence rather than a cause in becoming a father (Rilling, 2013). Researchers have proposed that the reduction of testosterone in a committed romantic relationship is related to "pair bonding" (attachment) and that "affiliative interactions with a partner may decrease testosterone levels" (Burnham et al., 2003, p. 121). I propose that these adaptive hormonal changes are a direct result of the implicit reciprocal synchronized right brain-to-right brain bodily-based affective attachment communications between the mother and the father, and then the infant and the father, especially in father–male toddler child play (see discussion earlier in this chapter). These interactions may have organizational, programming effects on the growth of paternal circuits in the father's brain, paralleling documented increased growth in the mother's brain in the postpartum months (P. Kim et al., 2010). Indeed, a recent functional magnetic resonance imaging (fMRI) study revealed that the father's brain is sensitive to childcare experiences, and that while maternal caregiving involves an "evolutionarily ancient" brain-hormone-behavior *subcortical-paralimbic* network involved in *emotional* processing, paternal caregiving activates a later developing brain-hormone-behavior *cortical* circuit involved in socio-*cognitive* understanding, mentalizing, and future planning (Abraham et al., 2014).

In the past, the physical sciences have focused on biological gender and the social sciences on psychological gender. At this point, however, updated models of gender differences are understood to represent a dynamic interaction between biological and social factors (Wood & Eagley, 2015). Current developmental interpersonal neurobiological models of early gender development indicate that in both males and females, there are different early emotional identifications around gender. In a common social scenario of a secure attachment, male and female infants/toddlers internalize a maternal estrogen-dominant imprinted and then a paternal androgen-dominant imprinted attachment relationship. In the second year, in both sexes, psychological gender (the sense of maleness or femaleness) is not only genetically encoded, but also epigenetically molded by early experiences with feminine and masculine caregivers. This allows resilient androgynous access to both affiliative, communal, expressive, and nurturant feminine aspects, as well as agentic and instrumental masculine aspects of the evolving personality (Bem, 1974, Spence & Helmreich, 1978). In this manner, optimal human male gender functioning in adulthood is associated with regulated testosterone levels that underlie adaptive sexual functions (Stoleru et al., 1993), pair bonding (van Anders, Goldey, & Kuo, 2011), and fathering (Gettler et al., 2011), as well as implicit power motivation and achievement motivation (Stanton & Schultheiss, 2009). The activational effects of this androgenic steroid are triggered at implicit levels in social contexts, like corticosteroids (Quirin et al., 2009), producing behavioral changes in seconds to minutes.

Confirming my earlier speculations (Schore, 1994), recent research now indicates that "Sex differences in orbitofrontal cortex activity may be due to organizational effects of gonadal hormones early in life. The behavioral and neurobiological differences between men and women are an expression of more general sex differences in the regulation of emotions" (van den Bos, Homberg, & de Visser, 2013, p. 95). There is now consensus that in adulthood, male and female brains use different strategies during emotional processing (Whittle et al., 2011), and that men's subjective affective experience is relatively more rooted in sensations from the world, whereas women's affective experience is more rooted in sensations from within the body (Moriguchi et al., 2014). This underlies the well-known social tendencies of males to utilize cognitive empathy while females access bodily-based affective empathy. The same socioemotional gender difference is also expressed in a general predisposition of males to autoregulate stress, while females use more interactive regulation ("tend and befriend"; Taylor et al., 2000). In parallel to and echoing this, the two genders also show different situational triggers and coping strategies in stress regulation. Men show greater adrenocortical responses to achievement challenges, whereas women show significant cortisol responses to social rejection stressors (Stroud, Salovey, & Epel, 2002).

Basic research now demonstrates that testosterone exerts differential effects in males and females, that in male adults the magnitude of the HPA response of corticosteroid release to stress is negatively related to plasma testosterone, that androgens inhibit the stress axis, and that testosterone can block stress-induced corticosteroid release, inducing anxiolytic effects and reducing fear (Bingham et al., 2011; Viau & Meaney, 1996). In light of the gender-specific interactions and mutual inhibition between the HPG and HPA axes, ongoing testosterone-driven aggression or sexual experience in males can transiently decrease stress reactions (Cunningham et al., 2012). On the other hand, cortisol can suppress circulating testosterone levels in normal adult men (Cummings, Quigley, & Yen, 1983; Doerr & Pirke, 1976), and so both testosterone and cortisol jointly regulate masculine dominance, an assertive and self-assured behavioral style that is mediated by the effects of these dual hormones on the neural activity in the orbitofrontal cortex and amygdala (Mehta & Josephs, 2010).

Furthermore, Ingalhalikar and colleagues (2014) demonstrated that male brains are structured to facilitate connectivity between perception and coordinated action as opposed to female brains, which are designed to facilitate communication between analytical and intuitive processing modes. These authors noted that male brains are optimized for communicating within hemispheres as opposed to female brains, which are optimized for interhemispheric communication. They concluded, "the developmental trajectories of males and females separate at a young age" (p. 823) and that these dominant forms "are established early on and preserved throughout the course of development" (p. 825). In total, the preceding pages of this chapter suggest that differences between the sexes in brain wiring patterns that account for *gender* differences in social and emotional functions are established at the very beginning of life, that the developmental programming of these differences are more than genetically coded but epigenetically shaped by the early social and physical environment, and that the adult male and female brains represent an adaptive *complementarity* for optimal *human* function.

CHAPTER 5

Early Right Brain Regulation and the Relational Origins of Emotional Well-Being

IN AN EDITORIAL in the *Journal of Child Psychology and Psychiatry* titled "Developmental Neuroscience Comes of Age," Leckman and March (2011) described "the phenomenal progress of the past three decades." Looking both into the past and into the future they boldly asserted,

> It has . . . become abundantly clear that . . . the in utero and immediate postnatal environments and the dyadic relations between child and caregivers within the first years of life can have direct and enduring effects on the child's brain development and behavior. . . . The enduring impact of early maternal care and the role of epigenetic modifications of the genome during critical periods in early brain development in health and disease is likely to be *one of the most important discoveries in all of science that have major implications for our field*. (p. 334, italics added)

Indeed, over this time period a large body of interdisciplinary research demonstrates that early brain development is not just genetically encoded; rather, it needs epigenetic social experiences. Scientists are now describing gene-environment interactions and offering models in which Mother Nature *and* Mother Nurture combine to shape human nature. These epigenetic factors in the social environment that affect genomic mechanisms are expressed within the mother-infant attachment relationship. Researchers as well as clinicians are eagerly looking for clinical applications of current knowledge about the critical biological and psychological aspects of early attachment experiences, both in optimal and nonoptimal relational contexts.

Toward that end, over the same three decades my contributions to the burgeoning field of developmental neuroscience have focused on the neurodynamics and psychodynamics of attachment, an essential evolutionary mechanism of early human development. My work in interpersonal neurobiology attempts to elucidate precisely how optimal *emotional* attachment experiences shape and sculpt the early developing "*emotional*" right brain, and thereby the origins of an enduring background sense of subjective *emotional* well-being. My studies in developmental affective neuroscience focus not only on the processing of socioemotional information but also on the regulation of bodily-based affective states, a central mechanism of the attachment dynamic. In parallel, my contributions in developmental neuropsychoanalysis and psychodynamic psychotherapy continue to explore the problem, how do relational experiences at the beginning of life, especially in intimate contexts, fundamentally influence the growth of the self's subjective, unconscious mind? Neuroscience thus lies at the core of what I have termed "regulation theory," an interpersonal neurobiological model of the development, psychopathogenesis, and treatment of the early forming emotional core of the subjective self.

The progression of regulation theory over these decades reflects the ongoing incorporation of the rapidly expanding body of research on the earliest stages of development into my writings. At the outset, in 1994 I began my first book with the assertion, "The understanding of early development is one of the fundamental objectives of science. The beginnings of living systems set the stage for every aspect of an organism's internal and external functioning throughout the life span" (Schore, 1994, p. 3). My work over the ensuing "decade of the brain" continued to report an increasing number of studies in this area, and by 2009 I offered an invited plenary address to the American Psychological Association, "The Paradigm Shift: The Right Brain and the Relational Unconscious" (Schore, 2009a). Subsequently, in 2012 I continued to track the paradigm shift from behavior, to cognition, to bodily-based emotion, and from the language functions of the left brain to the emotional functions of the right brain in both the research and clinical disciplines (Schore, 2012a). This transformation of our conceptualization of human development is being fueled by three converging paradigm shifting forces, and it has deepened our understanding of the origins of an essential adaptive capacity of human beings, a subjective sense of emotional well-being.

PARADIGM SHIFTS IN EARLY DEVELOPMENT

The first theme of the ongoing paradigm shift is expressed in the increasing trend of psychology, psychiatry, and neuroscience to simultaneously emphasize the *centrality of emotion* (even more than cognition) in the human experience. Building upon the neuroscience of the past century, in 1994 I described the neurobiological "primacy of affect"—that right brain affective processes operating at levels beneath conscious awareness are dominant in development, psychopathogenesis, and psychotherapy. Citing research over the ensuing 10 years, in 2003 I wrote that affective processes lie at the core of the self, and due to the intrinsic psychobiological nature of these bodily-based phenomena, models of human development, from infancy throughout the life span, were moving toward brain/mind/body conceptualizations (Schore, 2003a). By 2007, the editor of the journal *Motivation and Emotion* was asserting, "After three decades of the dominance of cognitive approaches, motivational and emotional processes have roared back into the limelight" (Ryan, 2007, p. 1).

This dictum also applied to developmental theory. Previous developmental psychological models had focused on the emergence of more complex *cognition* late in the first and into the second year. The significant increase in current knowledge in early human *relationships* clearly demonstrates that from the very beginning, the developing human is *emotionally* relating with the *social environment*, moving the emphasis from cognitive to emotional development. The concept of the "primacy of affect" has also affected the concept of "mental health" and its earliest expression, "infant mental health." Reflecting the paradigm shift, updated models of psychological well-being are now grounded in not cognitive but emotional well-being. For an overview of my more recent interdisciplinary studies of emotional development and the relational origins of emotional well-being, I refer the reader to Schore (2012a, 2012b, 2013a).

The second theme of the paradigm shift is the converging interest in a theoretical organizing principle that lies at core of every biological and psychological discipline—*self-regulation*, an essential mechanism of emotional processes. Again, at the very beginning of my studies, in *Affect Regulation and the Origin of the Self: The Neurobiology of Emotional Development*, I offered a psychoneurobiological model of emotional attachment dynamics centered in self-regulation (Schore, 1994). Applying this construct to developmental psychology as a whole, in 2002 Fonagy and Target boldly concluded that the whole of child development can be basically conceptualized as the enhancement of self-regulation. By this time, both scientists and mental health workers shared a common interest in affect and affect regulation (Schore, 2003a, 2003b). In 2008, Judith and I offered a succinct explication of "modern attachment theory":

> We suggest that in line with Bowlby's fundamental goal of the integration of psychological and biological models of human development, the current clinical and experimental focus on how affective bodily-based processes are nonconsciously interactively regulated . . . has shifted attachment theory to a regulation theory. (J. Schore & A. Schore, 2008, p. 9)

Since that time, my ongoing studies continue to offer interpersonal neurobiological models of the underlying mechanisms by which attachment promotes self-regulation and of how this emergent function in turn allows new and more complex and resilient relational interactions between the individual and the social environment. From infancy throughout all later stages of the life span, spontaneous, rapidly acting emotional processes are centrally involved in enabling the organism to regulate and thereby cope with stresses and challenges, thus resulting in emotional resilience and well-being.

The third theme of the paradigm shift is reflected in the previously mentioned explosion of developmental neuroscience research, especially in *developmental affective neuroscience*, and particularly studies of prenatal, perinatal, and postnatal stages that occur within the period of the human brain growth spurt—the last trimester of pregnancy through the second year.

The number of studies exploring the earliest stages of rapid dynamic brain development has significantly expanded, demonstrating that the rate of synaptogenesis in the developing infant's brain is a remarkable 40,000 new synapses every second, and that brain volume increases from 400 grams at birth to 1,000 grams at 12 months. Furthermore, studies on early brain lateralization reveal that during this period, the right brain develops before the left, which does not begin its growth spurt until the second year. Most important, the unfolding of epigenetic programs that guide early brain development over the perinatal and postnatal stages of human infancy occur within mother-infant attachment transactions. Indeed, a body of research supports the idea that attachment transactions influence the "early life programming of hemispheric lateralization" (Stevenson et al., 2008) that in turn generates the dominance of the right hemisphere in the first year of life (Chiron et al., 1997). In this manner, attachment interactions during critical periods of maturation of the early developing right brain indelibly affect the trajectory of later socioemotional development.

As a result of the paradigm shift, what had earlier been theoretical proposals only two decades previously are now accepted developmental organizing principles:

> A complex, dynamic story is unfolding of evolutionarily conserved genetic programs that guide mammalian brain development and how our *in utero* and our early postnatal interpersonal worlds shape and mold the individuals (infants, children, adolescents, adults and caregivers) we are to become. (Leckman & March, 2011, p. 333)

The interpersonal worlds that shape and fine-tune early brain development represent the interpersonal neurobiological underpinnings of essential adaptive functions of the early maturing right brain, and thereby an enduring capacity of emotional well-being.

With this introduction in mind, in the following I will briefly discuss recent interdisciplinary research that further supports regulation theory's assertion that optimal attachment experiences (secure attachment) facilitate the experience-dependent maturation of the developing "emotional" right brain and thereby a predisposition for emotional well-being in later stages of life. I shall conclude with some thoughts about the application of regulation theory to early intervention and prevention. Throughout, I will describe the progression of my work in developmental neuroscience over the past two decades. Here, as in all my writings, I continue to use the device of citing verbatim the current voices of clinicians studying the mind and neuroscientists studying the brain in order to demonstrate their agreement on the centrality of bodily-based affective phenomena and to generate a common language that addresses the subjective emotional realm, including emotional well-being.

OPTIMAL ATTACHMENT EXPERIENCES AND THE EARLY RELATIONAL ORIGINS OF EMOTIONAL WELL-BEING

Modern attachment theory articulates the progression of early developing right brain structures and survival functions over the prenatal, perinatal, and postnatal critical periods and stages of infancy. In 2001, Walker-Andrews and Bahrick asserted, "From birth, an infant is plunged into a world of other human beings in which conversation, gestures, and faces are omnipresent during the infant's waking hours. Moreover, these harbingers of social information are dynamic, multimodal, and reciprocal" (2001, p. 469). This description reflects a paradigm shift in our conception of infancy. Previous developmental psychological models had focused on the development of more complex *cognition* late in the first and into the second year. The significant recent increase in research in early human social development clearly demonstrates that from the very beginning, the developing human is *emotionally* relating with the social environment, moving the emphasis from cognitive to emotional development. The baby is a sentient being, capable of perception, sensation, and feeling, and thereby states of consciousness. Her emerging subjectivity (developing mind) is created in an intersubjective context in a social world. In the first year, before the onset of verbal language, she is communicating with her caregivers who are attempting to communicate with her. In order to process these nonverbal communications, the infant seeks proximity to mother, who must be subjectively perceived as predictable, consistent, and emotionally available.

In his initial exposition of attachment theory, Bowlby proposed that mother-infant attachment communications are "accompanied by the strongest of feelings and emotions, and occur within a context of facial expression, posture, tone of voice" (1969, p. 120). Following Bowlby's lead, in my first book (Schore, 1994) I suggested that during attachment episodes of *visual-facial, auditory-prosodic, and tactile-gestural* affective communications, the primary caregiver regulates the infant's internal states of peripheral and central arousal:

> The infant's early maturing right hemisphere, which is dominant for the child's processing of visual emotional information, the infant's recognition of the mother's face, and the perception of arousal-inducing maternal facial expressions, is psychobiologically attuned to the output of the mother's right hemisphere, which is involved in the expression and processing of emotional information and in nonverbal communication. (p. 63)

In order to process these nonverbal communications, the infant seeks proximity to the mother, who in an optimal context must be subjectively perceived as predictable, consistent, and emotionally available. During dyadic attachment transactions, the sensitive primary caregiver's right brain implicitly attends to, perceives (recognizes), appraises, and regulates nonverbal expressions of the infant's more-and-more intense states of positive and negative affective arousal. This model was consonant with an early exposition of Porges's polyvagal theory, also in 1994, that posited the face and voice are powerful conduits through which safety is communicated between the mother and infant, and that "the right hemisphere—including the right cortical and subcortical structures—would promote the efficient regulation of autonomic function via the source nuclei of the brain stem" (Porges, Doussard-Roosevelt, & Maiti, 1994, p. 175).

In 2001, I expanded this model in an article in the *Infant Mental Health Journal*, "Effects of a Secure Attachment Relationship on Right Brain Development, Affect Regulation, and Infant Mental Health." In that work, I detailed the neurobiology of a secure attachment, an exemplar of adaptive infant mental health, and focused on the primary caregiver's psychobiological regulation of the infant's maturing right-lateralized limbic-autonomic circuits. I asserted, "adaptive infant mental health can be fundamentally defined as the earliest expression of flexible strategies for coping with the novelty and stress that is inherent in human interactions. This efficient right brain function is a resilience factor for optimal development over the later stages of the life cycle" (Schore, 2001a, p. 7). Linking that paper to the theme of this one, infant mental health describes the first expression of an enduring subjective sense of emotional well-being. The emergent right brain functions of emotional well-being are thus forged in optimal right brain-to-right brain attachment communications in the first 2 years of life. Since 2001, a large body of developmental neurobiological research supports the hypothesis that the attachment mechanism is embedded in infant-caregiver right brain-to-right brain affective transactions.

Confirming this model of the critical importance of right brain-to-right brain attachment communications in the progressive social experience–dependent lateralization of the right brain, neuroscientists now document that the right brain hemisphere is dominant in human infants, that the strong and consistent predominance for the right hemisphere emerges postnatally, and that the mother's right hemisphere is more involved than the left in emotional processing and mothering. Studying structural connectivity asymmetry in the perinatal brain with newborn infants *at the beginning of the first year,* Michael Meaney and his colleagues concluded,

> In early life the right cerebral hemisphere could be better able to process . . . emotion (Schore, 2000; Wada & Davis, 1977). This idea appears consistent with our findings of rightward asymmetry in . . . limbic structures. . . . These neural substrates function as *hubs in the right hemisphere for emotion processes and mother and child interaction.* (Ratnarajah et al., 2013, p. 193, italics added)

Tronick's studies of infants *in the middle of the first year* demonstrated that 6-month-old infants use left-sided gestures generated by the right hemisphere in order to cope with the stressful face-to-face still-face paradigm. They interpreted these data as being "consistent with Schore's (2005) hypotheses of hemispheric right-sided activation of emotions and their regulation during infant–mother interactions" (Montirosso et al., 2012, p. 826).

Using near-infrared spectroscopy, Minagawa-Kawai and colleagues' study of infant mother attachment *at the end of the first year* documented, "Our results are in agreement with that of Schore (2000) who addressed the importance of the right hemisphere in the attachment system" (2009, p. 289).

As the securely attached infant enters toddlerhood in the second year, his or her interactively regulated right brain visual-facial, auditory-prosodic, and tactile-gestural communications become holistically integrated, allowing for the emergence of a coherent right brain emotional and corporeal implicit self-system. As mentioned in the beginning of this chapter, an essential function of the right brain subjective self is to unconsciously generate a background sense of emotional well-being, an implicit sense of security that operates beneath levels of conscious awareness. Like myself, the preeminent Australian psychiatrist Russell Meares posits that "The right side of the brain seems to be more involved than the left in the creation of an 'inner,' emotionally laden experience," and that the right brain self-system generates "a *background state of well-being*" (2012, p. 296).

Ongoing neuroscience research continues to describe the adaptive socioemotional functions of the right brain. According to Decety and Chaminade, "self-awareness, empathy, identification with others, and more generally intersubjective processes are largely dependent upon . . . right hemisphere resources, which are the first to develop" (2003, p. 591). At all later stages of human development, "The neural substrates of the perception of voices, faces, gestures, smells, and pheromones, as evidenced by modern neuroimaging techniques, are characterized by a general right-hemispheric functional asymmetry" (Brancucci et al., 2009, p. 895). This rapid perception of emotional stimuli takes place within a social context. In an overview of brain laterality research, Hecht asserted, "Mounting evidence suggests that the right hemisphere has a relative advantage over the left hemisphere mediating social intelligence—identifying social stimuli, understanding the intentions of other people, awareness of the dynamics in social relationships, and successful handling of social interactions" (2014, p.1). Social relationships are also contexts for right brain-to-right brain interactive regulation. A large body of studies indicates that over the life span, the right, and not left, lateralized prefrontal regions are responsible for the most complex regulation of affect and stress (Cerqueira, Almeida, & Sousa, 2008; Czeh et al., 2008; Schore, 1994, 2003a, 2003b, 2012a; Sullivan & Gratton, 2002; Wang et al., 2005).

Furthermore, my work in neuropsychoanalysis suggests that the right brain represents the biological substrate of the human unconscious. Writing in the neuropsychoanalytic literature on "Emotions, Unconscious Processes, and the Right Hemisphere," Gainotti (2006) concluded,

> The right hemispheres subserves the lower "schematic" level (where emotions are automatically generated and experienced as "true emotions") whereas the left hemisphere the higher "conceptual" level (where emotions are consciously analysed and submitted to intentional control). (p. 71)

Note that emotional well-being involves the adaptive functions of both the cortical and subcortical levels of the right hemisphere. In accord with this model of emotional well-being, Greenberg (2007) cited my work in his description of a fundamental implicit affect regulatory process performed by the right hemisphere that rapidly and automatically processes facial expression, vocal quality, and eye contact in a relational (social) context. In light of the fact that the right hemisphere is dominant for the nonverbal, holistic processing of emotional information and social interactions (Decety & Lamm, 2007; Semrud-Clikeman, Fine, & Zhu, 2011), neuroscience thus suggests that the often used concept of "emotional well-being" is more properly characterized as "socioemotional well-being."

Secure attachment is defined not only by a sense of safety but also by a positively charged curiosity that fuels the burgeoning self's exploration of novel socioemotional and physical environments. According to McGilchrist (2009), at all points of the life span what is *new* must first be present in the right hemisphere before it can come into focus for the left. It begins in wonder, intuition, ambiguity, puzzlement, and uncertainty on the right. In 1965, Rachel Carson, author of the groundbreaking and transformative *Silent Spring*, wrote *The Sense of Wonder*. Emphasizing the central role of emotions in early childhood, she stated,

> A child's world is fresh and new and beautiful, full of wonder and excitement. . . . If a child is to keep alive his inborn sense of wonder . . . he needs the companionship of at least one adult who can share it, rediscovering with him the joy, excitement and mystery of the world we live in. I sincerely believe that for the child, and for the parent seeking to guide him, it is not half so important to know as to feel. If facts are the seeds that later produce knowledge and wisdom, then the emotions and the impressions of the senses are the fertile soil in which the seeds must grow. The years of early childhood are the time to prepare the soil. It is more important to pave the way for the child to want to know than to put him on a diet of facts he is not ready to assimilate." (pp. 42–45)

OPTIMIZATION OF EMOTIONAL WELL-BEING: PSYCHOTHERAPY, EARLY INTERVENTION, AND PREVENTION

In marked contrast to the earlier described optimal growth-facilitating attachment scenario, in a relational growth-inhibiting early environment of attachment trauma (abuse or neglect), the primary caregiver of an insecure disorganized-disoriented infant induces traumatic states of enduring negative affect in the child (Schore, 2001b, 2003b). This caregiver is too frequently emotionally inaccessible and reacts to her infant's expressions of stressful affect inconsistently and inappropriately (massive intrusiveness or massively disengagement), and therefore shows minimal or unpredictable participation in the relational arousal-regulating processes. Instead of modulating, she induces extreme levels of stressful stimulation and arousal, very high in abuse or very low in neglect. Because she provides little interactive repair, the infant's intense negative affective states are long lasting. This enduring state of emotional distress associated with early relational trauma and insecure attachment is in contrast to the enduring background state of emotional well-being associated with more secure attachment histories.

Regulation theory offers a coherent, heuristic, and clinically relevant theory of how attachment trauma alters human emotional and social development. In my early contributions to this effort, in 1994 I proposed that the mother-infant attachment relationship affects the developing right hemisphere *for better or worse* and can either facilitate resilience to stress (emotional well-being) or create a predisposition to emotional dysregulation and thereby psychopathology. In a companion article in the previously mentioned 2001 volume of the *Infant Mental Health Journal,* I suggested that intense and enduring stress created in high-risk contexts of *relational trauma* represented social environments that generated not attachment regulation but dysregulation, as well as little play and unpredictable or inconsistent interactive repair (Schore, 2001b).

Soon after in 2002, I published "Dysregulation of the Right Brain: A Fundamental Mechanism of Traumatic Attachment and the Psychopathogenesis of Posttraumatic Stress Disorder" in the *Australian and New Zealand Journal of Psychiatry.* In that work, I delineated how relational trauma in early critical periods of brain development imprints a permanent physiological reactivity of the right brain, a predisposition for the characterological use of pathological dissociation, and a susceptibility to later disorders of affect regulation expressed in a deficit in coping with future socioemotional stressors. This deficit in right brain functions is expressed as an inefficient capacity for emotional well-being and resilience, especially at moments of relational, social stress. Since then, I have continued to offer both clinical and research studies that articulate the early interpersonal neurobiological origins of all psychiatric and personality disorders (for my more recent theoretical and clinical work on trauma and dissociation, see Schore, 2009b, 2012a, 2013b).

Psychotherapy as a Relational Intervention That Promotes Emotional Well-Being

In my book *The Science of the Art of Psychotherapy,* I continued to elaborate an evidence-based clinical model that explicates the change mechanisms involved not only in reducing symptomatic behavior and negative cognitions, but also in promoting emotional well-being. Referring to patients with histories of relational trauma (borderline personality disorder), my colleague Russell Meares (2012) observed,

> The fundamental experience of self is a right-hemispheric affair . . . when right-hemispheric function is diminished, so also are those features associated with the overarching concepts of self, including inhibitory control and a *background state of well-being*. (p. 296, italics added)

My ongoing studies in regulation theory attempt to update treatment models of psychotherapy with developmentally traumatized patients. All personality and psychiatric disorders represent disturbances of right brain intersubjectivity and affect regulation. An essential clinical principle of working with relational trauma and severe disturbances of affect regulation is that the empathic therapist helps the patient to reexperience relational trauma in affectively tolerable doses in the context of a safe environment, so that the overwhelming traumatic feelings can be regulated and adaptively integrated into the patient's emotional life (see the chapter on enactment in Schore, 2012a). The focus of treatment is not on retrieving an explicit memory of attachment trauma in the first year, but on the effects of early relational trauma on evolving "character structure," and deficits in adaptive right brain functions.

In accord with a relational psychodynamic model of psychotherapy, right brain processes that are reciprocally activated on both sides of the therapeutic alliance lie at the core of the psychotherapeutic change process (J. Schore, 2012). Meares (2012) described "a form of therapeutic conversation that can be conceived . . . as a dynamic interplay between two right hemispheres." In these emotionally charged therapeutic encounters, the therapist's right brain visual-facial, auditory-prosodic, and tactile-gestural capacities for the nonverbal communication and regulation of the patient's emotional self-states are critical to the change process of psychotherapy (see Chapter 3 of Schore, 2003a). Ogden and colleagues (2005) concluded that the psychotherapy change mechanism is not in verbal language exchanges but in the empathic clinician's *background* implicit, psychobiologically attuned, interactive affect regulation, a relational context that allows the patient to safely contact, describe, and regulate his or her inner subjective experience.

In working with patients who present with early right brain attachment trauma, therapeutic expertise is expressed not so much in uncovering verbal content by left brain interpretations that promote cognitive understanding as much as the clinician's relational psychobiological capacities in implicit right brain emotional and social functions. My ongoing studies continue to suggest that change in trauma therapy is not an analytic left brain "talking cure" but a right brain "relational affect communicating and regulating cure" (for the latest update of this model, see Schore, 2014b, "The Right Brain Is Dominant in Psychotherapy," and J. Schore and A. Schore, 2014, "Regulation Theory and Affect Regulation Psychotherapy: A Clinical Primer"). Thus, effective affect regulation therapy with infant, child, adolescent, and adult patients can act as a growth-facilitating environment that alters the right brain, and thereby potentially promote a more secure sense of emotional well-being. Note, in line with current relational trends in psychotherapy, well-being is more than an intrapersonal intrapsychic function, but also an interpersonal intersubjective phenomenon.

Early Intervention, Prevention, and the Promotion of Emotional Well-Being

My most recent writings on the interpersonal neurobiology of attachment and brain development have emphasized that early intervention during the human brain growth spurt, a period of maximal neuroplasticity, can also optimize the development of right brain emotional well-being. Developmental neuroscientists are now concluding,

> The large increase in total brain volume in the first year of life suggests that this is a critical period in which disruption of developmental processes, as the result of innate genetic abnormalities or as a consequence of environmental insults, may have long-lasting or permanent effects on brain structure and function. . . . Although the first year of life may be a period of developmental vulnerability, *it may also be a period in which therapeutic interventions would have the greatest positive effect.* (Knickmeyer et al., 2008, pp. 12179–12180, italics added)

Congruent with this proposal, researchers studying the developmental neurobiological basis of human attachment are asserting, "Understanding the motivational basis for healthy and at-risk parenting may open new theoretical vistas and clinical opportunities and may lead to the construction of more specific interventions that can target disruptions to maternal-infant bonding at an earlier stage and in a more accurate manner" (Atzil, Hendler, & Feldman, 2011, p. 11). Toward that end, in an overview of the field I described an ongoing trend:

> Recent models of early life trauma are altering their focus from deficits in later maturing conscious, verbal, explicit and voluntary behavior, to impairments of early maturing nonconscious, nonverbal, implicit and automatic adaptive social emotional functions. Developmental neuroscience is now moving from studies of later maturing left brain conscious verbal cognitive processes into the early preverbal development of adaptive emotion processing right brain systems in pre- and postnatal periods. (Schore, 2010, p. 144)

This description of the paradigm shift applies equally to clinical assessments of the early origins of emotional disturbance as well as emotional well-being.

For some time, I have been putting forth the argument that the mental health field needs to move more deeply into early prevention programs anchored in developmental neuroscience, especially affective neuroscience (Schore, 2001c). Toward that goal, in a number of current publications in both the clinical and research literatures I use regulation theory as a guide for formulating early assessments of secure and insecure mother-infant attachment relationships (Schore, 2012a, 2013a, 2014b; Schore & Newton, 2012). The previously described temporal sequence of rapid, spontaneous, implicit visual-facial, auditory-prosodic, and tactile-gestural affective communications over the first year represents a source generator of evidence-based assessments of developing right brain functions. This early intervention also includes evaluations of the dyadic attachment relationship's increasing regulatory and intersubjective functions, and thereby the ontogeny of the infant's emotional well-being over that period. In parallel, I also apply the theory to the assessment of the early stages of autism, a neurodevelopmental disorder characterized by significant alterations of evolving social and emotional functions of the early developing right brain. These severe deficits are expressed as profound intersubjective disturbances in interactive affect regulation in autistic infant-mother dyads (Schore, 2013a, 2014a), a poor interpersonal context for the generation of an enduring subjective sense of emotional well-being.

At the beginning of this chapter, I described the excitement in developmental neuroscience around current studies on the impact of early maternal care on brain development, "one of the most important discoveries in all of science that have major implications for our field." The groundbreaking advances in our understanding of the science of early development have larger implications for cultural and political systems as well as for family law (Schore & McIntosh, 2011). In an editorial in the journal *Science*, "A Focus on Child Development," Silver and Singer (2014) described the wider economic implications of early brain research for the development of not only the individual but also the culture:

> Recent advances in neuroscience indicate the importance of healthy brain development in the early years to human capital formation. . . . Investing in child development is the foundation for improved health, economic, and social outcomes. Not getting the early years "right" is linked to violent behavior, depression, higher rates of non-communicable disease, and lower wages, and it negatively affects a nation's gross domestic product. (p. 120)

I would add that in the very earliest critical periods of child development, investing in "healthy brain development" can optimize the attachment-driven, experience-dependent maturation of the right brain and thereby maximize the relational origins of emotional well-being across larger numbers of individuals within any particular culture.

In a recent UNICEF (2013) report, "Child Well-Being in Rich Countries," the international authors described the essential importance of early intervention and prevention:

> It is perhaps no longer necessary to argue the case for the importance of the early years. Advances in both neuroscience and social science have repeatedly confirmed that it is at this time that genetic potential interacts in infinitely complex ways with early experience to construct the neural pathways and connections that quickly become both the foundations and the scaffolding for all later development. . . . It is therefore at this time that the child's *wellbeing, health and development* are most in need of society's concern and protection. (p. 34, italics added)

In light of the current paradigm shift across disciplines from behavior, to cognition, to bodily-based emotion, a society's support of early intervention and prevention programs should focus less on assessments of later evolving left brain executive functions and the development of cognitive and language skills and more on early evolving right brain social and emotional well-being.

CHAPTER 6

The Development of the Right Brain Across the Life Span

What's Love Got to Do with It?

OVER THE PAST THREE DECADES, my work in interpersonal neurobiology has incorporated basic discoveries of developmental neuroscience to offer heuristic and clinically relevant models of optimal early development and the dyadic origins of later social and emotional well-being and of non-optimal early development and the origins of a predisposition to psychiatric and personality disorders. Furthermore, I have attempted to integrate these new findings of developmental neuroscience into a theoretical perspective that can be accessed to more deeply understand these rapidly expanding bodies of scientific data, and then to apply pragmatic applications of the theory to the mental health field. Toward that end, regulation theory models how early socioemotional development indelibly affects the brain/mind/body change mechanisms that are expressed at later points in the life span, including the change mechanisms embedded within the psychotherapy relationship (Schore, 1994, 2012, 2014).

At the core of all of my work is the critical role of the first human relationship, the attachment relationship between the mother and infant. In 1994, at the very beginning of *Affect Regulation and the Origin of the Self: The Neurobiology of Emotional Development*, I asserted, "The understanding of early development is one of the fundamental objectives of science. The beginnings of living systems set the stage for every aspect of an organism's internal and external functioning throughout the life span" (Schore, 1994, p. 3). Over the course of my subsequent studies, I have offered interdisciplinary evidence that supports the basic developmental principle that during critical periods of brain development, the developing brain is malleable, and that the early relationship with the mother shapes the baby's brain *for better or for worse.*

In this expansion of regulation theory, I utilize the perspective of interpersonal neurobiology and the data from recent advances in neuroscience in order to shed light upon perhaps the most essential characteristic of the human experience, the ability of humans to love an other, an adaptive function that fundamentally affects every aspect of an organism's internal and external functioning throughout the life span. I will argue that the paradigmatic expression of how the mother shapes the baby's brain *for the better* is expressed in an early bond of mutual love, and that this growth-promoting early emotional experience acts as a relational matrix for the emergence of the capacity to share a loving relationship with a valued other at later stages of life. Although the humanities have a long history of exploring this deepest expression of the human heart and mind, the idea that the brain sciences can be used to explain the subtleties and depths of human love has been controversial. Many share the fear that a reductionistic science will reduce the complexities of love to a neural synapse or to a collection of neurochemicals. My ongoing interdisciplinary work on emotion, a central component of love, disputes this idea.

The *Shorter Oxford English Dictionary* defines love as "a state or feeling," "*deep affection, strong emotional attachment.*" This raises the matter of the relationship of love to attachment, especially in light of the transformational impact of the shift of modern attachment theory from behavior and cognition to affect and an emotional bond between intimate individuals (Schore & Schore, 2008). Love is defined as (1) a noun: a feeling of tenderness, passion, and warmth; and (2) a verb: to feel love for another person—actions including expressions of physical affection, tenderness, and acts of kindness. The first usage implies love as an intense intrapersonal emotion, the second as a strong interpersonal emotional communication. The contrast in these two definitions mirror the ongoing shift from a "one-person" intrapsychic to a "two-person" interpersonal perspective in psychology, including the most prominent theory in developmental psychology: attachment theory. To understand the attachment origins of the capacity to receive, feel, and express the emotion of love for another, we need to utilize the perspective of *interpersonal* neurobiology in order to elucidate the functional *and* structural development of the early bonds of *mutual* love.

The mutual love between a mother and her infant is embedded in an optimal co-created, reciprocal, bodily-based, emotion-transacting attachment relationship. For three decades, I have offered interdisciplinary evidence to show that over the course of the critical periods of human infancy, right brain-to-right brain mutual, reciprocal attachment communications indelibly shape the experience-dependent maturation of the infant's early developing right brain and thereby influence the trajectory of its evolving functions for all later stages of development. In this manner, the relational mechanism of mutual love, "*strong emotional attachment*," is mediated by the mother's right brain interacting with the infant's right brain (Schore, 1994).

On the matter of a centrality of a mother's love, I would go as far as to say that most if not all mothers have the conscious intention of loving their babies. Yet one of the major findings of science is that many of the underlying processes involved in love operate at rapid time frames, unconsciously, at levels beneath awareness. For this reason, the relational psychobiological mechanisms that underlie mutual love can best be described by integrating observations and data from neurobiology and psychoanalysis, the science of unconscious processes. Toward that end, rather than describing love as an ideal mental state, I will suggest that love is embedded in a basic evolutionary mechanism located in the early developing emotion-processing right brain. A central purpose of this chapter is to describe the structural and functional ontogenetic development of this evolutionary system, much of which takes place at nonverbal bodily-based levels. In light of modern conceptions of nature-nurture interactions, I will describe how a loving early beginning can optimally epigenetically shape the basic evolutionary processes that are expressed in human infancy.

In the following sections of this chapter, I will utilize the dynamic bodily-based perspective of regulation theory in order to interpret a significant body of neuroimaging research on love in infancy and adulthood in order to more deeply understand the right brain attachment origins and underlying psychoneurobiological mechanisms of the capacity to form and maintain a strong emotional bond of mutual love. After an introduction and background, I will discuss recent developmental neuroimaging and conceptualizations of mother's love, a model of the initial emergence of mutual love at 2–3 months, and then recent adult neuroimaging and conceptualizations of adult love. In the final section, "The Right Brain and Mutual Love across the Life Span," I will integrate the research and clinical data to model the neuroanatomy, neuropsychology, and neuropsychoanalysis of this essential marker of what it means to be human.

INTRODUCTION AND BACKGROUND

Although love is mostly thought to be the province of the arts, poets and writers, actors, dancers, and musicians, from the very beginnings of modern biology and psychology, science has also explored its origins and emotional expressions. Indeed in his seminal work *The Expression of Emotions in Man and Animals*, Charles Darwin proposed, "The emotion of love, for instance that of a mother for her infant, *is one of the strongest of which the mind is capable*. . . . No doubt, as affection is a *pleasurable sensation*, it generally causes a gentle smile and some brightening of the eyes. A *strong desire* to touch the beloved is commonly felt" (1872/1965, pp. 224–225, italics added). Specifically referring to the origins of perhaps this most essential expression of the human species, he speculated, "The movements of expressions in the face and body . . . serve as the first means of communication between the mother and her infant; she smiles approval and thus encourages her child on the right path or frowns disapproval" (p. 385).

At the end of the 19th century, Sigmund Freud (1895/1953) began his pioneering studies in psychoanalysis and initiated the field's long history of interest in the essential role of love in human function and dysfunction. Referring to his evolving position on the developmental origins of love, I've suggested, "Although for much of his career [Freud] seemed ambivalent about the role of maternal influences in earliest development, in his very last work he stated, in a definitive fashion, that the mother-infant relationship "is unique, without parallel, established unalterably for a whole lifetime as the first and *strongest love-object* and the *prototype of all later love relations* (Freud, 1940/1964)" (cited in Schore, 2003a, p. 256, italics added)

Perhaps more than any of Freud's followers, Donald Winnicott studied the deepest origins of the capacity to love. He observed, "The early management of an infant is a matter beyond conscious thought and deliberate intention. It is something that becomes possible only through love" and that the mother "by expressing love in terms of physical management and in giving physical satisfaction enables the infant psyche to begin in the infant body" (Winnicott, 1975, p. 183). Thus, the early origins of love are expressed in the mother-infant experience of mutuality, and in this primordial context of mutual love, "The main thing is a communication between the baby and mother in terms of the anatomy and physiology of live bodies" (Winnicott, 1986, p. 258). Furthermore, Winnicott (1963) described two forms of love in the developing infant. "Quiet love" (Figure 6.1) is seen in moments when the mother holds and handles (soothes, comforts, caresses) the infant (for a visual representation, also see Figure A.7 in Schore, 2003). "Quiet love" has been characterized as "a mutual

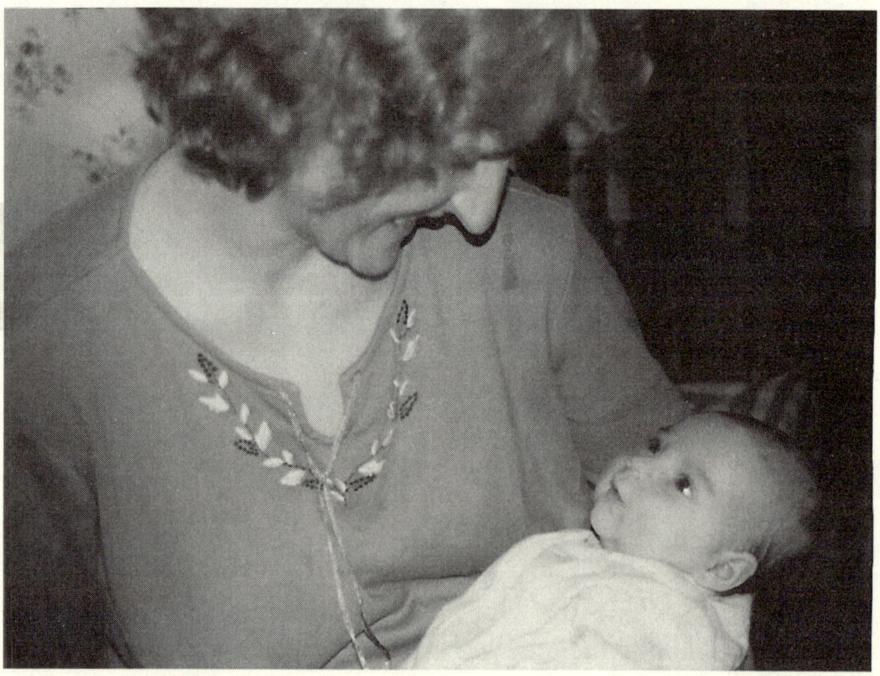

FIGURE 6.1 Quiet love. Courtesy of Sharon Austin.

dwelling of baby and mother where one and one make not two but one" (Ulanov, 2001, pp. 49–50). On the other hand, "excited love" occurs in moments of thrilling excitement and intense interest in interaction with the mother and contains an energetic potential (also see Figure 6.3 in Schore, 1994). As opposed to the "soothing" qualities of left cradling, right cradling is associated with the "arousing" emotional state of the "exciting" mother (Reissland, 2000). Indeed this author proposes that "mothers might, consciously or unconsciously, vary the side they cradle their child depending on whether they try to arouse or soothe the infant (p. 185).

In the middle of the past century, another of Freud's followers, John Bowlby (1953), began his seminal writings on what would become attachment theory in *Child Care and the Growth of Love.* In that volume, he asserted that a mother's love in infancy and childhood is as important for mental health as are vitamins and proteins for physical health. Following

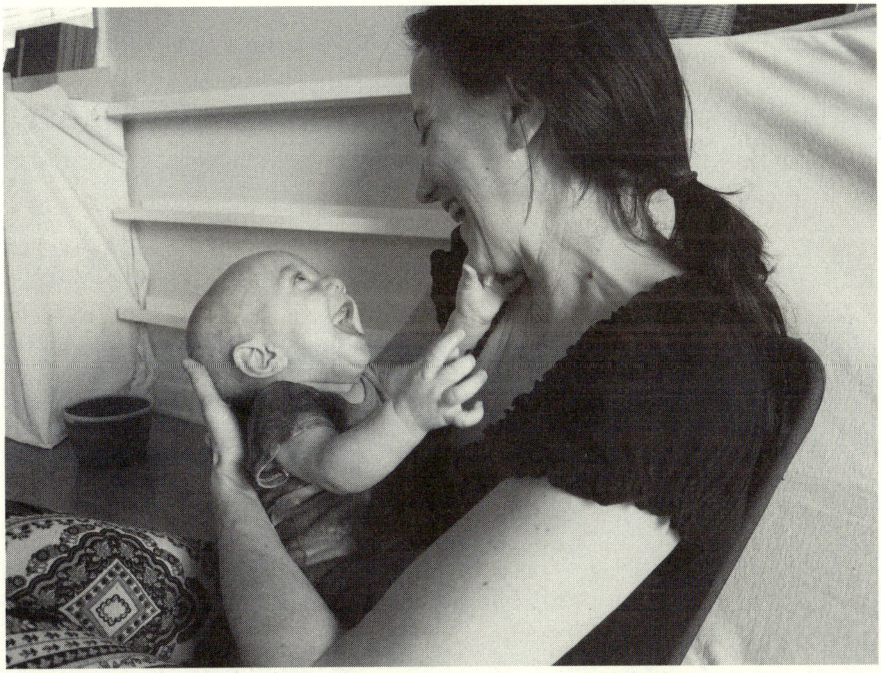

FIGURE 6.2 Excited love. Courtesy of Ruth Anne Hammond.

this explicit association of the origins of attachment and love, Ainsworth (1967) offered her classic *Infancy in Uganda: Infant Care and the Growth of Love*. In his later writings, Bowlby concluded, "Many of the most *intense emotions* arise during the formation, the maintenance, the disruption, and the renewal of attachment relationships. The formation of a bond is described as falling in love, maintaining a bond as loving someone, and losing a partner as grieving over someone" (1969, p. 130).

Also in mid-century, another of Freud's disciples, Erich Fromm, wrote the classic *The Art of Loving*, in which he described love as "the experience of union with another being" and "becoming one with another." In that volume, Fromm described what he deemed to be the central problem in individual development: "What meaning—in both women as well as men—does our longing for a mother have? What constitutes the bond to the mother?" (1956, pp. 26–27). He stated that motherly love is an unconditional affirmation of the child's life and needs, and that it is expressed in two different aspects:

> One is the care and responsibility absolutely necessary for the preservation of the child's life and his growth. The other aspect goes further than mere preservation. . . . Motherly love, in this second step, makes the child feel: it is good to have been born; it instills in the child the *love for life* and not merely the wish to remain alive. . . . Mother's love for life is as infectious as her anxiety. (pp. 46–47, italics in original)

Note the overlap between maternal "care" and Winnicott's "quiet love" and between Fromm's maternal support of the child's love for life and Winnicott's "excited" love that contains an energetic potential.

At about the same time, the humanist psychologist Abraham Maslow ranked "love and belongingness needs" in the middle of his motivational hierarchy and asserted that "belongingness needs do not emerge until food, hunger, safety, and other basic needs are satisfied, but they take precedence over esteem and self-actualization" (1968, p. 497). He also posited that "beloved people can be incorporated into the self" (1968, p. 103). Simultaneously another prominent psychologist, Harry Harlow (1958), contributed

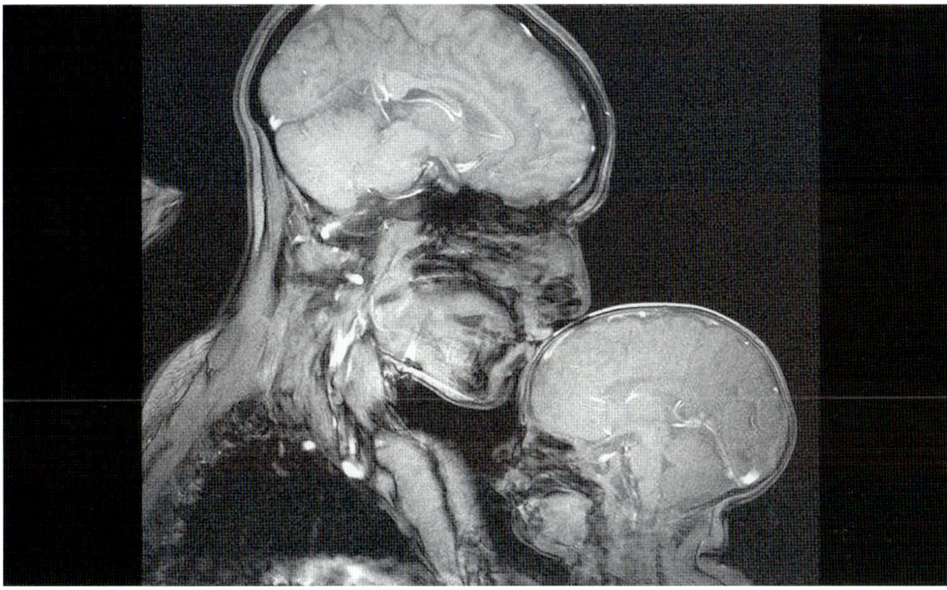

FIGURE 1.2 Mother and child in an MRI scanner. From Rebecca Saxe and Atsushi Takahashi | Department of Brain and Cognitive Sciences, MIT | Athinoula A. Martinos Imaging Center at the McGovern Institute for Brain Research, MIT.

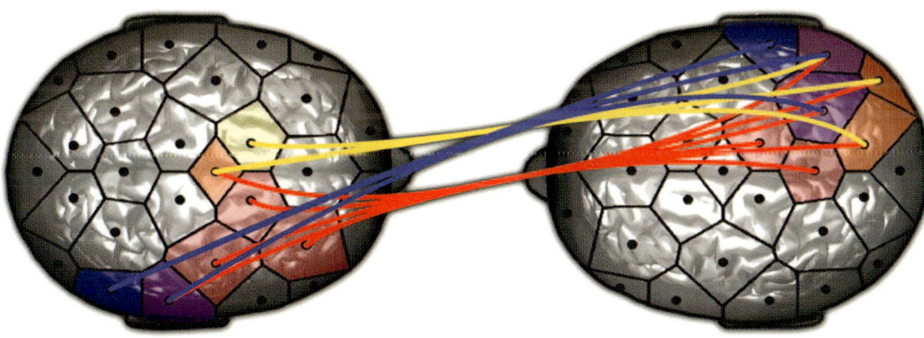

FIGURE 1.3 Right-lateralized interbrain synchronization of a spontaneous nonverbal communication. Adapted from "Toward a Two-Body Neuroscience" by Dumas (2011). Copyright 2011 by Landes Bioscience. Adapted with permission. See insert for color.

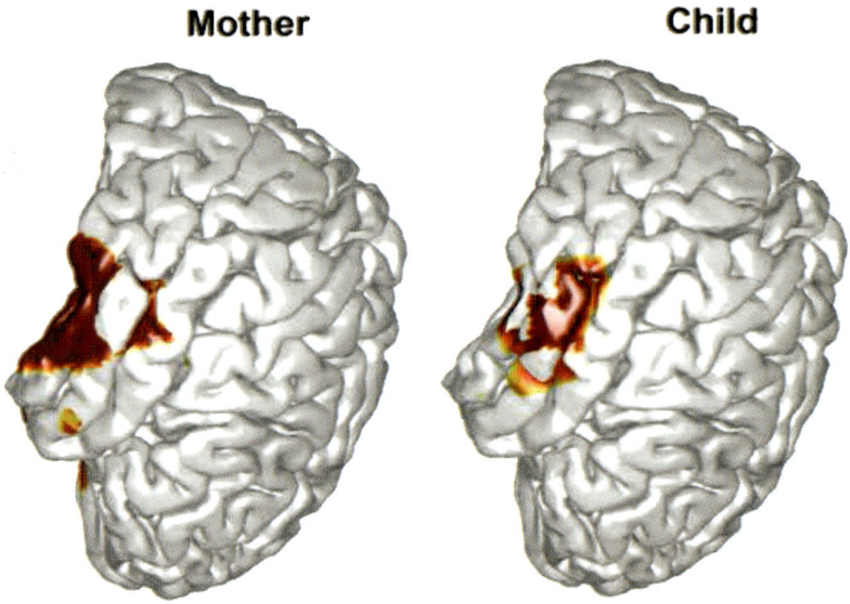

FIGURE 1.4 Brain responses of mother and child to vignettes of their interactions probing social synchrony. The brain responses of the child (right panel) and the mother (left panel) to episodes of own social synchrony were expressed in the right superior temporal sulcus. From Jonathan Levy et al. Perception of Social Synchrony Induces Mother-Child Gamma Coupling in the Social Brain. SCAN (2017) 12 (7): 1036-1046.

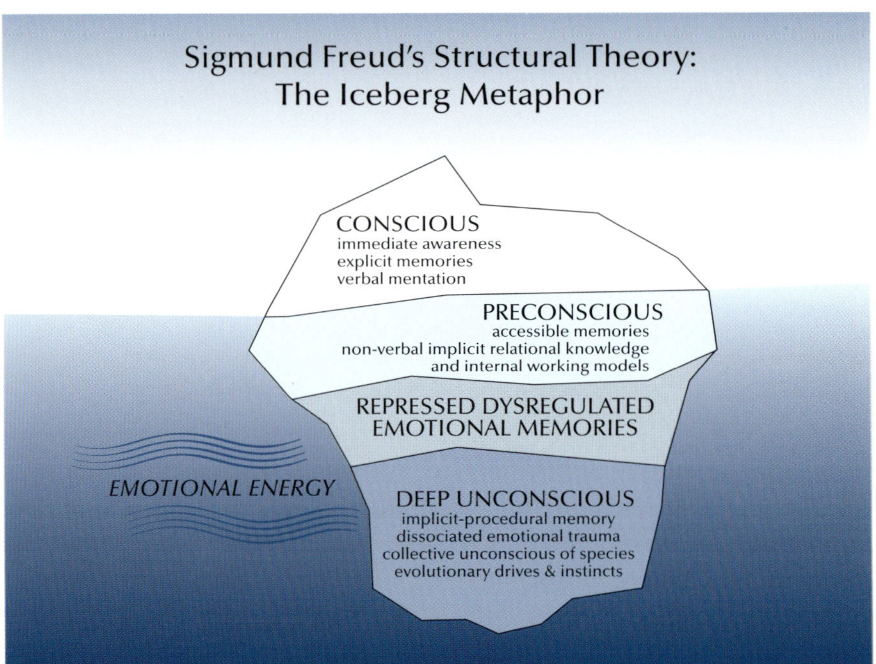

FIGURE 1.6 Revised update of Freud's iceberg metaphor.

an influential article, "The Nature of Love," in which he offered an overview of the field at the middle of the 20th century:

> Love is a wondrous state, deep, tender, and rewarding. Because of its intimate and personal nature it is regarded by some as an improper topic for experimental research. . . . Psychologists, at least psychologists who write textbooks, not only show no interest in the origin and development of love or affection, but they seem to be unaware of its very existence. . . . We know little about the fundamental variables underlying the formation of affectional responses and little about the mechanisms through which the love of the infant for the mother develops into the multifaceted response patterns characterizing love or affection in the adult. (p. 673)

Indeed, further advances in the scientific study of love, like emotions in general, were not available to science until the 1990s. In that decade, emotion finally became investigated by both researchers and clinicians. This period also began to forge links between brain and emotion, and in particular three neuroscientists began to offer models of the association of love and specifically the right brain. In his 1989 classic *The Triune Brain in Evolution,* Paul MacLean offered neurobiological studies indicating that in mammalian attachment transactions, the infant's thalamocingulate limbic system expresses emotional signals processed in the loving mother's right brain. In these intense emotional moments, the baby's expressions excite proprioceptive inputs that activate the mother's right postcentral and parietal regions, while auditory stimuli from the sounds of the baby's cooing and babbling are conveyed by her left ear to the right primary auditory area and the adjoining region of the temporal association cortex. He concluded, "For the mother the experience during pregnancy of the formless life within, could become after birth a sense of exteriorization and extension of the self that physiologically derives to a large extent from the right hemisphere" (MacLean, 1996, p. 435).

Also in the early 1990s, Rhawn Joseph proposed that two right-lateralized components of the limbic system, the amygdala and anterior cingulate, "are primary in regard to the development and maintenance of long-lasting social and emotional attachments . . . it is presumably the interaction of these limbic nuclei (coupled with the neocortex) that give rise to attachment and bonding behavior" (1990, p. 266). In *The Right Brain and the Unconscious,* he asserted that "The infant and child must experience love and nurturance, or the limbic nuclei will not develop normally" (1992, p. 133), and that "The right amygdala appears to be more greatly affected by early rearing experiences" (p. 132).

In this same period, I began to publish my own studies of the impact of early attachment on the early developing right brain. In my first book (Schore, 1994), I set forth the argument that the right orbitofrontal cortex acts as the control center of attachment, earlier described by Bowlby (1969). Expanding this model in my second book, *Affect Dysregulation and Disorders of the Self,* I offered the heuristic proposal, "The infant's right brain is tuned to dynamically self-organize upon perceiving certain patterns of facially expressed exteroceptive information, namely the visual and auditory stimuli emanating from the smiling and laughing joyful face of a *loving mother*" (2003a, p. 147). In concordance with MacLean and Joseph, I presented evidence showing that over the course of the first year, mutual emotional exchanges of interactively regulated heightened affective moments are imprinted into the amygdala, insula, cingulate, and orbitofrontal areas of the infant's developing right brain. I thus concluded, "the visual image of the *loving mother's* positive emotional face as well as the imprint of the mother's regulatory capacities are inscribed into the circuits of this lateralized prefrontal system" (p. 278).

Building upon the long-standing tradition of scientific interest in the development of love, in this chapter in the following sections I will discuss recent neuroimaging research on the effects of this "strong emotional attachment" on brain development in both infancy and adulthood. A large body of studies clearly demonstrate that at all stages of the life span, an attachment relationship that supports a loving emotional bond between two individuals is optimized when it is reciprocal and mutual. Overviewing attachment dynamics in adulthood, Baumeister and Leary emphasized "how important it is that caring, concern, and affection be *mutual and reciprocal*" and concluded, "Apparently, love is highly satisfying and desirable only if it is *mutual*" (1995, p. 514, italics added).

At present, a number of psychological and biological disciplines are experiencing a paradigm shift into a relational psychology and a relational brain (Schore, 2012). In parallel, both researchers and clinicians are moving from investigations of love as an emotional state within an individual to mutual love between two individuals. This shift is manifested in the study of love within a single mind/brain in a solitary context to mutual love that is communicated to a valued other in a relational context. That said, in both the intrapersonal and interpersonal perspectives, love is conceptualized as an intense emotion, indeed "one of the strongest of which the mind is capable," which when shared by another forms an "intense emotional union." All emotion is composed of two dimensions: valence (positive-negative, pleasant-unpleasant, approach-avoidance of discrete emotions) and arousal (intensity, energy, calm-excited). Furthermore, left-hemispheric activity is associated with moderate levels of cortical arousal, while right-hemispheric activity accompanies either high or low levels of cortical arousal. Shared right brain states of reciprocated mutual love thus generate the most intense states of emotional arousal and positive affects in the human experience.

A central thesis of this chapter dictates that all forms of mutual love arise from early affective experiences of mother-infant mutual love, and that these first appear at about 2–3 months. Furthermore, I suggest that mutual love in the very earliest and all later stages of development is expressed in two separate functional systems, Winnicottian "quiet love" and "excited love." In terms of regulation theory, the calming and soothing, dyadic context of "quiet love" represents the down-regulation of strong negative affect from a high-arousal, *sympathetic-dominant energy-expending state* to a low-arousal, *parasympathetic-dominant energy-conserving psychobiological state* expressed in comfort and relief from stress. "Quiet love" associated with left cradling represents Porges' (2011) ventral vagal system in the nucleus ambiguous of the right brain that is preeminent in the regulation of state by social engagement, as well as in the right-lateralized regulation of emotion and autonomic activity.

Furthermore, left cradling, an "unconscious" (Jones, 2014) attachment mechanism within "the first relationship" (Stern, 1977) imprints the critical period growth of circuits in the experience-dependent maturation of the socioemotional right brain in the perinatal and postnatal stages of infancy.

In earlier writings (Schore, 2012) I have suggested that attachment transactions directly influence the "early life programming of hemispheric lateralization and synchronization" (Stevenson et al., 2008, p. 852). I now suggest that left cradling and its bias for right hemispheric left visual field processing of human faces acts as an evolutionary mechanism by which the early social environment drives the epigenetic lateralization of various subcortical and cortical systems within critical periods of the developing right brain.

Indeed, there is now convincing evidence that left-sided cradling is associated with the functions of the right cerebral hemisphere (Sieratzki, & Woll, 1996; Reissland, 2000, Bourne & Todd, 2004; Huggenberger et al., 2009, Hendriks, van Rijswijk, & Omtzigt, 2011; Forrester et al, in press), especially in the emotional functions (including love). According to Suter and her colleagues (2007),

> the right hemisphere is superior in decoding of facial expressions and emotional stimuli. Cradling the baby on the left side in the left visual field therefore enhances the processing of its facial expressions and affective signals, resulting in an enhanced mother-child communication and monitoring of the infant's well-being. Yet, not only is the decoding of signals of the infant by its mother facilitated, but the child also has the advantage of being able to monitor the left side of its mother's face, which is more expressive than the right side (p. 16).

According to Manning et al. (1997) the tendency of mothers to cradle the infant on their left side "facilitates the flow of affective information from the infant via the let ear and eye to the center of emotional decoding, that is, the right hemisphere of the mother" (p. 327). I refer the reader to the photograph of the right-lateralized interbrain synchronization of left-cradling "quiet love" in Figure 6.1.

On the other hand, "excited love" that contains an energetic potential represents a transition into a regulated high-arousal, mutually accelerating, sympathetic-dominant energy-expending emotional state, expressed in expanding joy and excitement (see Figures 6.3 and 6.4 in Schore, 1994).

In other words, Winnicott's "quiet love" describes the down-regulation of intense, negatively valenced emotional arousal into a positively valenced calm, intensely pleasant state, while "excited love" describes the up-regulation of emotional arousal into an intensely positive excited and joyful state. Ultimately, "quiet love" and "excited love" need to be integrated in the personality structure.

Throughout the life span, these intense, nonverbal embodied expressions of the human heart are generated by subcortical limbic-autonomic circuits of the right brain, which are imprinted in the attachment relationship. Love between the mother and infant in early critical periods thus shapes the trajectory of development of the right brain in the later stages of life. All forms of the "extraordinary affect state" of mutual love share common activations of right-lateralized cortical-subcortical circuits that generate extremes of arousal, including amygdala, insula, cingulate, and orbitofrontal areas of the right brains of both members of a loving dyad. Mutual love can be understood as the interactive regulation of a shared, strong positive affective state that results from right brain-to-right brain resonance and amplification of intense emotional arousal. These evidence-based developmental models of mutual love that evolve from regulation theory are grounded in clinical studies and neurobiological research of the past century, and yet they are heuristic and testable in the current century's emergent neuroimaging research, which I shall now describe.

RECENT MATERNAL NEUROIMAGING AND CONCEPTUALIZATIONS OF MOTHER'S LOVE

In 2000, Arthur Janov published the scholarly tome *The Biology of Love,* in which he cited my work to argue that the right side of the brain acts as the hemisphere of love. Three years later, Sue Gerhardt (2004) offered *Why Love Matters. How Affection Shapes a Baby's Brain.* Also incorporating my work, she set forth the proposition that love is essential to brain development in the early years of life, particularly to the development of social and emotional brain systems. Beginning in this same year, a number of international neuroscience laboratories began to publish neuroimaging studies of love in mother-infant (as well as adult romantic) dyads. These new functional magnetic resonance imaging (fMRI) studies, carried out on four continents, now added to a large body of interdisciplinary research on the structural and functional development of the infant brain. Much of this infant imaging continues to focus on the infant brain's perceptual processing of maternal visual-facial, auditory-prosodic, and tactile-gestural communications. Many of these studies utilize not just static pictures but dynamic videos or auditory recordings of an infant's own mother.

In parallel to these infant investigations, over the same 10-year period there was a surge in maternal brain imaging. These studies attempted to maximize ecological validity using experimental stimuli that have real-world adaptive significance and subjective value to the mother. Instead of using photographs of mothers' babies, many use videos instead of images of static faces. Current neuroimaging research demonstrates that videos of both positively and negatively valenced social interactions directly activate right-hemispheric circuits (Semrud-Clikeman et al., 2011). Furthermore, the methodology usually includes scanning the mother's brain response to not just a generic infant face but to her infant's face. None of the studies utilize a psychological attachment assessment, but do describe "healthy mothers," whom I would assume to be securely attached to their infants. Most important, many also include a measure of the mother's subjective responses to their own infant's interpersonal cues. Note that hard science is not only attending to objective data but also carefully documenting subjective responses of the mother responding to her infant's attachment cues.

In a groundbreaking seminal study, "The Neural Correlates of Maternal and Romantic Love," Bartels and Zeki (2004) announced,

> The tender intimacy and selflessness of a mother's love for her infant occupies a unique and exalted position in human conduct . . . it provides one of the most *powerful motivations for human action*, and has been celebrated throughout the ages—in literature, art and music—as one of the most beautiful and inspiring manifestations of human behavior. (p. 1155, italics added)

In order to study "the long-lasting and pervasive influence of maternal love (or its absence) on the development and future mental constitution of a child," they offered an fMRI study of mothers viewing pictures of their own children's faces (as early as 9 *months*). They posited that this attachment cue would be associated with activity in cortical and subcortical sites in the mother's brain.

Bartels and Zeki reported that the "*extraordinary affect state*" of maternal love triggers activation in mother's lateral orbitofrontal cortex, medial insula, anterior cingulate, and fusiform cortex. Interpreting these data, they stated the lateral orbitofrontal cortex is activated by pleasant visual, tactile, and olfactory stimuli (such as the face of a mother's infant), while the anterior cingulate suggests "a potential link to the mother's feelings of empathy and urge to care for her infant" (p. 1163). Activation is also seen in the mother's insula while she is experiencing a subjective state of love for her infant. They noted this area is involved in the "gut feelings" of emotive states and in "limbic touch" that evokes pleasant feelings and regulates emotional, hormonal, and affiliative responses to caress-like, skin-to-skin contact between individuals (Olausson et al., 2002). Maternal love is also associated with heightened activity in cortical areas, the fusiform gyrus that reads facial expressions and increases attention to faces, as well as in subcortical ventral tegmental dopamine neurons associated with "highly rewarding experiences."

But Bartels and Zeki also pointed out that deactivations of brain areas are also important, as emotions are the product of both increases and decreases of activity in specialized regions. Deactivation is seen more in the right hemisphere, including in the mesial prefrontal cortex, the parietotemporal junction, and the temporal poles involved in "mentalizing" or "theory of mind." Note the deactivation of these cognitive functions during the subjective experience of maternal love. A second area in the temporal pole and amygdala indicates maternal love deactivates negative emotion, aggression and fear. They concluded, "Our findings of consistently activated and deactivated regions with attachment may be indicative of a fine balance between activity states of these regions that needs to be maintained to ensure a healthy social interaction" (2004, p. 1164).

The same year, Nitschke and colleagues (2004) published "Orbitofrontal Cortex Tracks Positive Mood in Mothers Viewing Pictures of Their Newborn Infants." In their introduction, they describe the subjective state of maternal love:

> Positive affect elicited in a mother toward her newborn infant may be one of the *most powerful and evolutionarily preserved forms of positive affect in the emotional landscape of human behavior*. . . . One form of positive emotion . . . is the affect that arises in a mother's relationship with her infant. Whereas reward paradigms capitalize on approach tendencies and pursuit of an appetitive goal, the form of positive emotion in maternal attachment is better characterized by warmth, nurturance, joy, and fulfillment. (p. 583, italics added)

Nitschke and colleagues documented that while a mother was in the scanner viewing photos of her own *3- to 5-month-old infant*, "Most mothers report *extremely strong* pleasant emotions when interacting with or thinking about their infants" (2004, p. 584). While observing a picture of their smiling infant (never before seen photo), mothers described their subjectivity as "loving" and "motherly." In this emotional state, the mother shows signal changes within the orbitofrontal cortex that linearly tracks "the *intensity* of positive emotions that may underlie maternal attachment. . . . The present study extends this work by highlighting the role of the orbitofrontal cortex in the representation of attachment-related positive affect (Bowlby, 1982)" (p. 590) (see Schore 1994, 2000, on orbitofrontal cortex as the control center of attachment). They concluded that individual differences in maternal orbitofrontal responses to positive stimuli "may have important relevance for happiness and well-being as well as clinical implications" (p. 590).

In the same year, Ranote and colleagues scanned mothers looking at videos of their own (vs. an unknown) *4- to 8-month-old infant*. They reported activation in the mother's brain in her right anterior inferior temporal cortex (involved in facial emotional recognition and expression) and right occipital gyrus (involved in visual familiarity), "consistent with previous findings reporting right sided effects of . . . face processing" (2004, p. 1827). Activation was also seen in the mother's amygdala. Noting a significant recent change in neurobiological conceptions of the amygdala, they stated, "The amygdala is commonly associated with the processing of fearful and unpleasant emotional stimuli, but has also been shown to play a part in processing of happy expressions of facial emotion" (p. 1828). Confirming a right-lateralization effect, they concluded, "In healthy new mothers, the viewing of own infants elicited activation in the ventral visual processing stream and cerebellum. This was more marked on the right and extended to polar temporal cortex. This is consistent with previous findings reporting right sided effects of visual object recognition and face processing" (p. 1827).

Continuing this emerging line of research, Leibenluft and colleagues offered an fMRI study of mothers looking at photographs of their 5- *to 12-year-olds*. Viewing one's own child activates amygdala, insula, anterior paracingulate cortex, and posterior superior temporal sulcus: "These activations may reflect . . . *intense attachment*" (2004, p. 225). Again, note all fMRI researchers commenting on the heightened energetic intensity of the mother's positive affective state. Strikingly, Leibenluft and colleagues reported that this strong response is seen in specifically the mother's right amygdala. They also cited studies showing amygdala activation in not only fear but also positive states, as well as during autonomic arousal and the imitation of facial expressions. Indeed, these data "suggest that mothers process the faces of children in a manner that differs in important ways from the manner in which they process the faces of adults" (p. 231). Speculating upon the mother's subjective state, they proposed, "The activations seen in this study may reflect the mixture of intense attachment and vigilant protectiveness that characterizes the maternal relationship but not . . . other close personal relationships" (p. 229).

Four years later, Noriuchi, Kikuchi, and Senoo published "The Functional Neuroanatomy of Maternal Love: Mother's Response to Infant's Attachment Behaviors" in *Biological Psychiatry.* They boldly asserted, "Maternal love is one of the most *powerful* motivations for the maternal behaviors of mothers to care for and protect their infants" (2008, p. 415). Furthermore, "Maternal love is essential for maternal behavior in which the mother makes sacrifices that are necessary to care for her infant day and night. Loving the infant is the dynamo that empowers her to maintain never-ending vigilance and sustain exhausting toil for the protection and nurture of her infant" (p. 418).

In this study, mothers of *16-month-old infants* were shown two videos of infant attachment behavior. In the first situation, the infant was smiling while playing with his or her mother, and in the second video, the infant was asking for her while being separated from his or her mother. Note this use of both a separation situation and a play situation parallels infant studies in the psychological sciences of evaluating attachment as maternal up-regulation of positive states and down-regulation of negative states. In the video of the play context, the smiling mother blew bubbles toward her infant, while in the video of separation context, the mother leaves the room and the infant is left alone "unduly distressed," crying and calling for mother. Noriuchi and colleagues noted, "While mothers may feel joyful by watching video clips of their own infant in the first situation, they may feel anxious and protective when shown video clips of their own infant in the second situation" (2008, p. 415). They posited maternal love and "strong emotional attachment" would be invariant regardless of whether the mother was expressing affectionate behavior or vigilance and protectiveness, the latter being "a *biologically essential mechanism for preservation of the human species*" (p. 415).

While watching the videos in the scanner, fMRI results indicated maternal love activates the mother's anterior insula, which is involved in "processing caress-like touch between individuals and is thought to be important for affiliative behaviors between the mother and infant" (Noriuchi and colleagues, 2008, p. 419). Maternal love also increased activity in the mother's right inferior frontal gyrus that recognizes her infant's facial expressions while viewing her infant's attachment behavior, calling for his or her mother. In this way, "the infant's attachment behaviors in the video stimuli were thought *to touch its mother's heart*, in which she felt her own infant's dynamic facial expressions and actions realistically" (p. 419, italics added). Note the reference to maternal autonomic functions.

In another important finding, Noriuchi and colleagues reported that maternal love is associated with activation of the mother's periaqueductal gray and right anterior cingulate, areas "involved in maternal response to infant's pain of separation" (2008, p. 421). They interpreted this as indicating the mother is paying attention to her infant, who is expressing strong attachment behaviors, and that she recognizes her infant's emotional and mental *states evoked by separation from herself.* They therefore concluded, "Positive emotions such as love and motherly feeling coexisted with negative ones such as anxious feeling and worry in the mother herself. In this complicated situation, the mother's emotional responses to her own infant might be appropriately regulated by monitoring her own emotional states and by inhibiting her excessive negative affects so as not to show negative expressions to her infant who is in distress" (pp. 422–423). Note the emphasis on the autoregulation of negative states in a loving, secure mother and also her ability to hold ambivalent feelings for the loved infant (see Schore, 1994, 2012).

In line with the earlier cited studies, Noriuchi and colleagues documented that maternal love activates the mother's right orbitofrontal cortex, which regulates both positive and negative affect. They stated that the orbitofrontal cortex plays an important role in the positive reward system (it receives ascending dopamine projections from the ventral tegmental area), and at the same time its activation reflects the selection of appropriate strategies for the mother to reduce the negative distress of her infant. This finding fits nicely with my ideas about the right orbitofrontal system encoding strategies of positive and negative affect regulation in the mother's internal working model of her relationship with her infant. In summary, they concluded, "the amount of love with which a mother interacts with her infant is highly influential on the stability of the mother-infant relationship and the quality of the mother-infant attachment" (2008, p. 415).

One year later in the journal *Cerebral Cortex*, Minagawa-Kawai and colleagues (2009) offered a near-infrared spectroscopy (NIRS) study of *12-month-old* infants responding to movies of their own mothers' smiling expressions and of the mothers watching movies of their own infants playing, and the authors also rated the mothers' emotional mood from 0 to 6 (6 = "most loving"). Note the age is the same as that in the classical attachment measure, the "strange situation." The infants showed activation in the right orbitofrontal cortex that is stronger when viewing their own mothers' smiles. On the other hand, mothers looking at their own infants also showed activation in the right orbitofrontal cortex. The authors speculated that if a mother shows higher right frontal activation in response to her infant, then her infant could also show larger activations as a result of his or her mother's stronger affection probably observed in their daily life. The authors noted that the orbitofrontal cortex both encodes and regulates the attachment system and that at 1 year of age, infants share similar neuronal functions with their mothers. With respect to the lateralization effect, they stated, "Our results are in agreement with those of Schore (2000) who addressed the importance of the right hemisphere in the attachment system" (p. 289). Thus, the attachment functions of the right orbitofrontal area develop within the social world between the caretaker and their infant. They concluded, "This type of emotional regulation is also a fundamental social skill to extend infants' social involvement beyond kinship and friendship, including *love*" (p. 291, italics added).

More recently Barrett and colleagues (2012) have reported an fMRI study demonstrating the importance of the mother's subcortical amygdala response to the facial affective signals of her *3-month-old infant*, the youngest age of these neuroimaging studies. Referring to the emotional parenting tasks specific to this early postpartum period, they noted that giving birth and becoming a mother is a "profound experience":

> Over the course of pregnancy and throughout the postpartum period, changes in levels of certain hormones likely influence the function of key brain regions to increase the likelihood that a mother is attracted to her baby, is attentive and sensitive to her baby's needs, learns from her experiences, and behaves appropriately . . . the early postpartum period is an inherently emotional and challenging time, associated with both *positive and negative affect*." (p. 253, italics added)

At 3 months postpartum, mothers viewed and affectively responded to photos of their own and unfamiliar infants' positive and negative facial expressions. Repeating the finding of other laboratories, Barrett and colleagues reported that mothers were more responsive to their own infants than to unfamiliar infants, for both positive and negative infant faces. On the basis of their observation that maternal responses to negative faces consisted of a mixture of positive and negative affect, they suggested that "an infant face does not have to be overtly 'happy' in order to function as a positive stimulus for mother" (2012, p. 263).

Neuroimaging data showed that although a number of areas of the mother's brain are activated while viewing photos of her own 3-month-old infant, two areas stand out to be centrally involved in maternal responsiveness: the anterior cingulate cortex and the basolateral amygdala and its connections to the temporal pole. Activation of a mother's right anterior cingulate by her infant's negative face (crying or fussing) reflects greater maternal distress. In line with the previously discussed studies on the role of the amygdala in positive emotions, Barrett and colleagues reported an increased maternal amygdala response by mothers to their infants' smiling faces that was associated with "positive feelings and attachment" and "more pro-social aspects of maternal responsiveness, feelings, and experience." Notably, this greater amygdala response was associated with "(1) lower maternal anxiety, lower parental distress, and fewer symptoms of depressed mood, and (2) more positive attachment-related feelings about her infant" (2012, p. 263).

INITIAL EMERGENCE OF MUTUAL LOVE AT 2–3 MONTHS

Note that the age of the infants cited in these neuroimaging studies spans 3–16 months. In fact, the choice of beginning these studies of maternal love at 3 months may be grounded in the emergence of dyadic, intense emotional interactions at this very time. Supporting this idea, developmental psychoanalysis and developmental psychology have long described the importance of the 2- to 3-month transition. In classic research, Stern (1985) described the transition from an early forming "emergent self" at birth into a "core self" at 2–3 months. He observed, "At the age of two to three months, infants begin to give the impression of being quite different persons. When engaged in social interaction, they appear to be more wholly integrated. It is as if their actions, plans, affects, perceptions, and cognitions can now all be brought into play and focused, for a while, on an interpersonal situation" (p. 69). With the onset of this emergent developmental function, the subjective social world is altered and interpersonal experience operates in a different domain, a domain of core-relatedness. He concluded that at this stage, the infant participates in shared "observable interactive events" involved in "bridging the infant's subjective world and the mother's subjective world" (p. 119), and that now "There are many ways being with an other can be experienced . . . such as merging, fusion . . . symbiotic states" (p. 100). Recall Trevarthen's (1979) protoconversation and primary intersubjectivity also emerge at 2–3 months, suggesting the onset of mutual love in association with primary intersubjectivity.

Confirming the 2- to 3-month transition, Miall and Dissayanake documented, "Over time, mothers subtly adjust their sounds and movements to what the baby seems to want (or not want), and to its changing needs and abilities. They gradually move from the gentle, cooing reassurance of the first weeks to trying to engage the baby in increasingly animated mutual play. At 8 weeks utterances and facial expressions have become more exaggerated, both in time and space" (2003, p. 342). In another study of this critical period of change of infant face, voice, and gesture, Dissanayake (2001) asserted,

> It should also be emphasized here that although mothers "talk" to their babies, the multimodal messages in early interactions are nonverbal. What mothers convey to infants are not their verbalized observations and opinions about the baby's looks, actions, and digestion—the ostensible content of talk to babies—but rather positive affiliative messages about their intentions and feelings: You interest me, I like you, I am like you, I like to be with you, You please me, I want to please you, You delight me, I want to communicate with you, I want you to be like me." (p. 91)

In the context of intense affect, these are the first communications of maternal love. More recently, Ammaniti and Galesse (2014) reported,

> From the second month after birth, parents and infant begin to show a temporal structure in their interactions. . . . In this period, the sharing of social gaze between parent and baby is the expression of coordinated interactions, which can occur between 30% and 50% of the time. At the same time, mutual gaze can be integrated with parents' and infants' affectionate touch. . . . At around 3 months, parents tend to touch their baby in an affectionate way and infants tend to respond with an intentional affectionate touch. (p. 147)

Note the increases of the mother's loving touch that emerge at this time period. On the other side of the loving dyad, Feldman and her colleagues describe increases in the child's expression of "affective touch" and "unintentional touch," an indicator of the free-floating closeness between mother and child (p. 1095).

During this same interval, the emotional bond between mother and infant is strengthened in the close physical contact and affectionate dyadic interactions that occur during infant breast-feeding. This interpersonal neurobiological context is associated with increased parasympathetic nervous system modulation and reduced stress and negative affect in both members of the dyad (Mezzacappa & Katlin, 2002). Mothers show increased touching, gazing, and affectionate responses during feeding, all associated with parasympathetic modulation, a form of "*quiet love.*" An fMRI study of breast-feeding at 3–4 months showed activation in the mother's right superior frontal gyrus and amygdala associated with increased maternal sensitivity (Kim et al., 2010).

In another publication, Feldman and colleagues offered a study of interaction synchrony between mothers and their 3-month-old infants during face-to-face interactions of free play. The authors described these "*intense moments within attachment relationships*: "during episodes of high positive arousal—for instance, *moments of vocal or affective synchrony which are accompanied by high positive energy*—the tightness of this biological synchrony increased . . . moments of social attunement without a rise in positive arousal, did not increase biological synchrony" (2011, p. 575, italics added). Note the characterization of a mutual state of "*high positive energy*" corresponds to an expression of "*excited love*" that contains "*an energetic potential*" in the mother and 3-month-old infant.

Integrating the studies in this section, I propose that the primordial expression of mutual love first appears at 2–3 months. In heightened moments of affect synchrony, vitality affects are amplified by interpersonal resonance, generating shared moments of intense positive arousal. In dyadic episodes of interactive repair, the contingently responsive mother who has misattuned to the infant's negative state adaptively psychobiologically re-attunes in a timely manner, thereby sharing states of down-regulated intense negative arousal. The loving mother now interactively regulates both states of sympathetic "excited love" and parasympathetic "quiet love," allowing the infant to begin to integrate these two differently embodied affective psychobiological states. These dual patterns of synchronized face-to-face, right brain-to-right brain state sharing occur in critical periods of the early developing right brain (Ratnarajah et al., 2013; Schore, 1994, 2012), and thus experiences of mutual love structuralize Stern's "core self" that appears at 2–3 months.

Furthermore, I suggest that the 2- to 3-month transition represents the onset of a critical period of experience-dependent maturation in the developing right-lateralized limbic system. In other writings, I have proposed that connections between the right basolateral amygdala and the right anterior cingulate—a corticolimbic structure associated with responsivity to social cues—come online, giving the infant greater capacities for intersubjectivity and for receiving nonverbal communications of caregiver interactive regulation (Schore, 2014b). Supporting this critical-period idea, research indicates that brain development in neonates is most rapid in the first 3 months, when the brain increases growth by 64% (Holland et al., 2014), and that the total number of cortical neurons in the human brain increases by 23% to 30% from birth to 3 months (Shankle et al., 1999).

Most intriguingly on the other side of the infant-mother dyad, research documents neuroplastic structural changes in the mother's brain during this same early postpartum period (Kim et al., 2010). This longitudinal study of the mother's brain by Kim and colleagues included two time points: 2–4 weeks postpartum and 3–4 months postpartum, and therefore over the onset of mutual love, 2–3 months. During this period, gray matter in the mother's brain increases in specifically her right insula, hypothalamus, anterior cingulate, and amygdala, as well as in the reward-associated mesolimbic dopamine nuclei in the substantia nigra. The authors concluded that interactions with the infant induce these structural changes, which are expressed in functional increases of maternal motivation and sensitivity to infant cues. Indeed, they reported these structural changes at 3–4 months "were predicted by a mother's positive perception of her baby at the first month postpartum. Thus, the mother's positive feelings for her baby may facilitate the increased levels of gray matter" (2010, p. 698, italics added). This clearly implies that the mother's intense positive feelings of love for her developing baby are associated with subsequent changes in her own brain.

These infant and maternal neurobiological data can be interpreted within the framework of interpersonal neurobiology's central principles that the structure and function of the mind and brain are shaped by experiences, especially those involving synchronized emotional relationships, and that brains align their neural activities in social interactions. This suggests an alignment between mother and infant right brain cortical-subcortical limbic-autonomic circuits during intense, strong, loving emotional transactions. At 2–3 months, the onset of mutual love, when the mother is falling in love with her baby, her right basolateral amygdala and anterior cingulate are undergoing neuroplastic reorganization, at the very same time when her infant's right basolateral amygdala and anterior cingulate are in a critical period of growth. During critical periods, genetic programs in specific brain regions significantly increase synthesis and methylation of DNA, the rate of which is epigenetically influenced by the social environment (Schore, 1994). In an overview of the emerging field of behavioral epigenetics, Miller described "the importance of a loving mother" (2010, p. 24, italics added). I suggest that from its relational onset in early infancy to all later points of the life span, mutual love, "the experience of union with another being," induces increases in the emotion-processing limbic system on both sides of any loving dyad, whether they be parent-infant, adult romantic, or intimate friendships.

MUTUAL LOVE IN EARLY AND LATE INFANCY AND THE INTERPERSONAL ORIGINS OF ADULT LOVE

The co-creation of mother-infant mutual love, a bond of "deep affection, strong emotional attachment," represents the expression of an instinctual evolutionary mechanism that is continually activated over the stages of human infancy and beyond. Although it emerges at 2–3 months, the loving mother's right brain-to-right brain up-regulation of positive and down-regulation of negative intense emotional arousal continues to shape the child's right subcortical-cortical circuits over the human growth spurt of the first 2 years of life. Across the stages of infancy, the infant's amygdala, anterior cingulate, and orbitofrontal cortex enter into critical periods of growth that are sensitive to and imprinted by events in the socioemotional environment (Schore, 2003, a,b; 2014b). In *intensely charged* synchronous affective communications of mother-infant love, the infant's right-lateralized limbic-autonomic system learns how to perceive and respond with *heightened perceptual awareness* to the mother's *spontaneous* facial, auditory, olfactory, and somesthetic affective expression (to consciously "take in" the look, sound, smell, and feel of the mother's love). In this manner the ongoing mother-infant attachment relationship acts as growth-facilitating intersubjective matrix of the adaptive capacity to enter into a shared state of mutual love with a valued other.

During the next developmental transition from infancy to toddlerhood, play behavior expands significantly. Research shows that at ten to thirteen-and-a-half months, a significant increase in positive emotion accompanies the neo-toddler's rapid neuromuscular development, gross motor ability, and upright locomotion. In the second year the mother switches from a mirroring object to a socialization agent, setting limits, and creating a context for the child's emerging autonomy (Schore, 1994). Fromm (1956) observes, "the real achievement of motherly love lies not in the mother's love for the small infant, but in her love for the growing child" (p. 47). The Danish philosopher Soren Kirkegaard described the attuned mother's support of the toddler's exploration and emerging autonomy:

> The loving mother teaches her child to walk alone. She is far enough from him so that she cannot actually support him, but she holds out her arms to him. She imitates his movements, and if he totters, she swiftly bends as if to seize him, so that the child might believe that he is not walking alone . . . and yet, she does more. Her face beckons like a reward, an encouragement. Thus, the child walks alone with his eyes fixed on his mother's face, not on the difficulties in his way. He supports himself by the arms that do not hold him and constantly strives towards the refuge in his mother's embrace, little supposing that in the very same moment that he is emphasizing his need for her, he is proving that he can do without her, because he is walking alone. (p. 462)

Over the stage of toddlerhood mother-infant "quiet" and "excited" mutual love epigenetically shape the right brain subjective self's capacity to empathically share an intensely embodied bond of emotional arousal with other humans than the mother, such as the father (see Schore, 1994). And yet in intensely emotional moments in the second year, the infant's early developing right hemisphere (Gupta et al., 2005), which is dominant over the course of human infancy (Chiron et al., 1997), continues to be imprinted by the output of the mother's right hemisphere, which is dominant for "emotional processing, and thus mothering" (Lenzi et al., 2009, p. 1131). This right brain-to-right brain interpersonal neurobiological mechanism continues to activate limbic-autonomic emotional circuits in later right brain growth spurts in childhood, adolescence, and adulthood (Thatcher, 1994, 1997), thereby allowing "the emotional brain" to develop to more complexity and "higher forms" of mutual love.

The bidirectional communications of embodied love between the mother and her infant is thus the developmental source of all later forms of sympathetic-dominant "excited love" (exhilaration or romantic infatuation) and parasympathetic-dominant "quiet love" (tender intimacy, spirituality). Indeed, there is now consensus from both developmental and adult researchers that "the biological basis of parental and romantic attachment share similar mechanisms" (Weisman, Feldman, & Goldstein, 2012, p. 533). This body of research is actively studying the commonalities of mutual love across the life span. Ammaniti and Gallese (2014) offered an evocative portrayal of Stern's model of the similar interpersonal expressions of love in early and later development:

> As Daniel Stern has written, expressions of love begin early in an astonishing way. Mother and child behavior overlaps with the behavior of two lovers. For example, mother and child look at each other without speaking, hold a physical closeness with faces and bodies in constant contact, display alterations in vocal expressions or synchrony of movements, and perform particular gestures like kissing each other, hugging, touching, and taking the face or the hands of the other. . . . When parents speak to their child, or lovers talk with one another . . . they emphasize the musicality of the words instead

> of the meaning, they use baby talk, and they express a wide range of nonverbal vocalizations. . . . Facial expressions assume a special register also, altering and emphasizing the facial mimic. There is also a choreography in the movements of mother and baby, like those of two lovers; *they move in synchrony, getting closer and more distant on the basis of a common rhythm.* (pp. 110–111, italics added)

Note the description of common right brain nonverbal facial, prosodic, and gestural expressions and right-lateralized interbrain synchronization of mutual love in both intimate relational contexts. These observations are confirmed by longitudinal developmental psychological research demonstrating that maternal sensitivity during the first 3 years of life is associated with "effectiveness of romantic engagement" during adulthood (Raby et al., 2015, p. 695).

In their seminal neuroimaging research Bartels and Zeki (2004) argued that maternal and romantic love share a crucial evolutionary purpose and a similar biological function; namely, the maintenance and perpetuation of the species, and thereby similar brain circuits. Alluding to "excited love," these authors noted that in both, attachment bonds are associated with "the power of love to motivate and exhilarate" (p. 1155). In an overview of more recent neuroimaging studies of the parental brain, Swain (2011) described essential "emotional circuits" in specifically the amygdala, cingulate cortex, orbitofrontal cortex, insula, and ventral tegmental dopaminergic reward area that support maternal parenting via "subcortical memory" that activates the expression of "caring impulses." Mutual love represents a context for an intense expression of "caring impulses" over the life span. The cortical and subcortical limbic circuits, especially right amygdala functions in extreme arousal and reward and therefore intense affective states, is expressed as a source of all later forms of "excited" and "quiet" love.

Following Freud's (1940/1964) speculation that the mother-child relationship is the prototype of all later love relations, Stern (1985) hypothesized that the early evolving "core self" is expressed in moments of "excited love" at later stages of life. Note his description of the "core self" in adulthood parallels Winnicott's "excited" love as thrilling excitement and intense interest in interaction: "The sense of being with an other with whom we are interacting can be one of the *most forceful experiences* of social life. . . . Falling in love provides a normal example. Lovers are not simply preoccupied with one another. The loved other is often experienced as an almost continual presence, even an aura, that can change almost everything that one does—heighten one's perception of the world or reshape and refine one's very movements" (Stern, 1985, p. 100, italics added). In parallel writings in the social psychological literature, Baumeister and Leary asserted that across the life span, interpersonal attachment bonds are associated with positive emotions, and that "the prototype of relationship formation is the experience of falling in love, which is typically marked by periods of *intense bliss and joy, at least if the love is mutual*" (1995, p. 305, italics added). Integrating this with the preceding sections on early development, I propose that early "excited love" of increased energetic potential evolves to intense, high-arousal romantic love and infatuation.

Neuroimaging studies now confirm this. Aron and his colleagues offered an fMRI study of individuals who are "intensely in love." Describing the state of "exited love," they observed, "Romantic love is . . . associated, particularly in early stages, with specific physiological, psychological, and behavioral indices. . . . These include emotional responses such as euphoria, *intense focused attention* on a preferred individual, obsessive thinking about him or her, emotional dependency on and craving for *emotional union* with this beloved, and *increased energy*" (2005, p. 327, italics added). In this state, activation is seen in subcortical dopamine-rich areas associated with reward and motivation, specifically the right (and not left) ventral tegmental area and the right postero-dorsal body and medial caudate nucleus. Amygdala activity was decreased, suggesting love reduces fearful responses. Notably, activity related to the length of the relationship was found in the right insula, the right anterior and posterior cingulate cortex, and the right posterior retrosplenial cortex.

This laboratory subsequently continued their study of "early stage *intense* romantic love" in female Chinese students (Xu et al., 2011). The students viewed photographs of the faces of their beloved while in the scanner, and the authors reported increases of activity in the right mid orbitofrontal cortex and decreases in the amygdala. Activity in the right subgenual area and right superior frontal gyrus was associated with subjective ratings of high relationship happiness at 18-month follow-up, suggesting that the more intensely rewarding a relationship is in its early stage, the more likely it will continue to be rewarding in later stages. Replicating this lab's earlier work (Fisher et al., 2002), they documented significant activation in the right ventral tegmental midbrain dopaminergic system. In that very first work, these authors also described "quiet love," in which the attachment system is associated with the maintenance of close proximity and intimacy. "In humans, adult male-female attachment (often called 'companionate love') is . . . characterized by feelings of calm, security, social comfort, and emotional union" (Fisher et al., 2002, p. 414). Unfortunately, no fMRI studies have been specifically done on the later stages of love and deep intimacy, and none have included a parallel measure on shifts of autonomic function.

That said, it is generally accepted that at the most fundamental level, early attachment experiences epigenetically shape the individual's capacity for functioning in close proximity to another; that is, the adaptive emotional capacity to share an intimate subjective state with a valued other. Porges and Carter concluded, "Although the brain retains plasticity and adaptability throughout life, early experience may set the parameters for that plasticity. Attachment may be said to set up social and emotional homeostasis, *designing future patterns for intimacy.* Emotional homeostasis resides in the subcortical brain structures and their links to cortical structures, all of which are shaped in early life" (2010, p. 13, italics added). The *Shorter Oxford English Dictionary* defines "intimate" as "of or pertaining to the inmost nature or fundamental characteristic . . . proceeding from concerning or relating to one's deepest thoughts or feelings." Reis and Shaver (1988) define intimacy as a process of an escalating reciprocity of self-disclosure in which each partner feels that his or her innermost self is validated, understood, and cared for by the other.

This mutual self-disclosure is more than verbal, mental, and conscious, it is nonverbal, intersubjective, and physiological, at levels beneath conscious awareness, and is expressed in tender loving moments of "union with another being." Recall, as opposed to the sympathetic dominant state of "excited" mutual love between mother and infant, "quiet" mutual love represents a shared interactively regulated transition in both from a sympathetic to a parasympathetic dominant state. Early experiences of "quiet" love evolve to the shared intimacy, deep warmth, and emotional union that characterizes all extremely close relationships. Bromberg (2011) terms this quiet form of intimacy as "The Nearness of You" after Hoagy Carmichael's and Ned Washington's lyrics.

Developmental researchers report similar patterns of affectionate touch between mother and infant, and conclude "children growing in the context of nonrestricted loving physical closeness appear to give more touch to their caregivers, a tendency likely to be internalized and transferred to significant others throughout life" (Feldman et al., 2004, pp. 1095–1096). In a more current developmental psychophysiological study of this earliest stage of mother-infant interaction, Feldman and colleagues observed, "the early experience of such *intense moments* within attachment relationships sets the possibility that *close relationships, throughout the life span*, may integrate the individual's affective state and physiological systems into an interpersonal event that affords the online coordination of physiological and social processes between two individuals within an attachment bond" (2011, p. 575). In other words, moments of intense intimacy of "quiet" mutual love involve a synchronized down-regulation of the autonomic nervous system. Shared moments of self-exposure and vulnerability in episodes of "quiet" mutual love may create the relational context for Fromm's (1956) description of "becoming one with another" and "the experience of union with another being." As mentioned earlier, Winnicottian "quiet love" has been characterized as "a mutual dwelling of baby and mother where one and one make not two but one" (Ulanov, 2001).

Also recall Maslow's (1968) proposal that "beloved people can be incorporated into the self." Baumeister and Leary suggested that "love aspires to a mutual dissolving of personal boundaries, leading to an egalitarian merging into a new whole" (1995, p. 522). This aspect of close relationships has been most extensively investigated by the psychological research of Elaine and Arthur Aron, authors of some of the neurobiological studies I cited earlier. They asserted, "The model treats love (the desire for a relationship with a particular other) as arising from a desire to expand the self by including that other in the self, as well as by associating expansion with that particular other" (E. Aron & A. Aron, 1996, p. 45). This enlargement of the self is mutual, and not at another's expense. They posited that in addition to love being emotional, it is also fundamentally motivational, and that love involves a motivation of expansion toward a state of wholeness and integration. They further suggested that a love experience will not expand the self if it cannot be integrated. Neurobiologically, this occurs in the "integrated self" that Kuhl, Quirin, and Koole (2015) locate in the right brain.

This conception of mutual love is consonant with the earlier developmental section of this chapter on the role of interpersonal resonance and reciprocal arousal amplification in intensely loving interactions, on the internalization of a neural representation of the mother interacting with the infant that is imprinted into the developing brain, and on the importance of the developing right brain's capacity to integrate dyadic experiences of "quiet" and "excited" love. I suggest that in adulthood, the sympathetic-dominant "excited love" of the earlier stage of romantic attachment and the parasympathetic-dominant "quiet love" of later stages of an intimate relationship must be integrated in order to form an adaptive capacity to be able to co-participate in both forms of mutual love. Throughout the life span, intensely positive and negative emotional experiences shared with a highly valued intimate other are internalized into the deeper levels of the right brain subjective self-system, thereby expanding a sense of self-integration. As in early development, these processes of expansion and integration occur mostly at levels beneath levels of conscious awareness. Recall Joseph's (1992) groundbreaking volume, *The Right Brain and the Unconscious.*

In my ongoing work in developmental neuropsychoanalysis, I continue to offer evidence to show that the loving mother's up-regulation of positive and down-regulation of negative emotional arousal imprints the right brain, the psychobiological substrate of human unconscious (see Schore, 2012, for recent updates). During its critical period of development of the deep levels of the psyche—the unconscious—the resonant and amplified and thereby intense emotional energy shared within the loving mother-infant dyad structuralizes the infant's evolving right brain unconscious. This allows the developing unconscious to attain more structural coherence and thereby more functional complexity. In a further progression of regulation theory, I suggest that at all points of the life span, in any heightened affective moment of mutual love, two deep unconscious systems are communicating, synchronizing, resonating, and co-regulating each other.

The ability to recognize right brain-to-right brain strong facial, visual, auditory, tactile, and olfactory signals of love from an other involves unconscious processes of perception and implicit memory. Forster, Epstude, and Ozelsel described "subtle or even unconscious reminders of love" (2009, p. 1479). The adaptive capacity to receive and express these intense regulatory signals of mutual love operates at rapid time frames and thereby unconscious levels. It is now established that the unconscious processing of emotional information is mainly subsumed by a right hemisphere subcortical route (Gainotti, 2012). In other words, at all later Eriksonian stages, the interpersonal signals of love are first perceptually processed unconsciously, automatically, effortlessly, at levels beneath conscious awareness, and they trigger changes in emotional arousal and internal state that produce the "neuroendocrine chemistry" of mutual love. Ultimately, these psychobiological experiences are incorporated into right brain autobiographical memory as what Ortigue and colleagues (2007) term an "unconscious representation of a loved one" that expands the self.

THE RIGHT BRAIN AND MUTUAL LOVE ACROSS THE LIFE SPAN

At the beginning of this chapter, I proposed that love is now conceptualized as an intense emotion, indeed one of the strongest of which the mind is capable, which when shared with an other forms an "intense emotional union." Utilizing the perspective of regulation theory, I proposed an interpersonal neurobiological model that attempts to shed further light on the related problems of how the adaptive capacity of human love first evolves in infancy and the psychoneurobiological mechanism by which a mother's love directly influences the right brain and right mind of an individual over the course of a lifetime. I suggested that during the critical periods of human infancy, the primordial expressions of mutual love are expressed in right brain-to-right brain reciprocal attachment communications between the loving mother and her developing infant. This seminal context of mutual love is expressed in two neurobiologically distinct motivational systems, "quiet love" and "excited love." Furthermore, I hypothesized that at all later developmental stages, the "strong emotional attachment" of mutual love activates extremes of arousal in the right-lateralized limbic system, especially the amygdala, insula, anterior cingulate, and orbitofrontal cortex of the right brains of both members of a loving dyad.

In his classic volume, Bowlby (1969) speculated about an attachment "biological control system" that regulates the limbic system and is structured as a "hierarchical mode of organization." Following this idea, I have suggested an ontogeny of this emotion-processing system in which a number of discrete limbic components come online and develop connectivity in a defined sequence in the first year (Schore, 2003, 2012). The model proposes that the neuroanatomy of the limbic system is characterized as a series of hierarchically organized "control systems" or "hubs" in the right amygdala, right anterior cingulate, and right orbitofrontal cortex (Schore, 2003a,b, 2012a, 2014). During their sequential critical periods of neurobiological maturation, ongoing mother-infant experiences of the "extraordinary affect state" of mutual love optimally imprint the connectivity of these subcortical and cortical circuits of the limbic system, thereby allowing for the emergence of an efficient and resilient socioemotional right brain.

Earlier I cited Joseph's (1992) speculations that in order for the limbic system to develop normally, the infant must experience love and nurturance, and that the right amygdala is greatly affected by early rearing experiences. Recent research confirms this. Olsavsky et al. (2013) document "a role for the amygdala in the dyadic and intense interaction between mother and child . . . in recognizing affective salience of the primary caregiver" (p. 2103). Todd and Anderson (2009) asserted that socialization tunes the amygdala in early development. These authors stated that the amygdala "is responsive to positive and arousing rather than to strictly negative events," and that it plays a central role in "regulating interpersonal distance." They observed that "People automatically regulate the distance between themselves and others on the basis of feelings of personal comfort," and referred to "invisible social force fields that regulate *close physical proximity*, suggesting that the amygdala is crucial for the sense of interpersonal space . . . the amygdala should be more active at *close interpersonal distances*" (p. 1217, italics added). In light of the documented facts that the right amygdala initiates an ultra-rapid high-speed detection of unconscious stimuli (Costafreda et al., 2008), and is associated with "subjective emotionality" (Ally, Hussey, & Donahue (2013), throughout life this aspect of mutual love is expressed at subjective levels beneath conscious awareness. As the previously discussed neuroimaging studies of both infants and adults indicate, the amygdala is centrally involved in all forms of very close relationships that share intense emotional states. I would add that the basolateral amygdala, which has extensive connections with the ventral tegmental area, regulates mesolimbic dopamine that activates the intensely positive reward states in mutual love.

A central theme running throughout this chapter dictates that the social context for the intergenerational transmission of the capacity to experience love in later life is embedded in the mutual love of the mother-infant attachment relationship. The accepted principle that "the biology of maternal behaviour is influenced by mothers' past and current experiences" (Barrett et al., 2012, p. 252) clearly implies that the mother's early experience with her own mother affects the manner in which she interactively regulates her infant. Furthermore, an interpersonal neurobiological perspective suggests that the early expressions of mutual love indelibly shape the experience-dependent maturation of the infant's early developing right brain, especially its emotion-processing subcortical and cortical limbic-autonomic circuits, and thereby influence the trajectory of its evolving functions over the life span. In other words, an early experience of "deep affection" with an intuitive loving mother enhances and optimizes the structural development of the right brain and its evolving functional expression in subsequent later Eriksonian stages of life.

In parallel to and consonant with my own work on the implicit, subjective self (Schore, 1994, 2003a,b, 2012), neuroscientists and social scientists are now delineating the adaptive functions of the right brain. For example, De Pisapia and colleagues demonstrated its involvement in "interpersonal competence," which encompasses "the capacity to interact and communicate with others, to share personal views, to understand the emotions and opinions of others, and to cooperate with others or resolve conflict should it occur" (2014, p. 1257). Hecht offered research indicating its involvement in "social intelligence": "Identifying social stimuli, understanding the intentions of other people, awareness of the dynamics in social relationships, and successful handling of social interactions" (2014, p. 8). More specifically, it supports trust, affiliation, empathy, fairness, and gratitude, all of which are manifestations of mutual love. Kuhl and colleagues depicted the essential operations of the right brain "integrated self": emotional connectedness, broad attention and vigilance, utilization of positively and negatively valenced felt feedback, unconscious generation and regulation of emotions, integration of negative experiences, extended resilience, and basic trust, which "develops during the first months of life in interaction with the primary caretaker" (2015, p. 125). These right brain functions are activated in all close, intensely emotional, intimate relationships.

According to Baumeister and Leary, "people seem to need frequent, affectively pleasant or positive interactions with the same individuals, and they need these interactions to occur in a framework of long-term, stable caring and concern" (1995, p. 520). Such interactions include both states of "excited" and "quiet" love, which are stored in different right brain implicit-procedural memory systems and must ultimately be integrated. All forms of mutual love, deep and lasting friendships, long-term romantic relationships, or shared, intimate spiritual connections involve a right brain-to-right brain reciprocal intersubjective context that implicitly communicates and interactively regulates strong positive and negative bodily-based affective states. Social science research now indicates that "invisible support" "under the radar" without full awareness is enacted between romantic partners in spontaneous face-to-face interactions (Howland & Simpson, 2010), and that this implicit and not explicit support provides the strength of a close relationship (Bolger & Amarel, 2007). The interpersonal neurobiological mechanisms of resonance and amplification of intense emotional arousal allow both members of all close relationships to experience the strongest subjective emotional states, and thereby to intersubjectively share with a valued other the intense pleasure and pain that accompany the most emotionally significant aspects of human life. This "experience of union with another being" in turn co-creates a subjective state of not only safety and trust, but also self-expansion, wholeness, and integration in both partners of a loving pair bond. The pursuit of mutual love is thus a major motivational system expressed from the early beginnings to the final stages of life.

Tying together the developmental and adult contexts, the psychoanalytic psychiatrist Daniel Stern (2004) described the special state of integrated assembly of feelings, behaviors, and thoughts that are associated with the intersubjective context of falling in love. Note the references to right brain nonverbal processes:

> Following are some of the elements of falling in love that are driven by an intersubjective motive (many of these are shared both by lovers and by parents with their young babies): Lovers can look into each others eyes, without speaking, for minutes on end—a sort of plunging through the "window of the soul" to find the interior other. . . . There is also an exquisite attention to the other's attentions and feelings, not only to read them correctly but even to anticipate them. There is a playfulness that involves much facial, gestural, and postural imitation. And there is the creating of a private world, a sort of privileged intersubjective space to which they have the keys. The keys are special words with specific meanings, secret abbreviations, sacred rituals and spaces, and so on. All these things create a psychological niche in which intersubjectivity can flourish. (pp. 108–109)

Another psychoanalytic psychiatrist, Henry Krystal (1988), in his classic text *Integration & Self-Healing*, concluded,

> Just as white light contains all the colors of the spectrum, so love encompasses all the feelings reflecting our living process. When we get a chance to observe it, as in self-healing or in promoting the expansion of the conscious recognition of our selfness, we are especially prone to equate it with life forces, or the full enjoyment of our identity and unity. Love is the affective state that is favorable to the achievement of the most comprehensive self-representation. (p. 78)

I suggest that the love between a mother and her infant communicated in "the first relationship" (Stern, 1977) represents an essential context in which we can observe the early events of the co-creation of human love and self-identity.

From its relational onset in early infancy mutual love increases right-lateralized emotional processing on both sides of any loving dyad, whether parent-child, adult romantic, or intimate friendships. This intimacy of both quiet and excited love is later expressed as a host of adaptive states of being, including a childlike capacity to be unselfconsciously playful with an equally animated other, thereby remaining "forever young," to be mutually creative when interacting with another open curious mind, to share private moments of daydreaming and imagination within a stimulating relationship, to jointly develop a unique shared spontaneous sense of humor with another private self, to laugh out loud with an emotionally engaged other with so much gusto that one nearly comes to tears, to be able to vulnerably communicate deeply personal hopes and dreams with a safe, trusted companion, to be capable of quietly reveling with another in the precious little pleasures of life, to respect the quiet solitude of the other, to share the joy of a love of being alive with another emotionally communicating subjective self, to be young at heart and loving within a highly valued, intensely close attachment bond, and to share a long lasting, mutually loving opposite or same sex relationship across the lifespan, wing to wing, oar to oar.

Early experiences of mutual love deeply imprint not only the individual but also the culture. In the last quarter of the past century, Donald Winnicott, with keen foresight, put forth the developmental principle, "If human babies are to develop eventually into healthy independent, and society-minded adult individuals, they absolutely depend on being given a good start, and this good start is assured by . . . the thing called love" (1975, p. 17). Thirty years later, Sue Gerhardt (2004) looked forward and asked:

> The babies who are born now and in the years to come will be the adults who nurse us in old age, who manage our industry, who entertain us, who live next door. What kind of adults will they be? Will they be emotionally balanced enough to contribute their talents, or will they be disabled by hidden sensitivities? Their early start, and

the degree to which they felt loved and valued, will surely play an important part in determining that. (p. 218)

In the same year, Bartels and Zeki underscored the importance of "the long-lasting and pervasive influence of maternal love (or its absence) on the development and future mental constitution of a child" (2004, p. 1155). The earliest stages of humanhood are critical because they contain the representations of our possible futures—they model the potential developmental extension of our individual and collective cultural identities, including those that value ourselves as loving human beings. Each society needs to nurture the beginnings of human life, on both a psychological and economic level. One pragmatic expression of this cultural support of the origins of the capacity for mutual love is a national policy on parental leave in the first year, now offered by almost every industrialized nation, but glaringly lacking in the United States.

But perhaps on an even more fundamental level, neuroscientists are currently asserting that the first expression of love, the one between a mother and her infant, represents "one of the most powerful and *evolutionarily* preserved forms of positive affect in the emotional landscape of human behavior" (Nitschke et al., 2004, p. 583), that "the phylogenetically ancient role of maternal care . . . appears to be underpinned by *evolutionarily ancient structures*" (Abraham et al., 2014, p. 9795), that the early appearing left cradling bias of mothers and infants that favors right hemispheric processing (Giljov, Karenina, & Malaschichev, 2018) represents "an *evolutionary facilitator of social cognition*" (Forrester et al., 2018), and that social epigenetic forces in the cultural environment can positively *or* negatively affect the *evolutionary mechanism of attachment* (Narvaez et al., 2013). Explicitly alluding to Charles Darwin's 1859 magnum opus, *The Origin of Species*, these scientists are now telling us that maternal love for the infant is "a biologically essential mechanism for the *preservation of the human species*" (Noriuchi et al., 2008, p. 415, italics added). We must now pay very careful attention to these essential messages of current developmental science.

CHAPTER 7

Playing on the Right Side of the Brain

An Interview with Allan N. Schore
Published in the American Journal of Play

ALLAN N. SCHORE has served on the clinical faculty of the Department of Psychiatry and Biobehavioral Sciences at UCLA's David Geffen School of Medicine since 1996 and has maintained a private clinical practice for more than four decades. He has contributed significant research to the disciplines of interpersonal neurobiology, affective neuroscience, psychiatry, psychoanalysis, psychotherapy and clinical social work, and infant mental health and trauma theory. He is best known for his integration of neuroscience and attachment theory, his idea of attunement between mothers and infants, his investigation of right-brain regulation of emotion, and his applications of neuroscience in psychoanalysis and models of psychotherapy. Given the Scientific Award from the Division of Psychoanalysis of the American Psychological Association in 2008, he is a prolific writer whose works include *The Science of the Art of Psychotherapy*, *Affect Regulation and the Origin of the Self*, *Affect Dysregulation and Disorders of the Self*, and *Affect Regulation and the Repair of the Self*. In this interview, he discusses his scholarly and clinical career in neuroscience and neuropsychoanalysis and the breakthroughs in brain science that have changed our understanding of lived experience.

American Journal of Play: Can you tell us something of your own early play?

Allan N. Schore: I think a childlike sense of playful wonder and exploration has been with me from my very beginnings. It's the way my mind works, and therefore a central core of my subjectivity. As a child, I treasured play, both physical and mental play, both solitary play that continually exercised my imagination and intersubjective play, where I eagerly shared my imagination with others. I have an intense curiosity that traces back to my early childhood in Manhattan in the late 1940s. Both of my parents recognized and cultivated this inquisitiveness. That George and Barbara were my parents was both a wonderful cosmic accident and my good fortune. My mother, a gifted homemaker, had the combination of being an extremely warm, affiliative, and sociable person yet at the same time a very strong force of personality. I have many memories of her building up my self-esteem and a strong positive sense of self, yet at other times setting strong limits and curbing my grandiosity. My father had a very pragmatic mind. But he was also a very sensitive and empathic man, with a capacity to form emotional bonds with what on the surface appeared to be very different types of people. I also have many memories of my strong attachments to both of them, and how they provided an emotional context that supported my playful activities and burgeoning creativity.

AJP: Did you consider your father a role model?

Schore: My father was a chemical engineer, an applied scientist, an international expert in metal finishing and water pollution, and had numerous patents on electroplating copper and gold recovery processes. In 1976, he received an award from the Environmental Protection Agency, "In recognition of having contributed major efforts and demonstrated a significant advancement in our nation's continuing struggle for environmental pollution abatement." The plaque hangs in my office. His work was always at the cutting edge, and even ahead of its time. His career, like mine, significantly changed at several points in his life. So I was exposed to the mind of a creative scientist who was continually translating advances in basic chemical science into practical applications. And yes, he was a role model.

And I constantly learned from him. When I was 21 and between college graduation and my post-graduate education, I spent about a year working with my father. At that time he was designing and building the first automated metal finishing systems and sold them to, among others, General Electric, General Motors, and IBM. On one occasion, in particular, he taught me something that was to become invaluable. We took a trip to Tampa, where he gave a sales presentation to build an automation system for Honeywell, the manufacturer of thermostats. I have a strong visual memory of the room, of my father in the center of a long table, facing seven engineers and executives. I saw him effortlessly field questions posed by a variety of experts—an electrical engineer, a chemical engineer, a mechanical engineer, a water pollution expert, and vice presidents from three different departments. He was going back and forth answering each of their technical questions, talking about the automation system in terms of its impact on all of these different fields, and then creatively integrating that information into a system specifically tailored to their needs.

Watching my father play the polymath's role, I thought, that's the professional mind that I admired and needed to nurture in myself—the one that knows the different languages of experts and communicates with a number of different professions. An ability to fluidly move between disciplines would become the model for my career as a scholar—a synthetic, integrative approach as opposed to more typical specialization and narrowing of one's interests in one's field. This evolved into the interdisciplinary perspective that characterized my work and led me to create a theoretical model that not only describes but integrates various scientific disciplines; for example, charting the points of contact between psychology and psychiatry, biology and chemistry.

AJP: When did you turn to the biology of emotion?

Schore: In 1970, when I began my career in psychotherapy, I worked closely with a large number and wide variety of patients to learn my craft. But over the next decade, another important aspect of my development occurred—my wife Judith and I created a family. Becoming a father to a daughter and then a son transformed me emotionally, particularly when they were infants. Their instinctual desire to play greatly impressed me. Early development, an area that had always intrigued me scientifically, played out before my eyes. I spent a good deal of time not only observing but naturally regressing into states of early parent-infant play.

Then in 1980, in my late thirties, I decided to cut back at work, thinking I might devote time to writing. I was unsure about my specific goal, but broadly I hoped to integrate biology and psychology by looking anew at the relationship between organic and functional disorders. It turned into a 10-year period of independent study, a decade before I would put pen to paper (to use a late-20th-century, now almost obsolete metaphor). My experience both as a patient in psychotherapy and a therapist with 10,000 dutiful hours of clinical work had not only allowed me to develop expertise and confidence in clinical psychology and neuropsychology but also had fueled an intense curiosity about the relational processes of psychotherapy. This curiosity led me to ask: How do minds and brains align with and shape other minds and brains? I left my clinical position at the Psychiatry Department at Kaiser Permanente and cut back my private practice from 5 to 3 days.

AJP: Did this give you the time you felt was needed?

Schore: Yes. For about three out of every four Saturdays, and over the course of 10 years, I explored the stacks of the California State University Northridge library—just a mile from home—like a child in a candy store (again pardon the mid-20th-century reference), roaming between its sections on psychology, psychiatry, biology, chemistry, and even the physical sciences. When my children Beth and David were old enough, they came along, riding their bicycles around the campus while I searched out books and journals and fed quarters to hungry copying machines. You might say, as my kids biked around campus, I played around in the stacks, led almost entirely by my long-nurtured curiosity and trusting absolutely to my intuition about what to read beyond the fields in which I had earned my degrees. I did not read the articles in the library; I brought them back where I could spend time analyzing and synthesizing them, expanding my earlier education, not by studying at a university, but by playing in my home. I enjoyed these long, playful states out there in the library and back at my home office: I was acting out in daily life my long-held wish to become a scholar of many disciplines.

AJP: How did independent exploration differ from formal study?

Schore: Once freed from the pressures of examinations—and with no need to explain or solve anything in particular and no need to publish—my mood became surprisingly positive, and I was imbued with the joy of learning new information from different fields. My confidence and intense curiosity increased as I realized I could master a variety of disciplines, and so I spent a number of years reading journals in not only psychology and psychiatry but also cell biology, neurochemistry, neurophysiology, and neuroanatomy. I looked especially closely at changes that took place over the early developmental periods of an organism's life span. Over time, I found that my creativity expressed itself not in linear, analytical intellectual work, but in the nonlinear, positively charged emotional play states I mentioned, states of flow which—though they wandered—lasted for long periods of time. In these creative play states, research often spawned excitement and joy. These, in turn, generated thought experiments that triggered novel solutions. I personally experienced how play facilitates the processing of novel but useful information, which improves creativity and increases the capacity to learn. In fact, throughout the 1980s, I fell routinely into both intellectual and emotional states of flow. You might say I had become something like the polymath I admired in my father. I certainly grew adept at moving between different scientific and clinical literatures and between studies of the brain and studies of the mind.

AJP: What did you discover during this time?

Schore: In every third or fourth notebook, I found myself recording patterns across fields, and I began to integrate different research literatures, especially developmental biology, developmental neurochemistry, and developmental psychology. Meanwhile, I shuttled between my study and consulting room where I concentrated more and more on the relational processes that lie at the core of psychotherapy. This work expanded my skills as a clinician-scientist, the term I found that best suited my emerging professional identity. As a clinician, I made careful observations about my patients' and my own subjectivities, especially about the emotional interactions between the two. But as a maturing scientist, I took careful note of the research I found convincing, research I would later use to develop an interdisciplinary theoretical model. I focused on the boundaries between fields and looked closely at the commonalities that lie beneath the surfaces of apparently unrelated phenomena. I became increasingly confident about theoretical concepts that cut across different sciences. Ultimately, I found that the construct of regulation lies at the core of chemistry, physics, and biology, and I knew that any overarching developmental or clinical model could be centered around this organizing principle. Hence my deep interest in the problem of self-regulation, a central dynamic of the human experience.

Halfway through my decade playing scholar, I had became absolutely confident that by creating a theoretical model of emotion and human relationships which integrated psychology and biology, I could alter the course of clinical theory and practice, and indeed science. And even though my self-image is basically that I am a modest man, again something I learned from my father, I became comfortable with that explicit sense of conviction and confidence, even certainty, in the power of the model my mind was creating.

AJP: How did you know when you had had enough independent study?

Schore: Over the years, the stack of legal-sized notepads grew 6 feet high and began to teeter precariously, which may have contributed to my intuitive sense that I needed to end my solitary investigation and finally write something. I had in mind a psychoneurobiological formulation of emotional development, both in early life and in the therapeutic process I was observing in my practice. It ultimately became my first book, *Affect Regulation and the Origin of the Self: The Neurobiology of Emotional Development.* Even before the book had hit the stands, I remember feeling the intense satisfaction of knowing that I had accomplished what I had set out to do.

AJP: How did your colleagues receive the book?

Schore: In 1994, after the book was published, I wrote letters to 60 researchers around the world—psychiatrists, psychoanalysts, neuroanatomists, neurochemists, brain researchers, cell biologists, developmental psychologists, and others I had cited, and I sent them copies of the book. By the end of the summer, about 50 had written back to congratulate me on the work and its interdisciplinary perspective. Of the positive notice I got, I was especially proud of the review in *British Journal of Psychiatry*, which called me a polymath. And I felt good, too, that there was an acceptance of my emphasis on developmental psychoanalysis and on the work of Sigmund Freud, who had fallen out of fashion in academia.

AJP: Can you speak about Freud's hope of creating a biology of the mind?

Schore: Recall that Freud originally trained as a neurologist, and he predicted that "we shall have to find a contact point with biology." In his 1895 *Project for a Scientific Psychology*, he attempted to construct a model of the human mind in terms of its underlying neurobiological mechanisms. It was in this endeavor "to furnish a psychology which shall be a natural science" that Freud introduced the theoretical concepts at the core of psychoanalysis, including ideas about regulation, the unconscious, development, and emotion. In the *Journal of the American Psychoanalytic Association*, I wrote in 1995 that advances in the interdisciplinary study of emotion indicated that the central role played by regulatory structures represented a confluence with Freud, and I called the time right for a rapprochement between psychoanalysis—the science of the unconscious mind—and neuroscience, the science of the brain.

AJP: Were you also still promoting Freud's therapeutic mission?

Schore: In the sense that I wanted to move Freud's *Project* forward. His original model of the psychodynamics of the psyche was influenced by the neuroscience of his time. Thus it was a drive-reduction model—the down-regulation of ego over id, or to put it less technically, of rational insight over emotion. For Freud, ideally, therapists should remain emotionally neutral and detached; we would say that the left hemisphere dominated their approach. In addition, the Cartesian mind-body split remained at the core of Freud's theory. Thus there was little room in Freud's drive-reduction theory for body-based positive emotions. Neither, crucially, was there room in Freud for their up-regulation and amplification in play states. His theory was essentially intrapsychic and not interpersonal. So he discounted states like mother-infant play.

Donald Winnicott's later emphasis on play broke away from classical psychoanalytic theory—so did relational psychoanalysis, which transformed the theory from a one-person psychology to a two-person psychology. As an argument for the power of integrating the psychological and the biological, the scientific and the clinical, *Affect Regulation and the Origin of the Self* was in part a response to and a taking up of Freud's *Project for a Scientific Psychology.*

Attachment theory, founded by the British psychoanalyst John Bowlby, represented his own attempt to reinstate Freud's *Project.*

Toward that end, Bowlby's theory integrated ethology—or behavioral biology—and developmental psychology. Focusing on emotional development, in *Affect Regulation*, I expanded upon Bowlby's idea that the major motivational system involved in the attachment dynamic was the mother's regulation of the infant's fear states (a concept borrowed from Freud). I suggested that instead, the attachment relationship regulates both distressing negative and playful positive states. I explored mother-infant play in early and late infancy, and I linked these experiences, which expose the child not only to improvements in learning capacity but also to brain development.

My first book thus represented a primal formulation of interpersonal neurobiology, a biopsychosocial perspective of human development that enables us to understand how the structure and function of the mind and brain are shaped by experiences, especially emotional relationships. Its interdisciplinary perspective also attempted to understand how brains align their neural activities in social interactions.

It was my first articulation of regulation theory, an interpersonal neurobiological model of the development, psychopathogenesis, and treatment of the implicit subjective self. And I am proud that the intersubjective brain-to-brain, mind-to-mind, body-to-body construct I explored in the book has subsequently been incorporated into the mental health professions as part of the ongoing relational trend in psychotherapy. In the book, I also outlined the core principles of modern attachment theory, which integrates biology, psychology, and psychiatry to conceptualize attachment transactions of early right brain-to-right brain socioemotional communications.

AJP: Did Freud influence your thinking in other ways?

Schore: Yes, principally in my work in the new field of neuropsychoanalysis—the study of the neurobiological development of the unconscious mind. My clinical experiences with patients and my own psychotherapy drove home for me, both objectively and subjectively, the essential nature of the unconscious in everyday life. And so I became intensely curious and interested in the unconscious and its essential psychic operations, 90% of which lies below the surface of the conscious 10% of the mind. For the past three decades, I have produced a large body of clinical and research data that indicate the right brain is the psychobiological substrate of the human unconscious. Over this period, a paradigm shift has occurred within the concept of the unconscious. In its updated reformulations, this central construct of psychoanalysis shifted from an intrapsychic unconscious that expresses itself in dreams at night to a relational unconscious in which, during everyday life, the unconscious mind of one individual communicates with the unconscious mind of another (right brain-to-right brain via an interpersonal neurobiology).

AJP: So what is the unconscious in your view?

Schore: I view the unconscious as essentially an emotion-processing regulatory system that acts rapidly beneath levels of awareness. And I have company in this point of view. In a chapter for *Adolescent Psychopathology and the Developing Brain* [2007], neuroscientists Don Tucker and Lyda Möller noted that the nonverbal emotional communication rooted in the right hemisphere suggested a domain of the mind much like the psychoanalytic unconscious that Freud described. The neurologist Guido Gainotti separated a schematic level in the right hemisphere that generates true emotions from a left brain that processes, analyzes, and controls emotions at a conceptual level. Russell Meares asserts that the brain's right side creates an "'inner,' emotionally laden experience" and a self-system that generates "a background state of well-being." And so there is now consensus that the conscious, surface "left mind" is located in the left brain, while we find the deeper unconscious "right mind" in the right brain.

AJP: Why did 20th-century behavioral and cognitive psychologists avoid accounting for emotion?

Schore: The dominant behavioral psychology for much of the past century emphasized overt behavior, which explains the reluctance among scientific researchers to peer into "the black box." The behaviorists thus basically banished the mind, the brain, and the body from their scientific study. They focused instead on voluntary behavior and conscious processes, and they aggressively attacked both Freud's unconscious and the concept of subjectivity. And because much of emotional processing occurs beneath levels of conscious awareness, they directed their attention away from affect.

AJP: What impact did this thinking have on thinking and research about play?

Schore: Behaviorists conceptualized play solely and narrowly as a behavior and not as an emotional state. In the 1980s, however, psychology's emphasis shifted to cognition, which legitimated the study of implicit, covert processes, and revalidated unconscious processes. Yet most saw cognition as a voluntary control mechanism of emotions, so here again they conceptualized play narrowly as the expression of cognitive processes. As a result, the deeper mechanisms of emotion, motivation, and play continued to be ignored. That said, I have written about an ongoing paradigm shift from the behavioral psychology (and behavioral psychotherapy) of the 1960s and 1970s to the cognitive psychology (and cognitive psychotherapy) of the 1980s to today's scientific exploration of body-based emotions, when therapy has become focused on affective psychobiological states.

This shift continues to affect thinking in neuroscience and neuropsychology—from investigating into the explicit, analytical, conscious, verbal, rational left hemisphere to refining our understanding of the implicit, integrative, unconscious, nonverbal, body-based emotional right hemisphere. A major theme of this paradigm shift finds expression in the increasing trend within psychology, psychiatry, and neuroscience to emphasize the centrality of emotion (even more than cognition) in the human experience, "the primacy of affect." Current psychobiological studies indicate that affects are not merely by-products of cognition—they have unique temporal and physiological characteristics that determine our internal experience of self more than thoughts do.

AJP: Does this new approach hold implications for the study of play?

Schore: The shift away from the narrow constraints of a strict behaviorism has sanctioned scientific study of internal states, and so it has created an environment that supports a new generation of methodologies that more directly access the proximal internal causes of overt behavior, including play behavior. The current paradigm shift has also served as an antidote to the Cartesian sundering of mind and body that has plagued psychology and psychiatry. For most of the past century, these models overemphasized symptomatic negative, fearful, and anxious behaviors and underemphasized affect-driven joyful play states. Furthermore, this movement of research from behavior to cognition to body-based emotion forged stronger connections among the disciplines of psychology, neuroscience, and psychiatry. They are all now focusing on affective phenomena, the essential components of body-based play states.

AJP: Tell us more about your interest in human development—do you think the old rule still holds that development before birth is genetic and development after birth is learned?

Schore: The shift from the verbal left to the nonverbal right brain has proven essential to our understanding of the preverbal stages of infancy. Research now questions previous views of development based solely on the ontogeny of cognitive language rather than emotional and social functions. That old rule you mention, still postulated by many scientists, turns out to be incorrect. Learning occurs in prenatal stages, *in utero*, between mother and fetus. For example, the emotional state of a mother affects her fetus: The amount of cortisol crossing the placenta affects the fetal genetic system.

This all makes more room for experience in neurological development. Indeed, a large body of interdisciplinary research has demonstrated that early brain development is not merely genetically encoded. Instead, such development depends especially on socioemotional experiences with the caregiver. Scientists now describe gene-environment interactions and offer models that show nature and nurture combining to shape human development. Epigenetic factors regulated by a social environment that directly affects genomic mechanisms, turning genes on and off, find expression in both the mother-fetal and the mother-infant attachment relationships.

AJP: When does the mother-infant attachment relationship actually begin?

Schore: We now think earlier and earlier. Over the past several years, developmental research has moved the beginning from late in the first year to the first stages of infancy. In the work I have published most recently in the *Infant Mental Health Journal* [2017], I emphasize that developmental studies now need to move even further back to the period of life before birth. This primordial period of human development has been mostly ignored by science. But a growing body of studies on fetal brain development argues against the long-held idea that a fixed, inborn temperament represents genetic factors first expressed at birth. Current research indicates instead that temperament at birth is a result of prenatally evolving epigenetic mechanisms that continue to be shaped or misshaped by the postnatal socioemotional environment. Thus in the earliest of human beginnings—the prenatal *and* postnatal stages of human development—the fetus and then the infant evolves through a succession of critical periods. In both the *in utero* and then extrauterine environments, experience-dependent stages of brain growth can both support or inhibit the development of more complex brain structure and function.

AJP: Tell us about the period after birth you call the process of attunement.

Schore: Secure attachment depends upon a mother's attunement not with her infant's cognition or behavior but instead with her infant's dynamic alterations of autonomic arousal, the energetic dimension of the child's affective state. And here the musical metaphor of attunement is both helpful and telling. To enter into this communication, a mother must be psychobiologically attuned to the dynamic crescendos and decrescendos of her infant's body-based internal states of peripheral autonomic nervous system arousal and central nervous system arousal. Through right brain-to-right brain nonverbal, visual-facial, auditory-prosodic, and tactile-gestural body-based affective communications, a caregiver and infant learn the rhythmic structure of the other and modify their behavior to fit that structure. Thereby they co-create a moment-to-moment, specifically fitted interaction. During this affective communication, an attuned mother synchronizes the spatiotemporal patterning of her sensory stimulation with her infant's spontaneous organismic rhythms. Through this contingent responsivity, a mother appraises the nonverbal expressions of her infant's internal arousal and affective states, regulates them, and communicates them back to her baby. Thus a mother's responses are finely attuned to the moment-to-moment changes in her infant's facial expression, vocalization, and body movement. Her own state is in turn affected by changes in her infant's state.

AJP: How can you tell when mother and infant are attuned?

Schore: The major indicators are pleasure and interest.

AJP: Then is attunement more a matter of feeling than thinking?

Schore: Psychobiological attunement is a right-brain process. In a 2011 article for *Neuroscience Research,* Shota Nishitani and his colleagues showed that the right (and not left) prefrontal cortex is involved when human mothers discriminate their infants' facial emotions. Importantly, secure mothers attune to both their infants' positive and negative facial communications. Studies of the mothers' EEG responses to videos of their own 5- to 8-month-old infants during free play show right frontal activation. In these peek-a-boo episodes, maternal affect matches infant joy. But the mothers' right frontal areas are also activated during episodes of infant distress. When they see their own infants in distress, mothers express negative affect matching—sadness, concern, irritability, and the absence of joy. In turn, this empathic, right brain-to-right brain attunement sets up a bidirectional relational context for mutual regulation—coregulation, if you will—of each of their affective states. This interactive regulation allows a shared positive affective state in both mother and child. These dynamics operate in the earliest forms of positive, emotionally charged mother-infant play, during which an attuned mother initially matches her internal state with her infant's state.

Mothers overtly express this matching in their facial expressions, tones of voice, and gestures to resonate with their children's body-based emerging subjectivity. For example, the temporal contour of a maternal nonverbal vocalization might match in a way that gives a sense of what a mother sees in her infant's face. This kind of matching is not imitation and it is not an exact copy—it is analogical. Her face and her voice represent analogues of the baby's state. As Donald Winnicott observed, a mother looks at her baby, and what she looks like is related to what she sees in her child. Furthermore, these implicit, rapid, spontaneous, intersubjective, and body-based nonverbal communications occur at levels beneath a mother's conscious awareness.

AJP: How does play help mothers and infants attune?

Schore: A caregiver, even one in whom the attachment bond is secure, will not always be perfectly attuned—indeed, studies show such attunement occurs less than 30% of the time. Instead, the "good-enough mother" can monitor the changes in her infant's state and alter her response as needed. She re-attunes. Recall that she is psychobiologically attuning not to her infant's external behavior but to the baby's internal rhythms of arousal. This interactive regulation of re-attunement brings the infant back into autonomic balance and homeostasis, reestablishing the feelings of safety and trust. The disruption of the attachment bond leads to a transient stressful response of negative affect and a temporary loss of safety and trust. In a pattern of interactive repair following dyadic misattunement—of disruption and repair—a secure bond lets the mother and infant transition fluidly from a positive attuned state to a negative misattuned state and back again. This repair process allows an infant to actively cope with negatively charged affects. In the process of overcoming interactive stress, the infant gains self-regulatory skills.

AJP: Does this process advance beyond coping and the building of skills? Does it go beyond repair?

Schore: Yes. Classical attachment theory once held that attachment was primarily protective and aimed at reducing an infant's fear. It made little mention of positive affects such as joy, excitement, and surprise. Modern attachment theory notes that mothers co-create a bond of emotional communication with infants by synchronizing with the rhythms of the infant's dynamic internal states. Attachment is thus fundamentally the communication and interactive regulation of emotion. The baby becomes attached to the psychobiologically attuned, regulating, primary caregiver who not only minimizes negative affect but also maximizes opportunities for positive affect. Regulated interactions with a familiar, predictable, primary caregiver create not only a sense of safety but also a positively charged curiosity that fuels the burgeoning self-exploration of novel socioemotional and physical environments.

AJP: Is this where play comes in?

Schore: Play, in fact, is a fundamental expression of the attachment regulatory dynamic. Attachment is not just the reestablishment of security after a dysregulating experience and a stressful negative state. It is also the interactive amplification of positive affects, as in play states. Play calms and soothes infants, and it modulates their stressful states of negative arousal, replacing stress with intense joy and excitement. The dual regulatory processes of affect synchrony embedded in play states and interactive repair embedded in soothing and calming moments that modulate states of negative arousal are the fundamental building blocks of attachment and its associated emotions. Synchrony and repair promote resilience and security.

AJP: Is play equally important in brain development?

Schore: Perhaps even more so. Attachment play imprints circuits during early critical periods of brain growth. We now have evidence that positive and negative affects activate different brain circuits. Play behavior transforms the physical environment into an enriched environment. Changes in cortical and subcortical synaptic development from exposure to enriched environments are associated with regulated, elevated levels of arousal. Mother-infant play, like all later forms of dyadic play, enhances behavioral flexibility through an increase in neural interconnectivity. And, in the first year of life, this enhanced plasticity occurs in the early developing nonverbal right brain, which develops before the verbal left.

AJP: What happens in this playful dialogue between mother and child?

Schore: Although the mother and infant begin to monitor each other's face at the infant's birth, an increasingly complex co-constructed communication system does not emerge between them for 2 or 3 months. During this same period, we see the onset of right brain-to-right brain protoconversations within the dyad. Colwyn Trevarthen notes that, in these initial transactions of primary intersubjectivity, a baby—attracted to her mother's voice, her gentle cooing, her reassuring facial expressions, and her gestures—replies spontaneously, affectionately, and playfully. In turn, a mother replies spontaneously and playfully to her baby's nonverbal communications. A traffic of visual, auditory-prosodic, and tactile signals pass between mother and infant that builds excitement and joyful pleasure, which the two express in facial expression, voice inflection, and body movements of posture and gesture. Infants note the sequence, rhythm, and pitch of the prosody (if not semantics) of the spoken word. Ellen Dissanayake also reports the emergence of increasingly animated mother-infant play at 8 weeks associated with exaggerated facial expressions and utterances that is based on surprise and uncertainty. A creative mother's nonverbal communications thus expose the infant to spontaneous, interpersonal novelty, and this helps an infant integrate external and internal sensations.

The benefits of play at this stage extend beyond sensory integration, and their effects propagate. During the first 2 or 3 months, mother-infant play experiences also help structure what Daniel Stern terms an unconscious core self. These spontaneous protoconversations of arousal-inducing play continue across the stages of infancy. Indeed, a major developmental task of an infant's first year increasingly involves more intense states of emotional arousal. And this system functions throughout the life span.

AJP: Do you consider this an evolutionary purpose of play?

Schore: Mother-infant play over the first year serves an essential adaptive function—it progressively increases the infant's tolerance for higher and higher levels of arousal that sustains more complex emotional, cognitive, and behavioral emergent functions. This adaptive function evolves as a result of early maternal sensitivity to, participation in, and regulation of the infant's highly stimulated states. Mutual gaze is known to be a powerful amplifier of arousal. Stern characterizes the level of intensity of the joyful, excited infant as extremely high, creating maximum levels of activation almost intolerable to the developing nervous system. He explains that joy arises from mutual regulation of social exchanges such as smiling, especially as it builds to giggling. Hilarity loves company, of course, as exuberant players pleasurably seek others with whom to share the fun.

AJP: How does play change the brain, and what does such change mean for growing infants?

Schore: Mother-infant play promotes human brain development during its initial 2-year growth spurt, a period of right-brain dominance. The right hemisphere is centrally involved in face-to-face protoconversations, the recognition of emotional faces. Two months marks the onset of a critical period during which visual experience—including play experiences—modify synaptic connections in the developing occipital cortex, the same time in which infants show right-hemispheric activation when exposed to a woman's face. Four-month-old infants presented with images of a female face gazing directly ahead show enhanced activity over right prefrontal areas. In these studies, at 6 months the infants showed a right-lateralized, left-gaze bias when they viewed a female face and significantly greater right-front temporal activation when they viewed their mothers' faces as opposed to the faces of strangers. Importantly, the development in the first year of more complex visual-affective functions allows infants to visually read their mothers' different affect states.

We should remember that face-to-face, emotional communications, including those embedded in early mother-infant play, are more than visual. They also have a particular sound, expressed in the right brain prosodic emotional tone of the voice—"motherese"—that a mother uses in play. Indeed, the right hemisphere dominates the processing of prosody and rhythm. With respect to auditory communications, a magnetic resonance imaging study of 1- to 3-day-old newborns reports that lullabies evoke right-hemispheric activation in their auditory cortices. Studies of the prosodic processing of emotional voices in 3-month-old infants show activation of the right temporoparietal region. Seven-month-old infants respond to emotional voices in a voice-sensitive region of their right superior temporal sulcus, and happy-sounding prosody specifically activates their right inferior frontal cortices.

AJP: Given your attunement metaphor, does the emotive, musical tone of motherese play any specific role in brain development?

Schore: The emotional quality of what infants hear in the early stages of infancy affects the development of the voice-processing areas of the right hemisphere, especially the temporal voice areas in the upper banks of the right superior temporal sulcus. Studies note the importance not of the verbal content but of the melody of a mother's voice, and whether she uses infant-directed or adult-directed speech in her interactions with her child, especially in both arousal-amplifying, playful contexts and arousal-reducing, calming and soothing contexts. This use of infant-directed speech is thus essential to the development of an infant's right-temporal areas. The corresponding burgeoning ability to read the emotional tones of the voice of others becomes an essential element of all later social relationships.

AJP: We have covered sight and sound, so how does touch affect infant play?

Schore: Mothers and their babies use interpersonal touch to communicate and regulate emotional information. And mother-infant play provides a relational context for this body-based, affective communication. Clinical research has demonstrated the essential role of maternal affective touch on human development in a child's first year. This research shows an infant's need for affectionate touch for healthy right-hemisphere development. Two decades ago, Jechil Sieratzki described the effects of touch on the developing right hemisphere. He asserted that the emotional impact of touch is more direct and immediate if we cradle infants on the left side of our bodies. Later studies reported that mothers tended to touch their 3-month-old infants' heads on their left cheeks. In the second year, as a securely attached infant becomes a toddler, his or her interactively regulated right brain-to-right brain visual-facial, auditory-prosodic, and tactile-gestural communications become more and more integrated, allowing for the emergence of a coherent, right-brain emotional and corporeal sense of self. How effectively this adaptive self-system alters its internal state depends on changes in the external environment, which allows for flexible and resilient behaviors in response to personally meaningful stressors.

AJP: Does this process benefit only infants?

Schore: No. The psychobiological attachment dynamic is expressed in all later developmental stages. Researchers now assert that we are biologically connected to those with whom we have close relationships. Homeostatic regulation between members of a dyad is a stable aspect of all intimate relationships throughout the life span. In all ensuing periods of human development, attachment dynamics find expression in right brain-to-right brain communications of affect and the interactive regulation of affective arousal. The evolutionary mechanism of attachment is, fundamentally, the regulation of biological synchronicity between and within organisms. This mechanism occurs most prominently at later points of shared, spontaneous, improvised, and emotionally rewarding moments of intimate contact, including intimate intersubjective play.

AJP: So players are like lovers?

Schore: Researchers note the similarity of mother-child play and interpersonal intimacy in the child's first year and in later development, especially in the right brain nonverbal facial, prosodic, and gestural expressions they share. Lovers speak to each other like parents speak to their young children. In both playful and intimate contexts, players and lovers will move close and in synchrony; they emphasize musicality over meaning, and, of course, they sometimes even employ baby talk.

AJP: Can you tell us more about early playful protoconversations?

Schore: Terry Marks-Tarlow points out that the right brain-to-right brain mother-infant protoconversation continues over the first year in play, songs, and chants such as peek-a-boo and "This Little Piggy." In this play, repetition in the mother's vocal utterances, facial expressions, and body movements coordinates the minds and brains of two bodies, regulating the infant emotionally and uniting mother and child temporally. Thus over the course of the first year, intersubjective play occurs in a relational context of mutual psychobiological regulation. Recent advances in developmental neuroscience and developmental psychology also clearly indicate that mother-infant play not only precedes but acts as a social-psychobiological crucible for later forming solitary play. Interpersonal neurobiology suggests that mother-infant play is more socioemotional than cognitive, and that, fundamentally, the underlying mechanism of this arousal-altering, pleasurable, rewarding activity facilitates the experience-dependent maturation of both the cortical and subcortical systems. This primordial form of play generates the neurobiological substrate on which all forms of play—mother- infant and solitary, spontaneous and controlled, active and passive—evolve.

At all points of the life span, spontaneous play represents an emergent property of an interactively regulated, nonlinear dynamic system. In this relational context, play expands an infant's tolerance of higher and lower states of arousal and broadens the regulatory boundaries and windows of arousal tolerance.

AJP: How does play entrain and elaborate the infant's emotional capacities?

Schore: During the first year, dyadic relational play expands the infant's affect array. The psychobiological mechanism embedded in mother-infant play allows the transformation of mildly pleasurable enjoyment into joy and the intensification of mildly pleasurable interest into excitement. In this context of regulated, accelerating, positive arousal, discrete affective states grow more complex. The relational context between a playful mother and her infant thus allows the infant's maturing brain to create an expanding variety of emotional states. In this early development of the self, the caregivers initially regulate emotion, but over the course of infancy, it becomes increasingly self-regulated as a result of neurophysiological development. This expansion of autoregulation allows more complex forms of solitary play.

Over the maturational course of infancy, the passive, immobile infant at the beginning of the first year becomes an active, upright, mobile being by its end. This structural development supports highly elevated levels of stimulation-seeking exploratory play generated by the mesocortical dopamine system to support locomotion and exploration. In other words, the enriched environment of intersubjective play during the first months is now accompanied by the enriched environment of the neo-toddler's full-body, active play. Indeed, at 10 months, with the appearance of upright locomotion and the functional onset of the orbital prefrontal cortex, fully 90% of maternal physical and verbal behavior consists of affection, play, and caregiving, and by 1 year of age, stimulation-seeking exploratory play time increases to as much as 6 hours of a child's day. These relational events represent the early origins of both passive and active play, and they are both influenced by a child's emotional transactions with—and regulated attachments to—a mother.

Research shows that at 10 to 13½ months, a significant increase in positive emotion accompanies the neo-toddler's rapid neuromuscular development, gross motor ability, and upright locomotion. But as the second year progresses, the social environmental niche of the caregiver-infant dyad changes dramatically. The process of socialization begins in earnest, and the mother's role shifts dramatically from mostly caregiver to socialization agent. Soon after the onset of exuberant upright locomotion, parental socialization focuses on discipline in addition to nurturant functions. That being the case, as my colleague Russell Meares points out, in optimal attachment contexts, the right brain-to-right brain protoconversation continues in the second year, a time when a toddler becomes acutely aware of others, develops a full, playful imagination, and grows eager for novel experiences. With the expansion of higher right brain functions and the onset of language, the intersubjective protoconversation now takes the form of intersubjective imaginative games, then intrasubjective, internalized dialogues, and then what Meares calls "conversational play." This creative game, which a toddler plays while alone, depends on make-believe, the expressive use of words, and analogy.

It is similar to Jean Piaget's symbolic play, but Meares describes it as analogical or protosymbolic play, which is imbued with the extra dimension of pleasure. The game consists of a miniature story, told as if to the child himself or herself but also to someone else, who is not there except as a feeling of the presence of the internalized, protoconversational mother. This earliest form of symbolic play allows the toddler to play with ideas and generate fantasies, including fantasied interactions with other selves. Studies now confirm that symbolic play and imagination are heavily influenced by right brain activation and that both of these processes are inhibited by shame.

AJP: Shame?

Schore: Yes, a number of authors have emphasized the growth-facilitating importance of small doses of shame in the socializing of the infant. In fact, this attachment emotion, which has been described as the primary social emotion, makes its initial appearance in the second year. Guided by the principle that all affects develop within an interpersonal context and that specific affects imply a particular form of relatedness, I proposed more than 25 years ago a prototypical model of shame based on an analysis of incipient shameful experiences. A toddler—in an activated, hyperstimulated, high-arousal state of stage-typical, ascendant excitement and elation—reattaches to a caregiver as in late infancy. Despite an excited expectation of a psychobiologically attuned, shared positive affect state with the mother and a dyadic amplification of the positive affects of excitement and joy, the infant unexpectedly encounters a facially expressed affective misattunement, an embarrassed or disgusted expression from the mother that triggers a sudden, shock-induced deflation and propels the infant into an intense, low-arousal state the infant cannot regulate. Shame represents this rapid transition from a preexisting, high-arousal, positive hedonic state to a low-arousal, negative hedonic state. And, true, shame blocks the play state and acts as a brake on a developing child's desire to be constantly at the center of his or her parents' attention. The key is then the mother's interactive repair of shame.

AJP: We have talked about a mother's influence, but how does play with a father affect an infant's self-regulation and brain development?

Schore: A major transition in the middle of the second year involves male and female toddlers in more complex interactions with their fathers. We have long established that a father's play with an infant is more arousing than a mother's. Although a mother's soothing play is essential to a child's attachment security, a father's arousing play can be critical to a child's competent exploration of the physical world. I have suggested that not only an infant's mother but a toddler's father has an effect on the growth of a baby's brain. I have proposed that in the middle of the second year, the structural development of a child's brain shifts from a maternal, experience-dependent maturation of an early developing right brain circuitry to a paternal, experience-dependent maturation of later developing, left-brain circuitry. Now a father becomes an important source of arousal induction and reduction, and his regulation of higher levels of stimulation influences the formation of the neural structures entering into a critical period of growth. Neuroimaging research demonstrates that although maternal caregiving involves an evolutionarily ancient, subcortical-paralimbic network engaged in emotional processing, paternal caregiving activates a later developing cortical circuit involved in sociocognitive understanding, mentalizing, and planning.

Researchers have shown that paternal care influences synaptic development in, for example, the somatosensory cortex of the left hemisphere. These studies indicate that paternal care significantly affects the development of play behavior, especially active, full-body play. Notably, Jaak Panksepp finds that juvenile rough-and-tumble play is critically affected by the father-child relationship. The father serves as a regulator of a toddler's increasingly expressed aggressive impulses (the "terrible twos"), and rough-and-tumble play (as opposed to the mother's earlier role in fear regulation). The 18-month-old toddler's increases in negativism ("no!"), an interpersonal behavior of noncompliance, is essential to the emergence of autonomy and to the expression of the child's developing interpersonal influence strategies. Indeed, the parents' emotional responsiveness to this is critical to the development of autonomy.

This same period represents the end of a right hemisphere growth spurt and a critical period of growth in the left hemisphere. From an interpersonal, neurobiological perspective, I have suggested that the paternal attachment system of father-toddler interactions forges imprints in the child's evolving left brain circuits, including the left dorsolateral prefrontal cortex and the left motor systems controlling voluntary movement. Very recent models of brain laterality hold that—in contrast to the right hemisphere's role in affiliation, empathy, trust, and social intelligence— the left hemisphere's role lies in power, dominance, control of others, and autonomy. Ideally, these two motivational systems, their affiliation and power, are sufficiently expressed and balanced.

AJP: How does autonomy emerge?

Schore: Emotion is initially regulated by caregivers, but over the course of the first 2 years, it becomes increasingly self-regulated as a result of neurophysiological development. Secure, interactively regulated attachment histories are imprinted into developing, right cortical-subcortical circuits in implicit-procedural memory, thus generating an internal working model of attachment that encodes strategies of affect regulation, strategies that nonconsciously guide the individual through interpersonal contexts. Consisting of a dual processes of self-regulation, these adaptive strategies are interactive regulation (the ability to flexibly regulate psychobiological states of emotions with other humans in affiliative contexts) and autoregulation (which occurs apart from other humans in autonomous contexts). For the rest of the life span, individuals under stress can down-regulate negative affect by turning to others for comfort or by engaging in private nonsocial activities. Similarly, they can share intense joy with others or experience it in a solitary state.

Parents often note that their toddler's independence seems to signal his or her emerging personality. In fact, depending on the interpersonal neurobiological attachment histories with their mothers and then their fathers, individual personalities (and genders) vary in the balance of the two mechanisms of self-regulation. Early social experiences of mutual intersubjective play of the developing mind and active physical play of the maturing body act as enriched environments for the creation of a flexible personality that employs either interactive regulation or autoregulation. That said, these adaptive, regulatory mechanisms derive from our earliest attachments to other human beings, and they are both forged and strengthened in various affect-regulating attachment experiences including play experiences.

AJP: What happens when something goes wrong? How does trauma impact development?

Schore: Regulation theory offers a comprehensive interpersonal neurobiological model for the development, psychopathogenesis, and treatment of the subjective self. Over the past three decades, I have used the interdisciplinary perspective of the theory to integrate data from developmental psychology, developmental neuroscience, developmental psychopathology, and child psychiatry to offer heuristic and clinically relevant models of psychopathogenesis. The contrast between the kind of optimal growth-facilitating attachment I have described and the relational, growth-inhibiting, early environment of attachment trauma that involves abuse and neglect (or both) is a stark one. In abuse or neglect, a primary caregiver induces traumatic states of enduring negative affect—of intense, overwhelming fear or sense of loss—in an insecure disorganized, disoriented infant. Such caregivers are misattuned and emotionally inaccessible and react inconsistently and inappropriately to their infants' expressions of stress with massive intrusiveness or utter disengagement. They therefore participate minimally or unpredictably in relational arousal-regulating processes, including intersubjective play. Instead of modulating these extreme levels of stress, they induce them. Because they provide little interactive repair, their intense negative affective states of stimulation and arousal—very high in cases of abuse, very low in cases of neglect—become long lasting. For an immature organism with undeveloped and restricted coping capacities, the primary caregiver is the major source of stress regulation and, therefore, a sense of safety. When danger instead of safety emanates from the attachment relationship, the homeostatic assaults have significant short- and long-term consequences on the maturing psyche and soma.

AJP: What consequences?

Schore: During these episodes of imprinted right brain-to-right brain relational trauma, a child matches the rhythmic structures of a mother's dysregulated states, and this synchronization registers in the ring patterns of the stress-sensitive cortical and limbic regions of an infant's brain, especially in the right brain, which is in a critical period of growth. The detrimental psychobiological impact of this intergenerational transmission of relational trauma is the altered metabolic processes that poorly sustain the critical period of growth of the developing right brain. Early attachment trauma (common in psychiatric and severe personality and psychiatric disorders such as borderline personality) imprints a permanent physiological reactivity of the right brain and a susceptibility to later disorders of affect regulation. This mechanism of frequently ruptured attachments and poor interactive repair generates a lasting impairment—an inefficient and limited ability of the right brain to regulate the stressors that later in life generate intense emotional states, both negative (affects such as fear, sadness, and shame) and positive (affects such as excitement and joy). When under stress, such personalities avoid turning to others for interactive regulation. Instead, they disengage from the social environment and rapidly enter into a state of defensive dissociative autoregulation. The inability to cope with emotional and social stressors finds expression in a lowered threshold for emotional turbulence, an increased tendency for defensive dissociation that blunts both negative and positive affect, and a hyperreactivity to novel events.

AJP: What kind of impact does such stress have on play?

Schore: The intense and enduring stress that arises in such psychopathogenetic socioemotional contexts is associated with histories of significantly reduced amounts of spontaneous play. In early right brain attachment trauma, the chronically dysregulated self does not seek but avoids spontaneously generated interpersonal novelty, a component of the protoconversation of mother-infant play, thereby generating highly repetitive defensive play. As I have already mentioned, early relational play imprints right brain circuits, especially dopaminergic circuits in their critical period of maturation during the first 2 years. Neglect and abuse interfere with the experience-dependent maturation of right-lateralized reward circuits as well as with the connections between the central and autonomic nervous systems. In this manner, the neural substrates of early protoconversational, intersubjective play and of later symbolic play fail to evolve, leading to enduring deficits in these adaptive, growth-promoting functions.

AJP: Have your therapy models changed in light of these insights?

Schore: Attachment trauma, inscribed not in left brain, verbally explicit memory but in right brain, nonverbally implicit memory, has become a central focus of developmentally oriented, emotionally focused psychotherapy—mine and others'—with children and adults. Psychotherapy with such patients attends to the severe dysregulation of affect as well as to the interpersonal and intrapsychic deficits that characterize the developmental self-pathologies associated with histories of relational trauma. In light of the commonality of nonverbal, intersubjective, implicit right brain-to-right brain emotion-transacting and -regulating mechanisms in the caregiver-to-infant and the therapist-to-patient relationship, developmental attachment studies have direct relevance to the treatment process.

Thus regulation theory is particularly relevant to therapy in cases of relational trauma. It provides an interpersonal, neurobiological model for the psychotherapeutic context. During treatment, an empathic therapist consciously and explicitly attends to a patient's verbalizations to diagnose and rationalize his or her dysregulating symptomatology. But an experienced therapist also listens and interacts at another, more subjective level, one that implicitly processes moment-to-moment socioemotional information at levels below awareness. Beneath the conscious verbal conversation of two left brains is the unconscious nonverbal protoconversation of two right brains. For a therapeutic alliance to work, a therapist must be felt by the patient to be in a state of vitalizing attunement. In other words, the crescendos and decrescendos of a therapist's affective state must resonate with a patient's similar state. An intuitively empathic therapist psychobiologically attunes to and resonates with a patient's shifting affective state, thereby co-creating with the patient a context in which the clinician can act as a regulator of the patient's physiology.

Recently, I have suggested that the right hemisphere is dominant in psychotherapy. Experiences of relational trauma and attachment dysregulation appear in the therapeutic alliance as clinical reenactments. From a neuropsychological perspective, rapid, implicit right brain-to-right brain nonverbal body-based, affective communications (facial expressions, tones of voice, and gestures) convey unconscious transference-countertransference transactions, which revive earlier attachment memories, especially of intensely dysregulated affective states. Russell Meares has also described a form of therapeutic conversation that can be conceived as a dynamic interplay between two right hemispheres. As in early development, the attachment dynamic of interactive repair and regulation of the patient's dysregulated affects are an essential mechanism of the therapeutic action.

AJP: From your perspective, what is the role of play in psychotherapy?

Schore: With respect to child psychotherapy, clinical models of play between therapist and patient have long been known to be effective with early trauma histories. According to the Association for Play Therapy, treatment involves "the systematic use of a theoretical model to establish an interpersonal process wherein trained play therapists use the therapeutic powers of play to help clients prevent or resolve psychosocial difficulties and achieve optimal growth and development." Studies of neurobiologically informed play therapy now integrate data from neuroscience and recent advances in theory, including my own work on attachment, attunement, and the right brain. These approaches focus on attachment trauma and stress the importance of the therapeutic relationship and the regulation of affective states. The paradigm shift I mentioned earlier now indicates that the role of the therapist is not to interpret children's play, but to co-create play contexts that can form an attachment, a bond of emotional communication and interactive regulation. We understand a child's defenses as strategies that minimize or avoid intolerable affects, and so we pay attention not only to conscious but also to unconscious affects.

AJP: Are you implying that the therapist needs to become a playmate?

Schore: In this sense: Spontaneous (more so than controlled) dyadic play can reenact attachment trauma, which is then communicated and regulated by the therapist. Play therapy also serves as a context for rupture and repair, which enables a child to cope with an array of negative affects and to generate novel solutions to interpersonal problems. The co-created therapeutic relationship thus allows children to tolerate and regulate not only negative emotions but also positive emotions, and it facilitates a more secure implicit, positive sense of self and emotional well-being.

AJP: Does this also have implications for therapy with adults?

Schore: The integration of neuroscience into clinical models instills an appreciation of the essential role of play in the "change process" of adult psychotherapy. For example, current neurobiologically informed models of music therapy—and dance and movement therapy and art therapy—now incorporate my work. But beyond these, traditional psychotherapists are also emphasizing the growth-facilitating affects of play. Let me paraphrase Winnicott's classic dictum: Psychotherapy happens in the overlap of the two play areas—that of the patient and that of the therapist. He said that, if the therapist can't play, he's not suitable for the work; and if a patient can't play, then something needs to be done to enable the patient to play—and after that, psychotherapy can begin. The reason playing was so essential, according to Winnicott, was that by playing, a patient was being creative.

With adults, therapy focuses on interactively regulating conscious and unconscious negative and positive affect, as well as facilitating the growth of the patient's symbolic, imaginative functions. Play allows the patient and therapist not only to discover but to nurture different and more complex aspects of the right brain self. That said, in all forms of psychotherapy— infant, child, and adult—many now agree that the emotion-expressing and -regulating attachment relationship between the patient and therapist is essential to therapeutic change.

This kind of therapy goes substantially beyond teaching patients coping skills. The practice of psychotherapy is fundamentally relational. The therapeutic alliance—the major vector of change—is essentially a two-person system for self-exploration and relational healing. At all points in the life span, this emotional growth of the self occurs in relational contexts. From infancy throughout life, spontaneous, rapidly acting emotional processes are centrally involved in enabling us to regulate—and, thereby, to cope with—stresses and challenges. These processes are thus an essential marker of mental health and emotional well-being.

AJP: If play changes the brain, should we assume that psychotherapy also changes the brain?

Schore: The way patients grow proves to be more than psychological. A large body of research indicates that therapy induces neuroplastic changes in the brain, especially in the emotion-processing right limbic system. The early developing right brain has later growth spurts. Psychotherapy-induced changes in the right brain allow the transformation of an insecure attachment into an "earned secure" attachment that encodes more efficient strategies of affect regulation. Researchers have concluded that although the left hemisphere specializes in coping with predictable representations and strategies, the right predominates in assimilating novel situations and interacting with a new environment. In addition to promoting cognitive changes, psychotherapy can boost emotional resilience, a central marker of mental health, which we consider an individual's ability to use in coping flexibly with the surprises and stresses inherent in human interactions.

AJP: Many consider surprise to be a key element of play. Does it also help psychotherapy?

Schore: Recall that attuned play amplifies joy, excitement, and yes indeed, surprise. A positive state in turn allows individuals to experience a situation as safe, to feel unrestrained, to take risks, to explore novel pathways, and to be creative. I've suggested that the positive arousal of surprise is central to all forms of exploration and play and is associated with increasing safety and trust. Psychoanalyst Philip Bromberg has written extensively about the critical role of "safe surprises" in therapy, calling it "interpersonal novelty" that allows the self to grow because neither party anticipates it. Instead, he claims, it is organized by what takes place between two minds and belongs to neither alone. He concludes that through the novelty and surprise of this reciprocal process therapeutic action takes shape, and that they account for the enhanced spontaneity and flexibility of a patient's personality resulting from successful therapy.

AJP: What new technologies have had an impact on your work?

Schore: For much of the past century, we based our knowledge about brain functions on anatomical studies of neurological patients, which excluded research on normal brains. EEG accessed only cerebral levels, offered poor resolution within cortical regions, and provided no access at all to subcortical areas. Then came the so-called "decade of the brain" in the 1990s, and researchers began using neuroimaging technologies such as functional magnetic resonance imaging (fMRI), technologies that could record brain activity with more local precision as it moves from a resting to an activated state during various human functions, both pathological and normal. We now have studies in real time of brain changes not only during cognitive and emotional functions but also during higher functions involving creativity, morality, and humor. In addition, these technologies reach deep subcortical brain structures such as the amygdala, hypothalamus, and brain stem. Recent neuroimaging studies of the central nervous system, along with updated measures of the autonomic nervous system, have greatly added to our knowledge of the mechanisms that lie beneath behavior, cognition, and affect.

Technological advances have enabled a major area of current research focusing on brain laterality. There is now agreement that each hemisphere is an independent system capable of different forms of attention and different forms of consciousness. Indeed, the differences between the two hemispheres are profound. Thus, we are using the current concept of hemisphericity to explore and understand not two halves of one brain, but dual right and left cortical-subcortical systems with unique structure-function relationships. In other words, the singular term "the brain" is imprecise—we're looking at a dual system.

Neuroimaging research has established that the right hemisphere is critical to the processing of social and emotional information such as facial recognition and deciphering nonverbal communication. These, of course, are central components of the attachment dynamic and face-to-face play. Facial emotions can be automatically appraised by the right brain at astonishing speed—within 30 milliseconds—and then spontaneously expressed a fraction of a second later. Advances in technology allow us to understand better very rapid spontaneous processes that occur beneath levels of conscious awareness. Attachment relationships shape circuits in the right brain during early and critical periods of right brain development.

AJP: Then are we the sum of our brain's early circuitry?

Schore: The story is more complicated. Adaptive attachment mechanisms endure over the course of the life span. Again, the right brain has later growth spurts affected by socioemotional experiences. Throughout life, the right brain, and not the left brain, is critical to survival functions such as the allocation of attention, the capacity to experience positive and negative emotions, the regulation of stress, and the ability to read the emotional states of other human beings empathically and intuitively. The right hemisphere specializes in pattern recognition—in the comprehension of faces, chords and complex pitch, graphic images, and voices. Over the life span, the right-lateralized prefrontal regions are responsible for the most complex regulation of affect and stress. Indeed, the right frontal cortex, more closely in touch with emotion and the body, is also the most sophisticated, extensive, and highly evolved part of the brain. Its basic social, perceptual, and regulatory functions are the foundations of later evolving higher human functions. Self-awareness and empathy depend on the circuits in the right hemisphere. And there, too, resides our ability to resolve social conflict. We perceive voices, sense smells and interpret pheromones, recognize faces, and interpret gestures on the right side. All these abilities play a role in interpersonal competence.

But recall that interpersonal neurobiology attempts to understand how the structure and function of the brain are shaped by experiences, especially those involving early emotional relationships. This perspective also attempts to understand how brains align their neural activities in social interactions. My work in developmental neurobiology specifically focuses on how the early developing right brain, the "emotional brain," is indelibly affected by emotional attachment relationships. But the right brain is also affected by later emotional attachments—close relationships, including deep friendships and mutual love.

It is important to note that although the attachment relationship shapes the early developing right brain, this hemisphere continues to enter growth spurts in later stages of life.

AJP: Let's return to the revolt against behavioral psychology. How does your new understanding of the right brain better equip us to understand the fast-acting neurodynamics of how we relate to others?

Schore: We can also see the paradigm shift from behavior to cognition to emotion in recent attachment research promoted by affective and social neuroscience, which is moving from the left to the right brain. Developmental neuroscience has moved beyond producing semantic, abstract studies of the attachment verbal narrative into real-time, ecologically valid studies of a mother's responsiveness. These studies on measuring the mother's response not to simple static images of generic infant faces but to videos of her right brain, dynamic, emotional reactions to her own infant. In parallel, neuroscientists are also beginning to study an infant's right brain responses to videos of his or her mother. The next step is to measure changes in both synchronizing brains and bodies as they align, synchronize, and emotionally interact. In other words, moment-to-moment, dynamic, right brain-to-right brain measures. We are moving from a one-brain neuroscience to a two-body and two-psychology understanding. A recent "hyperscanning" study of simultaneous fMRI brain images on both participants of a pair reports that establishing mutual understanding of novel signals synchronizes cerebral dynamics across the communicators' right temporal lobes. The interpersonal cerebral coherence occurred only in pairs with a shared communicative history. Not incidentally, this two-person psychology can also lead to a breakthrough in studying and understanding people involved in an intimate therapy relationship, or a loving couple, or indeed of free intersubjective play between familiar individuals within a close friendship.

AJP: How has the new understanding of the right brain advanced neuropsychoanalysis?

Schore: The neuroscience research on the nonverbal, fast-acting, implicit, nonconscious functions of the right brain has also affected the growth of neuropsychoanalysis—the study of the interpersonal neurobiological development of the unconscious mind. Iain McGilchrist, an authority on brain laterality, has noted that traditionally the right hemisphere has been "shrouded in darkness," silent, and, as he put it, "dumb." But recent neuroscience has shined light on this implicit realm of the human experience. We now have access to efficient, fundamental, ultrafast processes and rapid spontaneous phenomena that occur before and beneath conscious awareness. The right amygdala, the major fear center in the brain, for example, processes a facially expressed threat stimulus in well under 100 milliseconds. It takes another 400 milliseconds for the individual to be consciously aware of threats.

And we are this fast at grasping the nuances of complex social situations. The right prefrontal insula and anterior cingulate relay a fast intuitive assessment of complex social situations to allow the rapid adjustment of behavior in quickly changing and therefore uncertain social situations. Intuition, a knowledge that bypasses conscious reasoning, clearly implies right brain, not left brain, processing. Current brain research on human decision making articulates dual-process theories that clearly differentiate right-hemispheric intuition—which is fast, emotional, effortless, and creative—from left-hemispheric reasoning, which is slow, controlled, and effortful. We now conceptualize intuition as subjective experience associated with the use of knowledge gained through implicit learning and as direct knowing that seeps into conscious awareness without the conscious mediation of logic or rational process. Furthermore, by structurally locating circuits activated at various levels of implicit, unconscious process, neuropsychoanalysis has allowed us to explore the distinct dynamic of the preconscious, unconscious, and deep unconscious right brain functions.

AJP: This seems to return us to Freud's quest for a biology of the mind.

Schore: Indeed, yes it does. For the past three decades, I have offered research and clinical studies that support the idea that the essential functions of Freud's unconscious mind are localized in the right brain, the subjective implicit self. Freud distinguished early forming, unconscious, primary-process, nonverbal language functions from later forming, conscious, secondary-process language functions. There is now agreement that verbal, conscious, rational, and serial information processing takes place in the left hemisphere, whereas nonverbal, unconscious, holistic, and subjective emotional information processing takes place in the right. Freud was correct in positing that the deep unconscious (right) mind, which is highly visual, develops before the conscious surface (left) mind. We can now equate the early development of the unconscious with the ontogenesis of a right brain self-system that operates beneath conscious verbal levels.

Again, McGilchrist has marshaled a large body of evidence that indicates the right and left hemispheres create coherent, utterly different, and often incompatible versions of the world. And these world views establish competing priorities and values. He says that the conscious mind brings the world into focus and allows us to formulate thoughts in language. And crucially, he points out that the left brain is "aware of its own awareness." The left hemisphere also depends on denotative language and abstraction to manipulate what is known, fixed, static, isolated, decontextualized, explicit, disembodied, and general. But for all its remarkable command, the power of the left brain extends only so far. McGilchrist notes that these static, decontextualized facts, the province of the left brain, are ultimately lifeless.

In fact, we owe our appreciation of the lived world to the right hemisphere. In contrast to the left hemisphere, the right generates a world that consists of changing, evolving, interconnected, living individuals. The sense of the shifting social world often eludes our grasp; we know it only imperfectly, but it cares for us and gives us our lives. Naturally, the relationship between the two hemispheres is not always easy or harmonious. McGilchrist explores this tension in *The Master and His Emissary* [2009]. Alluding to Nietzsche's allegory, he portrays the right hemisphere as the Master. The left brain, the willful Emissary, seeks power, believes itself superior, and—in its ambition—sometimes betrays the Master, bringing both to harm. In his cautionary tale, McGilchrist convincingly argues that the left hemisphere increasingly takes precedence in the modern world, with potentially disastrous consequences.

I agree that present-day Western culture, even more so than in the past, overemphasizes left brain functions. Our cultural conceptions of both mental and physical health, as well as the aims of all levels of education, continue to stress rational, logical, analytical thinking at the expense of holistic, body-based, relational, right brain functions essential to homeostasis and survival. I would add that we see this trend in the current devaluation of spontaneous free play and the overemphasis on controlled, highly structured play. This left-hemispheric bias also overvalues active bodily exercise over mental activities and, thus, devalues playing with ideas and fantasy. And as we undervalue the symbolic play associated with the right brain, we diminish the unique powers of imagination, frustrate innovation, and starve the creative arts.

AJP: Returning to the beginning of this conversation, could you summarize the ways that regulation theory guided your work?

Schore: In 1994, I first articulated the basic organizing principles of regulation theory, and over the past three decades, I have expanded the theory. Note that what I am offering is a theory, a systematic exposition of the general principles of this science. I continue to argue that no theory of any human function can be restricted to a description of psychological processes. During that time, I continued to articulate three principles: First, that developmental theory must extend across the life span. Second, that it must integrate psychology and biology consonant with what we now know about biological structure and brain development. And third, that it must account for unconscious systems in everyday life that operate beneath awareness. The test of this theory is its success in generating experimental hypotheses that yield experimental research that can be applied clinically.

I then applied the lens of regulation theory to different aspects of the human experience. In my second and third books, *Affect Dysregulation and Disorders of the Self* and *Affect Regulation and the Repair of the Self* [both published in 2003], I focused on the problem of trauma, early brain development, psychopathogenesis, and affect dysregulation, as well as on the underlying right brain mechanisms involved in trauma that are reexpressed and repaired in affectively focused psychotherapy. In a subsequent volume, *The Science of the Art of Psychotherapy* [2012], I cited recent advances in neuroscience to support a new paradigm of psychotherapy that emphasized the essential role of both conscious and unconscious affects in treatment. I then outlined a clinical model of therapeutic enactments of relational trauma that can alter right brain circuits and allow psychotherapeutic changes in both the left and the right brain. I also applied the theory to pediatrics, psychiatry, family law and other cultural phenomena, and ethology when I investigated trauma in another big-brained mammal, elephants!

AJP: Where are you headed next?

Schore: I am now focusing on four other problems: the early interpersonal neurobiological origins of autistic spectrum disorders, and the subjects of gender, love, and creativity. Let me take these one at a time and begin with autism. All mental health fields now agree that infantile autism and disorganized insecure attachments are the most severe clinical expressions of early dysregulated social and emotional human development. A growing body of studies shows altered right brain maturation in these developmental psychopathologies. This has highlighted the need for a more effective neurobiologically informed model of differential diagnosis between these two disorders in infancy. Indeed, there is a strong if not urgent call in both autism and attachment literatures for updated, research-informed, clinically relevant interventions that can more effectively assess the mother-infant dyad during early periods of brain plasticity.

In 2013, I was approached by the editor of the *Journal of Infant, Child, and Adolescent Psychotherapy* to offer a neurobiological commentary on an upcoming article reporting the successful treatment of an attachment disorder over the first year. Citing both the infant-attachment and autism literatures, the author specifically posed the problem of differential diagnosis, a problem commonly encountered by clinicians who specialize in infancy. In response, I published two articles on the early interpersonal neurobiological assessment of attachment and autistic spectrum disorders. Studies indicate that the psychopathological processes leading to autism begin during fetal development due to genetic and untoward intrauterine influences of the social and physical environment, while disorganized attachments result from epigenetic mechanisms associated with stressful perinatal and postnatal social environments. The complex neurodevelopmental autistic disorders reflect altered connectivity and developmental derangement of the right brain, as opposed to attachment disorders that represent delayed connectivity or immaturity of the limbic-autonomic circuits of the right brain. Although both the analytic left hemisphere and holistic right hemisphere are affected by a common neuropathological process, at the core autism represents a severe impairment of the right-lateralized, implicit, cortical-subcortical self-system that acts unconsciously and automatically.

AJP: Does play have a role in this work as well?

Schore: Yes. Deficits in later developing pretend play are well documented, but I argue that deficits in the early spontaneous mother-infant play of protoconversation and intersubjectivity are central to the psychopathogenesis of autistic disorders. I have used neuroscience data to formulate an assessment model of a mother's right brain, an infant's right brain, and a mutually constructed right brain-to-right brain attachment relationship. Early assessments of high-risk dyads can easily transition into clinical interventions that potentially expand a mother's implicit capacities for interactive affect regulation—the core of the attachment dynamic—thereby creating a growth-facilitating environment for infant right brain development. This work suggests that modern attachment theory can act as a catalyst for the cross-fertilization of the attachment and autism worlds, one that can lead to more effective clinical intervention models. It also highlights the need for early prevention, including in the prenatal period.

And more recently, I have discussed the role of gender differences in autism. In my latest developmental writings in the *Infant Mental Health Journal*—"All Our Sons: The Developmental Neurobiology and Neuroendocrinology of Boys at Risk" [2017]—I cite a large body of research that indicates boys, more than girls, are at risk for autism, early onset schizophrenia, ADHD, conduct disorders, and externalizing psychopathologies. These disorders have increased significantly in recent years. To understand why boys are at risk, I use regulation theory as a model of the deeper psychoneurobiological mechanisms that underlie the vulnerability of the developing male. My central thesis posits that important gender differences appear between male and female social and emotional functions in the earliest stages of development and that these differences result not only from different sex hormones and social experiences but also in the rates of male and female brain maturation, specifically in the early developing right brain. Interdisciplinary research indicates that the stress-regulating circuits of the male brain mature more slowly than those of the female in the prenatal, perinatal, and postnatal critical periods, and that this dissimilarity is reflected in normal gender differences in attachment functions.

Because of maturational delay, developing males become more vulnerable over a longer period of time to stressors in the social environment—attachment trauma for example, as well as toxins in the physical environment, including endocrine disruptors such as pesticides and plasticizers that impair right brain development. In gender-related psychopathology, the early developmental neuroendocrinological and neurobiological mechanisms are involved in the increased vulnerability of males to the disorders I have mentioned, and they contribute to the recent widespread increase of these disorders in the United States.

AJP: You said that currently you are also looking at love and creativity. Does regulation theory and neuropsychoanalysis offer insights in the age-old preoccupations of artists and poets?

Schore: I am indeed turning my attention to a different interdisciplinary interface, the integration of neuroscience and the humanities. I stood on the shoulders of two giants in the history of science, Darwin and Freud, in a recent paper, "The Development of the Right Brain across the Life Span: What's Love Got to Do with It?"

Although love is mostly thought to be the province of the arts, of poets and writers, actors, dancers, and musicians, from the very beginnings of modern biology and psychology, science has also explored love's origins and emotional expressions. Indeed, in a work far ahead of its time, *The Expression of Emotions in Man and Animals* [1872], Charles Darwin noted that the power and the pleasurable sensation of love "causes a gentle smile and some brightening of the eyes" and "a strong desire to touch." Specifically referring to the origins of perhaps this most essential expression of the human species, he speculated, "the movements of expressions in the face and body . . . serve as the first means of communication between the mother and her infant; she smiles approval and thus encourages her child on the right path or frowns disapproval." At the beginning of the 20th century, Sigmund Freud began his pioneering studies in psychoanalysis and initiated the field's long history of interest in the essential role of love in human function and dysfunction. Referring to his evolving position on the developmental origins of love, I've suggested that although for much of his career Freud seemed ambivalent about the role of maternal influences in early development, in his very last work he definitively stated that the mother-infant relationship "is unique, without parallel, established unalterably for a whole lifetime as the first and strongest love-object and the prototype of all later love relations."

AJP: So what does love have to do with attachment theory?

Schore: Let's define the terms first. Love can be a noun denoting deep affection or a verb, to love, that describes the feeling of tenderness and passion that one lover communicates to another. The contrast in these two usages mirrors the ongoing shift from a one-person, intrapsychic to a two-person, interpersonal perspective in psychology, including the most prominent theory in developmental psychology: attachment theory. I used data from neuroscience to shed light on the ability of humans to love one another. The paradigmatic expression of this strongest of all emotions is forged in an attachment bond of mutual love between a mother and her infant, and this right brain-to-right brain, growth-promoting, emotional experience acts as a relational matrix for the emergence of the capacity to share a loving relationship with a valued other at later stages of life.

Consonant with Darwin's description of love as an emotional communication system, love is embedded in a basic evolutionary mechanism located in the early developing, emotion-processing right brain. The mutual love between the mother and the infant can optimally shape this evolutionary process. Neuroscientist Jack Nitschke and his colleagues in a 2004 article for *NeuroImage* declare that the first expression of love, the one between a mother and her infant, represents one of the "most powerful and evolutionarily preserved forms of positive affect in the emotional landscape of human behavior." As such, love proves essential for the preservation of the human species.

A significant body of neuroimaging research on love in infancy and adulthood points to how right brain attachment underpins the psychoneurobiological mechanisms of the capacity to form and maintain a strong emotional bond of mutual love with a valued other. Recent neuroimaging research of mother-infant love offers a model of the initial emergence of mutual love at 2 to 3 months, the period of the onset of protoconversation and dyadic play, as well as the neurodynamics of adult love. In a final section, "The Right Brain and Mutual Love across the Life Span," I integrate the research and clinical data to model the neuroanatomy, neuropsychology, and neuropsychoanalysis of this essential marker of what it means to be human.

AJP: Can love teach us more about the brain?

Schore: One of the major findings of brain science is that many of the underlying biological processes involved in mutual love operate at rapid time frames— and so unconsciously and at levels beneath awareness. For this reason, the relational psychobiological mechanism that underlies mutual love can best be described by integrating observations and data from not only neurobiology but also neuropsychoanalysis. It is now established that the unconscious processing of emotional information is mainly subsumed by a right hemisphere subcortical route. From the earliest stages of development, the adaptive capacity to receive and express the intense, body-based signals of mutual love operates spontaneously. In other words, at all later stages, the interpersonal signals of love are first perceptually processed unconsciously, automatically, effortlessly, at levels beneath conscious awareness, and they trigger changes in emotional arousal and internal state that produce the neuroendocrine chemistry of mutual love.

AJP: And what's play got to do with it?

Schore: This conception clearly suggests that intimate, spontaneous, intersubjective mother-infant play represents an important expression of mutual love. In fact, this idea is a central theme of another soon to be published work, "Early Right Brain Development: How Love Opens Creativity, Play, and the Arts," which I've written with Terry Marks-Tarlow, the guest editor of this issue of the *American Journal of Play* [see *Playground Creativity in Psychotherapy*].

AJP: That leads us to the final new subject you mentioned interested you—creativity.

Schore: As I have said throughout this interview, creativity has long been very meaningful to me, both personally and professionally. A large body of research implicates the right brain in creative processes, especially in the earliest stages where information is processed rapidly beneath conscious awareness. Indeed, research demonstrates that the initiatory stage of creative inspiration where sensorial, affective, and cognitive integrations take place rapidly at unconscious levels, as well as the ensuing stage of "incubation" and the emergence into consciousness of sudden insight, are both right lateralized. Neuroscientists Naama Mayseless and Simone G. Shamay-Tsoory offer evidence that the right frontal area mediates creativity while the left competes with or interferes with an original creative response. They suggest an antidote to this inhibition of the conscious mind and a surer route to creative production: reduce left frontal activity and surrender some cognitive control; open the right hemisphere to ambiguity and novelty, the source of creativity and imagination, and, thereby, to poetry, art, and music. To this I would add play, an essential process in artistic and scientific creativity.

Neuroscientists are converging on the principle that creativity helps us adapt to changing circumstances, develop novel solutions to problems (including interpersonal problems), and give value and purpose to human experience. Creativity, now considered a personality attribute, enables us the flexibility to cope with the social and emotional challenges to the right brain, integrated self at different stages of life and in changing cultural circumstances. This interpersonal neurobiological mechanism thus facilitates the growth and development of the socioemotional right brain, the human unconscious, throughout life.

The period of independent study I talked about earlier revealed to me that the process of both objective and subjective learning is a highly emotional one, and that studying body-based emotional processes cannot be done without also introspecting into my own self.

In essence, a central aspect of my recent work is an attempt to use my self-reflective awareness in order to understand my own creativity, not just its output, but its organizational processes. In neuropsychoanalytic terminology, these contributions are efforts of my left brain to understand my right brain, of making conscious what is unconscious. I'm reminded of Jung's dictum, "Man's task is to become conscious of the contents that process upward from the unconscious." In this lifelong search, Einstein tells us that "intellectual growth should commence at birth and cease only at death," and that "the true sign of intelligence is not knowledge but imagination."

References

Anders, S., Heinzle, J., Weiskopf, N., Ethofer, T., & Haynes, J. D. (2011). Flow of affective information between communicating brains. *NeuroImage, 54*, 439–446.

AAACP (American Academy of Child & Adolescent Psychiatry). (n.d.). *The campaign for America's kids.* Retrieved May 3, 2011, from http://www.campaignforamericaskids.org/

Abel, K. M., Dalman, C., Svensson, A. C., Susser, E., Dal, H., Idring, S., et al. (2013). Deviance in fetal growth and risk of autism spectrum disorder. *American Journal of Psychiatry, 170*, 391–398.

Abraham, E., Hendler, T., Shapira-Lichter, I., Kanat-Maymon, Y., Zagoory-Sharon, O., & Feldman, R. (2014). Father's brain is sensitive to childcare experiences. *Proceedings of the National Academy of Sciences USA, 111*, 9792–9797.

Adamec, R. E., Blundell, J., & Burton, P. (2003). Phosphorylated cyclic AMP response element bonding protein expression induced in the periaqueductal gray by predator stress; its relationship to the stress experience, behavior, and limbic neural plasticity. *Progress in Neuro-Psychopharmacology & Biological Psychiatry, 27*, 1243–1267.

Adriani, W., Seta, D. D., Dessi-Fulgheri, F., Farabollini, F., & Laviola, G. (2003). Altered profiles of spontaneous novelty seeking, impulsive behavior, and response to D-amphetamine in rats perinatally exposed to bisphenol A. *Environmental Health Perspectives, 111*, 395–401.

Afif, A., Bouvier, R., Buenerd, A., Trouillas, J., & Mertens, P. (2007). Development of the human fetal insular cortex: Study of the gyration from 13 to 28 gestational weeks. *Brain Structure and Function, 212*, 335–346.

Ainsworth, M. D. S. (1967). *Infancy in Uganda: Infant care and the growth of love.* Baltimore, MD: Johns Hopkins University Press.

Ainsworth, M. D. S., Blehar, M. C., Waters, E., & Wall, S. (1978). *Patterns of attachment: A psychological study of the strange situation.* Hillsdale, NJ: Erlbaum.

Albers, E. M., Beijers, R., Riksen-Walraven, M., Sweep, F. C. G., & De Weerth, C. (2015). Cortisol levels of infants in center care across the first year of life: Links with quality of care and infant temperament. *Stress* [Early Online], 1–10. doi:10.3109/10253890.2015.1089230

Alexander, G. M., & Saenz, J. (2011). Postnatal testosterone levels and temperament in early infancy. *Archives of Sexual Behavior, 40,* 1287–1292.

Allman, J. M., Watson, K. K., Tetreault, N. A., & Hakeem, A. Y. (2005). Intuition and autism: A possible role for Von Economo neurons. *Trends in Cognitive Science, 9,* 367–373.

Ally, B.A., Hussey, E.P., & Donahue, M.J. (2013). A case of hyperthymesia: rethinking the role of the amygdala in autobiographical memory. NeuroCase, 19, 166–181.

Ammaniti, M., & Gallese, V. (2014). *The birth of intersubjectivity.* New York, NY: Norton.

Ammaniti, M., & Trentini, C. (2009). How new knowledge about parenting reveals the neurobiological implications of intersubjectivity: A conceptual synthesis of recent research. *Psychoanalytic Dialogues, 19,* 537–555.

Angold, A., & Costello, E. J. (2006). Puberty and depression. *Child and Adolescent Psychiatry Clinics of North America, 15,* 919–937.

Apicella, F., Chericoni, N., Costanzo, V., Baldini, S., Billeci, L., Cohen, D., & Muratori, F. (2013). Reciprocity in interaction: A window on the first year of life in autism. *Autism Reearch and Treatment.* doi.org/10.1155/2013/705895

Aron, A., Fisher, H., Mashek, D. J., Strong, G., Li, H., & Brown, L. L. (2005). Reward, motivation, and emotion systems associated with early stage intense romantic love. *Journal of Neurophysiology, 94,* 327–337.

Aron, E. N., & Aron, A. (1996). Love and expansion of the self: The state of the model. *Personal Relationships, 3,* 45–58.

Atzil, S., Hendler, T., & Feldman, R. (2011). Specifying the neurobiological basis of human attachment: Brain, hormones, and behavior in synchronous and intrusive mothers. *Neuropsychopharmacology.* doi:10.1038/npp.2011.172

Baker, K. B., & Kim, J. J. (2004). Amygdalar lateralization in fear conditioning: Evidence for greater involvement of the right amygdala. *Behavioral Neuroscence, 118,* 15–23.

Bakermans-Kranenburg, M. J., & van IJzendoorn, M. H. (2009a). The first 10,000 Adult Attachment Interviews: Distributions of adult attachment representations in clinical and non-clinical groups. *Attachment & Human Development, 11,* 223–263.

Bakermans-Kranenburg, M. J., & van IJzendoorn, M. H. (2009b). No reliable gender differences in attachment across the lifespan. *Behavioral and Brain Sciences,* 32, 22–23.

Banzett, R. B., Mulnier, H. E., Murphy, K., Rosen, S. D., Wise, R. J. S., & Adams, L. (2000). Breathlessness in humans activates insular cortex. *NeuroReport 11,* 2117–2120.

Baranek, G. C.,Watson, L. R., Boyd, B. A., Poe, M. D., David, F. J., & McGuire, L. (2013). Hyporesponsiveness to social and nonsocial sensory stimuli in children with autism, children with developmental delays, and typically developing children. *Development and Psychopathology, 25,* 307–320.

Bargh, J. A., & Chartrand, T. L. (1999). The unbearable automaticity of being. *American Psychologist, 54*, 462–479.

Barker, D. J. P. (1998). *Mothers, babies and health in later life* (2nd ed.). London, UK: Churchill Livingstone.

Barker, D. J. P., Eiikkson, J. G., Forsen, T., & Osmond, C. (2002). Fetal origins of adult disease: Strength of effects and biological basis. *International Journal of Epidemiology, 31*, 1235–1239.

Baron-Cohen, S., Ring, H. A., Bullmore, E. T., Wheelwright, S., Ashwin, C., & Williams, S. C. R. (2000). The amygdala theory of autism. *Neuroscience & Biobehavioral Reviews, 24*, 355–364.

Baron-Cohen, S., O'Riordan, M., Jones, R., Stone, V., & Plaisted, K. (1999). A new test of social sensitivity: Detection of faux pas in normal children and children with Asperger syndrome. *Journal of Autism and Developmental Disorders, 29*, 407–418.

Barrett, J., Wonch, K. E., Gonzalez, A., Ali, N., Steiner, M., Hall, G. B., & Fleming, A. S. (2012). Maternal affect and quality of parenting experiences are related to amygdala response to infant faces. *Social Neuroscience, 7*(3), 252–268.

Bartels, A., & Zeki, S. (2004). The neural correlates of maternal and romantic love. *NeuroImage, 21*, 1155–1166.

Baumeister, R. F., & Leary, M. R. (1995). The need to belong: Desire for interpersonal attachments as a fundamental human motivation. *Psychological Bulletin, 117*, 497–528.

Bazhenova, O. V., Stroganova, T. A., Doussard-Roosevelt, J. A., Posikera, I. A., & Porges, S. W. (2007). Physiological responses of 5-month-old infants to smiling and blank faces. *International Journal of Psychophysiology, 63*, 64–76.

Beebe, B., Jaffe, J., Markese, S., Buck, K., Chen, H., Cohen, P., et al. (2010). The origins of 12-month attachment: A microanalysis of 4-month mother-infant interaction. *Attachment and Human Development, 12*, 3–142.

Beebe, B., & Lachmann, F. M. (1994). Representations and internalization in infancy: Three principles of salience. *Psychoanalytic Psychology*, 11, 127–165.

Beebe, B., Lachmann, F. M., Maekese, S., Buck, K. A., Bahrick, L. E., & Chen, H. (2012). On the origins of disorganized attachment and internal working models: Paper II. An empirical microanalysis of 4-month mother-infant interaction. *Psychoanalytic Dialogues, 22*, 352–374.

Behen, M. E., Muzik, O., Saporta, A. S. D., Wilson, B. J., Pai, D., Hua, J., et al. (2009). Abnormal fronto-striatal connectivity in children with histories of early deprivation: A diffusion tensor imaging study. *Brain Imaging and Behavior, 3*, 292–297.

Bekedam, D. J., Engelsbel, S., Mol, B. W., Buitendijk, S. E., & van der Pal-de Bruin, K. M. (2002). Male predominance in fetal distress during labor. *American Journal of Obstetrics and Gynecology, 187*, 1605–1607.

Bem, S. L. (1974). The measurement of psychological androgeny. *Journal of Consulting and Clinical Psychology, 42*, 155–162.

Benenson, J. F. (1993). Greater preference among females than males for dyadic interaction in early childhood. *Child Development, 64*, 544–555.

Benowitz, L. I., Bear, D. M., Rosenthal, R., Mesulam, M.-M., Zaidel, E., & Sperry, R. W. (1983). Hemispheric specialization in nonverbal communication *Cortex, 19,* 5–11.

Berg, R. (2009). Autism—an environmental health issue after all. *Journal of Environmental Health, 71,* 14–18

Bergman, K., Glover, V., Sarkar, P. Abbott, D. H., & O'Connor, T. G. (2010). In utero cortisol and testosterone exposure and fear reactivity in infancy. *Hormones and Behavior, 57,* 306–312.

Bernard, K., Peloso, E., Laurenceau, J. P., Zhang, Z. Y., & Dozier, M. (2015). Examining change in cortisol patterns during the 10-week transition to a new child-care setting. *Child Development, 86,* 456–471.

Berthier, M., Starkstein, S., & Leiguarda, R. (1987). Behavioral effects of damage to the right insula and surrounding regions. *Cortex, 23,* 673–678.

Bertrand, M., & Pan, J. (2013). The trouble with boys: Social influences and the gender gap in disruptive behavior. *American Economic Journal: Applied Economics, 5,* 32–64.

Bestelmeyer, P.E.G., Belin, P., & Grosbas, M-H. (2011). Right temporal TMS impairs voice detection. *Current Biology, 21,* R838–839.

Bilbo, S. D., Levkoff, L. H., Mahoney, J. H., Watkins, L. R., Rudy, J. W., & Maier, S. F. (2005). Neonatal infection induces memory impairments following an immune challenge in adulthood. *Behavioral Neuroscience, 119,* 293–301.

Bilbo, S. D., Smith, S. H., & Schwartz, J. M. (2011). A lifespan approach to neuroinflammatory and cognitive disorders: A critical role for glia. *Journal of Neuroimmune Pharmacology, 7,* 24–41.

Bingham, B., Gray, M., Sun, T., & Viau, V. (2011). Postnatal blockade of androgen receptors or aromatase impair the expression of stress hypothalamic-pituitary-adrenal axis habituation in adult male rats. *Psychoneuroendocrinology, 36,* 249–257.

Black, M., Hess, C. R., & Berenson-Howard, J. (2000). Toddlers from low-income families have below normal mental, motor, and behavior scores on the Revised Bayley Scales. *Journal of Applied Developmental Psychology, 21,* 655–666.

Blonder, L. X., Bowers, D., & Heilman, K. M. (1991). The role of the right hemisphere in emotional communication. *Brain, 114,* 1115–1127.

Bock, J., Murmu, R. P., Fredman, N., Leshem, M., & Braun, K. (2008). Refinement of dendritic and synaptic networks in the rodent anterior cingulate and orbitofrontal cortex: Critical impact of early and late social experience. *Developmental Neurobiology, 68,* 685–695.

Boisse, L., Moulhate, A., Ellis, S., & Pittman, Q. J. (2004). Long-term alterations in neuroimmune responses after neonatal exposure to lipopolysaccharide. *Journal of Neuroscience, 24,* 4928–4934.

Bolger, N., Kessler, R.C., & Zuckerman, A. (2000). Invisible support and adjustment to stress. *Journal of Personality and Social Psychology, 79,* 953–961.

Bolger, N., & Amarel, D. (2007). Effects of social support visibility on adjustment to stress: Experimental evidence. *Journal of Personality and Social Psychology, 92*, 458–475.

Booth, A., & Dabbs, J. M. (1993). Testosterone and men's marriages. *Social Forces, 72*, 463–477.

Boston Change Process Study Group. (2007). The foundational level of psychodynamic meaning: Implicit process in relation to conflict, defense and the dynamic unconscious. *International Journal of Psychoanalysis, 88*, 843–860.

Bourne, V. J., & Gray, D. L. (2009). Hormone exposure and functional lateralization: Examining the contributions of prenatal and later life hormonal exposure. *Psychoneuroendocrinology, 34*, 1214–1224.

Bourne, V. J., & Todd, B. K. (2004). When left means right: An explanation of the left cradling bias in terms of right hemisphere specializations. *Developmental Science, 7*, 19–24.

Bowlby, J. (1953). *Child care and the growth of love.* London, UK: Pelican.

Bowlby, J. (1969). *Attachment and loss, vol. 1: Attachment.* New York, NY: Basic Books.

Bowlby, J. (1973). *Attachment and loss, vol. 2: Separation, anxiety and anger.* New York, NY: Basic Books.

Bowlby, J. (1982). *Loss: Sadness and depression, Volume* 3. New York, NY: Basic Books.

Boyle, C. A., Boulet, S., Schieve, L. A., Cohen, R. A., Blumberg, S. J., Yeargin-Alsopp, M. N., et al. (2011). Trends in the prevalence of developmental disabilities in US children, 1997–2008. *Pediatrics, 127*, 1034–1042.

Bradshaw, G., & Schore, A. N. (2007). How elephants are opening doors: Developmental neuroethology, attachment, and social context. *Ethology, 113*, 426–436.

Brancucci, A., Lucci, G., Mazzatenta, A., & Tommasi, L. (2009). Asymmetries of the human social brain in the visual, auditory and chemical modalities. *Philosophical Transactions of the Royal Society of London. Series B, Biological Sciences, 364*, 895–914.

Brand, M., Eggers, C., Reinhold, N., Fujiwara, E., Kessler, J., Heiss, W.-D., & Markowitsch, H. J. (2009). Functional brain imaging in 14 patients with dissociative amnesia reveals right inferolateral prefrontal hypometabolism. *Psychiatry Research: Neuroimaging, 174*, 32–39.

Brazelton, T. B. (1973). *Neonatal behavior assessment scale.* Philadelphia, PA: Lippincott.

Brazelton, T. B., Koslowski, B., & Main, M. (1974). The origins of reciprocity: The early mother-infant interaction. In M. Lewis & L. A. Rosenblum (Eds.), *The effect of the infant on its caregiver* (pp. 49–76). New York, NY: Wiley Interscience.

Brazelton, T.B., & Cramer, B.G. (1990). *The earliest relationship.* Reading: Addison-Wesley.

Brenner, C. (1980), A psychoanalytic theory of affects. In R. Plutchik & H. Kellerman (Eds.), *Emotion: Theory, research, and experience* (Vol. 1). New York, NY: Academic Press.

Bretherton, I. (1985). Attachment theory: Retrospect and prospect. *Monographs of the Society of Research in Child Development*, 50 (1–2), 3–35.

Brettell, R., Yeh, P. S., & Impey, L. W. (2008). Examination of the association between male gender and preterm delivery. *European Journal of Obstetrics & Gynecology and Reproductive Biology, 141*, 123–126.

Bromberg, P. M. (2006). *Awakening the dreamer: Clinical journeys*. Mahwah, NJ: Analytic Press.

Bromberg, P. M. (2011). *The shadow of the tsunami and the growth of the relational mind*. New York, NY: Routledge.

Brown, J. S., Jr. (2009). Effects of bisphenol-A and other endocrine disruptors compared with abnormalities of schizophrenia: An endocrine-disruption theory of schizophrenia. *Schizophrenia Bulletin*, 35, 256–278.

Buck, R. (1994). The neuropsychology of communication: Spontaneous and symbolic aspects. *Journal of Pragmatics*, 22, 265–278.

Burnham, T. C., Chapman, J. F., Gray, P. B., McIntyre, M. H., Lipson, S. F., & Ellison, P. T. (2003). Men in committed, romantic relationships have lower testosterone. *Hormones and Behavior, 44*, 119–122.

Bush, G., Luu, P., & Posner, M. I. (2000). Cognitive and emotional influences in anterior cingulate cortex. *Trends in Cognitive Science, 4*, 215–222.

Buss, C., Davis, E. P., Class, Q. A., Gierczak, M., Patillo, C., Glynn, L. M., & Sandman, C. A. (2009). Maturation of the human fetal startle response: Evidence for a sex-specific maturation of the human fetus. *Early Human Development*, 85, 633–638.

Buss, K.A., Schumacher, J.R.M., Dolski, I., Kalin, N.H., Goldsmith, H.H., & Davidson, R.J. (2003). Right frontal brain activity, cortisol, and withdrawal behavior in 6-month-0ld infants. *Behavioral Neuroscience, 117*, 11–20.

Calkins, S. D., Dedmon, S. E., Gill, K. L., Lomax, L. E., & Johnson, L. M. (2002). Frustration in infancy: Implications for emotion regulation, physiological processes, and temperament. *Infancy*, 3, 175–197.

Call, J. D. (1978). Differential vulnerability and coping in boys and girls at birth. In E. J. Anthony, C. Koupernik, C. Chiland, A. Freud, & M. Mahler (Eds.), *The child in his family: Vulnerable children* (Vol. 4, pp. 145–171). New York, NY: Wiley.

Calnen, G. (2007). Paid maternity leave and its impact in breastfeeding in the United States: An historic, economic, political, and social perspective. *Breastfeeding Medicine*, 2, 34–44.

Carlson, V., Cicchetti, D., Barnett, D., & Braunwald, K. (1989). Disorganized/disoriented attachment relationships in maltreated infants. *Developmental Psychology*, 25, 525–531.

Carlsson, J., Langercrantz, H., Olson, L., Printz, G., & Bartocci, M. (2008). Activation of the right fronto-temporal cortex during maternal facial recognition in young infants. *Acta Paediatrica*, 97, 1221–1225.

Carson, R. (1962). *Silent spring*. New York, NY: Houghton Mifflin Harcourt.

Carson, R. (1965). *The sense of wonder*. New York, NY: Harper & Row.

Cerqueira, J. J., Almeida, O. F. X., & Sousa, N. (2008). The stressed prefrontal cortex. Left? Right! *Brain, Behavior, and Immunity, 22,* 630–638.

Challis, J., Newnham, J., Petraglia, F., Yeganegi, M., & Bocking, A. (2013). Fetal sex and preterm birth. *Placenta, 34,* 95–99.

Chartrand, T. L., & Bargh, J. A. (1999). The chameleon effect: The perception-behavior link and social interaction. *Journal of Personality and Social Psychology, 76,* 893–910.

Chawarska, K., Macari, S., & Shic, F. (2013). Decreased spontaneous attention to social scenes in 6-month-old infants later diagnosed with autism spectrum disorders. *Biological Psychiatry, 74,* 195–203.

Chelazzi, L., Bisley, & Bartolomeo, P. (2018). The unconscious guidance of attention. *Cortex, 102,* 1–5.

Chen, F., Zhou, L., Bai, Y., Zhou, R., & Chen, L. (2014). Sex differences in the adult HPA axis and affective behaviors are altered by perinatal exposure to a low dose of bisphenol A. *Brain Research, 1571,* 12–24.

Chen, L., & Hsiao, J. (2014). Right hemisphere dominance in nonconscious processing. *Journal of Vision, 14,* 1313. doi:10.1167/14.10.1313

Chi, J. G., Dooling, E. C., & Gilles, F. H. (1977). Gyral development of the human brain. *Annals of Neurology, 1,* 86–93.

Chiron, C., Jambaque, I., Nabbout, R., Lounes, R., Syrota, A., & Dulac, O. (1997). The right brain hemisphere is dominant in human infants. *Brain, 120,* 1057–1065.

Choate, J. V. A., Slayden, O. D., & Resko, J. A. (1998). Immunocytochemical localization of androgen receptors in brains of developing and adult male rhesus monkeys. *Endocrine, 8,* 51–60.

Clark, H.H., & Brennan, S.E. (1991). Grounding in communication. *Perspectives in Socially Shared Cognition,* 13, 127–149.

Clifton, V. L. (2010). Review: Sex and the human placenta: Mediating different strategies of fetal growth and survival. *Placenta, 24,* 533–539.

Commission on Children at Risk (2003). *Hardwired to connect. The new scientific case for authoritative communities.* New York, NY: Institute for American Values.

Conti, G., Hansman, C., Heckman, J. J., Novak, M. F. X., Ruggiero, A., & Suomi, S. J. (2012). Primate evidence on the late health effects of early-life adversity. *Proceedings of the National Academy of Sciences USA, 109,* 8866–8871.

Cooper, R. P.,&Aslin, R. N. (1990). Preference of infant-directed speech in the first month after birth. *Child Development, 61,* 1584–1595.

Costafreda, S. G., Brammer, M. J., David, A. S., & Fu, C. H. Y. (2008). Predictors of amygdala activation during the processing of emotional stimuli: A meta-analysis of 385 PET and fMRI studies. *Brain Research Reviews, 58,* 57–70.

Courchesne, E., Carper, R., & Akshoomoff, N. (2008). Evidence of brain overgrowth in the first year of life in autism. *Journal of the American Medical Association, 290,* 337–344.

Cowan, W. M. (1979). The development of the brain. *Scientific American, 241*(3), 113–133.

Cozolino, L. (2002). *The neuroscience of psychotherapy: Building and rebuilding the human brain.* New York, NY: Norton.

Craig, A. D. (2010). The sentient self. *Brain Structure & Funcion., 214*, 563–577.

Craig, A. D. (2011). Significance of the insula for the evolution of human awareness of feelings from the body. *Annals of the New York Academy of Science,, 1225*, 72–82.

Craig, A. D., Chen, K., Bandy, D., & Reiman, E. M. (2000). Thermosensory activation of insular cortex. *Nature Neuroscience, 3*,194–190.

Critchley, H. D., Mathias, C. J., & Dolan, R. J. (2002). Fear conditioning in humans: The influence of awareness and autonomic arousal on functional neuroanatomy. *Neuron, 33*, 653–663.

Crockenberg, S. C. (2003). Rescuing the baby from the bathwater: How gender and temperament (may) influence how childcare affects child development. *Child Development, 74*, 1034–1038.

Crowell, D. H., Jones, R. H., Kapuniai, L. E., & Nakagawa, J. K. (1973). Unilateral cortical activity in newborn humans: An early index of cerebral dominance? *Science, 180*, 205–208.

Cummings, D. C., Quigley, M. E., & Yen, S. S. (1983). Acute suppression of circulating testosterone levels by cortisol in men. *Journal of Clinical Endocrinology and Metabolism, 57*, 671–673.

Cunningham, R. L., Lumia, A. R., & McGinnis, M. Y. (2012). Androgen receptors, sex behavior, and aggression. *Neuroendocrinology, 96*, 131–140.

Curby, K., Willenbockel, V., Tanaka, J., & Schultz, R. (2010). Face processing in autism: Insights from the perceptual expertise framework. In I. Gauthier, M.Tarr, & D. Bub (Eds.), *Perceptual expertise: Bridging brain and behavior.* New York: Oxford University Press.

Czeh, B., Perez-Cruz, C., Fuchs, E., & Flugge, G. (2008). Chronic stress-induced cellular changes in the medial prefrontal cortex and their potential clinical implications: Does hemisphere location matter? *Behavioural Brain Research, 190*, 1–13.

Dadds, J. M., Jr., Jambrak, J., Pasalich, D., Hawes, D., & Brennan, J. (2010). Impaired attention to the eyes of attachment figures and the developmental origins of psychopathy. *Journal of Child Psychology and Psychiatry, 52*, 238–245.

Dadds, J. M., Jr., Jurkovic, G. J., & Frady, R. L. (1991). Salivary testosterone and cortisol among late adolescent male offenders. *Journal of Abnormal Child Psychology, 19*, 469–478.

Darwin, C. (1859/1958). *The origin of species.* New York, NY: Signet Classics.

Darwin, C. (1872/1965). *The expression of emotion in man and animals.* Chicago, IL: University of Chicago Press.

Darwin, C.R. (1877). A biographical sketch of an infant. *Mind*, 2, 286–294.

Davies, J. M. (1996). Dissociation, repression and reality: Testing in the countertransference. The controversy over memory and false memory in the psychoanalytic treatment of adult survivors of childhood sexual abuse. *Psychoanalytic Dialogues, 6*, 189–218.

Davis, M., & Emory, E. (1995). Sex differences in neonatal stress reactivity. *Child Development, 66*, 14–27.

Dawson, G., Osterling, J., Meltzoff, A. N., & Kuhl, P. (2000). Case study of the development of an infant with autism from birth to two years of age. *Journal of Applied Developmental Psychology, 21*, 299–313.

De Bellis, M. D., Keshavan, M. S., Beers, S. R., Hall, J., Frustaci, A., Masalehdan, J., Noll, A. M., & Boring, A. M. (2001). Sex differences in brain maturation during childhood and adolescence. *Cerebral Cortex, 11*, 552–557.

de Cock, M., Maas, Y. G. H., & van de Bor, M. (2012). Does perinatal exposure to endocrine disruptors induce autism spectrum and attention deficit hyperactivity disorders? Review. *Acta Paediatrica, 101*, 811–818.

de Graaf-Peters, V. B., & Hadders-Algra, M. (2006). Ontogeny of the human central nervous system: What is happening when? *Early Human Development, 82*, 257–266.

de Haan, M., Belsky, J., Reid, V., Volein, A., & Johnson, M. H. (2004). Maternal personality and infants' neural and visual responsivity to facial expressions of emotion. *Journal of Child Psychology and Psychiatry, 45*, 1209–1218.

de Heering, A., & Rossion, B. (2015). Rapid categorization of natural face images in the infant right hemisphere. *eLife, 4*. doi:10.7554/eLife.06564

de Kloet, E. R., Joëls, M., & Holsboer, F. (2005). Stress and the brain: From adaptation to disease. *Nature Reviews Neuroscience, 6*, 463–475.

de Lacoste, M.-C., Horvath, D. S., & Woodward, D. J. (1991). Possible sex differences in the developing human fetal brain. *Journal of Clinical and Experimental Neuropsychology, 13*, 831–846.

De Pisapia, N., Serra, M., Rigo, P., Jager, J., Papinutto, N., Esposito, G., Venuti, P., & Bornstein, M. H. (2014). Interpersonal competence in young adulthood and right laterality in white matter. *Journal of Cognitive Neuroscience, 26*, 1257–1265.

De Vries, G., & Simerly, R. B. (2002). Anatomy, development, and function of sexually dimorphic neural circuits in the mammalian brain. In D. W. Pfaff , A. P. Arnold, A. M. Etgen, S. E. Fahrbach, R. L. Moss, R. T. & Rubin (Eds.), *Hormones, brain, and behavior. Volume IV: Development of hormone-dependent neuronal systems* (pp. 137–191). San Diego, CA: Academic.

De Weerth, C., van Hees, Y., & Buitelaar, J. K. (2003). Prenatal maternal cortisol levels and infant behavior during the first 5 months. *Early Human Development, 74*, 139–151.

Decety J., & Chaminade, T. (2003). When the self represents the other: A new cognitive neuroscience view on psychological identification. *Consciousness and Cognition, 12*, 577–596.

Decety J., & Lamm, C. (2007). The role of the right temporoparietal junction in social interaction: How low-level computational processes contribute to meta-cognition. *Neuroscientist, 13*, 580–593.

Dehaene, S., Changeux, J.-P., Naccache, L., Sackur, J., & Sergent, C. (2006). Conscious, preconscious, and subliminal processing: A testable taxonomy. *Trends in Cognitive Sciences, 10,* 204–211.

Deth, R., Muratore, C., Benzecry, J., Power-Charnitsky, V. A., & Waly, M. (2008). How environmental and genetic factors combine to cause autism: A redox/methylation hypothesis. *Neurotoxicology, 29,* 190–201.

Devinsky, O. (2000). Right cerebral hemisphere dominance for a sense of corporeal and emotional self. *Epilepsy &Behavior, 1,* 60–73.

Di Renzo, G. C., Conry, J. A., Blake, J., DeFrancesco, M. K., DeNicola, N., Martin, J. N., Jr., et al. (2015b). International Federation of Gynecology and Obstetrics opinion on reproductive health impacts of exposure to toxic environmental chemicals. *International Journal of Gynecology and Obstetrics, 131,* 219–225.

Di Renzo, G. C., Picchiassi, E., Coata, G., Clerici, G., & Brillo, E. (2015a). Is there a sex to the placenta? *Journal of Pediatric and Neonatal Individualized Medicine,* 4(2), e040246

Di Renzo, G. C., Rosati, A., Sarti, R. D., Cruciani, L., & Cutuli, A. M. (2007). Does fetal sex affect pregnancy outcome? *Gender Medicine, 4,* 19–30.

Dimberg, U. (1982). Facial reactions to facial expressions. *Psychophysiology, 19,* 643–647.

Dimberg, U., & Ohman, A. (1996). Behold the wrath: Psychophysiological responses to facial stimuli. *Motivation and Emotion, 20,* 149–182.

Dissanayake, E. (2001). Becoming *Homo Aestheticus*: Sources of aesthetic imagination in mother-infant interactions. *SubStance, 94/95,* 85–103.

Dmitreva, J., Steinberg, L., & Belsky, J. (2007). Child-care history classroom composition, and children's functioning in kindergarten. *Psychological Science, 18,* 1032–1039.

Dobbing, J. (1974). The later growth of the brain and its vulnerability. *Pediatrics,* 53, 2–6.

Dobbing, J., & Sands, J. (1973). Quantitative growth and development of human brain. *Archives of Diseases of Childhood, 48,* 757–767.

Doerr, P., & Pirke, K. M. (1976). Cortisol-induced suppression of plasma testosterone in normal adult males. *Journal of Clinical Endocrinology and Metabolism,* 43, 622–629.

Doria, V., Beckmann, C. F., Arichi, T., Merchant, N., Groppo, M., Turkheimer, F. E., et al. (2010). Emergence of resting state networks in the preterm human brain. *Proceedings of the National Academy of Sciences USA, 107,* 20015–20020.

Dorpat, T. L. (2001). Primary process communication. *Psychoanalytic Inquiry,* 3, 448–463.

Doussard-Roosevelt, J. A., Joe, C. M., Bazhenova, O. V., & Porges, S. W. (2003). Mother-child interaction in autistic and nonautistic children: Characteristics of maternal approach behaviors and child social responses. *Developmental Psychopathology., 15,* 277–295.

Dubois, J., Benders, M., Cachia, A., Lazeyras, F., Leucher, R. H., Sizonenko, S. V., et al. (2008). Mapping the early cortical folding process in the preterm newborn brain. *Cerebral Cortex, 18*, 1444–1454.

Dumas, G. (2011). Towards a two-body neuroscience. *Communicative and Integrative Biology, 4*, 349–352.

Dumas, G., Nadel, J., Soussignan, R., Martinerie, J., & Garnero, L. (2010). Inter-brain synchronization during social interaction. *PLOS ONE, 5*, e12166.

Dundas, E., Gasteb, H., & Strauss, M.S. (2012). Left visual field biases when infants process faces: A comparison of infants at high- and low-risk for autism spectrum disorder. *Journal of Autism and Developmental Disorders, 42*, 2659–2668.

Dutra, L., Bureau, J.-F., Holmes, B., Lyubchik, A., & Lyons-Ruth, K. (2009). Quality of early care and childhood trauma. A prospective study of developmental pathways to dissociation. *Journal of Nervous and Mental Disease, 197*, 383–390.

Elsmen, E., Steen, M., & Hellstrom-Westas, L. (2004). Sex and gender differences in newborn infants: Why are boys at increased risk? *Journal of Men's Health and Gender, 1*, 303–311.

Enriquez, P., & Bernabeu, E. (2008). Hemispheric laterality and dissociative tendencies: Differences in emotional processing in a dichotic listening task. *Consciousness and Cognition, 17*, 267–275.

Eriksson, J. G., Kajantie, E., Osmond, C., Thornburg, K., & Barker, D. J. P. (2010). Boys live dangerously in the womb. *American Journal of Human Biology, 22*, 330–335.

Eskenazi, B., Marks, A. R., Bradman, A., Harley, K., Barr, D. B., Johnson, C., Morga, N., & Jewell, N. P. (2007). Organophosphate pesticide exposure and neurodevelopment in young Mexican-American children. *Environmental Health Perspectives, 115*, 792–798.

Evans, S. F., Kobrosly, R. W., Barrett, E. S., Thurston, S. W., Calafat, A. M., Weiss, B., et al. (2014). Prenatal bisphenol A exposure and maternally reported behavior in boys and girls. *NeuroToxicology, 45*, 91–99.

Evans-Storms, R. B., & Cidlowski, J. A. (1995). Regulation of apoptosis by steroid hormones. *Journal of Steroid Biochemistry and Molecular Biology, 53*, 1–6.

Fang, C. Y., Egleston, B. L., Brown, K. M., Lavigne, J. V., Stevens, V. J., Barton, B. A., Chandler, D. W., & Dorgan, J. F. (2009). Family cohesion moderates the relation between free testosterone and delinquent behaviors in adolescent boys and girls. *Journal of Adolescent Health, 44*, 590–597.

Feldman, J. F., Brody, N., & Miller, S. A. (1980). Sex differences in non-elicited neonatal behaviors. *Merrill-Palmer Quarterly, 26*, 63–73.

Feldman, R. (2010). The relational basis of adolescent adjustment: Trajectories of mother-child interactive behaviors from infancy through adolescence shapes adolescents' adaptation. *Attachment & Human Development, 12*, 173–192.

Feldman, R. (2012). Parent-infant synchrony: A biobehavioral model of mutual influences in the formation of affiliative bonds. *Monographs of the Society of Research in Child Development, 77*, 42–51.

Feldman, R. (2015a). Sensitive periods in human social development: New insights from research on oxytocin, synchrony, and high-risk parenting. *Development and Psychopathology, 27,* 369–395.

Feldman, R. (2015b). The adaptive human parental brain: Implications for children's social development. *Trends in Neurosciences, 38,* 387–399.

Feldman, R. (2016). The neurobiology of mammalian parenting and the biosocial context of human caregiving. *Hormones and Behavior, 77,* 3–17.

Feldman, R., Greenbaum, C.W., & Yirmiya, N. (1999). Mother-infant affect synchrony as an antecedent of the emergence of self-control. *Developmental Psychology,* 35, 223–231.

Feldman, R., Keren, M., Gross-Ruzval, O., & Tyano, S. (2004). Mother-child touch patterns in infant feeding disorders: Relation to maternal, child, and environmental factors. *Journal of the American Academy of Child and Adolescent Psychiatry,* 43, 1089–1097.

Feldman, R., Magori-Cohen, R., Galili, G., Singer, M., & Louzon, Y. (2011). Mother and infant coordinate heart rhythms through episodes of interaction synchrony. *Infant Behavior and Development, 34,* 569–577.

Feldman, R., Singer, M., & Zagoory, O. (2010). Touch attenuates infants' physiological reactivity to stress. *Brain and Behavior, 13,* 271–278

Ferber, S. G., Feldman, R., & Makhoul, I. R. (2008). The development of maternal touch across the first year of life. *Early Human Development, 84,* 363–370.

Fernald, A. (1989). Intonation and communicative interest in mother's speech to infants: is the melody the message? *Child Development, 60,* 1497–1510.

Fischer, K. W., & Pipp, S. L. (1984). Development of the structures of unconscious thought. In K. S. Bowers & D. Meichenbaum (Eds.), *The unconscious reconsidered* (pp. 88–148). New York, NY: Wiley.

Fisher, H. E., Aron, A., Mashek, D., Li, H., & Brown, L. L. (2002). Defining the brain systems of lust, romantic attraction, and attachment. *Archives of Sexual Behavior, 31,* 413–419.

Fizgerald, M. (2013). *Recent advances in autism spectrum disorders.* Rijeka, Croatia: In Tech.

Fonagy, P., & Target, M. (2002). Early intervention and the development of self-regulation. *Psychoanalytic Inquiry,* 22, 307–335.

Forrester, G.S., Davis, R., Mareschal, D., Malatesta, G., & Todd, B.K. (in press). The left cradling bias: An evolutionary facilitator of social cognition? *Cortex.*

Forster, J., Epstude, K., & Ozelsel, A. (2009). Why love has wings and sex has not: How reminders of love and sex influence creative and analytic thinking. *Personality and Social Psychology Bulletin,* 35, 1479–1491.

Freud, S. (1895). Project for a scientific psychology. In J. Strachey (Ed. and Trans.), *The standard edition of the complete psychological works of Sigmund Freud* (Vol. 1, pp. 281–397). London, UK: Hogarth Press. Standard Edition I: 281 397.

Freud, S. (1900/1953). The interpretation of dreams. In J. Strachey (Ed. & Trans.),

The standard edition of the complete psychological works of Sigmund Freud (Vols. 4 & 5, pp. 1–627). London, UK: Hogarth Press.

Freud, S. (1913/1958). On beginning the treatment. In J. Strachey (Ed. and Trans.), *The standard edition of the complete psychological works of Sigmund Freud*. London, UK: Hogarth Press.

Freud, S. (1915a/1957). Thoughts for the times of war and death. In J. Strachey (Ed. and Trans.), *The standard edition of the complete psychological works of Sigmund Freud* (Vol. 14, pp. 273–302). London, UK: Hogarth Press.

Freud, S. (1915b/1957). Repression. In J. Strachey (Ed. and Trans.), *The standard edition of the complete psychological works of Sigmund Freud*. London, UK: Hogarth Press.

Freud, S. (1920). A general introduction to psycho-analysis. In J. Strachey (Ed. and Trans.), *The standard edition of the complete psychological works of Sigmund Freud*. London, UK: Hogarth Press.

Freud, S. (1923/1961). The ego and the id. In J. Strachey (Ed. and Trans.), *The standard edition of the complete psychological works of Sigmund Freud* (Vol. 19, pp. 3–68). London, UK: Hogarth Press.

Freud, S. (1940/1964). An outline of psychoanalysis. In J. Strachey (Ed. and Trans.), *The standard edition of the complete psychological works of Sigmund Freud* (Vol. 23). London, UK: Hogarth Press.

Frodi, T., Stauber, F. Y., Schaaf, N., Koutsouleris, N., Scheuerecker, J., Ewers, M., et al. (2010). Amygdala reduction in patients with ADHD compared with major depression and healthy volunteers. *Acta Psychiatrica Scandinavia, 121*, 111–118.

Fromm, E. (1956). *The art of loving*. New York, NY: Harper & Row.

Gadea, M., Gomez, C., Gonzalez-Bono, R. E., & Salvador, A. (2005). Increased cortisol and decreased right ear advantage (REA) in dichotic listening following a negative mood induction. *Psychoneuroendocrinology, 30*, 129–138.

Gainotti, G. (2006). Unconscious emotional memories and the right hemisphere. In M. Mancia (Ed.), *Psychoanalysis and neuroscience* (pp. 151–173). Milan, Italy: Springer Milan.

Gainotti, G. (2012). Unconscious processing of emotions and the right hemisphere. *Neuropsychologia, 50*, 205–218.

Galin, D. (1974). Implications for psychiatry of left and right cerebral specialization: A neurophysiological context for unconscious processes. *Archives of General Psychiatry, 31*, 572–583.

Gallace, A., & Spence, C. (2010). The science of interpersonal touch: An overview. *Neuroscience and Biobehavioral Reviews, 34*, 246–259.

George, M. S., Parekh, P. I., Rosinsky, N., Ketter, T. A., Kimbrell, T. A., Heilman, K. M., Herscovitch, P., & Post, R. M. (1996). Understanding emotional prosody activates right hemispheric regions. *Archives of Neurology, 53*, 665–670.

Gerhardt, S. (2004). *Why love matters. How affection shapes a baby' s brain*. New York, NY: Brunner-Routledge.

Gerson, S. (2004). The relational unconscious: A core element of intersubjectivity, thirdness, and clinical process. *Psychoanalytic Quarterly*, 73, 63–98.

Geschwind, N. W., & Galaburda, A. M. (1987). *Cerebral lateralization: Biological mechanisms, associations and pathology.* Cambridge, MA: MIT Press.

Gettler, L. T., McDade, T. W., Feranil, A. B., &. Kuzawaa, C. W. (2011). Longitudinal evidence that fatherhood decreases testosterone in human males. *Proceedings of the National Academy of Sciences USA, 108*, 16194–16199.

Giljov, A., Karenina, K., & Malaschichev, Y. (2018). Facing each other: mammal mothers and infants prefer the position favouring right hemisphere processing. *Biology Letters* 14, 20170707. http://dx.doi.org/10.1098/rsbl.2017.0707

Giussani, D. A., Fletcher, A. J. W., & Gardner, D. S. (2011). Sex differences in the ovine fetal cortisol response to stress. *Pediatric Research, 69*, 118–122.

Gluckman, P. D., & Hanson, M. A. (2004). Living with the past: Evolution, development, and patterns of disease. *Science, 305*, 1733–1736.

Gollwitzer, E. S., & Marsland, B. J. (2015). Impact of early-life exposures on immune maturation and susceptibility to disease. *Trends in Immunology, 36*, 684–696.

Gordon, I., Vender Wyk, B. C., Bennett, R. H., Cordeaux, C., Lucas, M. V., Eilbott, J. A., et al. (2013). Oxytocin enhances brain function in children with autism. *Proceedings of the National Academy of Science, USA, 110*, 20953–20958.

Gore, A. C. (2008). Developmental programming and endocrine disruptor effects on reproductive neuroendocrine systems. *Frontiers in Neuroendocrinology, 29*, 358–374.

Gore, A. C., Balthazart, J., Bikle, D., Carpenter, D. O., Crews, D., Czernichow, P., et al. (2014). Reprint of: Policy decisions on endocrine disruptors should be based on science across disciplines: A response to Dietrich et al. *Hormones and Behavior, 65*, 190–193.

Grandjean, P., & Landrigan, P. J. (2014). Neurobehavioral effects of developmental toxicity. *Lancet Neurology, 13*, 330–338.

Grandjean, P., & Ozonoff, D. (2013). Transparency and translation of science in a modern world. *Environmental Health, 12*, 70. http://www.ehjournal.net/content/12/1/70

Granger, D. A., Hood, K. E., Ikeda, S. C., Reed, C. L., & Block, M. L. (1996). Neonatal endotoxin exposure alters the development of social behavior and the hypothalamic-pituitary-adrenal axis in selectively bred mice. *Brain, Behavior, and Immunity, 10*, 249–259.

Gray, P. B., Yang, C-F. J., & Pope, H. G., Jr. (2006). Fathers have lower salivary testosterone levels than unmarried men and married non-fathers in Beijing, China. *Proceedings in Biological Science, 273*, 333–339.

Greenberg, L. S. (2007). Emotion coming of age. *Clinical Psychology Science and Practice, 14*, 414–421.

Greenough, A., Langercrantz, H., Pool, J., & Dahlin, I. (1987). Plasma catecholamine levels in preterm infants. Effect of birth asphyxia and Apgar score. *Acta Paediatrica Scandinavica, 76*, 54–59.

Greulich, W. W., Crimson, C. S., & Turner, M. L. (1953). The physical growth and development of children who survived the atomic bombing of Hiroshima or Nagasaki. *Journal of Pediatrics, 43,* 121–145.

Griffin, J. E., & Wilson, J. D. (1998). Disorders of the testis. In E. Braunwald, A. S. Fauci, D. L. Kasper, S. L. Hauser, D. L. Longo, & R. Jameson (Eds.), *Harrison's principles of internal medicine* (14th ed., pp. 1–13). New York, NY: McGraw-Hill.

Gross, J. J. (2008). Emotion and emotion regulation: Personality processes and individual differences. In O. P. John, R. W. Robins, & L. A. Pervin (Eds.), *Handbook of personality: Theory and research* (pp. 701-724). New York, NY, US: Guilford Press.

Grossmann, T., Johnson, M. H., Farroni, T., & Csibra, G. (2007). Social perception in the infant brain: Gamma oscillatory activity in response to eye gaze. *Social Cognitive & Affective Neuroscience, 2,* 284–291.

Grossmann, T., Oberecker, R., Koch, S. P., & Friederici, A. D. (2010). The developmental origins of voice processing in the human brain. *Neuron, 65,* 852–858.

Gruver-Yates, A. L., & Cidlowski, J. A. (2013). Tissue-specific actions of glucocorticoids on apoptosis: A double-edged sword. *Cells, 3,* 203–223.

Gudsnik, K., & Champagne, F. A. (2012). Epigenetic influence of stress and the social environment. *ILAR Journal, 53,* 279–388.

Guedeney, A., & Fermanian, J. (2001). A validity and reliability study of assessment and screening for sustained withdrawal in infancy: The alarm distress scale. *Infant Mental Health Journal, 22,* 559–575.

Guedeney, A., Foucault, C., Bougen, E., Larroque, B., & Mentre, F. (2008). Screening for risk factors of relational withdrawal behavior in infants aged 14–18 months. *European Psychiatry, 23,* 150–155.

Guendelman, S., Goodmann, J., Kharrizi, M., & Lahiff, M. (2014). Work-family after childbirth: The association between employer-offered leave characteristics and maternity leave duration. *Maternal and Child Health Journal, 18,* 200–208.

Gunnar, M. R. (2000). Early adversity and the development of stress reactivity and regulation. In C. A. Nelson (Ed.), *The Minnesota symposium on child psychology: Vol. 31. The effects of early adversity on neurobehavioral development* (pp. 163–200). Mahwah, NJ: Erlbaum.

Gunnar, M. R. & Quevedo, K. (2007). The neurobiology of stress and development. *Annual Review of Psychology, 58,* 145–173.

Gunnar, M. R., Kryzer, E., van Ryzin, M. J., & Phillips, D. A. (2010). The rise in cortisol in family day care: Associations with aspects of care quality, child behavior, and child sex. *Child Development, 81,* 853–870.

Gunnar-Vongnechten, M. R. (1978). Changing a frightening toy into a pleasant toy by allowing the infant to control its actions. *Developmental Psychology, 14,* 157–162.

Gupta, R. K., Hasan, K. M., Trivedi, R., Pradhan, M., Das, V., Parikh, N. A., & Narayana, P. A. (2005). Diffusion tensor imaging of the developing human cerebrum. *Journal of Neuroscience Research, 81,* 172–178.

Hall, G. B. C., West, C. D., & Szatmari, P. (2007). Backward masking of reduced subcortical amygdala engagement in autism. *Brain & Cognition, 65*, 100–106.

Ham, J., & Tronick, E. (2006). Infant resilience to the stress of the still-face: infant and maternal psychophysiology are related. *Annals of the New York Academy of Sciences, 1094*, 297–302.

Hamann, S. (2005). Sex differences in the responses of the human amygdala. *Neuroscientist, 11*, 288–293.

Hammond, G. L., Koivista, M., Kouvalainen, K., & Vihko, R. (1979). Serum steroids and pituitary hormones in infants with particular reference to testicular activity. *Journal of Clinical Endocrinology and Metabolism, 49*, 40–44.

Handa, R. J., Burgess, L. H., Ker, J. E., & O'Keefe, J. A. (1994). Gonadal steroid hormone receptors and sex differences in the hypothalamo-pituitary-adrenal axis. *Hormones and Behavior, 28*, 464–476.

Hanson, J. L., Chung, M. K., Avants, B. B., Shirtcliff, E. A., Gee, J. C., Davidson, R. J., & Pollak, S. D. (2010). Early stress is associated with alterations in the orbitofrontal cortex: A tensor-based morphometry investigation of brain structure and behavioral risk. *Journal of Neuroscience, 30*, 7466–7472.

Harlow, H. (1958). The nature of love. *American Psychologist, 13*, 673–685.

Hassin, R. R. (2013). Yes it can: On the functional abilities of the human unconscious. *Perspectives in Psychological Science, 8*, 195–207.

Hassin, R. R., Bargh, J. A., Engell, A. D., & McCulloch, K. C. (2009). Implicit working memory. *Consciousness and Cognition, 18*, 665–678.

Hayward, C., & Sanborn, K. (2002). Puberty and the emergence of gender differences in psychopathology. *Journal of Adolescent Health, 30*(Suppl. 4), 49–58.

Hazlett, H., Poe, M., Gerig, G., Smith, R., Provenzale, J., Ross, A., et al. (2005). Magnetic resonance imaging and head circumference study of brain size in autism: Birth through age 2 years. *Journal of the American Medical Association, 62*, 1366–1376.

Haznedar, M. M., Buchsbaum, M. S., Wei, T.-C., Hof, P. R., Cartwright, C., Bienstock, C. A., et al. (2000). Limbic circuitry in patients with autism spectrum disorders studied with positron emission tomography and magnetic resonance imaging. *American Journal of Psychiatry, 157*, 1994–2001.

Hecht, D. (2014). Cerebral lateralization of pro- and anti-social tendencies. *Experimental Neurobiology, 23*, 1–27.

Helton, W. S., Dorahy, M. J., & Russell, P. N. (2011). Dissociative tendencies and right-hemisphere processing load: Effects on vigilance performance. *Consciousness and Cognition, 20*, 696–702.

Hendriks, A. W., van Rijswijk, M., & Omtzigt, D. (2011). Holding-side influences on infant's view of mother's face. *Laterality, 16*, 641–655.

Heritage, A. S., Stumpf, W. E., Sar, M., & Grant, L. D. (1980). Brainstem catecholamine neurons are target sites for sex steroid hormones. *Science, 207*, 1377–1379.

Herlenius, E., & Lagercrantz, H. (2001). Neurotransmitters and neuromodulators during the early human development. *Early Human Development, 65*, 21–37.

Hermoye, L., Saint-Martin, C., Cosnard, G., Lee, S.-K., Kim, J., Nassogne, M.-C., et al. (2006). Pediatric diffusion tensor imaging: Normal database and observation of the white matter maturation in early childhood. *NeuroImage, 29,* 493–504.

Hernstein, M.J. (2002). Touch: Its communicative functions in infancy. *Human Development, 45,* 70–94.

Hertenstein, M. J., & Campos J. J. (2001). Emotion regulation via maternal touch. *Infancy, 2,* 549–566.

Hertsgaard, L., Gunnar, M., Erickson, M. F., & Nachimias, M. (1995). Adrenocortical responses to the strange situation in infants with disorganized/disoriented attachment relationships. *Child Development, 66,* 1100–1106.

Hess, E. H. (1975). The role of pupil size in communication. *Scientific American, 233*(5), 110–112, 116–119.

Hesse, E., & Main, M. (1999). Second-generation effects of unresolved trauma as observed in nonmaltreating parents: Dissociated, frightened, and threatening parental behavior. *Psychoanalytic Inquiry, 19,* 481–540.

Hines, M., Constantinescu, M., & Spencer, D. (2015). Early androgen exposure and human gender development. *Biology of Sex Differences, 6*(3). doi:10.1186/s13293-015-0022-1

Hittelman, J. H., & Dickes, R. (1979). Sex differences in neonatal eye contact time. *Merrill-Palmer Quarterly, 25,* 171–184.

Hoffman, E. L., & Bennett, F. C. (1990). Birth weight less than 800 grams: Changing outcomes and influences of gender and gestation number. *Pediatrics, 86,* 27–34.

Hoistad, M., & Barbas, H. (2009). Sequence of information processing for emotions through pathways linking temporal and insular cortices with the amygdala. *NeuroImage, 40,* 1016–1033.

Holden, C. (2005). Sex and the suffering brain. *Science, 308,* 1574–1577.

Holland, D., Chang, L., Ernst, T. M., Curran, M., Buchtal, S. D., Alicata, D., et al. (2014). Structural growth trajectories and rates of change in the first 3 months of infant brain development. *JAMA Neurology, 71*(10), 1266–1274. doi:10.1001/jamaneurol.2014.1638

Hoover, E., Cook, K., Plain, R., Sanchez, K., Waghiyi, V., Miller, P., et al. (2012). Indigenous peoples of North America: Environmental exposures and reproductive justice. *Environmental Health Perspectives, 120,* 1645–1649.

Hoppe, K. D. (1977). Split brains and psychoanalysis. *Psychoanalytic Quarterly, 46,* 220–244.

Howes, C., & Olenick, M. (1986). Family and childcare influences on toddler's compliance. *Child Development, 57,* 202–216.

Howland, M., & Simpson, J.A. (2010). Getting in under the radar: A dyadic view of invisible support. *Psychological Science,* 21, 1878–1885.

Hugdahl, K. (1995). Classical conditioning and implicit learning: The right hemisphere hypothesis. In R. J. Davidson & K. Hugdahl (Eds.), *Brain asymmetry* . Cambridge, MA: MIT Press.

Huggenberger, H.J., Suter, S.E., Reijnen, E., & Schachinger, H. (2009). Cradling side preference is associated with lateralized processing of baby facial expressions in females. *Brain and Cognition, 70*, 67–72.

Humphrey, T. (1968). The development of the human amygdala during early embryonic life. *Journal of Comparative Neurology, 132*, 135–166.

Hutchinson, J. B. (1997). Gender-specific steroid metabolism in neural differentiation. *Cellular and Molecular Neurobiology, 17*, 603–626.

Hyson, M., & Tomlinson, H. B. (2014). *The early years matter: Education, care, and the well-being of children, birth–8*. New York, NY: Teachers College Press.

Ikeda, T., Tokuda, T., Monden, Y., Mizushima, S.G., Nagashima, M., Kyutoku, Y., et al. (2018). Hypoactivation of the right prefrontal cortex underlying motor-related inhibitory deficits in children with autism spectrum disorder: A functional near-infrared spectroscopy study. *Japanese Psychological Research* doi: 10.1111/ jpr,12204

Ikezuki, Y., Tsutsumi, O., Takai, Y., Kameei, Y., & Taketani, Y. (2002). Determination of bisphenol A concentrations in human biological fluids revels significant early prenatal exposure. *Human Reproduction, 17*, 2839–2841.

Ingalhalikar, M., Smith, A., Parker, D., Satterthwaite, T. D., Elliott, M. A., Ruparel, K., et al. (2014). Sex differences in the structural connectome of the human brain. *Proceedings of the National Academy of Sciences USA, 111*, 823–828.

Insel, T. R., & Fenton, W. S. (2005). Psychiatric epidemiology. It's not just about counting anymore. *Archives of General Psychiatry, 62*, 590–592.

Institute of Medicine. (2015). *Transforming the workforce for children birth through 8: A unifying foundation*. Washington, DC: IOM.

Ionta, S., Martuzzi, R., Salomon, R., & Blanke, O. (2014). The brain network reflecting bodily self-consciousness: a functional connectivity study. *Social and Cognitive Neuroscience, 9*, 1904–1919.

Iturria-Medina, Y., Perez Fernandez, A., Morris, D. M., Canales-Rodriguez, E. J., Haroon, H. A., Garcia Penton, L., et al. (2011). Brain hemispheric structural efficiency and interconnectivity rightward asymmetry in human and nonhuman primates. *Cerebral Cortex, 21*, 56–67.

Jacques, C. & Rossion, B. (2009). The initial representation of individual faces in the right occipito-temporal cortex is holistic: Electrophysiological evidence from the composite face illusion. *Journal of Vision*, 9, 1–16.

Janov, A. (2000). *The biology of love*. New York, NY: Prometheus Books.

Jasmin, K.M., McGettigan, C., Agnew, Z.K., Lavan, N., Josephs, O. Cummins, F. et al. (2016). Cohesion and joint speech: Right hemisphere contributions to synchronized vocal production. *Journal of Neuroscience*, 36, 4669–4680.

Jean, A. D. L., Stack, D. M., & Fogel, A. (2009). A longitudinal investigation of maternal touching across the first 6 months of life: Age and context effects. *Infant Behavior & Development*, 32, 344–349.

Jessen, S., & Grossmann, T. (2014). Unconscious discrimination of social cues from eye whites in infants. *Proceedings of the National Academy of Science, USA, 111*, 16208–16213.

Jones, S. (2014). Maternal cradling bias and early communicative interactions: Implications for early identification of children at risk. *Infant Behavior and Development*, 37, 722–728.

Jones, W., & Klin, A. (2013). Attention to eyes is present but in decline in 2-6-month-old infants later diagnosed with autism. *Nature, 504*, 427–431.

Joseph, R. (1982). The neuropsychology of development: Hemispheric laterality, limbic language, and the origin of thought. *Journal of Clinical Psychology*, 38, 4–33.

Joseph, R. (1990). *Neuropsychology, neuropsychiatry, and behavioral neurology*. New York: Plenum Press.

Joseph, R. (1992). *The right brain and the unconscious: Discovering the stranger within*. New York, NY: Plenum Press.

Joseph, R. (1996). *Neuropsychiatry, neuropsychology, and clinical neuroscience* (2nd ed.). Baltimore, MD: Williams & Wilkins.

Jostmann, N.B., Kuole, S.L., Vander Wulp, N.Y., & Fockenberg, D.A. (2005). Subliminal affect regulation: The moderating role of action-versus state-orientation. *European Psychologist*, 10, 209–217.

Jung-Beeman, M., Bowden, E. M., Haberman, J., Frymiare, J. L., Arambel-Liu, S., Greenblatt, R., Reber, P. J., & Kounios, J. (2004). Neural activity when people solve verbal problems with insight. *PLOS Biology*, 2, 500–510.

Kalsched, D. (2005). Hope versus hopelessness in the psychoanalytic situation and Dante's *Divine Comedy. Spring*, 72, 167–187.

Kane, J. (2004). Poetry as right hemispheric language. *Journal of Consciousness Studies, 11*, 21–59.

Kanner, L. (1943). Autistic disturbances in affective contact. *Nervous Child*, 2, 217–250.

Kasprian, G., Langs, G., Brugger, P., Bittner, M., Weber, M., Arantes, M., et al. (2011). The prenatal origin of hemispheric asymmetry: An in utero neuroimaging study. *Cerebral Cortex, 21*, 1076–1083.

Katz, M., Liu, C., Schaer, M., Parker, K. J., Ottet, M.-C., Epps, A., et al. (2009). Prefrontal plasticity and stress inoculation-induced resilience. *Developmental Neuroscience, 31*, 293–299.

Kawai, K., Nozaki, T., Nishikata, H., Aou, S., Takii, M., & Kubo, C. (2003). Aggressive behavior and serum testosterone concentration during the maturation process of male mice: The effects of fetal exposure to bisphenol A. *Environmental Health Perspectives, 111*, 175–178.

Keehn, B., Vogel_Farley, V., Tager-Flusberg, H., & Nelson, C.A. (2015). Atypical hemispheric specialization for faces in infants at risk for autism spectrum disorder. *Autism Research*, 8, 187–198.

Kierkegaard, S. (1846). *Purity of heart*. New York: Harper and Row.

Kigar, S. L., & Auger, A. P. (2013). Epigenetic mechanisms may underlie the aetiology of sex differences in mental health. *Journal of Neuroendocrinology, 2013*, 1141–1150.

Killeen, L. A., & Teti, D. M. (2012). Mothers' frontal EEG asymmetry in response to infant emotional states and mother-infant emotional availability, emotional experience, and internalizing symptoms. *Development and Psychopathology, 24*, 9–21.

Killgore, W. D., Oki, M., & Yurgelun-Todd, D. A. (2001). Sex-specific developmental changes in amygdala responses to affective faces. *NeuroReport, 12*, 427–433.

Kim, J., Lyoo, I. K., Estes, A. M., Renshaw, P. F., Shaw, D. W., Friedman, S. D., et al. (2010). Laterobasal amygdalar enlargement in 6- to 7-year-old children with autism spectrum disorder. *Archives of General Psychiatry, 67*, 1187–1197.

Kim, P., Leckman, J. F., Mayes, L. C., Feldman, R., Wang, X., & Swain, J. E. (2010). The plasticity of human maternal brain: Longitudinal changes in brain anatomy during the early postpartum period. *Behavioral Neuroscience, 124*, 695–700.

Kime, K. E., Vinson, G. P., Malor, P. W., & Kilpatrick, R. (1980). Adrenal-gonadal relationships. In L. Chester-Jones & I. W. Henderson (Eds.), *General comparative and clinical endocrinology of the adrenal cortex* (Vol. 3, pp. 183–264). New York, NY: Academic Press.

Klein, S. L. (2004). Hormonal and immunological mechanisms mediating sex differences in parasite infection. *Parasite Immunology, 26*, 247–264.

Knickmeyer, R. C., Gouttard, S., Kang, C., Evans, D., Wilber, K., Smith, J. K., et al. (2008). A structural MRI study of human brain development from birth to 2 years. *Journal of Neuroscence.*, 28, 12176–12182.

Koike, T., Tanabe, H.C., Okazaki, S., Nakagawa, E., Sasaki, A., Shimada, K., et al. (2016). Neural substrates of shared attention as social memory: A hyperscanning functional magnetic resonance imaging study. *NeuroImage, 125*, 401–412.

Konrath, S. H., Chopik, W. J., Hsing, C. K., & O'Brien, E. (2014). Changes in adult attachment styles in American college students over time: A meta-analysis. *Personality and Social Psychology Review, 18*, 326–348.

Koole, S., & Jostman, N.B. (2004). Getting a grip on your feelings: Effiects of action orientation and external demands on intuitive affect regulation. *Journal of Personality and Social Psychology*, 87, 974–990.

Korner, A.F. (1974). The effect of the infant's state, level of arousal, sex, and ontogenetic stage on the caregiver. *Journal of Reproductive and Infant Psychology, 10*, 53–63.

Krystal, H. (1988). *Integration & self-healing: Affect, trauma, alexithymia*. Hillsdale, NJ: Analytic Press.

Kuhl, J., Quirin, M., & Koole, S. L. (2015). Being someone: The integrated self as a neuropsychological system. *Social and Personality Psychology Compass*, 9, 115–132.

Kuhlen, A.K., Allefeld, C., & Haynes, J.D. (2012). Content-specific coordination of listeners' to speakers' EEG during communication. *Frontiers in Human Neuroscience, 6*, 266

Kunzler, J., Braun, K., & Bock, J. (2015). Early life stress and sex-specific sensitivity of the catecholaminergic systems in prefrontal and limbic systems of *Octodon degus*. *Brain Structure and Function, 220,* 861–868.

Lambe, E. K., Krimer, L. S., & Goldman-Rakic, P. S. (2000). Differential postnatal development of catecholamine and serotonin inputs to identified neurons in prefrontal cortex of rhesus monkeys. *Journal of Neuroscience, 20,* 8780–8787.

Lane, R. D., Ahern, G. L., Schwartz, G. E., & Kaszniak, A. W. (1997). Is alexithymia the emotional equivalent of blindsight? *Biological Psychiatry, 42,* 834–844.

Lanius, R. A., Vermetten, E., & Pain C. (Eds.). (2010). *The impact of early life trauma on health and disease: The hidden epidemic.* Cambridge, UK: Cambridge University Press.

Lanius, R. A., Williamson, P. C., Bluhm, R. L., Densmore, M., Boksman, K., Neufeld, R. W. J., Gati, J. S., & Menon, R. S. (2005). Functional connectivity of dissociative responses in posttraumatic stress disorder: A functional magnetic resonance imaging investigation. *Biological Psychiatry, 57,* 873–884.

Lanphear, B. P. (2015). The impact on toxins on the developing brain. *Annual Review of Public Health, 36,* 211–230.

Lavelli, M., & Poli, M. (1998). Early mother-infant interaction during breast- and bottlefeeding. *Infant Behavior & Development, 21,* 667–684.

Layard, R., Clark, A. E., Cornaglia, F., Powdthavee, N., & Vernoit, J. (2014) What predicts a successful life? A life-course model of well-being. *Economic Journal, 124,* F720–F738. doi:10.1111/ecoj.12170

Leckman, J. F., & March, J. S. (2011). Editorial: Developmental neuroscience comes of age. *Journal of Child Psychology & Psychiatry, 52,* 333–338.

Lee, H. J., Chattopadhyay, S., Gong, E. Y., Ahn, R. S., & Lee, K. (2003). Antiandrogenic effects of bisphenol A and nonylphenol on the function of androgen receptor. *Toxicological Science, 75,* 40–46.

Lehtonen, J., Kononen, M., Purhonen, M., Partanen, J., & Saarikoski, S. (2002). The effects of feeding on the electroencephalogram in 3- and 6-month-old infants. *Psychophysiology, 39,* 73–79.

Lemche, E., Giampietro, V. P., Surguladze, S. A., Amaro, E. J., Andrew, C. M., Williams, S. C. R., et al. (2006). Human attachment security is mediated by the amygdala: Evidence from combined fMRI and psychophysiological measures. *Human Brain Mapping 27,* 623–635.

Lenzi, D., Trentini, C., Pantano, P., Macaluso, E., Iacaboni, M., Lenzi, G. I., et al. (2009). Neural basis of maternal communication and emotional expression processing during infant preverbal stage. *Cerebral Cortex, 19,* 1124–1133.

Levenson, R. W., & Gottman, J. M. (1983). Marital interaction: Physiological linkage and affective exchange. *Journal of Personality and Social Psychology, 45,* 587–597.

Levy, J., Goldstein, A., & Feldman, R. (2017). Perception of social synchrony induces mother-child gamma coupling in the social brain. *Social Cognitive and Affective Neuroscience, 2017,* 1036–1046.

Liebenluft, E., Gobbini, M. I., Harrison, T., & Haxby, J. V. (2004). Mothers' neural activation in response to pictures of their children and other children. *Biological Psychiatry, 56,* 225–232.

Llorente, R., Lopez Gallardo, M., Berzal, A. L., Prada, C., Garcia-Segura, L. M., & Viveros, M.-P. (2009). Early maternal deprivation in rats induces gender-dependent effects on developing hippocampal and cerebellar cells. *International Journal of Developmental Neuroscience, 27,* 233–241.

Loman, M. M., & Gunnar, M. R. (2010). Early experience and the development of stress reactivity and regulation in children. *Neuroscience and Biobehavioral Reviews, 34,* 867–876.

Lombardo, M. V., Chakrabarti, B., Bullmore, E. T., Sadek, S. A., Pasco, G., Wheelwright, S. J., et al. (2010). Atypical neural self-representation in autism. *Brain, 133,* 611–624.

Ludwig, M., & Field, T. (2014). Touch in parent-infant mental health. In K. Brandt, B.PD. Perry, S. Seligman, & E. Tronick (Eds.), *Infant and early childhood mental health. Core concepts and clinical practice* (pp. 237–247). Arlington, VA: American Psychiatric Association.

Lutchmaya, S., & Baron-Cohen, S. (2002). Foetal testosterone and eye contact in 12-month-old human infants. *Infant Behavior and Development, 25,* 327–335.

Lutchmaya, S., Baron-Cohen, S., & Raggart, P. (2002). Human sex differences in social and non-social looking preferences at 12 months of age. *Infant Behavior and Development, 25,* 319–325.

Lyons-Ruth, K. (1999). The two-person unconscious: Intersubjective dialogue, enactive relational representation, and the emergence of new forms of relational organization. *Psychoanalytic Inquiry, 19,* 576–617.

Lyons-Ruth, K., Bronfman, E., & Parson, E. (1999). Frightened, frightening, and atypical maternal behavior and disorganized infant attachment strategies. In J. Vondra & D. Barnett (Eds.), *Atypical patterns of infant attachment: Theory, research, and current directions.* Monographs of the Society for Research in Child Development, *64*(3, Serial No. 258).

Lyons, D. M., Afarian, H., Schatzberg, A. F., Sawyer-Glover, A., & Moseley, M. E. (2002). Experience-dependent asymmetric variation in primate prefrontal morphology. *Behavioural Brain Research, 136,* 51–59.

Lyons, T., & Fitzgerald, M. (2013). *Recent advances in autism spectrum disorders.* Rijeka, Croatia: In Tech.

Maccoby, E. E., & Jacklin, C. N. (1974). *The psychology of sex differences.* Stanford, CA: Stanford University Press.

MacDonald, H. Z., Beeghly, M., Grant-Knight, W., Augustyn, M., Woods, R. W., Cabral, H., et al. (2008). Longitudinal association between infant disorganized attachment and childhood posttraumatic stress symptoms. *Development and Psychopathology, 20,* 493–508.

MacLean, P. D. (1989). *The triune brain in evolution. Role in paleocortical functions.* New York, NY: Plenum Press.

MacLean, P. D. (1996). Women: A more balanced brain. *Zygon, 31,* 421–439

Main, K. M., Mortenson, G. K., Kaleva, M. M., Boisen, K. A., Damgaard, I. N., Chellakooty, M., et al. (2006). Human breast milk contamination with phthalates and alterations of endogenous reproductive hormones in infants three months of age. *Environmental Health Perspectives, 114,* 270–276.

Main, M., Kaplan, K., & Cassidy, J. (1985). Security in infancy, childhood, and adulthood: A move to the level of representation. *Monographs of the Society of Research in Child Development,* 50, 1–2.

Main, M., & Solomon, J. (1986). Discovery of an insecure-disorganized/disoriented attachment pattern: Procedures, findings and implications for the classification of behavior. In T. B. Brazelton & M. W. Yogman (Eds.), *Affective development in infancy* (pp. 95–124). Norwood, NJ: Ablex.

Main, P. A. E., Angley, M. T., O'Doherty, C. E., Thomas, P., & Fenech, M. (2012). The potential role of the antioxidant and detoxification properties of glutathione in autism spectrum disorders: A systematic review and meta-analysis. *Nutrition & Metabolism,* 9, 35.

Manini, B., Cardone, D., Ebisch, S. J. H., Bafunno, D., Aureli, T., & Merla, A. (2013). Mom feels what her child feels: thermal signatures of vicarious autonomic response while watching children in a stressful situation. *Frontiers in Human Neuroscience,* 7, 299. http://doi.org/10.3389/fnhum.2013.00299

Manning, J.T., Trivers, R.L., Thornhill, R., Singh, D., Denman, J., Eklo, M.H., et al. (1997). Ear asymmetry and left-side cradling. *Evolution and Human Behavior, 18,* 327–340.

Maras, A., Laucht, M., Gerdes, D., Wilhelm, C., Lewicka, S., Haack, D., Malisova, L., & Schmidt, M. H. (2003). Association of testosterone and dihydrotestosterone with externalizing behavior in adolescent boys and girls. *Psychoneuroendocrinology,* 28, 932–940.

Markowitsch, H. J., Reinkemeier, A., Kessler, J., Koyuncu, A., & Heiss, W.-D. (2000). Right amygdalar and temporofrontal activation during autobiographical, but not fictitious memory retrieval. *Behavioral Neurology, 12,* 181–190.

Mashal, N., Faust, M., Hendler, T., & Jung-Beeman, M. (2007). An fMRI investigation of the neural correlates underlying the processing of novel metaphoric expressions. *Brain and Language, 100,* 115–126.

Maslow, A. H. (1968). *Toward a psychology of being.* New York, NY: Van Nostrand.

McCarthy, M. M., Auger, A. P., Bale, T. L., De Vries, G. J., Dunn, G. A., Forger, N. G., et al. (2009). The epigenetics of sex differences in the brain. *Journal of Neuroscience,* 29, 12815–12823.

McClelland, E. E., & Smith, J. M. (2011). Gender specific differences in the immune response to infection. *Archivum Immunologiae et Therapiae Experimentalis,* 59, 203–213.

McClure, E. B. (2000). A meta-analytic review of sex differences in facial expression processing and their development in infants, children, and adolescents. *Psychological Bulletin, 126,* 424–453.

McCormick, C. M., Furey, B. F., Child, M., Sawyer, M. J., & Donohue, S. M. (1998). Neonatal sex hormones have "organizational" effects on the hypothalamic-pituitary-adrenal axis of male rats. *Developmental Brain Research, 105,* 295–307.

McEwen, B. S. (2007). Physiology and neurobiology of stress and adaptation: Central role of the brain. *Physiological Reviews, 87,* 873–904.

McEwen, B. S., & Gianaros, P. J. (2011). Stress- and allostasis-induced brain plasticity. *Annual Review of Medicine, 62,* 431–445.

McGilchrist, I. (2009). *The master and his emissary.* New Haven, CT: Yale University Press.

McLaughlin, J. T. (1978). Primary and secondary processes in the context of cerebral hemispheric specialization. *Psychoanalytic Quarterly, 47,* 237–266.

McMillen, M. M. (1979). Differential mortality by sex in fetal and neonatal deaths. *Science, 204,* 89–91.

McWilliams, N. (2018). Core competency two: Therapeutic stance/attitude. In R.E. Barsness (Ed.), *Core competencies of relational psychoanalysis: A guide to practice, study, and research* (pp. 87–103). New York, NY: Routledge.

Meaney, M. J., Stewart, J., Poulin, P., & McEwen, B. S. (1983). Sexual differentiation of social play in rat pups is mediated by the neonatal androgen-receptor system. *Neuroendocrinology, 37,* 85–90.

Meaney, M. J., Szyf, M., & Seckl, J. R. (2007). Epigenetic mechanisms of perinatal programming of hypothalamic-pituitary-adrenal function and health. *Trends in Molecular Medicine, 13,* 269–277.

Meares, R. (2012). *A dissociation model of borderline personality disorder.* New York, NY: Norton.

Meares, R. (2016). *The poet's voice in the making of mind.* New York, NY: Routledge.

Meares, R., Schore, A. N., & Melkonian, D. (2011). Is borderline personality disorder a particularly right hemispheric disorder? A study of P3a using single trial analysis. *Australian & New. Zealand Journal of Psychiatry, 45,* 131–139.

Mehta, M. A., Golembo, N. I., Nosarti, C., Colvert, E., Mota, A., Williams, S. C. R., et al. (2009). Amygdala, hippocampal and corpus callosum size following severe early institutional deprivation: The English and Romanian adoptees study pilot. *Journal of Child Psychology and Psychiatry, 50,* 943–951.

Mehta, P. H., & Josephs, R. A. (2010). Testosterone and cortisol jointly regulate dominance: Evidence for a dual-hormone hypothesis. *Hormones and Behavior, 58,* 898–906.

Melnyk, S., Fuchs, G. J., Schulz, E., Lopez, M., Kahler, S. G., Fussell, J. J., et al. (2012). Metabolic imbalance associated with methylation dysregulation and oxidative damage in children with autism. *Journal of Autism & Developmental Disorders, 42,* 367–377.

Mento, G., Suppiej, A., Altoe, G., & Bisiacchi, P. S. (2010). Functional hemispheric asymmetries in humans: Electrophysiological evidence from preterm infants. *European Journal of Neuroscience, 31,* 565–574.

Merikangas, K. R., He, J. P., Burstein, M., Swanson, S. A., Avenevoli, S., Cui, L., et al. (2010). Lifetime prevalence of mental disorders in U.S. adolescents: Results from the National Comorbidity Survey Replication—Adolescent Supplement (NCS-A). *Journal of the American Academy of Child & Adolescent Psychiatry, 49*, 980–989.

Mesiano, S., & Jaffe, R. B. (1997). Developmental and functional biology of the primate fetal adrenal cortex. *Endocrinological Reviews, 18*, 378–403.

Mezzacappa, E. S., & Katlin, E. S. (2002). Breast-feeding is associated with reduced perceived stress and negative mood in mothers. *Health Psychology, 21*, 187–219.

Miall, D., & Dissanayake, E. (2003). The poetics of baby talk. *Human Nature, 14*, 337–354.

Miller, B. L., Seeley, W. W., Mychack, P., Rosen, H. J., Mena, I., & Boone, K. (2001). Neuroanatomy of the self. Evidence from patients with frontotemporal dementia. *Neurology, 57*, 817–821.

Miller, G. (2010). The seductive allure of behavioral epigenetics. *Science, 329*, 24–27.

Miller, L. (1986). Some comments on cerebral hemispheric models of consciousness. *Psychoanalytic Review, 73*, 129–144.

Miller, L. (1991). Freud's brain: Neuropsychodynamic foundations of psychoanalysis. New York, NY, US: Guilford Press.

Minagawa-Kawai, U., Matsuoka, S., Dan, I., Naoi, N., Nakamura, K., & Kojima, S. (2009). Prefrontal activation associated with social attachment: Facial-emotion recognition in mothers and infants. *Cerebral Cortex, 19*, 284–292.

Minagawa, Y., Matsuoka, S., Dan, I., Naoi, N., Nakamura, K., & Kojima, S. (2009). Prefrontal activation associated with social attachment: Facial-emotion recognition in mothers and infants. *Cerebral Cortex, 19*, 284–292.

Minagawa, Y., Xu, & Moimoto, S. (2018). Toward interactive social neuroscience: Neuroimaging real-world interactions in various populations, *Japanese Psychological Research*, https://doi.org/10.1111/jpr.12207

Miodovnik, A., Engel, S. M., Zhu, C., Ye, C., Soorya, L. V., Silva, M. J., Calafat, A. M., & Wolff, M. S. (2011). Endocrine disruptors and childhood social impairment. *Neurotoxicology, 32*, 261–267.

Miyazaki, M., Fujii, E., Saijo, T., Mori, K., Hashimoto, T., Kagami, S., et al. (2007). Short-latency somatosensory evoked potentials in infantile autism: Evidence of hyperactivity in the right primary somatosensory area. *Developmental Medicine & Child Neurology, 49*, 13–17.

Moffitt, T. E. (1993). Adolescence-limited and life-course-persistent antisocial behavior: A developmental taxonomy. *Psychological Review, 100*, 674–701.

Money, J., & Ehrhardt, A. A. (1972). *Man and woman, boy and girl*. Baltimore, MD: Johns Hopkins University Press.

Monk. C. S., Weng, S. J., Wiggins, J. L., Kurpati, N., Louro, H. M. C., Carrasco, M., et al. (2010). Neural circuitry of emotional face processing in autism spectrum disorders. *Journal of Psychiatry & Neuroscience, 35*, 105–114.

Montirosso, R., Borgatti, R., & Tronick, E. (2010). Lateral asymmetries in infants' regulatory and communicative gestures. In R. A. Lanius, E. Vermetten, & C. Pain (Eds.), *The impact of early life trauma on health and disease: The hidden epidemic* (pp. 103–111). Cambridge, UK: Cambridge University Press.

Montirosso, R., Cozzi, P., Tronick, E., & Borgatti, R. (2012). Differential distribution and lateralization of infant gestures and their relation to maternal gestures in the face-to-face still-face paradigm. *Infant Behavior & Development, 35*, 819–828.

Moore, G.A., & Calkins, S.D. (2004). Infants' regulation in the still-face paradigm is related to dyadic coordination of mother-infant interaction. *Developmental Psychology, 40*, 1068–1080.

Moore, G.A., Hill-Soderlund, A.L., Propper, C.B., Calkins, S.D., Mills-Koonce, W.R., & Cox, M.J. (2009). Mother-infant vagal regulation in the face-to-face still-face paradigm is moderated by maternal sensitivity. *Child Development, 80*, 209–223.

Morgan, B., Hunt, X., Sieratzki, J., Wol, B., & Tomlinson, M. (2018) Atypical maternal cradling laterality in an impoverished South African population. *Laterality: Asymmetries of Body, Brain, Cognition.* https://doi.org./10.1080/1357650X.2018.1509077

Moriguchi, T., Touroutoglou, A., Dickerson, B. C., & Barrett, L. F. (2014). Sex differences in the neural correlates of affective experience. *Social Cognitive and Affective Neuroscience, 9*, 591–600.

Morris, J. S., Ohman, A., & Dolan, R. J. (1999). A subcortical pathway to the right amygdala mediating "unseen" fear. *Proceedings of the National Academy of Science, U.S.A., 96*, 1680–1685.

Mosconi, M. W., Cody-Hazlett, H., Poe, M. D., Gerig, G., Gimpel-Smith, B. A., & Piven, J. (2009). Longitudinal study of amygdala volume and joint attention in 2- to 4-year-old children with autism. *Archives of General. Psychiatry, 66*, 509–516.

Moszkowski, R.J., Stack, D.M., Giriuard, N., Field, T.M., Hernadez-Reif, M., & Diego, M. (2009). Touching behaviors of infants of depressed mothers during normal and perturbed interactions. *Infant and Behavior Development, 32*, 183–194.

Munson, J., Dawson, G., Abbott, R., Faja, S., Webb, S. J., Friedman, S. D., et al. (2006). Amygdalar volume and behavioral development in autism. *Archives of General Psychiatry, 63*, 686–693.

Muratori, F., Apicella, F., Muratori, P., & Maestro, S. (2011). Intersubjective disruptions and caregiver-infant interactions in early autistic disorder. *Research in Autism Spectrum. Disorders, 5*, 408–417.

Mustieles, V., Perez-lobato, R., Olea, N., & Fernandez, M. F. (2015). Bisphenol A: Human exposure and neurobehavior. *NeuroToxicology, 49*, 174–184.

Nagy, E. (2006). From imitation to conversation: The first dialogues with human neonates. *Infant and Child Development, 15*, 223–232.

Nagy, E., Kompagne, H., Orvos, H., & Pat, A. (2007). Gender-related differences in neonatal imitation. *Infant and Child Development, 16*, 268–276.

Nakagami, A., Negishi, T., Kawasaki, K., Imai, N., Nishida, Y., Ihara, T., et al. (2009). Alterations in male infant behaviors towards its mother by prenatal exposure to bisphenol A in cynomolgus monkeys (*Macaca fascicularis*) during early suckling period. *Psychoneuroendocrinology, 34,* 1189–1197.

Nakamura, M., Nestor, P. G., McCarley, R. W., Levitt, J. L., Hsu, L., Kawashima, T., et al. (2007). Altered orbitofrontal sulcogyral pattern in schizophrenia. *Brain, 130,* 693–707.

Naoi, N., Minagawa-Kawai, Y., Kobayashi, A., Takeuchi, K., Nakamura, K., Yamamoto, J., & Kojima, S. (2011). Cerebral responses to infant-directed speech and the effect of talker familiarity. *NeuroImage, 59,* 1053–8119.

Narvaez, D., Panksepp, J., Schore, A. N., & Gleason, T. R. (2013). *Evolution, early experience and human development: From research to practice and policy.* New York, NY: Oxford University Press.

Nathanielsz, P. W. (1998). *Life before birth: The challenge of prenatal development.* New York, NY: W. H. Freeman.

Negishi, T., Kawasaki, K., Suzaki, S., Maeda, H., Ishii, Y., Kyuwa, S., et al. (2004). Behavioral alterations in response to fear-provoking stimuli and tranylcypromine induced by perinatal exposure to bisphenol A and nonylphenol in male rats. *Environmental Health Perspectives, 112,* 1159–1164.

NICHD (National Institute of Child Health and Human Development) Early Child Care Research Network. (1998). Early child care and self-control, compliance and problem behavior at 24 and 36 months. *Child Development, 69,* 1145–1170.

Nishitani, S., Doi, H., Koyama, A., & Shinohara, K. (2011). Differential prefrontal response to infant facial emotions in mothers compared with non-mothers. *Neuroscience Research, 70,* 183–188.

Nishizuka, M., & Arai, Y. (1981). Sexual dimorphism in synaptic organization in the amygdala and its dependence on neonatal hormone environment. *Brain Research, 212,* 31–38.

Nishizuka, M., & Arai, Y. (1983). Regional differences in sexually dimorphic synaptic organization of the medial amygdala. *Experimental Brain Research, 213,* 422–426.

Nitschke, J. B., Nelson, E. E., Rusch, B. D., Fox, A. S., Oales, T. R., & Davidson, R. J. (2004). Orbitofrontal cortex tracks positive mood in mothers viewing pictures of their newborn infants. *NeuroImage, 21,* 583–592.

Noordzij, M. L., Newman-Norlund, S. E., de Ruiter, J. P., & Hagoort, P. (2009). Brain mechanisms underlying human communication. *Frontiers in Human Neuroscience,* 3, 14. doi:10.3389/neuro.09.014.2009

Nordahl. C. W., Scholz, R., Yang, X., Buonocore, M. H., Simon, T., Rogers, S., et al. (2012). Increased rate of amygdala growth in children aged 2 to 4 years with autism spectrum disorders. *Archives of General Psychiatry, 69,* 53–61.

Noriuchi, M., Kikuchi, Y., & Senoo, A. (2008). The functional neuroanatomy of maternal love: Mother's response to infant's attachment behaviors. *Biological Psychiatry,* 2008, *63,* 415–423.

Nummenmaa, L., Glerean, E., Viinikainen, M., Jaaskelainen, Hari, R., & Sams,

M. (2012). Emotions promote social interaction by synchronizing brain activity across individuals. *Proceedings of the National Academy of Sciences USA, 109,* 9599–9604.

O'Connor, M. J., Sigman, M., & Brill, N. (1987). Disorganization of attachment in relation to maternal alcohol consumption. *Journal of Consulting and Clinical Psychology, 55,* 831–836.

Ogden, P., Pain, C., Minton, K., & Fisher, J. (2005). Including the body in mainstream psychotherapy for traumatized individuals. *Psychologist-Psychoanalyst, 25,* 19–24.

Olausson, H., Lamarre, Y., Backlund, H., Morin, C., Wallin, B. G., Starck, G., et al. (2002). Unmyelinated tactile afferents signal touch and project to insular cortex. *Nature Neuroscience, 5,* 900–904.

Olsavsky, A.K., Telzer, E.H., Shapiro, M., Humphreys, K.L., Flannery, J., Goff, B., & Tottenham, N. (2013). Indiscriminate amygdala response to mothers and strangers after early maternal deprivation. *Biological Psychiatry, 74,* 853–860.

Ongur, D., & Price, J. L. (2000). The organization of networks within the orbital and medial prefrontal cortex of rats, monkeys, and humans. *Cerebral Cortex, 10,* 206–219.

Orlinsky, D. E., & Howard, K. I. (1986). Process and outcome in psychotherapy. In S. L. Garfield & A. E. Bergin (Eds.), *Handbook of psychotherapy and behavior change* (3rd ed., pp. 311–381). , New York, NY: Wiley.

Ortigue, S., Bianchi-Demicheli, F., Hamilton, A. F., & Grafton, S. T. (2007). The neural basis of love as a subliminal prime: An event-related functional magnetic resonance imaging study. *Journal of Cognitive Neuroscience, 19,* 1218–1230.

Osofsky, J. D., & O'Connell, E. J. (1977). Patterning of newborn behavior in an urban population. *Child Development, 48,* 532–536.

Palanza, P., Howdeshell, K. L., Parmigiani, S., & vom Saal, F. S. (2002). Exposure to low dose of bisphenol A during fetal life or in adulthood alters maternal behavior in mice. *Environmental Health Perspectives, 110,* 415–422.

Panagiotidou, E., Zerva, S., Mitsiou, J., Alexis, M. N., & Kitraki, A. (2014). Perinatal exposure to low-dose bisphenol affects the neuroendocrine stress response in rats. *Journal of Endocrinology, 220,* 207–218.

Papousek, M. P. (2007). Communication in infancy: An arena of intersubjective learning. *Infant Behavior & Development, 30,* 258–266.Parmigiani, S., Palanza, P., & vom Saal, F. K. (1998). Ethotoxicology: An evolutionary approach to the study of environmental endocrine-disrupting chemicals. *Toxicology and Industrial Health, 14,* 333–339.

Parsons, C. E., Young, K. S., Murray, L., Stein, A., & Kringelbach, M. L. (2010). The functional neuroanatomy of the evolving parent–infant relationship. *Progress in Neurobiology, 91,* 220–241.

Paulus, M. P., Rogalsky, C., Simmons, A., Feinstein, J. S., & Stein, M. B. (2003).

Increased activation in the right insula during risk-taking decision making is related to harm avoidance and neuroticism. *NeuroImage, 19,* 1439–1448.

Pedersen, J. F. (1980). Ultrasound evidence of sexual differences in fetal size in first trimester. *BMJ, 281,* 1253.

Perera, F., Vishnevetsky, J., Herbstman, J. B., Calafat, A. M., Xiong, W., Rauh, V., & Wang, S. (2012). Prenatal bisphenol exposure and child behavior in an inner-city cohort. *Environmental Health Perspectives, 120,* 1190–1194.

Perini, T., Ditzen, B., Hengartner, M., & Ehlert, U. (2012). Sensation seeking in fathers: The impact on testosterone and paternal investment. *Hormones and Behavior, 61,* 191–195.

Peters, S., Jolles, D. J., Van Duijvenvoorde, A. C. K., Crone, E. A., & Peper, J. S. (2015). The link between testosterone and amygdala-connectivity in adolescent alcohol use. *Psychoneuroendocrinology, 53,* 117–126.

Phillips, D. I. (2007). Programming of the stress response: A fundamental mechanism underlying the long-term effects of the fetal environment? *Journal of Internal Medicine, 261,* 453–460.

Phillips, S., King, S., & DuBois, L. (1978). Spontaneous activities of female versus male infants. *Child Development, 49,* 590–597.

Pileggi, L-A., Malcolm-Smith, S., Hoogenhout, M., Kevin, G.F., & Solms, M. (2013). Cradling bias is absent in children with autism spectrum disorders. *Journal of Child and Adolescent Mental Health, 25,* 55–60.

Porges, S. W. (1997). Emotion: An evolutionary by-product of the neural regulation of the autonomic nervous system. *Annals of the New York Academy of Sciences, 807,* 62–77.

Porges, S. W. (2011). *The polyvagal theory. Neurophysiological foundations of emotions, attachment, communication, self-regulation.* New York, NY: Norton.

Porges, S. W., & Carter, C. (2010). Neurobiological bases of social behavior across the life span. In M. E. Lamb, A. M. Freund, & R. M. Lerner (Eds.), *The handbook of life-span development, Vol 2: Social and emotional development* (pp. 9–50). Hoboken, NJ: John Wiley & Sons.

Porges, S. W., Doussard-Roosevelt, J. A., & Maiti, A. K. (1994). Vagal tone and the physiological regulation of emotion. *Monographs of the Society for Research in Child Development, 59,* 167–186.

Powles, W. E. (1992). *Human development and homeostasis.* Madison, CT: International Universities Press.

Quirin, M., Gruber, T., Kuhl, J., & Dusing, R. (2013). Is love right? Prefrontal resting brain asymmetry is related to the affiliation motive. *Frontiers in Human Neuroscience, 7,* 902. doi:10.3389/fnhum.2013.00902

Quirin, M., Kazen, M., Rohrmann, S., & Kuhl, J. (2009). Implicit but not explicit affectivity predicts circadian and reactive cortisol: Using the implicit positive and negative affect test. *Journal of Personality, 77,* 401–426.

Raby, E. K., Rosiman, G. I., Fraley, R. C., & Simpson, J. A. (2015). The enduring predictive significance of early maternal sensitivity: Social and academic competence through age 32 years. *Child Development, 86*, 695–708.

Ranote, S., Elliott, R., Abel, K. M., Mitchell, R., Deakin, F. W., & Appleby, L. (2004). The neural basis of maternal responsiveness to infants: An fMRI function. *NeuroReport, 15*, 1825–1829.

Ratnarajah, N., Rifkin-Graboi, A., Fortier, M. V., Chong, Y. S., Kwek, K., Saw, S.-M., Godfrey, K. M., Gluckman, P. D., Meaney, M. J., & Qui, A. (2013). Structural connectivity in the neonatal brain. *NeuroImage, 75*, 187–194.

Raz, A. (2004). Anatomy of attentional networks. *Anatomical Record, 281B*, 21–36.

Raznahan, A., Lee, Y., Stidd, R., Long, R., Greenstein, D., Clasen, L., et al. (2010). Longitudinally mapping the influence of sex and androgen signaling on the dynamics of human cortical maturation in adolescence. *Proceedings of the National Academy of Sciences USA, 107*, 16988–16993.

Redcay, E., Dodell-Feder, D., Pearrow, M. J., Manros, P. L., Kleiner, M., Gasbrielli, J. D. E., & Saxe, R. (2010). Live face-to-face interaction during fMRI: A new tool for social cognitive neuroscience. *NeuroImage, 50*, 1639–1647.

Reis, H. T., & Shaver, P. (1988). Intimacy as interpersonal process. In S. Duck (Ed.), *Handbook of personal relationships: Theory, research, and interventions* (pp. 367–389). Chichester, UK: Wiley.

Reissland, N. (2000). The cradling bias in relation to pitch of maternal child-directed language. *British Journal of Developmental Psychology, 18*, 179–186.

Reissland, N., Hopkins, B., Helms, P., & Williams, B. (2009). Maternal stress and depression and the lateralization of infant cradling. *Journal of Child Psychology and Psychiatry, 50*, 263–269.

Ribaudo, J. (2016). Restoring safety: An attachment-based approach to clinical work with a traumatized toddler. *Infant Mental Health Journal, 37*, 80–92.

Richardson, M.J., Marsh, K.L., Isenhower, R.W., Goodman, J.R., & Schmidt, R.C. (2007). Rocking together: dynamics of intentional and unintentional interpersonal coordination. *Human Movement Science, 26*, 867–891.

Riecker, A., Ackermann, H., Wildgruber, D., Dogil, G., & Grodd, W. (2000). Opposite hemispheric lateralization effects during speaking and singing at motor cortex, insula and cerebellum. *NeuroReport, 11*, 1997–2000.

Rifkin-Graboi, A., Bai, J., Chen, H., Bak'r Hameed, W., Sim, L. W., Tint, M. T. et al. (2013). Prenatal maternal depression associates with microstructure of right amygdala in neonates at birth. *Biological Psychiatry, 74*, 837–844.

Rilling, J. K. (2013). The neural and hormonal bases of human parental care. *Neuropsychologia, 51*, 731–747.

Rossignol, D. A., Genuis, S. J., & Frye, R. E. (2014). Environmental toxicants and autism spectrum disorders: A systemic review. *Transcultural Psychiatry, 4*, e360.

Rubin, B. S. (2011). Bisphenol A: An endocrine disruptor with widespread exposure and multiple effects. *Journal of Steroid Biochemistry and Molecular Biology, 127*, 27–34.

Rutter, M. (1978). Diagnosis and definition of childhood autism. *Journal of Autism & Childhood Schizophrenia.*, *8*, 139–161.

Ryan, R. (2007). Motivation and emotion: A new look and approach for two reemerging fields. *Motivation and Emotion*, *31*, 1–3.

Sabbagh, M. A. (1999). Communicative intentions and language: Evidence from right-hemispheric damage and autism. *Brain and Laguage*, *70*, 29–69.

Sabbagh, M. A. (2004). Understanding orbitofrontal contributions to theory-of-mind reasoning: Implications for autism. *Brain & Cognition*, *55*, 209–219

Saif, Z., Hodyl, N. A., Stark, M. J., Fuller, P. J., Cole, T., Lu, N., & Clifton, V. L. (2015). Expression of eight glucocorticoid receptor isoforms in the human preterm placenta vary with fetal sex and birthweight. *Placenta*, *36*, 723–730.

Saint-Georges, C., Mahdhaoui, A., Chetouani, M., Cassel, R. S., Laznik, M.-C., Apicella, F., et al. (2011). Do parents recognize autistic deviant behavior long before diagnosis? Taking into account interaction using computational methods. *PLOS ONE*, *6*, e22393.

Sajaniemi, N., Suhonen, E., Kontu, E., Rantanen, P., Lindholm, H., Hyttinen, S., et al. (2011). Children's cortisol patterns and the quality of the early learning environment. *European Early Childhood Education Research Journal*, *19*, 45–62.

Salva, O.R., Regolin, L., Mascalzoni, E., & Vallortigara, G. (2012). Cerebral and behavioral asymmetries in animal social recognition. *Comparative Cognition and Behavior Reviews*, 7, 110–138.

Sandler, J., & Sandler, A.-M. (1986). On the development of object relations and affects. In P. Buckley (Ed.), *Essential papers on object relations* (pp. 272–291). New York, NY: New York University Press.

Sapolsky, R. M. (1996). Why stress is bad for your brain. *Science*, *273*, 749–750.

Saugstad, L. F. (1998). Cerebral lateralization and rate of maturation. *International Journal of Psychophysiology*, *28*, 37–62.

Saxe, R., & Wexler, A. (2005). Making sense of another mind: The role of the right temporo-parietal junction. *Neuropsychologia*, *43*, 1391–1399.

Schepman, A., Rodway, P., & Pritchard, H. (2016). Right-lateralized unconscious, but not conscious, processing of affective environmental sounds. *Laterality: Asymmetries of Body, Brain and Cognition*, *21*, 606–632. doi:10.1080/13576 50X.2015.1105245

Schiffer, F., Teicher, M., & Papanicolaou, A. (1995). Evoked potentials evidence for right brain activity during recall of traumatic memories. *Journal of Neuropsychiatry and Clinical Neuroscience*, *7*, 169–175.

Schleussner, E., Schneider, U., Amscheidt, C., Kahler, C., Haueisen, J., & Seewald, H.-J. (2004). Prenatal evidence of left-right asymmetries in auditory evoked responses using fetal magnetoencephalography. *Early Human Development*, *78*, 133–136.

Schneider, S., Peters, J., Bromberg, U., Brassen, S., Menz, M. M., Miedl, S. F., et al. (2011). Boys do it the right way: Sex-dependent amygdala lateralization during face processing in adolescents. *NeuroImage*, *56*, 1847–1853.

Schore, A. N. (1991). Early superego development: The emergence of shame and narcissistic affect regulation in the practicing period. *Psychoanalysis & Contemporary Thought*, 14(2), 187–250.

Schore, A. N. (1996). The experience-dependent maturation of a regulatory system in the orbital prefrontal cortex and the origin of developmental psychopathology. *Development and Psychopathology*, 8, 59–87.

Schore, A. N. (1997). Early organization of the nonlinear right brain and development of a predisposition to psychiatric disorders. *Development and Psychopathology*, 9, 595–631.

Schore, A. N. (2000). Attachment and the regulation of the right brain. *Attachment and Human Development*, 2, 23–47.

Schore, A. N. (2001). The effects of relational trauma on right brain development, affect regulation, and infant mental health. *Infant Mental Health Journal*, 22, 201–269.

Schore, A. N. (2001). The Seventh Annual John Bowlby Memorial Lecture, Minds in the making: Attachment, the self-organizing brain, and developmentally-oriented psychoanalytic psychotherapy. *British Journal of Psychotherapy*, 17, 299–328.

Schore, A. N. (2001a). The effects of a secure attachment relationship on right brain development, affect regulation, and infant mental health. *Infant Mental Health Journal*, 22, 7–66.

Schore, A. N. (2001b). The effects of relational trauma on right brain development, affect regulation, and infant mental health. *Infant Mental Health Journal*, 22, 201–269.

Schore, A. N. (2001c). Contributions from the decade of the brain to infant mental health: An overview. *Infant Mental Health Journal*, 22, 1–6.

Schore, A. N. (2002). Dysregulation of the right brain: A fundamental mechanism of traumatic attachment and the psychopathogenesis of posttraumatic stress disorder. *Australian & New Zealand Journal of Psychiatry*, 36, 9–30.

Schore, A. N. (2003) *Affect dysregulation and disorders of the self.* New York, NY: Norton.

Schore, A. N. (2005). Attachment, affect regulation, and the developing right brain: Linking developmental neuroscience to pediatrics. *Pediatrics in Review*, 26, 204–211.

Schore, A. N. (2009). Relational trauma and the developing right brain. An interface of psychoanalytic self psychology and neuroscience. *Annals of the New York Academy of Science , 1159*, 189–203.

Schore, A. N. (2009). Attachment trauma and the developing right brain: Origins of pathological dissociation. In P. F. Dell, & J. A. O'Neil (Eds.), *Dissociation and the dissociative disorders: DSM-V and beyond* (pp. 107–141). New York, NY: Routledge.

Schore, A. N. (2009a, August 8). The paradigm shift: The right brain and the relational unconscious. Invited plenary address to the American Psychological Association 2009 Convention, Toronto, Canada. Retrieved September 16, 2009, from http://www.allanschore.com/pdf/SchoreAPAPlenaryFinal09.pdf

Schore, A. N. (2010). Synopsis of section on "Biological approaches to early life trauma." In R. A. Lanius, E. Vermetten, & C. Pain (Eds.), *The impact of early life trauma on health and disease: The hidden epidemic* (pp. 142–147). Cambridge, UK: Cambridge University Press.

Schore, A. N. (2012). *The science and art of psychotherapy.* New York, NY: Norton.

Schore, A. N. (2012b). Bowlby's "environment of evolutionary adaptedness." Recent studies on the interpersonal neurobiology of attachment and emotional development. In D. Narvaez, J. Panksepp, A. N. Schore, & T. R. Gleason (Eds.), *Evolution, early experience and human development. From research to practice* (pp. 31–73). New York, NY: Oxford University Press.

Schore, A. N. (2013). Regulation theory and the early assessment of attachment and autistic spectrum disorders: A response to Voran's clinical case. *Journal of Infant Child & Adolescent Psychotherapy, 12,* 164–189.

Schore, A. N. (2013b). Relational trauma, brain development, and dissociation. In J. D. Ford & C. A. Courtois (Eds.), *Treating complex traumatic stress disorders in children and adolescents, Scientific foundations and therapeutic models* (pp. 3–23). New York, NY: Guilford Press.

Schore, A. N. (2014). The right brain is dominant in psychotherapy. *Psychotherapy, 51,* 388–397.

Schore, A. N. (2014a). The right brain is dominant in psychotherapy. *Psychotherapy, 51,* 388–397.

Schore, A. N. (2014b). Early interpersonal neurobiological assessment of attachment and autistic spectrum disorders. *Frontiers in Psychology, 5,* article 1049. doi:10.3389/fpsyg.2014.01049

Schore, A. N. (2015a). Book review, *The emotional life of your brain,* by Richard Davidson and Sharon Begley. *Psychoanalytic Psychology, 32,* 539–547.

Schore, A. N. (2015b). Plenary address, Australian Childhood Foundation Conference. Childhood trauma: Understanding the basis of change and recovery. Early right brain regulation and the origin of emotional wellbeing. *Children Australia, 40,* 104–113.

Schore, A. N. (2017). All our sons: The developmental neurobiology and neuroendocrinology of boys at risk. *Infant Mental Health Journal, 38,* 15–52.

Schore, A. N. (2017). Modern attachment theory. In S. N. Gold (Ed.), *APA handbook of trauma psychology: Vol. l. Foundations in knowledge.* Washington, DC: American Psychological Association.

Schore, A. N. (in press). *Right brain psychotherapy.* New York, NY: Norton.

Schore, A. N., & McIntosh, J. (2011). Family law and the neuroscience of attachment, part l. *Family Court Review, 49,* 501–512.

Schore, A. N., & Newton, R. P. (2012). Using modern attachment theory to guide clinical assessments of early attachment relationships. In J. E. Bettmann & D.

Friedman (Eds.), *Attachment-based clinical work with children and adolescents* (pp. 61–96). New York, NY: Springer.

Schore, A.N. (in press). *The development of the unconscious mind.* New York, NY: Norton.

Schore, J. (2012). Using concepts from interpersonal neurobiology in revisiting psychodynamic theory. *Clinical Social Work Journal,* 82, 90–111.

Schore, J. R. & Schore, A. N. (2008). Modern attachment theory: The central role of affect regulation in development and treatment. *Clinical Social Work Journal,* 36, 9–20.

Schore, J. R., & Schore, A. N. (2010). Clinical social work and regulation theory: Implications of neurobiological models of attachment. In S. Bennett & J. K. Nelson (Eds.), *Adult attachment in clinical social work* (pp. 57–75). New York, NY: Springer.

Schore, J. R., & Schore, A. N. (2014). Regulation theory and affect regulation psychotherapy: A clinical primer. *Smith College Studies in Social Work, 84,* 178–195.

Schumann, C. M., Barnes, C. C., Lord, C., & Courchesne, E. (2009). Amygdala enlargement in toddlers with autism related to severity of social communication impairments. *Biological Psychiatry, 66,* 942–949.

Schumann, C. M., Bauman, M. D., & Amaral, D. G. (2011). Abnormal structure or function of the amygdala is a common component of neurodevelopmental disorders. *Neuropsychologia, 49,* 745–759.

Schuurs, A. H., & Verheul, H. A. (1990). Effects of gender and sex steroids on the immune response. *Journal of Steroid Biochemistry,* 35, 157–172.

Schwartz, C. E., Kunwar, P. S., Greve, D. N., Kagan, J., Snidman, N. C., & Bloch, R. B. (2012). A phenotype of early infancy predicts reactivity of the amygdala in male adults. *Molecular Psychiatry, 17,* 1042–1050.

Schwarz, J. M., & Bilbo, S. D. (2012). Sex, glia, and development: Interactions in health and disease. *Hormones and Behavior, 62,* 243–253.

Selevan, S. G., Kimmel, C. A., & Mendola, P. (2000). Identifying critical windows of exposure for children's health. *Environmental Health Perspectives Supplements, 108,* 451.

Semrud-Clikeman, M., Fine, J. G., & Zhu, D. C. (2011). The role of the right hemisphere for processing of social interactions in normal adults using functional magnetic resonance imaging. *Neuropsychobiology, 64,* 47–51.

Shankle, W. R., Rafii, M. S., Landing, B. H., & Fallon, J. H. (1999). Approximate doubling of numbers of neurons in postnatal cerebral cortex and in 35 specific cytoarchitectural areas from birth to 72 months. *Pediatric and Developmental Pathology,* 2, 244–259.

Shankle, W. R., Rafii, M. S., Landing, B. H., & Fallon, J. H. (1999). Approximate doubling of numbers of neurons in postnatal human cerebral cortex and in 35 specific cytoarchitectural areas from birth to 72 months. *Pediatric and Developmental Pathology,* 2, 244–259.

Sharpe, R. M. (2008). Additional effects of phthalate mixtures on fetal testosterone production. *Toxicological Science, 105*, 1–4.

Shelton, J. F., Hertz-Picciotto, I., & Pessah, I. N. (2012). Tipping the balance of autism risk: Potential mechanisms linking pesticides with autism. *Environmental Health Perspectives, 120*, 944–951.

Shirtcliff, E. A., Granger, D. A., & Likos, A. (2002). Gender differences in the validity of testosterone measured in saliva by immunoassay. *Hormones and Behavior, 42*, 62–69.

Shockley, K., Santana, M.V., & Fowler, C.A. (2003). Mutual interpersonal postural constraints are involved in cooperative conversation. *Journal of Experimental Psychology, 29*, 326–332.

Sholl, S. A., & Kim, K. L. (1990). Androgen receptors are differentially distributed between right and left cerebral hemispheres of the fetal male rhesus monkey. *Brain Research, 516*, 122–126.

Siegel, D. J. (1999). *The developing mind: Toward a neurobiology of interpersonal experience.* New York, NY: Guilford Press.

Sieratzki, J. S., & Woll, B. (1996). Why do mothers cradle their babies on the left? *Lancet 347*, 1746–1748.

Silver, K. L., & Singer, P. A. (2014). Editorial, A focus on child development. *Science, 345*, 120.

Sisk, C. L., & Zehr, J. L. (2005). Pubertal hormones organize the adolescent brain and behavior. *Frontiers in Neuroendocrinology, 26*, 163–174.

Skinner, M. K. (2016). Epigenetic transgenerational inheritance. *Nature Reviews Endocrinology, 12*, 68–69.

Sparks, B. F., Friedman, S. D., Shaw, D. W., Aylward, E. H., Echelard, D., Artru, A. A., et al. (2002). Brain structural abnormalities in young children with autism spectrum disorder. *Neurology, 59*, 184–192.

Spence, J. T., & Helmreich, R. L. (1978). *Masculinity & femininity: Their psychological dimensions, correlates, and antecedents.* Austin: University of Texas Press.

Spitzer, C., Barnow, S., Freyberger, H. J., & Grabe, H. J. (2007). Dissociation predicts symptom-related treatment outcome in short-term inpatient psychotherapy. *Australian and New Zealand Journal of Psychiatry, 41*, 682–687.

Spitzer, C., Wilert, C., Grabe, H.-J., Rizos, T., & Freyberger, H. J. (2004). Dissociation, hemispheric asymmetry, and dysfunction of hemispheric interaction: A transcranial magnetic approach. *Journal of Neuropsychiatry and Clinical Neuroscience, 16*, 163–169.

Stack, D.M. (2001). The salience of touch and physical contact during infancy: Unraveling some of the mysteries of the somesthetic sense. In G.B. Bremmer & A. Fogel (Eds.), *Blackwell handbook of infant development: Social, emotional, and communicative development* (pp. 351–378). Malden, MA: Blackwell Publishers.

Stanilou, A., Markowitsch, H. J., & Brand, M. (2010). Psychogenic amnesia. A malady of the constricted self. *Consciousness and Cognition, 19*, 778–801.

Stanton, S. J., & Schultheiss, O. C. (2009). The hormonal correlates of implicit power motivation. *Journal of Research in Personality, 43*, 942–949.

Stephens, G.J., Silbert, L.J., & Hasson, U. (2010). Speaker-listener neural coupling underlies successful communication. *Proceedings of the National Academy of Science, USA, 107*, 14425–14430.

Stern, D.N. (1977). *The first relationship.* Cambridge, MA: Harvard University Press.

Stern, D. N. (1985). *The interpersonal world of the infant.* New York, NY: Basic Books.

Stern, D. N. (2004). *The present moment in psychotherapy and everyday life.* New York, NY: Norton.

Stevenson, C. W., Halliday, D. M., Marsden, C. A., & Mason, R. (2008). Early life programming of hemispheric lateralization and synchronization in the adult medial prefrontal cortex. *Neuroscience, 155*, 852–863.

Stoleru, S. G., Ennaji, A., Cournot, A., & Spira, A. (1993). LH pulsatile secretion and testosterone blood levels are influenced by sexual arousal in human males. *Psychoneuroendocrinology, 18*, 205–218.

Stoner, R., Chow, M. L., Boyle, M. P., Sunkin, S. M., Mouton, P. R., Roy, S., et al. (2014). Patches of disorganization in the neocortex of children with autism. *New England Journal of Medicine,.370*, 1209–1219.

Storey, A. E., Walsh, C. J., Quinton, R. L., & Wynne-Edwards, K. E. (2000). Hormonal correlates of paternal responsiveness in new and expectant fathers. *Evolution and Human Behavior, 21*, 79–95.

Stroud, L. R., Salovey, P., & Epel, E. S. (2002). Sex differences in stress responses: Social rejection versus achievement motivation. *Biological Psychiatry, 52*, 318–327.

Sullivan, R. M., & Dufresne, M. M. (2006). Mesocortical dopamine and HPA axis regulation: Role of laterality and early environment. *Brain Research, 1076*, 49–59.

Sullivan, R. M., & Gratton, A. (2002). Prefrontal cortical regulation of hypothalamic-pituitary-adrenal function in the rat and implications for psychopathology: Side matters. *Psychoneuroendocrinology, 27*, 99–114.

Sun, T., Patoine, C., Abu-Khalil, A., Visvader, J., Sum, E., Cherry, T. J., et al. (2005). Early asymmetry of gene transcription in embryonic human left and right cerebral cortex. *Science, 308*, 1794–1798.

Suter, S.E., Huggenberger, H.J., & Schachinger, H. (2007). Cold pressor stress reduces left cradling preference in nulliparous human females. *The International Journal of the Biology of Stress, 10*, 45–51.

Swain, J. E. (2011). The human parental brain: In vivo neuroimaging. *Progress in Neuro-Psychopharmacology & Biological Psychiatry, 35*, 1242–1254.

Symonds, L. L., Gordon, N. S., Bixby, J. C., & Mande, M. M. (2006). Right-lateralized pain processing in the human cortex: An fMRI study. *Journal of Neurophysiology*, 95, 3823–3830.

Tanabe, H.C., Kosaka, H., Saito, D.N., Koike, T., Hayashi, M.J., Izuma, K., et al. (2012). Hard to "tune in:" neural mechanisms of live face-to-face interaction with high-functioning autistic spectrum disorder. *Frontiers in Human Neuroscience*, doi: 10.3389/fnhum.2012.00268

Tanaka, M., Nakaya, S., Katayama, M., Leffers, H., Nozawa, S., Nakazawa, R., Iwamoto, T., & Kobayashi, S. (2006). Effect of prenatal exposure to bisphenol A on the serum testosterone concentration of rats at birth. *Human & Experimental Toxicology, 25,* 369–373.

Tanner, J. (1978). *Foetus into man.* Cambridge, MA: Harvard University Press.

Taylor, D. C. (1969). Differential rates of cerebral maturation between sexes and between hemispheres. *Lancet, 294*(7612), 140–142.

Taylor, S. E., Klein, L. C., Lewis, B. P., Gruenwald, T. L., Gurung, R. A., & Updegraff, J. A. (2000). Biobehavioral responses to stress in females: Tend-and-befriend, not fight-or-flight. *Psychological Review, 107,* 411–429.

Telkemeyer, S., Rossi, S., Koch, S. P., Nierhaus, T., Steinbrink, J., Poeppel, D., Obrig, H., & Wartenburger, I. (2009). Sensitivity of newborn auditory cortex to the temporal structure of sounds. *Journal of Neuroscience, 29,* 14726–14733.

Thatcher, R. W. (1994). Cyclical cortical reorganization: Origins of human cognitive development. In G. Dawson & K. W. Fischer (Eds.), *Human behavior and the developing brain* (pp. 232–266). New York, NY: Guilford Press.

Thatcher, R.W. (1996). Neuroimaging of cyclical cortical reorganization during human development. In R.W. Thatcher, G. Reid Lyon, J. Rumsey, N. Krasnegor, (Eds.), Developmental neuroimaging. Mapping the development of brain and behavior (pp. 91–106). San Diego, CA: Academic Press.

Thierry, G., Vihman, M., & Roberts, M. (2003). Familiar words capture the attention of 11-month-olds in less than 250 ms. *NeuroReport, 14,* 2307–2310.

Thordstein, M., Lofgren, N., Flisberg, A., Lindecrantz, K., & Kjellmer, I. (2006). Sex differences in electrocortical activity in human neonates. *NeuroReport, 17,* 1165–1168.

Todd, R. M., & Anderson, A. K. (2009). Six degrees of separation: The amygdala regulates social behavior and perception. *Nature Neuroscience, 12,* 1217–1218.

Toga, A. W., & Thompson, P. M. (2003). Mapping brain asymmetry. *Nature Reviews Neuroscience, 4,* 37–48.

Tops, M., Russo, S., Boksem, M. A. S., & Tucker, D. M. (2009). Serotonin: Modulator of a drive to withdraw. *Brain and Cognition, 71,* 427–436.

Tottenham, N., Hare, T. A., Millner, A., Gilhooly, T., Zevin, J. D., & Casey, B. J. (2011). Elevated amygdala response to faces following early deprivation. *Developmental Science, 14,* 190–204.

Trainor, L. J., Austin, C.M., & Desjardins, R. N. (2000). Is infant-directed speech prosody a result of the vocal expression of emotion? *Psychological Science, 11,* 188–195.

Trevarthen, C. (1979). Communication and cooperation in early infancy: A description of primary intersubjectivity. In M. Bullowa (Ed.), *Before speech: The beginning of interpersonal communication* (pp. 321–348). New York, NY: Cambridge University Press.

Trevarthen, C. (1990). Growth and education of the hemispheres. In C. Trevarthen

(Ed.), *Brain circuits and functions of the mind* (pp. 334–363). Cambridge, UK: Cambridge University Press.

Trevarthen, C. (1993). The self born in intersubjectivity: The psychology of an infant communicating. In U. Neisser (Ed.), *The perceived self: Ecological and interpersonal sources of self-knowledge* (pp. 121–173). New York, NY: Cambridge University Press.

Trevarthen, C. (1996). Lateral asymmetries in infancy: Implications for the development of the hemispheres. *Neuroscience and Biobehavioral Reviews, 20,* 571–586.

Trevarthen, C., & Daniel, S. (2005). Disorganized rhythm and synchrony: Early signs of autism and Rett syndrome. *Brain Development, 27,* S25–S34.

Tronick, E. (1989). Emotions and emotional communication in infants. *American Psychologist, 44,* 112–119.

Tronick, E. (2007). *The neurobehavioral and social-emotional development of infants and children.* New York, NY: Norton.

Tronick, E., & Reck, C. (2009). Infants of depressed mothers. *Harvard Review of Psychiatry, 17,* 147–156.

Tronick, E., & Gianino, A. (1986). Interactive mismatch and repair: Challenges to the coping infant. *Zero to Three,* 3, 1–6.

Tronick, E.Z. (1989). Emotions and emotional communication in infants. *American Psychologist, 44,* 112–119.

Tsakiris, M. (2010). *My* body in the brain: A neurocognitive model of body-ownership. *Neuropsychologia, 48,* 703–712.

Tsakiris, M., Costantini, M., & Haggard, P. (2008). The role of the right temporo-parietal junction in maintaining a coherent sense of one's body. *Neuropsychologia, 46,* 3014–3018.

Tucker, D. M., & Moller, L. (2007). The metamorphosis. Individuation of the adolescent brain. In D. Romer & E. F. Walker (Eds.), *Adolescent psychopathology and the developing brain. Integrating brain and prevention science* (pp. 85–102). Oxford, UK: Oxford University Press.

Turnbull, O., & Collins, P. (2000). Lateral cradling preferences and the mother-infant interaction: investigating a group of mothers experiencing difficulties. Masters thesis, University College, London.

Twenge, J. M., Gentile, B., DeWall, C. N., Ma, D., Lacefield, K., & Schurtz, D. R. (2010). Birth cohort increases in psychopathology among young Americans, 1938–2007: A cross-temporal meta-analysis of the MMPI. *Clinical Psychology Review, 30,* 145–154.

U.S. Department of Labor, Bureau of Labor Statistics. (2014, June 17). *American time use survey (ATUS), 2003–2010, multi-year data.* Retrieved from http://doi.org/10.3886/ICPSR24943.v2

Uddin, L. Q., & Menon, V. (2009). The anterior insula in autism: Under-connected and under-examined. *Neuroscience & Biobehavioral Reviews,* 33, 1198–1203.

Uddin, L. Q., Supekar, K., Lynch, C. J., Khouzam, A., Phillips, J., Feinstein, C., et al. (2013). Salience network-based classification and prediction of symptom severity in children with autism. *JAMA Psychiatry.* doi:10.1001/jamapsychiatry.2013.104

Ulanov, A. B. (2001). *Finding space. Winnicott, God, and psychic reality.* Louisville, KY: Westminster John Knox Press.

Ulfig, N., Setzer, M., & Bohl, J. (2003). Ontogeny of the human amygdala. *Annals of the New York Academy of Sciences, 985,* 22–33.

Ungar, T. (2017). Neuroscience, joy, and the well-infant visit that got me thinking. *Annals of Family Medicine, 15,* 80–83.

UNICEF Office of Research. (2013). *Child well-being in rich countries: A comparative overview.* Innocenti Report Card 11. Florence, Italy: UNICEF Office of Research.

Updegraff, K. A., Booth, A., & Thayer, S. M. (2006). The role of family relationship quality and testosterone levels in adolescents' peer experiences: A biosocial analysis. *Journal of Health Psychology, 20,* 21–29.

van Anders, S. M., Goldey, K. L., & Kuo, P. X. (2011). The steroid/peptide theory of social bonds: Integrating testosterone and peptide responses for classifying social behavioral contexts. *Psychoneuroendocrinology, 36,* 1265–1275.

Van Bokhoven, L., van Goozen, S. H. M., Van Engeland, H., Schaal, B., Arsenault, L., Seguin, J. R., et al. (2006). Salivary testosterone and aggression, delinquency, and social dominance in a population-based longitudinal study of adolescent males. *Hormones and Behavior, 50,* 118–125.

van den Bos, R., Homberg, J., & de Visser, L. (2013). A critical review of sex differences in decision-making tasks: Focus on the Iowa Gambling task. *Behavioural Brain Research, 238,* 95–108.

Van Eden, C. G., Uylings, H. B. M., & Van Pelt, J. (1984). Sex-differences and left-right asymmetries in the prefrontal cortex during postnatal development in the rat. *Developmental Brain Research, 12,* 146–153.

Vandell, D. L., Belsky, J., Burchinal, M., Steinberg, L., Vandergrift, N., & NICHD Early Childcare Research Network. (2010). Do effects of early childcare extend to age 15 years? Results from the NICHD study of early childcare and youth development. *Child Development, 81,* 737–756.

Vandenberg, L. N., Chahoud, I., Heindel, J. J., Padmanabhan, V., Paumgartten, F. J., and Schoenfelder, G. (2010). Urinary, circulating, and tissue biomonitoring studies indicate widespread exposure to bisphenol A. *Environmental Health Perspectives, 118,* 1055–1070.

Vauclair, J., & Donnot, J. (2005). Infant holding biases and their relations to hemispheric specializations for processing facial emotions. *Neuropsychologia, 43,* 564–571.

Vervloed, M.P.J., Hendriks, A.W., & Van der Eijnde, E. (2011). The effects of mothers' past infant-holding preferences on their adult children's face processing lateralization. *Brain and Cognition,* 75, 248–254.

Viau, V., & Meaney, M. J. (1996). The inhibitory effect of testosterone on hypothalamic-pituitary-adrenal responses to stress is mediated by the medial preoptic area. *Journal of Neuroscience, 16,* 1866–1876.

Volbrecht, M. M., Lemery-Chafant, K., Askan, N., Zahn-Waxler, C., & Goldsmith, H. H. (2007). Examining the familial link between positive affect and empathy development in the second year. *Journal of Genetic Psychology, 168*, 105–129.

Volpe, J. J. (2000). Overview: Normal and abnormal human brain development. *Mental Retardation and Developmental Disabilities Research Reviews, 6*, 1–5.

Voran, M. (2013). The protest of a 6-month-old girl: Is this a prodrome of autism? *J. Infant Child & Adolesscent Psychotherapy.*, *12*, 139–155.

Wada, J. A., & Davis, A. E. (1977). Fundamental nature of human infant's brain asymmetry. *Canadian Journal of. Neurological Science. 4*, 203–207.

Walker-Andrews, A. S., & Bahrick, L. E. (2001). Perceiving the real world: Infants' detection of and memory for social information. *Infancy*, 2, 469–481.

Wang, J., Korczykowski, M., Rao, H., Fan, Y., Pluta, J., Gur, R. C., McEwen, B. S., & Detre, J. A. (2007). Gender differences in neural response to psychological stress. *SCAN*, 2, 227–239.

Wang, J., Rao, H., Wetmore, G. S., Furlan, P. M., Korczykowski, M., Dinges, D. F., & Detre, J. A. (2005). Perfusion functional MRI reveals cerebral blood flow pattern under psychological stress. *Proceedings of the National Academy of Sciences USA, 102*, 17804–17809.

Ward, I. L., & Weisz, J. (1984). Differential effects of maternal stress on circulating levels of corticosterone, progesterone, testosterone in male and female rat fetuses and their mothers. *Endocrinology, 114*, 1635–1644.

Ward, I. L., Ward, O. B., Affuso, J. D., Long, W. D., French, J. A., & Hendriks, S. E. (2003). Fetal testosterone surge: Specific modulations induced in male rats by maternal stress and/or alcohol consumption. *Hormones and Behavior, 43*, 531–539.

Washburn, T. C., Medaris, D.N., Jr., & Childs, B. (1965). Sex differences in susceptibility to infections. *Pediatrics, 35*, 57–74.

Watt, D.F. (1986). Transference: A right hemispheric event? An inquiry into the boundary between psychoanalytic metapsychology and neuropsychology. *Psychoanalysis and Contemporary Thought*, 9, 43–77.

Watt, D.F. (1990). Higher cortical functions and the ego: Explorations of the boundary between behavioral neurology, neuropsychology, and psychoanalysis. *Psychoanalytic Psychology*, 7, 487–527.

Watt, D. F. (1998). Affect and the limbic system: Some hard problems. *Journal of Neuropsychiatry, 10*, 113–116.

Weatherill, R.P., Almergi, J.B., Levendosky, A.A., Bogar, G.A., von Eye, A., & Harris, L.J. (2004). Is maternal depression related to side of infant holding? *International Journal of Behavioral Development, 28*, 421–427.

Weaver, I. C., Cervoni, N., Champagne, F. A., D'Alessio, A. C., Sharma, S., Seckl, J. R., et al. (2004). Epigenetic programming by maternal behavior. *Nature Neuroscience, 7*, 847–854.

Weber, A. M., Harrison, T. M., & Steward, D. K. (2012). Schore's regulation theory: Maternal-infant interaction in the NICU as a mechanism for reducing the effects of allostatic load on neurodevelopment in premature infants. *Biological Research in Nursing, 14*, 375–386.

Weinberg, J., Sliwowska, J. H., Lan, N., & Hellemans, K. G. C. (2008). Prenatal alcohol exposure: Foetal programming, the hypothalamic-pituitary-adrenal axis and sex differences in outcome. *Journal of Neuroendocrinology, 20*, 470–488.

Weinberg, M., Tronick, E., Cohn, J., & Olson, K. (1999). Gender differences in emotional expressivity and self-regulation during early infancy. *Developmental Psychology, 35*, 175–188.

Weinstock, M. (2005). The potential influence of maternal stress hormones on development and mental health of the offspring. *Brain Behavior and Immunity, 19*, 296–308.

Weisman, O., Feldman, R., & Goldstein, A. (2012). Parental and romantic attachment shape brain processing of infant cues. *Biological Psychiatry, 89*, 533–538.

Weiss, B. (2011). Endocrine disruptors as a threat to neurological function. *Journal of the Neurological Sciences, 305*, 11–21.

Weisz, J., & Ward, I. L. (1980). Plasma testosterone and progesterone titers of pregnant rats, their male and female fetuses, and neonatal offspring. *Endocrinology, 196*, 306–316.

Welberg, L. A., & Seckl, J. R. (2001). Prenatal stress, glucocorticoids and the programming of the brain. *Journal of Neuroendocrinology, 13*, 113–128.

Werner, E. A., Myers, M. M., Fifer, W. P., Cheng, B., Fang, Y., Allen, R., & Monk, C. (2007). Prenatal predictors of infant temperament. *Developmental Psychobiology, 49*, 474–484.

Wexler, B. E., Warrenburg, S., Schwartz, G. E., & Janer, L. D. (1992). EEG and EMG responses to emotion-evoking stimuli processed without conscious awareness. *Neuropsychologia, 30*, 1065–1079.

Whittle, S., Yucei, M., Yap, M. B. H., & Allen, N. B. (2011). Sex differences in the neural correlates of emotion: Evidence from neuroimaging. *Biological Psychology, 87*, 319–333.

Williamson, M., Bingham, B., & Viau, V. (2005). Central organization of androgen-sensitive pathways to the hypothalamic-pituitary-adrenal axis: Implications for individual differences in responses to homeostatic threat and predisposition to disease. *Progress in Neuropsychopharmacology and Biological Psychiatry, 29*, 1239–1248.

Winnicott, D. W. (1963). The development of the capacity for concern. *Bulletin of the Menninger Clinic, 27*(4), 167.

Winnicott, D. W. (1975). *The child, the family, and the outside world*. Harmondsworth, Middlesex, UK: Penguin.

Winnicott, D. W. (1986). *Home is where we start from*. New York, NY: Norton.

Winson, J. (1990). The meaning of dreams. *Scientific American, 263*(5), 86–96

Wittling, W. (1997). The right hemisphere and the human stress response. *Acta Physiologica Scandinavica, Supplement, 640*, 55–59.

Wolff, J. J., Gu, H., Gerrig, G., Elison, J. T., Styner, M., Gouttasrd, S., et al. (2012). Differences in white matter fiber tract development present from 6 to 24 months in infants with autism. *American Journal of Psychiatry, 169*, 589–600.

Wood, W., & Eagley, A. H. (2015). Two traditions of research on gender identity. *Sex Roles, 73*, 461–473.

Xu, X., Aron, A., Brown, L., Cao, G., Feng, T., & Weng, X. (2011). Reward and motivation systems: A brain mapping study of early-stage intense romantic love on Chinese participants. *Human Brain Mapping, 32*, 249–257.

Yang, C. F., Chiang, M. C., Gray, D. C., Prabhakaran, M., Alvarado, M., Juntti, S. A., et al. (2013). Sexually dimorphic neurons in the ventromedial hypothalamus govern mating in both sexes and aggression in males. *Cell, 153*, 896–909.

Yang, Y., & Raine, A. (2009). Prefrontal structural and functional brain imaging findings in antisocial, violent, and psychopathic individuals: A meta-analysis. *Psychiatry Research: Neuroimaging, 174*, 81–88.

Yildirim, B. O., & Derksen, J. J. L. (2012). A review of the relationship between testosterone and life-course persistent antisocial behavior. *Psychiatry Research, 200*, 984–1010.

Yildirim, B. O., & Derksen, J. J. L. (2013). Systematic review, structural analysis, and new theoretical perspectives on the role of serotonin and associated genes in the etiology of psychopathy and sociopathy. *Neuroscience and Biobehavioral Reviews, 37*, 1254–1296.

Yirmiya, N., & Charman, T. (2010). The prodrome of autism: Early behavioral and biological signs, regression, peri- and post-natal development and genetics. *Journal of Child Psychology & Psychiatry, 51*, 432–458.

Yirmiya, N., & Ozonoff, S. (2007). The very early autism phenotype. *Journal of Autism & Developmental Disorders, 37*, 1–11.

Yovel, G. (2016). Neural and cognitive face-selective markers: An integrative review. *Neuropsychologia, 83*, 5–13.

Yu, Q., Ouyang, A., Chalak, L., Jeon, T., Chia, J., Mishra, V., et al. (2016). Structural development of human fetal and preterm brain cortical plate based on population-averaged templates. *Cerebral Cortex, 26*, 4381–4391.

Zahn-Waxler, C., Shirtcliff, E. A., & Marceau, K. (2008). Disorders of childhood and adolescence: Gender and psychopathology. *Annual Review of Clinical Psychology, 4*, 275–303.

Zaslow, M. S., & Haynes, C. D. (1986). Sex differences in children's responsiveness to psychosocial stress: Toward a cross-context analysis. In M. Lamb, & B. Rogoff (Eds.), *Advances in developmental psychology* (Vol. 4, pp. 289–337). Hillsdale, NJ: Erlbaum.

Zeitlin, J., Saurel-Cubizolles, M. J., De Mouzon, J., Rivera, L., Ancel, P. Y., Blondel, B., & Kaminski, M. (2002). Fetal sex and preterm birth: are males at greater risk? *Human Reproduction, 17*, 2762–2668.

Zhou, R., Bai, Y., Yang, R., Zhu, Y., Chi, X., Li, L., et al. (2011). Abnormal synaptic plasticity in basolateral amygdala may account for hyperactivity and attention-deficit in male rat exposed perinatally to low-dose bisphenol-A. *Neuropharmacology, 60*, 789–798.

Zoeller, R.T., Brown, T. R., Doan, L. L., Gore, A. C., Skakkebaek, N. E., Soto, A. M., Woodruff, T. J., & Vom Saal, F. S. (2012). Endocrine-disrupting chemicals and public health protection: A statement of principles from the Endocrine Society. *Endocrinology, 153*, 4097–4110.

Index

ALSO AVAILABLE FROM

THE NORTON SERIES ON INTERPERSONAL NEUROBIOLOGY

The Birth of Intersubjectivity: Psychodynamics, Neurobiology, and the Self
Massimo Ammaniti, Vittorio Gallese

Neurobiology for Clinical Social Work: Theory and Practice (Second Edition)
Jeffrey S. Applegate, Janet R. Shapiro

Mind–Brain–Gene
John B. Arden

The Heart of Trauma: Healing the Embodied Brain in the Context of Relationships
Bonnie Badenoch

Being a Brain-Wise Therapist: A Practical Guide to Interpersonal Neurobiology
Bonnie Badenoch

The Brain-Savvy Therapist's Workbook
Bonnie Badenoch

The Neurobiology of Attachment-Focused Therapy
Jonathan Baylin, Daniel A. Hughes

Coping with Trauma-Related Dissociation: Skills Training for Patients and Therapists
Suzette Boon, Kathy Steele, and Onno van der Hart

Neurobiologically Informed Trauma Therapy with Children and Adolescents: Understanding Mechanisms of Change
Linda Chapman

Intensive Psychotherapy for Persistent Dissociative Processes: The Fear of Feeling Real
Richard A. Chefetz

Timeless: Nature's Formula for Health and Longevity
Louis Cozolino

The Neuroscience of Human Relationships: Attachment and the Developing Social Brain (Second Edition)
Louis Cozolino

The Neuroscience of Psychotherapy: Healing the Social Brain (Second Edition)
Louis Cozolino

Why Therapy Works: Using Our Minds to Change Our Brains
Louis Cozolino

From Axons to Identity: Neurological Explorations of the Nature of the Self
Todd E. Feinberg

Loving with the Brain in Mind: Neurobiology and Couple Therapy
Mona DeKoven Fishbane

Body Sense: The Science and Practice of Embodied Self-Awareness
Alan Fogel

The Healing Power of Emotion: Affective Neuroscience, Development & Clinical Practice
Diana Fosha, Daniel J. Siegel, Marion Solomon

Healing the Traumatized Self: Consciousness, Neuroscience, Treatment
Paul Frewen, Ruth Lanius

The Neuropsychology of the Unconscious: Integrating Brain and Mind in Psychotherapy
Efrat Ginot

10 Principles for Doing Effective Couples Therapy
Julie Schwartz Gottman and John M. Gottman

The Impact of Attachment
Susan Hart

Art Therapy and the Neuroscience of Relationships, Creativity, and Resiliency: Skills and Practices
Noah Hass-Cohen and Joanna Clyde Findlay

Affect Regulation Theory: A Clinical Model
Daniel Hill

Brain-Based Parenting: The Neuroscience of Caregiving for Healthy Attachment
Daniel A. Hughes, Jonathan Baylin

Sex Addiction as Affect Dysregulation: A Neurobiologically Informed Holistic Treatment
Alexandra Katehakis

The Interpersonal Neurobiology of Play: Brain-Building Interventions for Emotional Well-Being
Theresa A. Kestly

Self-Agency in Psychotherapy: Attachment, Autonomy, and Intimacy
Jean Knox

Infant/Child Mental Health, Early Intervention, and Relationship-Based Therapies: A Neurorelational Framework for Interdisciplinary Practice
Connie Lillas, Janiece Turnbull

Play and Creativity in Psychotherapy
Terry Marks-Tarlow, Marion Solomon, Daniel J. Siegel

Clinical Intuition in Psychotherapy: The Neurobiology of Embodied Response
Terry Marks-Tarlow

Awakening Clinical Intuition: An Experiential Workbook for Psychotherapists
Terry Marks-Tarlow

A Dissociation Model of Borderline Personality Disorder
Russell Meares

Borderline Personality Disorder and the Conversational Model: A Clinician's Manual
Russell Meares

Neurobiology Essentials for Clinicians: What Every Therapist Needs to Know
Arlene Montgomery

Borderline Bodies: Affect Regulation Therapy for Personality Disorders
Clara Mucci

Neurobiology and the Development of Human Morality: Evolution, Culture, and Wisdom
Darcia Narvaez

Brain Model & Puzzle: Anatomy & Functional Areas of the Brain
Norton Professional Books

Sensorimotor Psychotherapy: Interventions for Trauma and Attachment
Pat Ogden, Janina Fisher

Trauma and the Body: A Sensorimotor Approach to Psychotherapy
Pat Ogden, Kekuni Minton, Clare Pain

The Archaeology of Mind: Neuroevolutionary Origins of Human Emotions
Jaak Panksepp, Lucy Biven

The Polyvagal Theory: Neurophysiological Foundations of Emotions, Attachment, Communication, and Self-regulation
Stephen W. Porges

The Pocket Guide to Polyvagal Theory: The Transformative Power of Feeling Safe
Stephen W. Porges

Foundational Concepts in Neuroscience: A Brain-Mind Odyssey
David E. Presti

Right Brain Psychotherapy
Allan N. Schore

The Development of the Unconscious Mind
Allan N. Schore

Affect Dysregulation and Disorders of the Self
Allan N. Schore

Affect Regulation and the Repair of the Self
Allan N. Schore

The Science of the Art of Psychotherapy
Allan N. Schore

Mind: A Journey to the Heart of Being Human
Daniel J. Siegel

The Mindful Brain: Reflection and Attunement in the Cultivation of Well-Being
Daniel J. Siegel

The Mindful Therapist: A Clinician's Guide to Mindsight and Neural Integration
Daniel J. Siegel

Pocket Guide to Interpersonal Neurobiology: An Integrative Handbook of the Mind
Daniel J. Siegel

Healing Moments in Psychotherapy
Daniel J. Siegel, Marion Solomon

Healing Trauma: Attachment, Mind, Body and Brain
Daniel J. Siegel, Marion Solomon

Love and War in Intimate Relationships: Connection, Disconnection, and Mutual Regulation in Couple Therapy
Marion Solomon, Stan Tatkin

How People Change: Relationships and Neuroplasticity in Psychotherapy
Marion Solomon and Daniel J. Siegel

The Present Moment in Psychotherapy and Everyday Life
Daniel N. Stern

The Neurobehavioral and Social-Emotional Development of Infants and Children
Ed Tronick

The Haunted Self: Structural Dissociation and the Treatment of Chronic Traumatization
Onno Van Der Hart, Ellert R. S. Nijenhuis, Kathy Steele

Prenatal Development and Parents' Lived Experiences: How Early Events Shape Our Psychophysiology and Relationships
Ann Diamond Weinstein

Changing Minds in Therapy: Emotion, Attachment, Trauma, and Neurobiology
Margaret Wilkinson

For all the latest books in the series, book details (including sample chapters), and to order online, please visit the Series webpage at wwnorton.com/Psych/IPNB Series